KEYS TO SUCCESS
READER

Joyce Bishop

Mary Jane Bradbury

Julie Wheeler

Prentice Hall

Upper Saddle River, New Jersey 07458

Library of Congress Cataloging-in-Publication Data

Bishop, Joyce (Joyce L.), 1950–
    Keys to success reader / Joyce Bishop, Mary Jane Bradbury, Julie Wheeler.
        p.   cm.
    Includes index.
    ISBN 0-13-010799-9
    1. College student orientation—United States.   2. College majors—United States.   3. Vocational guidance—United States.   4. Success in business—United States.   5. Success—United States.
    I. Bradbury, Mary Jane.   II. Wheeler, Julie.   III. Title.
    LB2343.32.B57   1999
    378.1'98—dc21   98-45121
                                                                                    CIP

Publisher: Carol Carter
Acquisitions Editor: Sue Bierman
Managing Editor: Mary Carnis
In-House Liaison: Glenn Johnston
Production: Holcomb Hathaway, Inc.
Director of Manufacturing and Production: Bruce Johnson
Manufacturing Buyer: Marc Bove
Editorial Assistant: Michelle M. Williams
Marketing Manager: Jeff McIlroy
Marketing Assistant: Barbara Rosenberg

© 1999 by Prentice-Hall, Inc.
A Simon & Schuster Company
Upper Saddle River, New Jersey 07458

Printed in the United States of America

10 9 8 7 6 5 4 3 2 1

ISBN 0-13-010799-9

Prentice-Hall International (UK) Limited, London
Prentice-Hall of Australia Pty. Limited, Sydney
Prentice-Hall Canada Inc., Toronto
Prentice-Hall Hispanoamericana, S.A., Mexico
Prentice-Hall of India Private Limited, New Delhi
Prentice-Hall of Japan, Inc., Tokyo
Simon & Schuster Asia Pte. Ltd., Singapore
Editors Prentice-Hall do Brazil, Ltda., Rio de Janeiro

Brief Contents

CONTENTS

From Start to Finish:
Helping You Through

Whether you are a traditional student, fresh out of high school, or an adult student returning after a long break, or a career changer, dissatisfied with your current career and searching for a new one, you will find the help you need in this book.

In crafting this book, we took into account all of the diverse needs you may have as you make your way through your college education. Each chapter was written by an expert in the topic it discusses, and was designed to help you discover more about yourself, your own needs, and the assets that you bring to your learning experience.

Navigating Uncharted Waters:
Finding the Tools to Help You

Since this book is so diverse in its audience, we have divided it into three sections for your perusing pleasure. The first section, "Student Success," is filled with topics that will help you wade your way through all the challenges college has to offer. This section will be helpful for most students, though some of the chapters, such as the chapter on transition from high school to college, have a pointed audience.

The second section, "Success Across the Disciplines," is an exploration of majors and the jobs that come out of those majors. As the titles suggest, each chapter explores a different area of study, and includes tips for success in school, and in a related career. For instance, the chapter on majoring in liberal arts will guide you through each of the liberal arts majors and help you to decide which will be most useful to you in your academic success as well as in your career.

The final section, "Advice for Career Changers," is tailored to people who are returning to school to prepare for a new career, but who have been in the workforce already. Much like adult learners returning to school, career changers have experience in the workforce. This section focuses on the intricacies of that world and some tips on succeeding in it. For example, you will find a chapter on corporate culture that will help you decide what kind of environment you need to be satisfied.

The Resource Supermarket

Since some of the material in this book is geared toward students making the transition from high school to college, and some toward adult learners and students ready to make the leap into the workforce, not everything in this book will be right for everyone. Just like when you go to the supermarket, you wouldn't want to buy every item. Perhaps you don't like creamed corn, but you adore asparagus. The point is that they are both there for you to choose from. This book embraces the same concept. If you need to know more about the field of business and what you might be able to look forward to if you pursue that field, peruse the chapter that covers business majors. Or, if you are looking forward to your career and want to know how to sustain your marketability, you've come to the right place if you read the chapter on becoming indispensable.

Just remember, like the supermarket, this book offers enough ingredients to make a successful college experience, and a successful career. But if you don't combine them thoughtfully and use them wisely, they will simply be a pile of ingredients that will eventually become stale and useless.

PART 1

Student Success

1 HOW COLLEGE IS DIFFERENT FROM HIGH SCHOOL
Making a Smooth Transition

In this chapter, you will explore answers to the following questions:

➤ How does residence life in a dorm differ from commuter campus life?

➤ How can you choose a course schedule that will suit you?

➤ How do you budget your money, and generally manage your finances?

➤ How do you make time your friend?

➤ Where do you go for help when you need it?

➤ How will you benefit from the diversity you will encounter in college?

? Thinking It Through

Check those statements that apply to you right now:

❑ I don't expect college to be much different from high school.

❑ I worry that college will be a much bigger challenge for me academically and socially than high school was.

❑ I'm undecided whether to live in a dorm, an apartment, or at home while attending school.

❑ I need help tailoring my class and study schedule to take best advantage of my time and "peak learning times."

❑ When I think about budgeting my own money and managing my finances, I worry that I'm not ready.

❑ I would like to know more about the resources that are available to help me while I'm in college.

GROW

HOW COLLEGE IS DIFFERENT FROM HIGH SCHOOL
Making a Smooth Transition

The transition from high school to college may be your most significant life transition to date. While the two *are* similar, they are also very different. High school required a fairly strict structure imposed by both your parents and the school. Classes were mandatory, homework assigned, reading tested, and attendance taken; you were ushered from one step to the next. Bells told you when to walk in the halls, when to be seated at your desk, and when to leave. The way behavior is controlled, Pavlov might have operated the high school system as a human experiment in classical conditioning.

Most college students, some of whom are away from home entirely, experience an incredible freedom. Some see that freedom as a license to party, skip classes, and stay out late. College, however, makes you learn to fend for yourself in ways you may never before have had to consider. No one says, "Do this" and "Be there." That's a definite advantage, right? Just remember, however, that with control comes responsibility.

MAKING CHOICES

Your college career will be filled with choices. Many of these are discussed in this chapter. But when you step up to the plate, remember you are in college to succeed, so make choices that will help you do so. For example, you must choose where to live, when to go to class, how to manage your finances, and how, when, and if to study.

Granted, you've been faced with choices before: taking drugs, having sex, and ditching class. Your choices may have been just as important, but now no one will bail you out when you screw up. You're on your own, and it's up to you to go to class. No one will call your parents to tell on you, and you won't have to go to the principal's office, but you must still be accountable. All the freedom and none of the fun, right? That doesn't have to be the case. You can have a blast making your own decisions, especially when you start seeing them pay off. OK. Lecture over; the commentary light is off. Let's see what you have to do to get through.

JUMPING INTO A BIGGER POND

In high school, if you had a problem with your transcript, grades, or schedule, chances are scads of people ushered you through it and made certain it was resolved. But all those people were probably under one roof. Now you will have to deal with staff in various buildings and departments to handle different situations. Perhaps one department handles administrative duties such as providing transcripts, another houses your professor's office, and yet another holds the office of the dean of your department.

What if you need only one tiny change in your transcript? You may have to go to the transcript office to see what is required, then to the professor who says, "No changes made without a note from the dean," who says, "Must hear from the professor first," and then it's back to the transcript office to have your B changed to the B+ you really deserved! Seem a bit convoluted? Just be prepared for your academic community to be spread over a larger geographical area, not across the hall and around the corner as in high school.

RESIDENCE AND COMMUTER CAMPUS LIFE

College atmospheres vary from campus to campus, but all will be different from high school. Most college communities are similar to small cities, and it will take some time to get your bearings.

Residence Hall Living

Living in a residence hall can help ease the transition from your parents' home to being on your own. The halls are usually less expensive than living on your own; most provide meal plans, so you don't have to grocery shop and prepare meals. They also come with built-in support systems. In addition to being a source for many new friends, they offer the help of resident (live-in) assistants.

Living in the hall also assists you in keeping a balance between your social and academic life. When you live in a community as tightly knit as a residence hall, there are often people with whom to study, walk to the store, and just hang out when you need a break. Also, if you're having problems in school or your personal life, you'll frequently find other students with similar challenges.

With the Internet on most college campuses now, residence halls often have interconnected computers so students can "talk" with one another without having to roam the halls in the middle of the night. For example, let's say you have a question on your microbiology term paper assignment. Not every neighbor in your hall will be able to help you. You can link into the college's computer system, however, and perhaps find a *chat room* where other students are discussing that topic.

But residence hall life consists of other people besides friends and companions. You must still live with these people. It may sound trivial, and you may think, "I've slept away from home before. It's not going to be a problem!" That's a great attitude to have. You may want to take into consideration, however, that this will be your first time living away from home for an extended period of time. Clean sheets will no longer appear in the linen closet as if by magic. The clothes you dropped in front of the washing machine will not appear in your room, folded and pressed. Parents won't wake you when you sleep late. And most of all, say good-bye to privacy!

For at least one year you may be living in a residence hall with hundreds of others, in a small room with another person (most likely someone you have never met before), in a new city you are not familiar with. You will eat cafeteria food that may send you away screaming in horror. Doesn't sound so neat, does it? But sooner than you think you will adjust. The noise in the hall will become part of the day (and night). The city will become familiar to you as you scout out interesting stores and coffee shops. You'll learn that going to the cafeteria on a particular day is certain disaster, and you'll plan your day accordingly. And your roommates? They may get on your nerves in the beginning, but you'll soon realize some advantages of roommates—for instance, being less afraid of scary movies.

Commuter Campus Living

Of course, there is more than one way to get a college education. Living in a residence hall may be a good way to feel connected, but it's also expensive. When going away to school is not an alternative, you can still live at home or in an apartment and attend a "commuter campus." This is becoming a more common decision for new students. While the costs of tuition are skyrocketing, the costs of living on campus can surpass them.

Commuter campuses are different. People may not always be available to help you, but these campuses are an excellent place to get an education. You will find similar classes, professors, and degrees, but you will not have the same "campus experience" as living in a residence hall. Perhaps you're saying, "I can't stand this cubicle-type living with hundreds of people." That can be true. But you can also miss out on the camaraderie that takes place in residence halls.

Though the dormitory and commuter lifestyles are different, they are meant to satisfy the same need: education. Depending on how you learn and what your options are, it may be the perfect way for you to get an education.

CHOOSING YOUR MAJOR

In high school, you had a set schedule, you had to take your "solid" classes, and with the remaining time, you did what you wanted. You didn't have to choose what you wanted to do for the rest of your life, and you may not have cared. One of the biggest differences between high school and college is that you must now declare a major: You will be given a list of required classes, and when you have completed those (and your core requirements), you are armed with a degree and a direction. Sounds pretty simple, right? Not necessarily. Choosing your major is not a decision to be taken lightly, as it will affect the rest of your life. If you haven't a clue about what you want to do, don't worry. College is the place to decide it, and you'll have all the resources you'll need. Consider taking diverse courses such as science, psychology, and English, those that will both count toward graduation requirements and allow you to test the waters to find your niche in life. (Remember when you are choosing a major to *enjoy* what you are studying, because you will be immersed in it for a long time.)

CHOOSING A SCHEDULE THAT WORKS FOR YOU

It can be difficult at first to narrow down when and what classes to take. Some students schedule them all on Tuesdays and Thursdays, cramming as much "schooltime" into each day as possible, then spending the remaining days working, studying, and trying to recover from the long days at school. Other students spread their classes over the entire week, giving themselves plenty of time for lunch breaks and study.

Peak Learning Times

The first thing to discover is *when* you learn best. A night owl won't want a class at 8:00 in the morning. This could prove torturous. Also, if you can't think when you're hungry, schedule a break for lunch so you can make it through your afternoon classes. (If you fall into a deep slumber following lunch, a 1:00 class might be a mistake.)

Use the information you already have about yourself ("I'm a night owl") to plan a schedule. The only way to test your schedule is to follow it. Therefore you may have to spend a semester or two "in practice."

Studying is also a big part of peak learning times. You may already know—and if you don't, you will soon learn—how you study. Some students say if they can't focus on a problem in the first five minutes of studying, they may as well get up and do something else, because studying then will do them little good. If you study best in long increments, leave several hours free before an upcoming test. Or if you can concentrate for only an hour, set aside an hour a night until the test to prepare yourself. Finding a place to study is also important. If you need perfect silence to study, the library would be a better choice than the cafeteria.

Classes Can Be Fun? Surviving Your Schedule

To lighten a grueling schedule, plan one "fun" class every semester. Some may count toward your core requirements as electives. One fun class every semester is important because it gives you an opportunity to relax and unwind from your required classes, provides credit, and allows you to learn about something that interests you. The more these classes vary from your regular class schedule, the better. Who knows? Astrogeology may give you great story ideas for your creative writing class.

Most universities offer some classes for credit, not for a grade. You register for the class on a pass/fail basis, and as long as you don't fail, you don't have to worry about getting a good grade. Determine if you will need these classes in the future, because chances are they won't count toward your major or graduation requirements (for anything other than electives). And don't be too upset when you get an A in the class and it doesn't count. The pass/fail status will take the pressure off you and allow you to have a good time.

Kristine Jenner, a senior at the University of Colorado at Denver, used this system to get through school. "It felt good to have classes I could just sit back and enjoy. I got pass/fail grades for them, but didn't have to be constantly submerged in my major. It was a lifesaver at times."

Another reason to take classes outside your major is that, if you end up in a career field you hate, you may be able to make a smoother transition into another field. You may even find something in your fun classes worth dedicating your life to. (Better to discover that while you're still in school than to be ten years into your career, miserable, and have to start over.)

HONING YOUR TALENTS

Even if you have already chosen your major, or you still don't have any clue, the skills you learn in college will serve you well in the rest of your life. Even if you are a biochemistry major, your freshman composition class will come in handy when you are writing that lab abstract that you still haven't managed to get out of doing. On the other hand, if you are a criminology major, you may want to pay special attention to the scientific processes you will learn in your biology class, as they can give you insight into logic and patterns.

Writing Effectively

Since learning to write effectively is essentially learning to communicate effectively, this is a skill you can use no matter what you decide to do. College students in every major still haven't convinced their professors they shouldn't need to write research papers, so be prepared when your history professor assigns you a ten-page paper on the Revolutionary War.

After graduation, especially in business, it is essential to be able to communicate your ideas. Throughout your career, you'll be doing more writing than you might have expected. You'll probably write memos, letters, reports, and proposals. If you can communicate your ideas more effectively than the next person, you will be seen as more competent.

Speaking Skills

Since you will have to not only write, but also speak during your college career (and possibly later in your professional career), you may as well become good at it early.

Standing in front of a roomful of people staring back at you can be pretty intimidating, but the more you do it, the more comfortable you will feel. If you start out slowly, your first experience talking in front of your peers won't necessarily be the one where you pass out because you forgot to breathe.

One way to practice your speaking skills is in class discussions. First, have your peers help you. You can usually speak from your desk, and only some of the students will turn and look at you. You'll feel more comfortable, get your opinion heard for the class to discuss, and you'll have practiced speaking in front of people. (That wasn't so hard, was it?)

Another way to practice your speaking skills is to join activities where you will get to speak with, as well as to, other people in the group. This provides a built-in support system and comfortable place to work on your skills.

Of course, many other ways exist to become experienced at public speaking. Be creative and discover ways to practice your skills to become an excellent communicator.

BOUGHT AND PAID FOR: MANAGING YOUR FINANCES

Many students start college with the independence bug in their ears and shiny, new credit cards in their pockets. This can be mistaken as a license to shop. Credit card companies know this. It's not that they're out to get you in credit trouble, but if you overspend and have to pay them more interest than you will on your first house, they're not upset. That's why they approach you when you turn eighteen. But there's no need to run screaming from the credit card application. Get *one* credit card, charge on it a little every month, pay it off *every* month (thus avoiding interest or finance charges altogether), and you will be surprised at how friendly these little pieces of plastic can be. Where most college students get into trouble is charging items they can't afford to avoid going into debt with loans. School loans, however, are much less expensive in the long run than credit cards. Remember, school loans are usually available at very reasonable rates of interest. And more important, payments and interest accrual are typically deferred until you are out of school.

If you do use a credit card, the monthly statement can help you keep track of what you are buying and how much you're spending. You may be shocked to look back over your bills for the last six months and add up how much you've really spent. For this reason, you also need a budget—or you may still be sunk.

BUDGET? YOU'VE GOT TO BE KIDDING!

It's no joke. Budgets are for everyone, and the sooner you start one, the better off you will be. One young woman considers herself lucky because her mother was kind enough to cut off her mindless spending at age 14, when she was given $100 a month to buy everything she could possibly need. From that moment, she understood the limitations of money and the importance of keeping within a budget.

Budgets are simple. In one column list your income (e.g., loans, parents, jobs) and in another, your expenses (e.g., rent, car, food). Then subtract to find the difference. For example, if your total income for the month is $1,000 and your expenses are $1,200, you need to delete something. Can you cut any expenses? Perhaps seeing three movies a week is something you could sacrifice. That doesn't mean you must sit home alone in the dark with only bread and water. If necessary, ask Mom and Dad for a bit more money or apply for an additional loan. Most students, however, can cut unnecessary spending.

Another "expense" is *savings*. If you put a minimum of 10 percent of your income into savings every month, you will have a nest egg for the proverbial rainy day most of us have already experienced. This is not the rainy day when you *must* party. Your entertainment budget should cover that. Reserve your savings for when you are sick and can't go to work or for staples like food when you find yourself short that month. Or you can use it for that much-needed vacation during the summer. (OK, that comes awfully close to the much-needed party.) The point is that it's there if you need it.

Keep this money separate from that with which you pay your monthly bills. It's almost too much of a temptation to have extra funds so accessible. This will be a good time to open a savings account, and "pay into it" every month, just as you would a bill. Once it becomes a habit, you won't even miss the money.

Now that you've tackled the budget issue, you must have time to do everything required of you.

TIME IS YOUR FRIEND—OR IS IT?

In college, you may find a vast amount of time for yourself. Managing your time is an important lesson to learn early. In high school, your schedule was planned for you. In college, it's all up to you. Some days you may have one class at 8:00 P.M., and other days you may have four classes from 11:00 A.M.. to 6:00 P.M. You will probably have more time not actually spent in class or doing homework than you did in high school. *Free-time* is a tricky phrase, however, because much of it is not really "free." If it's not used correctly, you pay for it later. Use free time for studying, writing papers, organizational and sports activities, meals, exercise, a part-time job, and fun. With all this time on your hands, much like Luke Skywalker with "the force," you have the chance to use your time for good or evil (i.e., productively or wastefully).

The right mix of work and fun is important. You can be gung ho about your education, lock yourself in a room at night, and pore endlessly over books and notes. That is one effective, though abysmally boring, way to get good grades. The flip side of that attitude is not worrying about classes at all and trying your best to break the world's record for most parties attended by one student in a school year. This presents just one problem: you will never break the record because you'll be kicked out of school at the end of the first semester. Remember: college is not solely for helping you grow academically; it also helps you grow socially. It is the person who knows when to work and when to play who will get the most out of college.

Develop a schedule to follow from the time you get up until the time you go to bed. Before you go to bed at night, think of the things you have to accomplish the next day, and include them in a your schedule. For example: 7:00 A.M., wake up; 8:00 A.M., eat breakfast; 8:30 A.M., history class, etc. Continue this for one week. Then determine how your use of time is different from your days without a schedule. Do you feel as if you are accomplishing more with your time?

For people who may not like that kind of rigidity in their life, develop a bulleted list titled "Things To Do." Every night take ten minutes to go over your syllabi and calendar to see what must be done the next day. Is it handing in a political science paper, going over budget proposals for an organization, or seeing a counselor for advice about a class?

As you go through the day, cross off each completed item from the list. At the end of each day, you will find great satisfaction in seeing what you have done. This is one of the keys to *excelling* in college, rather than just getting through it. These are not, however, the only ways to manage your time. Perhaps you'll find another way that suits you better. The important thing to remember is that being organized helps you see things more clearly and makes forgetting things like assignments and deadlines less likely. You have 24 hours in a day; make them work to your advantage.

WHERE TO GO FOR HELP

It is essential to know what resources are available on and off campus. A resource is a person, place, organization, or anything that has the potential of providing you with information that may be vital to you at some point. Knowing your resources in advance allows you to save time. Many resources are available to you in college.

Professors. They not only teach classes but can recommend other good courses and professors. Visit your professor (preferably during office hours). This is extremely important. One of the many complaints professors walk into class with is, "No one came to my office this week." They're required to offer a certain numbers of office hours every week, and they have to be there! Can you imagine how boring and lonely that is? Office hours are a great time to introduce yourself and discuss problems. It is always a good idea for you to get to know your professors and let them match your name with your face. This may lead them to give you the benefit of the doubt concerning your grades and help them feel more comfortable writing a letter of recommendation for you should you go on to graduate, medical, or law school. Remember that there are too many students in one class for the professor to approach you; you must take the first step. Always try to foster a good relationship with your teacher.

Academic counselors. Counselors can be helpful in many ways. They offer information about activities, courses, professors, and procedures that are part of campus life. Don't be afraid to approach them. They are there to help you. Usually there is a bevy of counselors on campus, but once again it is up to you to make an appointment with one. Try to see a counselor early in the year, and visit on a regular basis. Counselors try to make navigating and understanding campus life simpler for you.

They can also help you figure out what courses should be taken for which major and when. Every year, inevitably, some seniors are told they can't graduate because they're missing a required course or lack credits. Consulting with your counselor throughout your college career can help you avoid being one of them. You can go to counselors for advice about almost anything. They can put you in contact with people who have information, and they can be helpful in finding sources of financial aid.

Organizations.   Probably existing on your campus are dozens of clubs and organizations with various foci, including clubs for cartoonists, jugglers, and ultimate Frisbee players, as well as those for writers, biology enthusiasts, and chess players. Look also for cultural groups, student government organizations, and the school paper(s). These groups can be a great way to meet new people, including your college faculty and staff, and learn about campus government and events.

You may also be able to get valuable experience in a field of interest. If you want to be a biologist, working in a biology lab can be useful to help you decide if you love lab work (an important part of biology) or if you hate it and want to move in a different direction. The experience you gain with organizations can also be a good addition to your resume. When employers see extracurricular activities on your resume, they know you're interested and willing to take the initiative to get involved.

Another major advantage in joining an organization is the opportunity to network; that is, to get to know people who know people and so on. You may not see the results of your networking efforts immediately, but you would be amazed at how many times a member has a friend who can help with "this" or a parent who can suggest "that." Organizations keep you tied to the larger network of the college community, while also providing contact with other students. Active participation can help you build contacts among students and faculty, and it looks great on graduate and medical school applications, as well as your resume.

Libraries and computer centers.   You are unlikely to graduate from college without using both the library and computer center on a regular basis. Most libraries today have not only books but also computer systems that make information more accessible to students. Some library computers (1) offer the ability to search CD-ROM databases for certain subjects, (2) allow a computerized search of the library's card catalog, and (3) supply Internet access. Computer centers may offer the Internet, math programs, and the latest in computer software to make writing papers and other assignments easier and less hassle for you.

Health centers and gymnasiums.   Students need to exercise their bodies as well as their minds. Thus you can find gymnasiums on many college campuses. Many have weight-training equipment, stationary bikes, Stairmasters, and facilities for swimming, basketball, volleyball, and racquetball. They may also offer classes such as aerobics. Gyms are also an excellent way to meet people interested in the same things as you. It is always nice to have someone to work out with, and if you start early meeting people who like racquetball or aerobics as much as you do, you may find a friendship that helps you stay healthy.

Health centers can help you get, or stay, well—with physicians who examine you and offer medical prescriptions. They understand that students often have limited budgets and sometimes no insurance, so they will likely have prescriptions at reduced rates, and walk-in hours when there is no charge. They are among the most convenient forms of health care, and their staff serve as campus health educators.

Other students.   Chances are, no matter what problem you're having, somebody else has encountered it before. And who better to help you solve a problem than someone who has already solved it? For example, if you have a language requirement at your college and you're not certain of your options, someone who has already explored those options will likely save you a lot of time and energy in research. They may also save you from taking a class that won't fulfill requirements—and ending up short of hours in that area.

Since your fellow students are your support system, discussing your problems with them and finding you're not alone can be comforting. No one likes to feel they're the only one in the world who has failed a class, and if you talk to someone who has done so, you may get insider tips for next time.

Resources can also provide ties to the college you may not have had before. If you were transported to a strange land, would you like a map of the sites and information booths or would you like to "feel your way" around? Those who choose to feel their way have my best wishes. But those of you who do not like feeling lost when it's not necessary can look to deans, professors, and clubs, all as part of a map to help you get your bearings so you know where you are and what path to take to get where you want to go. Many colleges and universities have school directories that make it easy to find out where people are and what functions are handled by which departments.

Keeping Track of Information

Get a folder. Gather all the information you can about deans, professors, classes, counselors, and anything else pertaining to school. Included in this folder should be a map of the campus. Thus if you need to visit your professor during office hours and her syllabus says her office is in the Plaza Building, Room 102, and you didn't know there *was* a Plaza Building, you won't have to make a phone call to her. Look at your map and be on your way.

After you have gathered all of this information—ideally, as early as possible—you will have a handy resource to make finding information on campus even easier. This will be helpful for classes or for keeping track of the people with whom you've had contact on campus. You'll become a pro at navigating your school.

If you have a list of all of the telephone numbers you use often, for example, your major department, the advising office, records and registration office, bursar's office, gymnasium, health center, then you will not have to waste time when you have a problem. The last thing you need is something else to do in order to fix it.

DIFFERENT STROKES: RESPECTING DIVERSITY

At home, you probably went to school with people whose cultural attitudes were somewhat similar to yours. College, however, is a cornucopia of people who speak different languages, who are part of different cultures, and who practice different customs. Instead of refusing to acknowledge or respect others' way of life, you can try to learn from them, to foster understanding, and to make this aspect of college a fun, exciting part of your life. Tolerance is necessary in college. Coming in contact with different people, you encounter their feelings and ideas. You won't get along with everyone, but making the effort to do so and respecting a person enough to hear their opinions and share your own counts for a lot. This can be a wonderful chance to broaden your horizons and to exchange knowledge and ways of looking at things you may never have had before. College is not just about sitting in a lecture hall, taking notes, and regurgitating information onto an exam. It is about learning and teaching. It is about thinking about things in new ways. It is about exchanging knowledge, one of the most rewarding and fulfilling things we will ever have a chance to do.

IN THE END

When it comes down to it, college is all about experience. If you let yourself experience it to the fullest, you will gain the most knowledge and understanding of yourself and the world around you. Good luck, and may you have the best experience of your life.

Applications & Exercises

1. Facing Your Uncertainties

You probably had certain fears and uncertainties when you entered college. First, make a list of all of your fears and determine if they have been alleviated. Is there anything that still concerns you about your college experience? Then make a list of people who can help you. Search them out.

_____

_____

_____

_____

2. Managing Time

Create a schedule and follow it for a week. Do you feel more organized? Would you like to have this kind of structure every week? What did you discover about how you spend your time and how you could be more efficient? Write down your observations and make any necessary changes to your schedule.

_____

_____

_____

3. Watching Progress

Start a folder and place your writing in it. After you have included several papers, go back and look at how your writing has changed from when you first set foot in college. How have you grown as a writer? What do you still have to work on?

_____

_____

_____

4. Watching Money

Now that you know how to make a budget, it's time to do it. List your income and expenses, and create a budget you can live with. Now follow it for one week. What changes should you make? Have you begun to see a change in the amount of money still remaining in your wallet?

_____

_____

_____

2 THE ADULT LEARNER RETURNS TO COLLEGE

Tips on Reentry

In this chapter, you will explore answers to the following questions:

➤ How can I return to school and still manage the rest of my priorities?

➤ What do I need to know right away when I go back to school?

➤ It has been so long since I was a student, how will I assimilate?

➤ What will my family and coworkers think about my return to college?

➤ What skills should I review?

❓ Thinking It Through

Check those statements that currently apply to you:

❑ I am not sure why I am going back to school, but I know I need to do it.

❑ I am afraid that I won't be up to par as a student after being in the workforce for so long.

❑ I don't know what to expect when I go back to school.

❑ After seeing my options in the workforce, I am more prepared than ever to go back and earn my degree.

ENRICH

2

THE ADULT LEARNER RETURNS TO COLLEGE
Tips on Reentry

►SO YOU'RE RETURNING TO SCHOOL

Today's college campus looks dramatically different from most campuses 25 years ago. Adult learners—typically 25 years of age or older with work experience between high school and college—are everywhere. The number of adult learners increased by 22 percent between 1985 and 1995, while enrollment tapered to a 13 percent increase among students below age 25 (National Center for Educational Statistics). You're certainly not alone. Obviously, some campuses have more returning students than others, but in most classrooms you will find yourself surrounded by adult students who have a life and work background from which to draw when applying classroom theories to real-life experiences.

WHY AM I RETURNING TO SCHOOL?

Some of you are glad to be returning to school. It's a chance to do something for yourself for a change. Maybe your morning routine is to wake up, make breakfast, pack lunches for the family, and then try to get everyone to the bus and to work on time. Or perhaps you are at home with a sick child or an elderly parent—or maybe you're ill yourself. Many people spend the day living by someone else's agenda at work—punching a real or imaginary time clock to satisfy a supervisor. Or perhaps you enjoy your work—you work because you really love what you do. And some of you just wish you had a job.

Whatever the circumstances, many of you view returning to school as something you do for yourself. It's the dream of a college degree or a chance to change careers altogether.

On the other hand, a few of you would rather do just about anything than return to a classroom. Many return to school for economic survival—the need for an income after a divorce or after losing a job. Your boss may have asked you to upgrade your skills by taking classes—it's almost impossible to keep pace with current changes in technology without some type of retraining. Some of you are financing your own education, and others have economic support from your employer.

For Your Consideration

List all the reasons you returned to school. Try to list every possible reason you returned to the classroom and identify why these reasons may have driven you (job, dreams, finances, things people have said to you about earning a degree, etc.).

_____

_____

_____

_____

_____

_____

_____

_____

_____

_____

Whether it was your choice or someone else's, the fact is that you *are* in school, so let's talk about making this a worthwhile experience. This chapter provides a discussion of valuable skills you already possess and those you'll need when returning to the classroom.

TURNING EVERYDAY SKILLS INTO HELPFUL TOOLS FOR THE CLASSROOM

Many adult learners have been out of high school for a number of years, and some never graduated from high school but instead completed high school requirements through the GED exam. When you last attended school, you may have been an excellent student or not. Fortunately, many adult learners find that they have developed lifelong learning skills that enable them to succeed more easily when they return to school.

Let's take a look at basic skills many adult learners already possess.

You have purpose—you know why you are in school. Having a purpose is half the battle. You probably had to think long and hard about returning to school, and you may have had to consider how this change would impact a family, a partner, or at least how it would impact the time you have for yourself. In addition, you are probably paying the bills for your education, and that may mean large student loans or even giving up a new pair of Nikes for your child. Nancy, an adult learner with teenage children, had no doubts about her reasons for returning to school. She was there to learn. Nancy remembers the time she registered for an accounting class a week after the term had started. She realized that she had missed too much information, so she decided to drop the course, study a little more, and then take it again. "A D or C would never make me happy," she reflected. "I really need to understand the material, so I will try to learn what I can on my own and then take it again." Returning students know why they returned to school, and they usually have the advantage of a very determined spirit.

Your life experiences will be a resource in the classroom. When first returning to school, it's common for adult learners to be slightly intimidated by the youth and enthusiasm of younger students. Don't shortchange yourself. Yvonne had worked with her husband for about 18 years when she decided to return to school. She recalls that the day before she enrolled in classes she was "scared . . . terrorized. It was like . . . can I cut the mustard? Can I do it? Can I go back to school at age 40 with a crowd of 18-year-olds?" It doesn't take long to discover that your work and home experiences will be applicable to what you study in the classroom. In fact, many faculty members encourage returning students to share examples from their daily lives to illustrate points made in class.

You have learned the skill of working with others. It is possibly the most valuable skill brought to college by adult learners: the ability to work with others. By now you have learned through work, the military, community groups, or other life experiences how necessary it is to work well with other people. It is rare for adults to complete a work assignment or project without any involvement from others. These skills will be invaluable in the classroom. There are several reasons to develop good relationships with students in your classes. For example, you will find that students within your major may be in several of your classes. This provides a good opportunity to develop study groups or study partners. Seek out students who bring a variety of skills to your study group. Some classmates bring organizational skills, some are good at presentations, and others have superior writing skills. Successfully coordinating the group's efforts will come from your past experience of working with others.

Classmates may also provide social outlets. For students with spouses or significant others, this can offer both partners additional support. Sometimes the student's partner feels excluded from the academic world that has opened for the student. By getting to know other students' friends, both partners can build a support group. New friends can trade off hosting group study sessions, or students with families can host multifamily outings.

The decision to return to school was likely not an easy one. The more support relationships you create and maintain, the more successful you will become. Friends at work and at home can help to maintain balance in your life, and it is essential that you nurture those relationships.

Following are some specific life skills you can use in the classroom:

➤ Many of you use a computer in your current job, so that's a basic skill you may already possess.

➤ You may eventually take a business or accounting class. Consider how these subjects relate to your life. What about the years you've managed a household budget, or the treasury for your church or community group? Haven't you read and reread those IRS booklets and learned to complete your own tax forms? Those are all practical, hands-on skills that few 18-year-olds possess.

➤ When the classroom discussion relates to international issues or to cultural diversity, you probably know more than the typical 20-year-old. You may have had years of experience working with men and women from different cultures or racial and ethnic groups, so you have examples to share from your experience.

➤ Many of you read the local newspaper every day. You and your instructor (and, possibly, other adult learners) may be the only ones in the class who really know what's happening in your city or town. Often those topics will arise in class, and you will be ahead of the game. You may also want to pick up a copy of the college newspaper when you are on campus—then you will have both the campus and community bases covered.

➤ You have probably had years of practice working on teams or in work groups through your job or in community organizations. You understand the economic realities of having to work effectively as a group. When you are placed in classroom work groups, you will have the well-developed team skills to complete the classroom assignment.

➤ You've also had plenty of practice learning time management skills. Many of you have juggled a full-time job and child-rearing. Now that you are adding one or more classes to your schedule, you may need to modify some of your current activities. We'll talk about this later, but the fact is . . . you have learned to make adjustments in the past and you can do it again.

For Your Consideration

Identify life skills that you have developed in adulthood. Think about why each of these skills is important to your success as you return to school.

WHAT LEARNING SKILLS SHOULD YOU REVIEW?

For many returning students, it has been several years since you were in a class-room. Whether or not you were a successful student, you will need to brush up on some of the following learning skills that may have become rusty. (If you have children in high school or college, ask them to help you remember the basics. You will enjoy the added benefit of helping them practice using their knowledge.)

Reading

Practically every course you take will require that you understand what you read. Reading textbooks can be a lot different than reading novels. Many of you will be required to take a freshman placement test in reading, English, and math. If you are placed in a remedial reading class, don't complain. Take advantage of this opportunity to practice reading different types of texts under the instruction of a faculty member. If you become a more effective reader during your first year in school, it will be to your advantage when you hit a term with several "heavy reading" courses.

Writing

You will be asked to write papers in over half of the classes you take, and it is essential that you understand how to present a logical and grammatically correct paper. If you have questions about writing a good paper, get help in the beginning. You may be able to take advantage of a free writing lab on campus. There are remedial English courses offered on most campuses, or you can brush up by reviewing a writing and grammar manual suggested by your instructor or found in the campus bookstore.

Computer Know-How

Computer skills will save you endless time and energy if you learn basic word processing and research tools. Most campuses offer computer labs for students who do not have access to a computer. There are a number of important ways you will use the computer in your classes:

➤ Most instructors expect papers to be typed. By typing your papers on a word processor, you can easily make changes if you find mistakes at the last minute. In addition, you will have a copy of the paper in the computer or

The Rules of "Netiquette"

E-mail is increasing in popularity every day; and just like the rules of etiquette, there are a few important rules of "netiquette." Netiquette is derived from a combination of two words—Internet and etiquette.

1. Be very careful that you say only what you intend to say in an e-mail message. In fact, it is important to reread every e-mail message before you press the SEND key. *You* know the intention of your words, but the recipient of your message does not have the benefit of your facial expressions or the tone of your voice. Before sending the note, try reading the message as if you were the recipient. The reader will not have all the background information you possess, and the note may be misunderstood if your words are not carefully chosen.

2. Likewise, be careful in the notes you send to your instructors. It is difficult to explain why, but most Internet users will agree that there is a false sense of familiarity in an e-mail message. These messages are usually more informal than a typed epistle on a letterhead. For example, you may disagree with something the faculty member said in class and you decide to follow up the classroom discussion with a quick e-mail note. Before you know it, the e-mail exchange has escalated to a serious disagreement, which you never intended.

3. Be respectful of your instructor's time. E-mail provides an excellent opportunity for many students to ask a quick question for clarification on an assignment or to let your faculty member know that you will not be in class one evening. Unless a bulletin board discussion area is provided on a course's Web site, most faculty members do not have time to engage in lengthy exchanges with all of their students. If your instructor answers your e-mail note with an extensive response, enjoy the exchange and move on. Do not expect that the instructor's response will be so lengthy every time or that the instructor has time to sit at the computer and engage in e-mail dialogue with you every day.

4. Finally, there are a couple of standard rules for Internet exchange:
   ➤ Avoid writing uppercase words in your e-mail notes. SENTENCES IN CAPITALS INDICATE THAT YOU ARE ANGRY AND ARE YELLING YOUR MESSAGE.
   ➤ Avoid profanity or strong negative language in your e-mail messages to another person. Among Internet users, this is called *flaming*.

5. If you are interested in additional perspectives on the culture of Internet exchanges, enter the word "netiquette" in a Web search and read more about the subject on the Web links.

on disk for later use. Often, you can use paragraphs or references from one paper in another class.

➤ The world is literally at your fingertips when you research topics through the World Wide Web (WWW) or by using one of many CD-ROM research tools offered in your campus library.

➤ Was your child ill and you had to miss class? Or were you late to class because of work? You may wish to correspond with your instructors and classmates through the Internet. You can ask where to locate the classroom information you missed or even apologize for being late.

➤ Several schools have e-mail/Internet accounts for students through a campus server. This permits access from home or work as well as from on-campus computers. Students have the capability to access libraries as well as to correspond with faculty, staff, and other students.

Math

If you took math classes in high school, you may be able to pick up a high school algebra, geometry, or calculus book for a quick review. For most returning students, however, a more formal math review of some type is necessary because math is so easily forgotten when you do not use it every day. Look in your campus bookstore and academic support centers for refresher or skill-building texts, such as the series from Prentice Hall, *Learning Express*.

Math Anxiety

Math Anxiety is probably the most common complaint among returning students. If math anxiety is not your problem, be thankful, because many returning students passionately dread that first math course. Marilyn returned to school at age 47. She relates that the only time she considered quitting school was because of a math-related class. "I just thought," she said, "you've come so far to give it up now . . . and I'm sure glad I didn't quit."

To place math in perspective, think of your life as a series of math problems. Look at all the things you do now that relate to numbers. You learned to do these things. They may not have been easy, but you have probably mastered some or all of them.

➤ Do you pay your taxes? your bills each month? and your loans?

➤ Do you balance your checkbook?

➤ How about that family budget? Do you have one?

➤ Have you ever bought a house or had a house built? That took lots of math know-how.

➤ Do you know everything there is to know about counting calories and fat grams?

For Your Consideration

Create your own math word problems with your daily experiences. You will probably be surprised to see how many "math" problems you work each day! For example, here is a sample problem many of us calculate each time we go to the grocery store:

> *Problem:* If you know that there are 9 fat calories in every gram of fat, how many calories of fat are there in a candy bar with 12 grams of fat (listed on the wrapper)? The total number of calories in the bar is 180. What percentage of fat calories are in the bar?

PRACTICAL TIPS ON BECOMING A GOOD STUDENT

The following helpful hints come directly from adult learners who are currently enrolled in post-secondary school.

➤ *Find a quiet place to study.* When you were young, your parents probably tried to get you to study without the TV on or the radio blasting. Find a quiet place for yourself and ask your family to honor that study space. It may be in your bedroom or in the corner of a big walk-in closet you convert to a study. Keep supplies in your special study area so that you will not have to spend valuable study time searching for the things you need (see box below). Also find a quiet place to study at school, close to your classes, in case you have a little unexpected study time before class.

➤ *Get to know your professors.* Introduce yourself on the first day of class, and ask questions when you do not understand the material. Most faculty members enjoy having the experience of a returning student in the class.

Supplies for Your Study/Work Area

➤ Dictionary, thesaurus (If there is a computer in your work area, you can access these tools through your word processing program.)
➤ Pens, pencils, and a pencil sharpener
➤ Highlighter
➤ Note pads
➤ Tape
➤ Paper clips

And if you have a computer:
➤ Computer paper and envelopes
➤ Extra printer cartridges
➤ Blank formatted disks

You can help keep their classroom current by sharing examples from your work situations.

➤ *Take an orientation tour of the library.* You will need to understand the design and layout of the library when you begin to research your first paper. However, you may not have time to take the tour then (or it may not be offered).

➤ *Try to study at least two to three hours for each hour you are in class.* Utilize break times between classes, children's homework time at home, and lunch hours at work.

➤ *Use campus tutors for your challenging classes.* Quite often campus tutors provide free services. At the first of each term, call to see if there are tutors for the classes in which you are enrolled and check the times they are available. Also, find out what services are available in the academic or learning support centers.

➤ *Try to be a good classmate.* Sometimes returning students have a lot to say; according to some younger students, adult learners have a reputation for talking too much in class. Certainly, you should speak up in class, but it is not necessary to answer *every* question the instructor asks. If you sense that this may be a problem for you, monitor what you say. Pay attention to how often other students speak, and gauge yourself by the class norms of participation.

HOW TO ACCESS IMPORTANT CAMPUS RESOURCES

Most adult learners have accomplished things independently for several years. They are accustomed to asking the right questions of the right people—locating a financial institution for car or house loans, using company benefits such as health insurance, investigating child care options, or establishing a checking account. This experience is invaluable on a college campus. Let's consider ways to find and use the resources available on your campus.

Admissions

The very beginning of your academic search process probably began with the college admissions or recruiting office. Your admissions counselor knows all the resources available on campus and can be consulted well after enrollment in referring you to other campus resources. After all, this is where basic campus information was first made available to you—through campus catalogs and other school publications.

Student Affairs/Dean of Students

The dean of students' office also offers a wealth of information regarding campus activities and organizations, housing options (including campus housing, off-campus housing, special arrangements for students with families, and guest housing), health care, counseling, and career guidance and placement services.

Again, these are professionals who specialize in assisting students and making referrals to other departments when student needs can be met elsewhere. When you encounter difficulties or when you realize that your campus fails to offer essential services for adult learners, let these staff members know.

Academic Advising/Counseling

Academic advising is usually offered within your major department or field of study. At larger schools, first-year students may be placed with advisors for undeclared or undecided majors until they pass a number of courses in an area called the *core curriculum*—English, math, history, etc. The composition of these required core courses varies according to the mission of the college or university, but the core curriculum is always listed in the college catalog. An academic advisor is critical to a student's academic progress—the advisor will assist you in building a plan to meet all requirements for your major. The advisor will help you to determine prerequisites (courses needed in a sequence) and corequisites (courses which must be taken during the same term). Algebra is an example of a prerequisite that usually must be taken before beginning calculus. An example of a corequisite may be a writing lab that must be scheduled the same term as Freshman Composition.

It is important to remember that some classes are not offered every term. Academic advisors help with planning not only for the next term but also for your entire academic career. They know which courses are offered only once a year, and they can assist in evaluating which transfer credits can be used to meet current course requirements. Get to know your academic advisor well, and take advantage of her knowledge of the campus curriculum.

Faculty Members

Most faculty enjoy having adult learners in their classrooms because returning students are usually more prepared and more fully engaged in classroom discussions. You should view faculty as partners in your college experience. Seek them out during office hours when you have a question. On some campuses, faculty members double as academic advisors, and this is especially helpful when you move into your major.

Some instructors also hire students as research assistants; this may be an excellent opportunity to work with an expert in your field of study. As a research assistant or an intern, your ideas are often sought and enjoyed. Sometimes there is a stipend or additional academic credit offered. In order to access these opportunities, however, it is important to get to know the faculty members on your campus. Take every occasion you can to get to know your instructors.

Clubs/Organizations

Many campuses have a recognized student organization for returning students, providing a rich resource for the adult learner. These clubs were developed to help adult students find colleagues, but they also serve as a united voice for representing returning students' concerns to campus administrators. Most campuses first recognized the needs of "non-traditional" students because of organizations like S.O.T.A. (Students Older Than Average or Students Over Traditional Age). Many problems have been brought to the attention of administrators, but policy changes and increased services have usually come through the efforts of recognized student groups. There may be an organization for returning students on your campus—check with your campus student affairs office for information.

Financial Aid Office

The financial aid department at your college will assist you in locating available grants and loans. Just as you do when taking out home or auto loans, review all terms and repayment conditions closely. Most student loans require reasonable academic progress and require you to take a certain number of class hours/credits each term. Talk with your financial aid counselor regarding loan conditions that must be met to prevent early repayment penalties.

Housing

If your campus does not have a department of housing or residence life, it is likely that the office of student affairs maintains community housing information. Often the office maintains updated listings of apartments, houses, and rooms available for rent. If on-campus housing is available through your college or university, there may be several special options for adult learners. Some campuses offer housing for students with families, while others have special housing set aside for returning students—sometimes in a residence hall and sometimes in university-owned apartments. Still other colleges offer guest housing for students who attend night classes and need housing only one or two nights a week.

Other Services

Most full-time and many part-time students are required to pay a standard student services fee each academic term. If you pay this fee, check closely to see what services are covered. You may find that some or all of the following services are offered free or at a nominal cost:

➤ *Health center services.* This may include reduced pharmacy rates, annual physicals at a significantly reduced cost, immunizations, a women's clinic, and sometimes dental service. If your college does not have a health center, the student affairs office will have community information regarding health options. Which clinics offer services on a sliding pay scale? Are there local clinics which offer discounts for preventive care such as flu shots, mammograms, etc.? Your student affairs or dean of students' office should have the answers to these questions.

➤ *Recreation/leisure services.* Some campuses offer recreational services for your entire family. The student activities office may offer on-campus movies, speakers, picnics, and athletic events. Occasionally, there are even special on-campus events or theater productions offered at a reduced rate. Many returning students complain that their mandatory student fees cover services they never use, so investigate the leisure schedules for ways to utilize the services for which you have already paid. Check for reduced-rate family passes to services such as the campus pool, camping equipment rental, and even softball or soccer leagues.

➤ *Tutors.* As mentioned earlier, your institution may have tutors available at a low or even no cost. In addition to students who tutor face-to-face, some schools have on-line tutors who can be accessed until late in the evening.

➤ *Learning disabilities clinic.* Many adult learners discover that they have a slight or serious learning disability in one or more areas. This may hinder the processing of math problems or keep you from succeeding in a foreign language class. Some campuses offer special services for students with learning disabilities, and this assistance can make the difference between failing or succeeding in school. If you have any reason to believe that you have a learning disability, do not let your pride get in the way. Talk with one of the counselors and seek the help you need to achieve your academic goals. (This may also explain why earlier educational experiences were such a struggle for you.)

➤ *Counseling center.* College counselors are trained to deal with serious psychological issues but most of their time is spent helping with regular life issues like the ones you face. When returning to school, you encounter a wide variety of transitions. Your family may not be fully supportive of your return to school, or the financial pressure may be much greater than you expected. The return to school may have even had a negative impact on your weight or on your eating habits. Many campus counseling services offer couples counseling, even if your partner is not a student. Take advantage of the counseling center on your campus. It may be the last time you will ever have an opportunity for free counseling. Seeking outside assistance with the transition to college is not only common but is also a healthy choice.

➤ *Employment/career services.* Employment and career counseling are also offered at most colleges. Career centers offer assistance with resume construction, career exploration, on-campus interviews, and other career issues, such as:

  ➤ *Jobs.* Due to scheduling conflicts, some students eventually choose to leave their current jobs for positions that allow more time for academics. As a service to students, many campuses maintain current listings of available part-time and full-time jobs.

  ➤ *Services for spouses.* Another area of employment services is in the area of assistance for spouses or partners of enrolled students. Job leads may be generated for students and held for them exclusively for the first few weeks of the term. After that time, spouses or partners are invited to review leads. Workshops for interviewing skills and resume writing are often available not only for students but for partners as well. By offering employment assistance to students' spouses or partners, increased financial options are provided for students' families. This service was requested by adult learners, and some campuses responded. If your campus does not offer such services, ask administrators to consider it.

  ➤ *Career counseling.* Another aspect of career services—career counseling—will assist you in keeping abreast of opportunities within your field of interest. What do companies expect in terms of academic

Check Your Pride at the Door!

Returning to school has a unique impact on each student, but one thing many students say is that they often feel very young and foolish again. You may be accustomed to being in charge—either in your workplace or at home. You know where things are located and you know how to get the job done. Returning to school provides an opportunity to swallow your pride and let others help you for a change!

➤ *Ask for help when you need it.* Utilize campus tutors, writing labs, and math labs. Ask your own children for help on the computer. Together, you'll probably learn something you both need to know.

➤ *Don't let it get to you if an instructor treats you like you don't know anything.* Most faculty members are there to teach, and they will do everything in their power to help you learn. However, just like at work or in your own family, there is always a jerk or two. Just chalk it up as a chance to face the challenge of dealing with a difficult person. Also, don't forget to give an honest course evaluation on the helpfulness (or lack of helpfulness) of the instructor.

➤ *And again, use campus resources . . .* you've probably paid for them!

preparation and work experience for specific positions? How does your current employer's benefits and salary compare to others? What other careers exist for you when you have completed your degree? What are the qualifications for certain degrees? Are there pre-employment steps such as drug testing, background checks, or aptitude tests for applicants? Career/placement counselors will assist you with specific information for all of these career possibilities.

JUGGLING EVERYTHING: TIME AND FINANCIAL MANAGEMENT IN YOUR HECTIC WORLD

Managing all the parts of your life will probably be one of the most challenging aspects of returning to school. Many returning students are employees, parents, partners, members of civic or church groups, caregivers for sick or elderly parents, and many other roles. You have probably learned to juggle numerous priorities and to accomplish several things at the same time. For example, a project may be due at work the same week your child is in a school play and your spouse or partner is away on business.

Time

It is inevitable—a return to school will impact how you divide your time. You may have established a routine that has been in place for several years, and now you must squeeze classes and study time into your family calendar. Most

instructors expect you to spend 2 to 3 hours studying for each hour you are in class. You are the only one who can decide how to allocate the time for all your responsibilities. Take a look at an annual calendar. Are there times during the year when the weeks are packed with activities and increased responsibilities? Are there times of the year when you may have to work overtime on your job? Look at building your course schedule around the times that may be more hectic. For example, work at a vending company may be more demanding on weekends during the fall football season. In this case, you may wish to schedule your classes on Tuesdays and Thursdays, leaving the weekends and Mondays free.

Use a home calendar to include all important dates—exams, business trips, school events, family outings, etc. Planning is the key to meeting all your commitments. Consult with your family when you plan the calendar. Have everyone in your household refer to the calendar and update it regularly. Schedule time to study each week, and record that study time on the calendar. Children may join you during a portion of your study time to complete their homework. The more your family or roommates understand and are involved in reaching your goals, the more supportive they can be by understanding the time demands you face.

Of course, there simply may not be time to do it all. Prioritizing activities and goals is critical. It may be necessary to give up the twice-a-week softball league while you complete your course work. Perhaps you could serve as a substitute for the league. However, scheduling time to spend with others is important in maintaining a balance in your life. School and work cannot be the only areas demanding your time and attention. Relaxation, exercise, rest, and socializing are all important to mental and physical health. In exchange, your work and academic performance will be positively affected. It is difficult for everyone when you return to school, but by spending time with your family and friends, you offer them the recognition that they remain as important to you as your new academic goals. Hopefully, this will encourage their respect for your time needed for preparing for class, and they will be less likely to see school as a competition for your time and attention.

For Your Consideration

Divide a sheet of paper into three columns. At the top of the first column, put the words *Essential Activities.* These are the things you *must* do. Essential activities or tasks are different for everyone. Your values help determine what you see as essential. You are the only one who can decide which tasks you simply cannot live without. The second column is called *Important, But Not Essential.* These are the activities or tasks that are important, but you can live without them if necessary. Over the third column, place the words *Not Essential.* These are the activities you currently do, but you can probably do without while you are taking classes. List all the activities and responsibilities in your life, and then place each item in one of the three columns.

After you've completed the chart, sit down with the people who are affected by the way you spend your time (your spouse, partner, children, roommate, etc.). Share the information on this chart, and check to see which tasks, if any, they are willing to assume either indefinitely or until you finish school.

Finances

Whether you are in school or not, finances play a major role in most people's lives. You may have planned for your return to school by establishing a budget, giving up some of the luxuries you enjoy, or perhaps even some of the necessities of life. Regardless of how well you have planned, financial shifts occur. Your spouse or significant other may suddenly be laid off at work, or you may have unexpected car repairs. When financial changes occur, many students draw back from school, working long hours to cover the unexpected debts. It is easy to think you will return to school when the crisis passes, but the more time a student fails to make academic progress toward a degree, the less likely he is to return at all.

Before you decide to take time off from your school work, consider the options available to you. All colleges and universities have financial aid counselors who can assist you in establishing budgets; identifying and applying for loans, grants, and other types of aid; and understanding the financial consequences of your decisions.

Other resources may be available at your place of employment. During the last decade, academic financial assistance has been on the increase as a company benefit to the workforce. Assistance may take the form of complete or partial tuition payments or flexible scheduling. Some companies select employees to take course work as a condition of promotion. Others offer to pay for courses directly related to the employee's current job description. Still others reimburse tuition at the end of a term if a minimum grade point average is earned.

If you seek financial assistance from your employer, you should fully understand the conditions that accompany the assistance. You may be expected to continue working for that company for several years if you accept the company's financial assistance. If an employee leaves the company prior to the length of time specified, he may be required to repay the financial assistance. Your employer's human resources department should be able to review both opportunities and company expectations for assistance.

In the best possible circumstances, you have the full support of your family or those closest to you. Almost any return to school will impact family finances, and it helps to have family support when tighter budgets are required. Both you and others affected may need occasional reminders of why you decided to return to school and of the opportunities your education will offer when you meet your academic goals.

Again, utilize campus services. Refer to your campus newspaper or student activities calendar for free or low-cost events. If the gym you have been using is not in your new budget, don't neglect exercise and recreation. You may find that there are special options open to you as a student. Campus outdoor recreation opportunities often include camping trips, rafting, and skiing, which become more affordable to students. Sporting events often hold seating just for students, so your friends may be able to attend "the big game" only as your guest! Because so many adult learners are returning to the campus, events for children and families have become campus traditions. On-campus residence halls host Halloween trick-or-treat parties and Easter egg hunts. Service organizations sometimes sponsor "parents' night out," when members provide child care so that parents can have an evening to themselves. A few campuses offer minimal cost day care services for children of students.

There are a wide variety of financial options available to students, so take time to investigate every possibility before you decide to leave school. The long-term benefits may be a worthwhile payoff.

SUMMARY

Your decision to return to school was probably not an easy one. The skills you already possess will serve as incredible resources during this adventure. In fact, look at this time as an adventure! There are others on this trip who will help you succeed. There are others who shared in the decision and who are supportive of your efforts. They will continue to be vital to your success. Keep them involved in your life. They will offer balance as well as helping to keep you from second-guessing your commitment. Share your ideas with faculty, and share suggestions for service improvements with campus staff members. You will gain as much as you offer to your college experience.

Initially, you may think you've taken on too much. As time passes, however, new responsibilities will begin to fall in with the natural pace of your life. The class work and responsibilities will become more routine. During interviews with returning students, the one thing so many of them said was that their motto had become "Don't sweat the small stuff." Do what you can, but don't be so hard on yourself. And above all . . . enjoy this experience!

Applications & Exercises

Key to Self-Expression: Discovery Through Journal Writing

Summarize the discussions you have with the following groups of people about how your return to school affects the relationship:

1. Family Discussion Questions

1. With a parent returning to school, how will the daily routine at home specifically change?

   _____

   _____

2. What chores can be redistributed (varies with age of children)?

   _____

   _____

3. How will financial change affect specific spending practices and allowances?

   _____

   _____

4. What are some no- or low-cost activities available for families in your community and on campus?

   _____

   _____

5. How can your family keep track of important dates and events such as tests, parent/teacher conferences, plays, athletic events, etc., each week and each month?

   _____

   _____

6. How can the family best designate study times and places in the home?

   _____

   _____

7. Who else is available for help—extended family, friends, college resources?

   _____

   _____

2. Spouse/Partner Discussion Questions

1. What changes can be done with daily routines to help balance school and work schedules?

   _____

   _____

2. What chores can be redistributed?

_____

_____

3. How will returning to school affect finances and what changes should be made with regards to spending?

_____

_____

4. How can we expect changing time demands to affect our time together?

_____

_____

5. How can you involve your partner in the educational process so that they better understand new things being learned and experienced?

_____

_____

6. What low- or no-cost events are available to couples?

_____

_____

7. What future goals are available when the educational goal is achieved?

_____

_____

_____

3. Discussion Questions for Your Boss/Supervisor

1. When are tests and exams scheduled for each class?

_____

_____

2. What courses best prepare me for advancement?

_____

_____

3. What courses/programs would help the company by having a trained employee enrolled?

_____

_____

4. What assistance, be it financial or release time, is available?

_____

_____

4. Discussion Questions for Your Coworkers

1. What is college like and what are you learning in the classes?

_____

_____

2. Would other coworkers be interested in coming to campus for an open house?

_____

_____

3. Would coworkers be interested in attending a campus event—athletics, concerts, lectures, etc.?

_____

_____

4. Would a coworker be interested in having the name of your admissions counselor or academic advisor?

_____

_____

Keys to Cooperative Learning: Building Teamwork Skills

Small Group Exercise (3-4 students)

List the top 3 areas where you would benefit from a resource (campus or community). Share these with your group and ask for ideas and suggestions of where to find assistance. Have each member offer one idea for each area listed and rotate so each group member gets the chance to specify 3 areas.

_____

_____

_____

_____

Critical Thinking

Design a monthly calendar with members of your household for dates to remember which are important. What was listed and by whom? What activities listed by others surprised you as being important? How did you prioritize when there were conflicts? Did you notice a pattern of one person's events usually overriding others? Did you notice that someone else was usually compromised? If either of these occurred, should the calendar be redone?

_____

_____

_____

_____

3 INTERNSHIPS
How to Get Them and Do Well Once You're Hired

In this chapter, you will explore answers to the following questions:

➤ Why do you want an internship?

➤ How can you best explore your options?

➤ Where can you find internships?

➤ How do you arrange summer internships and internships during school?

➤ How do you interview successfully for an internship?

➤ Can you create an internship where one doesn't exist?

➤ How do you prepare a resume for an internship?

❓ Thinking It Through

Check those statements that apply to you right now:

❑ At times I feel as if what I'm learning in college may do me no good at all.

❑ My past employers have been somewhat intolerant of my school schedule.

❑ I'd like to learn more about the career path I'm considering now, while I'm in school.

❑ I believe I could be an asset to a company in an internship role.

❑ I could use help revising my resume before seeking an internship.

❑ I would value being able to "practice professionalism" in a real work environment.

P R A C T I C E

MOCK INTERVIEWS

JOB S

NETWORKIN

USING THE I

DEVELOP A PL

RESEARCH POTE

The Career Center

328-4220 X4235

2nd Floor -
Crosby Student Center

CAR
SER
SER

INTERNSHIPS

ACTIVE LEARNING & EXPLORING

CREATES FOCUS & MOTIVATION

PROFESSIONAL CREDENTIALS

R

EMP
SCHO

E

INTERNSHIPS
How to Get Them and Do Well Once You're Hired

At times in your college career, you may feel as if what you are learning may do you no good at all. That is a normal fear—and sometimes a justified one. You won't use everything you learn in college. But how do you determine what will be useful and what won't? One way to test what you are learning, get credit for it, and gain real-world experience for your resume while still in college is with an internship.

What is an internship? An internship is on-the-job work experience in any of a variety of settings. Internships can take place in a corporate, non-profit, or any other environment. They may be paid or unpaid, continuing or by semester, structured or independent, available in summer, winter, spring, or fall, and in your state or another. This chapter will discuss the "ins" and "outs" of internships, how to get them, what's there, what to do once you've been hired, and how to leave gracefully. When you're finished with this chapter, you'll be a pro.

WHY DO YOU WANT AN INTERNSHIP?

Several questions may pop into your mind about your inexperience, your fear of your chosen profession, and the necessity of holding down a job. But once you have experienced the environment of an internship, you will be grateful for the insight concerning what you can accomplish during school and when you get out.

Have you ever had an employer insist on dictating your school schedule to meet their needs? Or not understanding when you have a class you need to take to graduate? Most students with jobs run up against these kinds of scheduling problems and many others. A little-discussed fact about internships is that people who ask for interns, ask for students. These employers (1) understand that students often have the most up-to-date knowledge about their industries, and (2) are likely to have the same zest for knowledge that you do. In addition, they understand that you are trying to educate yourself. They respect your role as a student as much as you respect their roles in the industry. In most cases, this makes for a mutually beneficial relationship between employer and intern.

Since you are in a learning environment, chances are you'll have your "hands on" much more within the company and industry than someone hired to do one task in a specific area. You'll have more opportunities to learn about the company as a whole and be able to make educated decisions about your life with that knowledge.

Throughout the years, standards held by hiring employers have been steadily raised. With the widening range and number of internships available to students, employers are expecting college graduates to come to them as ready-made experts in their industry. Therefore internships render students, as well as recent graduates, more employable from the very beginning. But let's not think only about your employer. What about you? The more you learn while still in school, the easier will be the transition to your first "real" job.

It's often difficult to get a job without experience—and to get experience without a job. Internships will help solve that problem because employers usually expect little or no experience from the interns. These are places to learn and get a jump start on the game of life.

Now that you have the drive and determination necessary, you have to know what you want to do.

EXPLORING YOUR OPTIONS

The first step in finding a great internship is deciding on a professional area. You don't need to know right now what you want to do for the rest of your life, but this process can help you get some clues. First, write down all the things you like to do and are good at—in school or out. This will give you a starting point. If you've always known what you've wanted to do, skip this section.

For those, however, who are traveling in the fog of life, unable to determine a direction (which includes the majority of students), career centers exist on most campuses. Staff of the career center will help you narrow your interests, explore your options, and create a fantastic resume. Available are personality tests (only to give you an idea, not absolutes), resume-writing workshops, and lots of other help. Now all you need to know is where to go for the job, right? Unfortunately, there's more to it than that.

TESTING THE WATERS

Even after you decide what you want to do, the job itself can be different from what you've always thought it would be. For this reason, it's good to keep your mind open, taking each option one at a time. Diversity in your college education, as well as your life, may be more helpful than anything else. Internships have helped many students (who thought they had a set path to the future) determine they didn't want anything to do with their chosen career field. This may seem like starting at square one, but if you decide early you dislike what you have been training to do, you still have a choice to rework your major or choose another to prepare you for an alternate career. Sometimes narrowing the field is the best way to choose what you want to do. (If at first you don't succeed . . .) With an internship, you have learned something about yourself, and possibly you've been paid, and received credit; all are successes in themselves.

Internships are not always what they seem, however. With different jobs, expect different experiences. Internships range from a quasi-classroom experience to the deep end of the corporate pool where you're left to sink or swim. One of the best ways to ensure you will not only swim, but enjoy and excel in your internship, as in life, is to decide you *will*—and try your best to do so.

WHERE TO FIND INTERNSHIPS

Now that you've decided to take the plunge, where do you look to find the perfect internship for you? It's important to remember that internships, like the best jobs, will not come looking for you. You must make the effort. Many sources, however, are available to help you.

Most schools have a department offering information on internships. Some even combine the career center and internship office into one in order to streamline the process. When you go, take information about yourself such as the classes you've taken, what you want to do, and when you can begin. (You will also need a resume.) Now don't turn around and run. Starting this process as early as possible will make your transition from school to work less painful.

According to Kristy Adams of the Center for Internships, University of Colorado at Denver, the hardest part in getting an internship is getting in touch with the people who can help you. Go to the center and ask for what you want, and then follow up. Internships (both paid and unpaid) are constantly available, waiting for someone to snatch them up. Most are great opportunities for students.

Internships also tend to turn up unexpectedly in your major department. Staff and advisors may have connections with companies offering internships in your field, and they can help you become prepared.

The Internet may provide more diverse information on internships than any other source. It knows no city or state boundaries, so if you're looking for something in a different location, surf's up.

Books, a more traditional source of information, are a valuable resource on internships throughout the country. Some include (1) *Peterson's Internships,* published by Peterson's, (2) *The Princeton Review Student Advantage Guide to Summer Programs,* published yearly by Random House, and (3) Sara Gilbert's *Internships: The Hotlist for Job Hunters,* published by Macmillan. These and many others written both by private authors and companies like Peterson's are available in your library.

Before you dive in though, decide when you'll have time. You may think, "I don't have time for sleep, so how can I make time for an internship?" Luckily, several options exist.

SUMMER INTERNSHIPS

In summer, most students must work. Why not combine your summer job with experience working in an internship where you test the waters of your chosen career? Summer internships are a great way to pave the road ahead—or when at a dead end, to put up detour signs and move on down the road.

Since some companies need extra help each summer, you might secure an ongoing job—possibly available to you even after graduation. Rusty Ablin, an engineering student at the University of Illinois, landed a summer internship at an engineering firm in Colorado, his home state, between his first and second years. He worked through the summer, loving his job, and was asked to return the next summer. After working there for the remaining summers in his college career, he graduated and returned to a full-time job.

All internships won't be like that, but one internship will often lead to another from the experience you'll gain and connections you'll make. After all, once you've completed an internship in an industry, you'll have more experience than many other students.

Summer Internships Away from Home

Who said you must stay home and work? Internships exist throughout the country and the world. These opportunities are open to you no matter where you live or go to school. A summer internship away from home is a good way to test a geographical area, not only an industry. For instance, if you move to New York City from Sandpoint, Idaho, and find yourself in a state of panic, you can return home to re-think your career. It's not long-term, and chances are, if you're determined enough, you will find work in your field wherever you choose to settle; but it's nice to explore your options.

Have you heard travel and diversity during college will help you as much as your classroom education? It's true. During your internship, you will have time to explore the area and see more than you would as a tourist. That means no expensive last-minute hotels and no skipping an historical site because you're going to be in the area for only a day. Plus, you'll be getting paid for sightseeing. If you can't afford to travel in fine style, you can't beat this alternative.

Nonpaid Summer Internships

Since you will probably have more time during summer, you may want to devote a few hours a day or week to a nonpaid apprenticeship. Your first thought may be "Why take a nonpaying job instead of one that pays?" Many companies offer internships for no salary when they know the positions are in high demand and the experience provided is a sufficient draw. Television news stations often offer these types of opportunities. Students line up outside their doors, as they're excellent places to start a career in broadcasting. These stations may provide

some paid internships and also continued work for outstanding students after the internship is over; after all, you've been trained, tested, and confirmed as worth the effort spent. (Consider it a long job interview for the job of your life.) Even if you are not sure you can afford to take a nonpaid internship, glance through the jobs offered in case an incredible opportunity presents itself.

INTERNSHIPS DURING SCHOOL

Sometimes a job during school is financially necessary. More and more students are paying for their own education, juggling school, work, and family. Finding time for yet another responsibility can be difficult. An internship can be the perfect opportunity to consolidate many duties into one. Several do pay, and many schools allow credit for internships. Often, students can get upper division elective credit within their majors through internships. Check with the internship center on your campus. Your major department may also have ideas about how to get as much credit for your hard work as possible.

In addition to saving you time, your internship may prove helpful in some of your classes. If the information you're learning in class is similar to the work you're doing in your job, you may have a leg up—in both. Practical application supports classroom theory. For example, a tough class in advertising that requires drafting copy and layout may be easier after an apprenticeship.

The best bosses let you get your hands dirty and will teach you what no classroom may. Also, learning the industry's organizational patterns helps students juggle high-level classes with greater ease.

WINTER INTERNSHIPS

In addition to the longer internships in summer and during school semesters, many companies have opportunities for project work during winter breaks. It may not be enough to give you an idea about the industry as a whole, but it will provide experience, insight into the company's atmosphere and work ethic, and possibly future job opportunities.

INTERNSHIPS AFTER GRADUATION

Internships are a valuable resource for jobs even after graduation. If you are still exploring career options when you graduate, take advantage of the resources on your campus: the career center/internship office, job postings on campus, and professors closely connected to the industry. Staying aware of the jobs available may give you a tip for an internship that may blossom into a full-time job.

INTERVIEWING

You've decided what you want to do and when you can do it. Now you have to get the job. Interviewing can be the most difficult part of the process, but it can also be the most helpful in landing you the perfect internship.

Whether you can barely remember your name when talking to new people or you're the best public speaker in the world, the best way to prepare yourself is to practice. The career center/center for internships can give you helpful tips on interviewing, and you do the rest.

For this you will need a good friend to listen and role-play to create an interviewing environment. Sit down beforehand and list your accomplishments, failures, learning experiences, and anything else that's made you who you are.

The most important thing to remember when interviewing is to *relax.* Breathe calmly and try to create a positive first impression. Your purpose is to communicate effectively to your prospective employer (1) why you would be good for the job, (2) your eagerness to learn, (3) your prior experience, and (4) your related extracurricular activities.

Don't babble, say "um," chew gum, or pick at your nails. Remember to breathe, and you'll do fine.

LOST AND FOUND: HOW TO CREATE AN INTERNSHIP WHERE NONE EXISTS

What if you've completed the process and haven't turned up a single internship that interests you? (Possibly the company you have your heart set on working for doesn't offer them.) Joyce Wheeler, manager for a Denver publishing company, said the best companies never have to advertise they are hiring; they get enough applications without lifting a finger. The same is true of internships. A company may offer internships, but if they are in such demand, they may not have to ask for people to fill them. But just because a company doesn't have to advertise doesn't mean they don't hire. It simply means they choose interns and employees from their stock of unsolicited resumes. This can be your opportunity to prove you have the initiative to ask for what you want, and if they don't need anyone, they'll usually keep your resume on file for when they do. Even if nothing comes of it, you've invested only some paper and an envelope.

What if the company you've hoped to work for since childhood has never offered an internship? See it as a challenge. Just because they haven't doesn't mean they've rejected the idea. Perhaps they don't know about student programs. They may be merely waiting for someone like you to provide the idea.

How do you go about it? First, convince yourself. Write out all the reasons you deserve an internship with this company and the benefits it will provide for you. Then decide how to persuade the company. Write down all the benefits an internship will have for them. The internship center may be able to help you, but consider these arguments: As an intern, you can be taught about the overall company and become a floater who can take up the slack where help is needed. Also, since interns are generally up-to-date on the industry, you can help the company remain on the cutting edge. In addition, after your graduation, the company may need to fill a full-time, permanent position: They won't have to train someone new, and they know you will do a good job.

Be creative. Add anything to convince a prospective employer that hiring an intern (more specifically, you) is a good idea.

After you've listed the reasons interns are assets, get someone to listen to you. Write a letter, call and ask for an interview, or talk with the internship office to get help—and, better yet, do all three. Now, that's initiative. It may be intimidating at first, but prospective employers will appreciate it, and you may end up with a great internship and a fabulous job.

KEEPING TRACK

Unlike other jobs, with an internship you may be responsible for what you have learned in order to receive credit through your college or university. You may be required to keep a journal of what you have done and give samples of the work you produce. This is necessary for your school to be certain your internship is a learning experience, but it can also be helpful to you. In your search for a job after school (or during school, as many students begin job hunting before graduation), it will be helpful to show you can do what you are being hired for. Start a portfolio now and add to it every time you complete an impressive piece of work, instead of frantically piecing it together when an employer asks the week before the interview for samples of your work.

Even if you are not getting credit and you think you may never open your portfolio again, it's useful to maintain a paper trail. This will help when your boss asks to take a second look at something you did previously—that you may have otherwise thrown away. ("Remember that press release you wrote last February? We want to produce something similar to that.") Saving copies (paper or on diskette) means you don't have to relearn what you've already done. It's a good practice to get into early.

An inevitable part of internships is making mistakes. Being new on a job is a learning experience, and with so much new information, you are bound to cross a few wires. In comes your paper trail. Tracking your mistakes, along with your successes, can help you discover what you did wrong and what steps to take to correct your mistakes and avoid making them again.

But mistakes aren't always bad. Being able to figure out how and why you made one can uncover problems with the "system" and perhaps solve even larger problems for the company.

RESUMES

An internship can even help you more than another job. Not only will an apprenticeship provide experience to add to a resume, but internships, paid or not, show you have the initiative to take control of your life, decide what you want to do, and take measures to accomplish that goal.

Because internships will probably be the most important jobs you have during college, put them right up front on your resume. They are your best selling point. Place them under *accomplishments, job experience,* or *internships,* and explain your duties in detail. (Leave out "fetching coffee," etc., or generalize them into "additional duties.") Sometimes, however, menial work can show you're willing to work your way up from the bottom.

PRACTICE PROFESSIONALISM

The corporate workplace can be different from anything you have ever experienced in school. The environment may be different, the dress code strict, and the people more conventional. Going from "student" to "professional" can be more complex than buying a new skirt or tie. It may require an attitude change to help you grow into corporate life, whether you want to or not.

One way to get "practice" in an environment unfamiliar to you is through internships. In some work environments, you may feel comfortable and thrive, while in others you may feel you will never adjust. Your surroundings at work can be very important to your overall happiness. You may discover that a job where you are permitted to wear casual clothing makes you feel lax about your work, and you would prefer more structured, formal attire. Or you may find your cubicle gives you too little privacy—or too much. A practice environment can give you a good idea of what you must have to be happy.

NETWORKING

On the job, you will probably come into contact with people from other companies in your industry. Although they may not be helpful to you now, file them in your mind, or literally, in a notebook or card file for later contact. With these people, make your abilities apparent, try to create long-term connections (with as many as possible), and don't neglect them. They may be able to assist you later, and it will help if they remember you.

MOVING ON

Now you've completed the internship and learned all about the job. You're ready to move on. Stop. Are you forgetting your internship is a learning experience? And now it's evaluation time. The most effective way to evaluate an internship is to sit down with your boss and talk about what you did right and wrong, how you improved, and what you can do to make yourself more marketable in the future. This is also a good time to suggest improvements to your employer so the next intern will not have to climb the same mountains. You may get as much from your evaluation as you did from the experience itself.

It's time to leave, but don't go jetting out the door, never to look back. Turn around and remember that the people in your field are those who can help you most. These are people with whom you want to keep in touch. Will they have jobs in the future that interest you? Do they know others in the industry who can help you land a job (internship or permanent)? Will they give you a good reference? These people can help you place yourself in the spotlight of your career. Let them.

Applications & Exercises

1. Creative Explorations

You have just landed your dream job. You walk into your office. Describe what you see. What is your first assignment? (This is an exercise to help identify your interests, the kind of work you enjoy, and the type of environment you thrive in. Have a good time and be creative, but remember you are trying to determine what you may want to do, not win a contest for "the most far-out job ever.")

_____

_____

_____

_____

2. Finding Your Way

Locate the career center/center for internships on your campus. Call them and ask for information. Find out how to get the ball rolling toward your eventual success.

➤ What are their procedures?

_____

_____

➤ What do they need from you?

_____

_____

➤ How can you help yourself?

_____

_____

➤ When can you start the process?

_____

_____

3. Building Your Contact List

Since you will probably have to make at least one contact yourself, make a list of how an internship will help both you and your prospective employers. Then call a company in your industry and ask to speak to the manager in charge of hiring. Run your ideas by her to see if you are convincing. You may even secure an internship. If not, try again.

_____

_____

_____

_____

4 MAKING THE SCHOOL TO WORK TRANSITION

Success Skills for the Real World

In this chapter, you will explore answers to the following questions:

➤ Where do you start and how do you avoid surprises?

➤ What is corporate culture and how does it affect you?

➤ What are some ways of handling conflict in the workplace?

➤ How do you "work smart," managing time and information wisely?

➤ Can you prepare for performance reviews?

➤ Is it possible to "create" a successful lifestyle?

❓ Thinking It Through

Check those statements that apply to you right now:

❏ I've been successful in school but I'm not sure if that will translate into success in the workplace.

❏ I'm concerned about making a good first impression and having my coworkers like me.

❏ One minute I think I'll make a good employee and the next I'm worried about telling my boss off or alienating a client.

❏ Although my communication skills are okay, I need help with presentations and basic writing skills.

❏ I don't use time as effectively as I'd like.

❏ I'm not sure how I would define "success."

SUCCEED

MAKING THE SCHOOL TO WORK TRANSITION
Success Skills for the Real World

Congratulations on taking a major step toward a brighter future! You have just passed through the institutional hallways of higher learning. And whether you recently graduated from college or completed courses to round out your education, the decision to broaden your knowledge and skill base was a good one.

You are now ready to embrace a new challenge: applying what you've learned to your chosen field. The school-to-work process is a **transition,** a passage from one stage to another. The kind of transition we will be dealing with is the one you will make from the world of academics to the "real" world of work.

"Hey, wait a minute!" you may be thinking. "I am already in the real world. I worked my way through college holding down a job." You're right. Perhaps for you the world of work is nothing new. You've worked your way through college, maybe even year-round, managing both school and employment simultaneously. You may even have children. You've experienced the added pressure of juggling school, work, and child care. Whew! It took enormous amounts of discipline and diligence to get where you are today. Hats off to you! In any case, you know what it takes to find and keep a job.

Furthermore, you have effectively conquered many other transitions, such as the one from high school to college, from job to studies, and likely even from one job to another. But the transition we are talking about is the one from college into a full-fledged career. That's why you've taken courses or earned a degree. You want more than a job; you're seeking a career. Are you ready for this challenge?

Whether you realize it or not, you have been preparing for this rite of passage all your life. It actually started long before you entered college. For example, if you were on a committee to decorate a bulletin board in third grade, you learned something from that experience —group dynamics, art appreciation, visualization, spatial relationships, meeting deadlines, pleasing the boss (your teacher) while pleasing the coworkers (your classmates), marketing the finished product, aesthetics, and sharing the blame and credit.

All that from cutting out a few fish from green construction paper, you say? Definitely. And the more you worked with other people, the more you learned about them and yourself. All these learning experiences along the way from childhood until now have prepared you for this climactic moment: the pursuit of a lasting, satisfying career.

In fact, that's the message of this chapter. Our purpose is to show you how to take the things you already know, but may not realize you do, and turn them into a solid career-building body of knowledge.

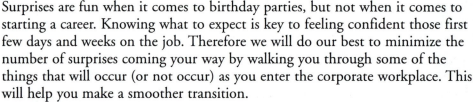

STARTING POINTS

Surprises are fun when it comes to birthday parties, but not when it comes to starting a career. Knowing what to expect is key to feeling confident those first few days and weeks on the job. Therefore we will do our best to minimize the number of surprises coming your way by walking you through some of the things that will occur (or not occur) as you enter the corporate workplace. This will help you make a smoother transition.

In order to make this transition successful, it's important to understand where you have come from and where you are going. You have just come from college or some other institution of higher learning. You are now going into the labor force. Being aware of some of the very real differences between school and work as a career—and taking steps to prepare for them—will help you successfully adjust to the changes about to take place.

Let's go back to when you started college. How would you describe your alma mater to a friend who's thinking about going there? You would probably tell her about the great computer science department and how your philosophy professor opened your mind to new ways of thinking. You might say the chemistry lab was a drag, the art department was cool, and the cafeteria food wasn't too bad. You might talk about the town, the tutoring program, and sports. But what are you leaving out? You're leaving out everything you had to adjust to so you could simply function in college—any college.

Like what? Like registering for classes. Your friend may not have done that yet. Or like where to park, catch a commuter train, or get a meal ticket. You also left out what to do if you can't stand your professor, how to drop and add a class, how to study, where to get used textbooks, or whether you can tape record lectures. You'd probably leave this information out for a few reasons.

First, you learned it early at school and then forgot about it. You took it for granted. Second, some of it was such a hassle that you'd rather not even remember it. And third, that's not why you went to school. All that stuff is just *stuff.* But if you think back, it was confusing getting used to it the first time around.

That's the way it is in business, too. Businesspeople forget to tell you these things for the same reasons: they take it for granted, they don't want to think about it, and it's just stuff—not the main deal. Understanding these things ahead of time, however, can make the path down career lane less rocky. The skills you learned in college, as well as your experiences, can be transferred into the world of work. This chapter will help you make those school-to-work connections. So take a deep breath, heave a sigh, open the door of the great big building full of employed adults and walk inside. Welcome to the career world, corporate style!

LEARNING THE ROPES

Those first few weeks on the job can be overwhelming. Knowing what to expect will help alleviate stress and make you feel more assured. Here are a few things you can count on happening right from the start.

On your very first day, you will probably need to report to the human resources department to complete forms. *Read everything given to you.* Then ask questions. Your humanities professor was right: there's no such thing as a dumb question. Clarify anything that seems vague, especially in regard to your benefits program. Find out when the benefits begin. Most health insurance plans, for example, don't kick in for at least 30 days, so be prepared.

The bigger the company the more likely you'll have an orientation period lasting from one day to one week. During this time, you'll be taken through the paces—the company history, the role of the company in the industry, greetings by top management, and all categories of employee life as outlined by the employee handbook.

Smaller companies may not have an orientation class or employee handbook. Instead, an office manager or other administrative personnel will introduce you to office protocol. Be sure to listen and take note of her instructions. Again, ask questions if anything is unclear.

FORGET THE RED-CARPET TREATMENT

On your first day of work, everyone will be happy to see you. You are going to do something new and exciting. Everyone will be nice to you and make an effort to make you feel welcome. Right? Don't count on it. As in other jobs you've held, you will be treated cordially, but you can forget the fanfare.

Some people will make a big deal about your arrival. Good people exist in every organization. They will go out of their way to greet you and make your life easy. Remember these folks when you need help learning to do something like requisitioning materials.

Other employees may see you as a threat, especially in the corporate world where—for most—climbing the ladder is of supreme importance. To them, you're another body they must climb over to get to the top. To some, it's just another day at the job and you're just another face in the hallway. As you get to know them, however, you'll discover they are not rude. It's just that meeting the new kid on the block isn't high on their priority list. Don't take it personally. While your first day is a big deal to you, to almost everyone else it's just another workday.

MAKING A GOOD FIRST IMPRESSION

People are quick to make a judgment when meeting someone for the first time. You can make a lot of ground with someone by your first impression. On the other hand, it's hard to recover from a bad first impression. This is true both inside and outside the classroom.

Make the first move to introduce yourself to people. If you see someone coming to talk to you, greet him as he approaches you. Always say your name if you haven't seen him in a long time or are not certain if he remembers you. People forget names all the time. If the tables are turned and you forget their name, reintroduce yourself; they may offer their name again.

Another way to make a positive impression on the people you meet—and learn something in the process, too—is to handle their questions quickly and politely, then turn the conversation around to them. We all love to talk about ourselves. Find out what they do at the company, how long they've been there, and so on. Ask about the people in the pictures on their desk. Comment on artwork and memorabilia they have in their offices. By doing this you learn a lot about the roles of other people in the company. In a business setting, very few people greet you at the door, say "hello," and jump right into business. Be human and loosen things up. It's easier to deal with people when you treat them as people.

YOUR FIRST ASSIGNMENT

Even though you're no longer in school, you'll continue receiving assignments. Your boss will probably start you out on one project. You might work on it alone or with a team. Be as flexible as you can. Remember this important ground rule: Make certain you understand the assignment before you begin. Don't be afraid to clarify what you have to do. It's better to clarify than sit at your desk and realize you don't really know what "it" is, and she wants "it" done when she returns in two days. Ask questions. Then, when you think you understand, repeat what she said (or what you think she said). She will either agree wholeheartedly or verbally give you minor changes or corrections.

Remember those college deadlines? You had to turn in a paper by a certain date. The same is true here. Ask for a deadline if the boss doesn't give you one. Some bosses are vague. ("Oh, when you get around to it.") If she can't be pinned down, take a stab and suggest one yourself. (Give yourself enough time; don't go for a quick turnaround to impress her.) "What about first thing Thursday morning?" She agrees. Done. Write it down.

If the assignment warrants it, make an appointment with her "first thing" Thursday morning to turn in your work. In fact, if she doesn't set up regular times to meet with you, initiate this system—the way you did with college professors to be certain you were hitting the mark.

SUCCEEDING ON THE JOB

Just because you've reached your goal of finding a job doesn't mean your goal-setting days are over. Now that you're a fully functioning professional, it's time to set new goals.

The world of work is similar to college. Begin by looking at where you want to be in your career. Map out a course for your professional development and establish goals that relate to your career. Ask yourself, "What do I want to accomplish in this position? What do I want to learn from it? Where do I want to be one year from now and three years from now?" Think of managing your career just as you did your college experience, or as you would your own business.

CORPORATE CULTURE

As you probably know, different companies operate in different ways. They all have their own distinct "personalities." From sociology class, we tend to think of *cultures* as groups of people with modes of behavior, styles of dress, and philosophies in common. Corporations have their own cultures. Certain companies expect, even demand, their employees dress a certain way. Men may not be allowed to wear sport coats, only suits, and not brown suits but dark blue ones. Other companies might not care if their employees wear suit coats at all, even though the nature of the work is about the same.

You won't find everything you need to know in an orientation class or employee handbook. Important details, such as who calls the shots and how corporate politics are played, must be learned elsewhere. Who are the people who have the real power and influence in your company? What tips and short-cuts do you really need to do your job effectively? This is information you must find out on your own.

If you attended a large university, you may have had very little personal interaction with your professor and none at all with the president of the school. Your professor may have taught hundreds of students at one time using a microphone in an auditorium. Smaller campuses tend to be less formal, and you can easily mingle with the educational staff.

Companies operate in a similar way. In some office buildings, senior management rarely interacts with staff; in others there may be a friendly interchange of conversation and ideas. Again, this is an aspect of corporate culture. Picking up on what's acceptable and following suit will help you work more efficiently. For example, does your organization communicate through formal meetings or water-cooler chats and hallway gatherings? Look at old memos, proposals, letters, and contracts. Learn how the company communicates and what's considered normal. Ask to see a contract or order and see how it's produced. Do you have authority to make decisions on your own or must you see a supervisor and seek approval?

MONEY AND TIME

Two things every company values are money and time. Discern how your company views both. With regard to money, is it a frugal company where conservation is high on their list of *dos?* Or is it a company that throws some caution to the wind and spares no expense for equipment and travel?

Time really is money and companies spend it in different ways. Advertising agencies, law firms, and other types of businesses bill their clients at hourly rates. Some expect you to account for every moment. Others may allow you to come and go pretty much as you please, as long as the work gets done. Look around the company and follow other people's leads. Do people work weekends? It may not be required, but is it expected? Do people take a late or early lunch? Does the office clear out at 5:30 or do people stick around until 6:45 when the boss leaves? As the new kid on the block, always be the first person to arrive in the office and don't be the first to leave. Everyone notices when you come in late or leave early.

HITCH YOUR WAGON TO A STAR

The best way to learn is by doing. You may have studied computers from a textbook, but it wasn't until you began using the mouse that you became adept at manipulating a computer program.

Often you can do the work, but you want to improve. In that case, the next best thing is to watch those who have mastered it. Find a mentor. From whom can you learn the most? You probably did this in college by noticing the exceptional student (it may have been you!) and studying with her once in a while. Do the same in your office situation. Watch who it is people truly listen to and whose opinions are valued at meetings. Who do people ignore? Who is respected? If a boss consistently interrupts or contradicts a certain person, yet listens patiently and attentively to someone else, you can easily spot who ranks high on the totem pole.

Once you've figured out who to emulate, ask these "stars" if you can sit in with them while they make phone calls or attend meetings. Listen to them on the phone and observe how they treat their customers and interact with management.

You've heard the phrase "Birds of a feather flock together." Management often buys this. Consider how easily cliques formed at school. It seems people like to be around others like them. The lesson here is: watch who you are seen with and associate with. Don't hang out with an employee who has a reputation for being crude and lazy or you will be similarly identified. Let those with sterling reputations and high performance rub off on you. If that person's career takes off, you might go along for the ride. You become grouped in that category by association.

RELATIONSHIPS: GETTING ALONG IN THE REAL WORLD

Certain relationships are unique to the professional world. Dealing with superiors, bosses, coworkers, clients, and subordinates or being a member of a team can pose special challenges that require relational skills.

A Word About Bosses

"Even if you've had a boss before in some other job, this will be different because now you're working in a job that will be part of your career. You'll have stronger opinions about how to do your job than you did about delivering pizzas," explains Garrett Soden, author of *I Went to College for This?*. He suggests you view your boss as a customer. "Treat your boss as you would a client who is paying for your services. If you expect a promotion somewhere down the road, do what it takes to make your boss a satisfied customer," says Soden.

Managers are often master jugglers. It's not uncommon for them to have many projects at once. Therefore respect your boss' time. When relating something to your boss, spare her the details initially. If it's something where minutia are not important, get right to the point.

Notice that business plans often include **executive summaries.** An executive summary is a brief synopsis of the report, sort of like Cliffs Notes. Give your boss the Cliffs Notes version of a situation. Provide enough detail so he fully understands what you're saying. If he wants more detail, he will ask. If you need extended time to explain something, schedule an appointment and let him know how much time you will need. On the day of the appointment, don't extend the promised time frame.

The job of a manager quite obviously is to . . . well, manage. That can mean many things, but one of them is to help you correct your mistakes and help steer you in the right direction.

Don't get defensive when you're criticized or someone gives you advice. Constructive criticism from your English professor helped you master the language. Also, a self-righteous attitude and fragile ego do not play well with bosses and managers.

When you receive criticism or advice, ask your boss how he would have handled it. A good manager will tell you this anyway, but if a situation is heated or you feel you are getting dumped on, put it in his court. Find out if he's been in similar situations and how he dealt with them.

Your job is to make the boss look good and shield her from surprises. Bosses hate surprises. Head problems off at the pass. If you know that sales numbers are going to look bad or something will not work out, don't wait for it to happen and watch the boss freak out. Soften the blow and prepare her. If you provide your boss with small progress reports, you will prevent her from having to come to you to ask what is going on or to put you on the spot.

The American work ethic—work hard and opportunity will come—is still valuable, but needs an addition: "Work hard, *use your people skills,* and opportunity will come." In a letter to the editor of *Fortune* magazine, industrial psychologist Michael Mercer commented on how it takes much more than results and effort to make it today. "Being highly competent plus fifty cents will only get you a cup of coffee. Being highly competent plus making a superb impression on the people who make or break your career can eventually get you $100,000 annually."

Remember that your boss has a career plan and path, just as you do. He is trying to promote himself, just as you are. Your boss can promote you, recommend you, teach you, look out for you, and generally help catapult your career. But remember that he is trying to advance. Don't put all your efforts into one person. Spread yourself around the organization and become known. Do things for other people and become known to managers and heads of other departments.

How to Handle Clients

The key to dealing successfully with clients, customers, and patrons is quite simple and straightforward, yet takes considerable effort. The most important rules for having successful client relationships are to tell the truth and treat the client fairly. If you have their respect and trust, you will more likely have their business. If you don't know the answer to something, don't bluff your way through it or give false information, only to come back later to correct it. If you don't know right then, say so. "I'm sorry. I don't know, but I'll find the correct answer for you."

Say what you mean and mean what you say.   Don't say *challenge* when you mean *problem*. You don't fool anybody. The client may not like what you have to say or may even disagree with you, but she will definitely respect you. Don't be known as someone who rides the fence. Know your position and stick to it.

Don't act as if you are interested only in their money or service.   You are dealing with other human beings. There is no easier sale in the world than repeat business and referrals from happy customers. Your reputation extends far beyond your immediate clients. People are more likely to tell someone about *bad* service and products than good.

How to Work in Teams

While in college you probably worked in study groups. This experience will serve you well now. Often in your career you will work with a partner, on a committee, or as a member of a group or department. As you know, groups have special dynamics requiring particular skills to accomplish tasks. Being a team player does not mean sacrificing yourself. It means being a contributor, participating, and sharing. A common problem for many groups or teams is a lack of direction and focus. As one of its members, help the team develop a goal. Is it to brainstorm ideas? To increase sales? To devise a new pricing policy? To design a project?

Another problem typically cropping up in groups is *leadership*. When groups form, there may be an assigned leader, or one may arise from the team members, but clear-cut responsibilities must be determined and delegated. Will leadership be shared? Will one person be a facilitator? Your responsibility as a group member is to be certain those issues are addressed, so the group can focus on goals.

Some people go on ego trips when they're in groups. They take too much ownership and operate like dictators. Don't be intimidated. Hold your ground if you believe in your ideas. In turn, make people substantiate their claims or ideas. If you see someone getting run over or being apprehensive about participating, try to make him comfortable. Ask him what he thinks.

How to Handle Peers and Coworkers

How employees work with peers is becoming increasingly important in the workplace. Your success in dealing with coworkers demonstrates your leadership abilities. Being a leader means providing an example your peers can respect. Making a smooth school-to-work transition involves learning how to work well with your colleagues.

According to Barbara Reinhold, author and career coach, "Eighty percent of career failures have to do with personality and communication issues." It really is the little things that count with people. People like to be appreciated. Don't you? If a coworker has performed well, helped you out of a pinch, or done you favor, write him a note of appreciation or take him to lunch.

Handling Conflict

Because we live in families, work with other people, and often have roommates in college and later, we all face conflict. One roommate might be a "neatnik," while the other is messy. Their different living habits can become a breeding ground for conflict. Whether it's a disagreement or a full-fledged argument, civil rules for resolving conflict without damaging the relationship do exist.

Use the passive voice.   It's so easy to start blaming someone in an argument. "You did this. It's your fault." When conflict arises don't use the word *you*. When people hear *you* in a heated situation, they feel attacked. Instead of saying, "You did it wrong," use passive phrases: "This needs some modification." You're saying the same thing, but not attacking.

Do it on your own terms.   You can't please everyone all the time, and not everyone will please you. When you are upset, think before you speak. Use the old-fashioned method of anger control: take a deep breath, exhale, and count to ten. Confront the person on your own terms. Be direct, always keeping in mind, however, that *you* make mistakes, too. Get it off your chest and then forget it.

Let people save face.   Keep conflict and disagreement with clients or bosses nonconfrontational. Don't try to press a point too much with clients or they won't come back. Don't hammer your boss into letting you have your own way or you'll never get it again. Being a good, tough negotiator doesn't mean you win and they lose.

COMMUNICATION SKILLS

One reason you completed school is because you have the ability to communicate. You communicated with a variety of people in a variety of ways: in person, one-to-one, over the phone, in writing, and in group discussions. You even used body language to communicate. Communication was central to your success in school. Likewise, the skill most critical to career success is communication. This section will help you tailor your communication skills for the work environment.

People skills are paramount. No matter what you do, at some point in your career you will interact with people. You will write, listen, maybe even speak in front of a group.

"You might think that a company like Microsoft would be full of 'propeller heads' with Ph.D.s and their heads in the clouds. Sure, you can find that. But, surprisingly, you have people who have degrees in English, French, history, and other disciplines that seem totally unrelated to software," writes Bradley G. Richardson of *Jobsmarts for Twentysomethings.* "You can teach anyone the num-

bers and the technical aspects of something, but you can't always teach people how to communicate," states Richardson.

Your Professional Presence

Communicating effectively involves much more than what you say. It's also how you say it. Your delivery, tone, and nonverbal gestures affect how your message is received.

Keep your voice even and steady.   Speaking smoothly and at a moderate pace makes people feel more comfortable and helps you be understood. If you are so excited you speed up and start running words together, you'll make the other person nervous. If you are speaking in a flat monotone, you will have to periodically wake her up. Find a happy medium.

Don't slouch or lean on furniture.   Try not to look as though you're at your kitchen table. As your mother said, "Sit up straight." Act like you *want* to be there. If you're slumping in your chair or fidgeting, it's obvious you want to be somewhere else.

Make people notice you.   Consultant Debra Benton, in her book *Lions Don't Need to Roar,* recommends pausing for a second upon entering a room or meeting. It sounds corny, but you create a presence. If you are late and just arriving, let people see you. Don't try to slink into the room so no one notices. You're noticed anyway. Remember, you can get away with a lot if you act with confidence—as though you know what you're doing.

Presentation Tips

Studies have shown that one of the greatest fears of Americans is the fear of speaking in public. Chances are high that at some time during your career you may be asked to speak in public. Here's a brush-up course on how to give a spectacular presentation.

The first step is to identify your audience to tailor your presentation to them. You'll also need to know how many people will be there, what kind of equipment you will need (e.g., chalkboard, overhead projector, microphone), and how long you have to speak.

Never wing a speech.   You will be nervous enough being in front of an audience, so practice at home in front of a mirror, or better yet, a friend. Even pros who have done it a thousand times practice because they still get butterflies.

People prepare speeches differently. No set way to do so exists, but one of the most effective is to develop an outline with key points you want to make, such as statistics typed or handwritten on a 3 × 5 note card.

Place everything you need on the podium beforehand.   Have a glass of water handy. You may not need it, but you don't want to have a coughing spell and lose your momentum by asking someone to get you a drink.

Let the audience know you will take questions at the end. If someone interrupts you, tell them you can meet with them afterwards to discuss their question further, or simply remind them you will field questions when you are finished. It's your show, so keep it on track.

Speaking to your audience. You don't need to scream, but be certain the folks sitting in back can hear you. Make eye contact with audience members. Find some friendly faces in the crowd. Key in on these people and look at them to gauge how you are doing. From time to time, scan the audience and look at everyone. This gives the impression of involving people and personalizing your presentation. Don't be self-conscious or act cautiously. Speak with authority, as if you know what you're talking about. Remember, some things you may feel are really noticeable, the audience can't see or doesn't care about.

Listening Skills

When listening to someone, give them your full attention. Without the necessary information, it's easy to jump to conclusions or make judgments. Think about what they said and then say what you mean. When you choose your words wisely, they will have more impact. The person respected for his opinions chooses opportunities to say something appropriate for the moment. When speaking, the goal is to impart something beneficial to the person with whom you're talking, instead of parroting a canned response. You can respond effectively only by listening.

Writing Skills

You may have dreaded writing term papers in college and thought once you were out of school your writing days would be over. You can't, however, escape writing in our age of information. Every industry has a different way to write and correspond. During your first few days on the job, ask if you can see old letters, reports, memos, or anything else you may have to write. Then study them. This will ease you into the task of writing when it is warranted.

The first thing to realize about writing is there's always room for improvement. One surefire way to improve your writing skills is to read good writing. It serves as an example for you to follow. Also, reading will improve your structure and grammar. If your writing skills are lacking, write letters to your family, keep a journal, and write thank-you notes instead of calling. As with so many other things, you become a better writer by doing it.

Meetings

If you served on a committee in school, you're familiar with meetings. You may have gone to regularly scheduled staff meetings at your previous job. This prior experience will come in handy now, because in the corporate workplace, meetings are a way of life.

The main purpose of meetings, of course, is to share information by catching everyone up on what everyone else is doing. As a new employee, arrive on time, don't talk too long (if at all, as newcomers are often not expected to contribute information at the first meeting or two), bring the items your boss told you to bring, provide enough copies for everyone, make sure charts are large enough to be easy to read, and take notes. Taking notes obviously means you will need a notepad and pen. It's also a good idea to bring your calendar/organizer to record the date of the next meeting and other office-related events.

Getting Noticed: Become Your Own Public Relations Firm

You are always selling yourself and your ideas. When you convinced your study group to take on the cleaner air technology assignment, you were selling your idea. And the interviews that landed you the job you now have were a process of selling yourself. The key to rising quickly and being promoted in the real world is to make your achievements and accomplishments known to the people who matter and can influence your career.

Don't toot your own horn, but in the course of conversation, let people know what project you're working on. Tell them how you closed a certain deal, managed a thorny situation with a client, or achieved something unprecedented.

Another way to do this without being obvious is to ask for advice. Tell your boss you are working on certain projects and would like an opinion. This way the boss knows what you are up to and will keep an eye out to see how his advice turned out.

Be different.   Keeping a high profile and being noticed takes constant effort. Always be on the lookout for ways to stand out and be different. Not "weird-different," but unique. Look for things others don't think of or ways to do them differently within your own style.

Volunteer for other assignments.   Remember those extra-credit assignments you could volunteer for back in school? The same principle still applies. Volunteering for projects not already assigned to you is an excellent way to impress your boss and earn brownie points. Volunteer for committees, teams, or task forces. Ask to make presentations at company meetings and functions. Reflect frequently on your role in the organization and how you can enhance what should already be a positive image.

After you have a few successes under your belt and are comfortable in your new position, take a few chances to show what you can do. Get noticed by seeking high-visibility, high-reward jobs. You might say, "Why would I do that? It's an opportunity to fail in front of everyone." That's just it. The more risk there is, the greater the possible reward. If you accept a very risky task, people expect you to fail. If you don't succeed, so what? You haven't disappointed anyone. No harm done. On the other hand, if you accept a challenge and succeed, you look like a hero. Win or lose, you can't go wrong taking the risk. Management will look at you favorably for getting in there and giving it a shot.

Volunteering for assignments *outside* your department.   With your boss' permission, help organize the company blood drive or annual picnic. It's a way to get out of your cubicle and into view of people from other departments.

Offer to write for the company newsletter.   Ask someone who writes well to edit it for you. You belonged to clubs and organizations in school that enhanced your education. Act along those same lines now. The knowledge you receive will help you better understand your field, thereby stocking your mental quiver with valuable information to write about. As your writing skills improve and your knowledge base expands, submit material to magazines in your field.

Make yourself a resource.   Perhaps you were one of the few students who knew about a local "cyber" cafe offering computer time. Transfer this same helpfulness to your new job. Become an expert at something people need. You might know a special procedure or have technical experience in an area. Always have an open-door policy by making yourself available to answer questions and offer help. Even keeping up with the office grapevine can make you a resource. Whether it's a peer or your boss, make yourself invaluable.

Dealing cards.   Always carry business cards with you and remember to give plenty of them away. When you meet someone, offer them your card. Spread your name around with people and make certain they know it.

As important as giving your card to someone is, also be sure you get hers. Write notes on the back of her card to serve as a memory jogger. It's also a nice gesture to develop the habit of dropping a short note after meeting someone. It can say as little as, "I enjoyed meeting you last week. Stay in touch." It may seem insignificant, but the small gestures are what stand out in people's minds.

WORKING SMARTER

Managing time and information can become overwhelming very quickly. No doubt you've already had lots of practice juggling school work, social engagements, and job schedules. Your classes were structured, and typically you knew what was expected of you. Career work is often less structured, and therefore presents its own time-management challenges. Yes, you will have a job description to follow with deadlines to keep, but the rest may be entirely up to you. In order to make a smooth transition, you'll now need to apply the juggling skills you practiced in school with a little more rigor. One thing is certain: To keep all the balls in the air, you need a system.

Have Only One (Really Good) Calendar

A common trap people get into is to keep several calendars. They maintain one at the office, carry a "DayTimer," and have a wall calendar at home. Consequently, they write something down on one and then forget to look at it. None are consistent. Keep only one calendar in which you write down everything. Select one that allows you to manage your time and keep your schedule and any pertinent information in one place. Use your calendar, not only to manage your schedule, but to keep phone numbers, addresses, and notes at your fingertips.

Use Your "Downtime" Wisely

Downtimes are moments, for instance, when you are commuting on a train or bus, traveling in an airplane, having your car repaired, or waiting in the doctor's office. View these pockets of time as opportunities to organize your life or accomplish tasks.

Work on an ongoing project or read. Always keep a notepad and pen with you to write ideas or map a strategy for the next day. Take newspapers and magazines with you when running errands that involve a wait. Listen to books-on-tape in your car. A million distractions can control your time; don't let them control you.

Poor Time Management

Here are a few ways to *waste* precious time:

- ➤ Working without a plan or list
- ➤ Killing ants instead of elephants: small-priority items over high-priority items
- ➤ Trying to do everything: not delegating
- ➤ Trying to do everything perfectly instead of just getting it done.
- ➤ Failing to control interruptions.
- ➤ Not thinking ahead.

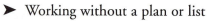

MANAGING INFORMATION

A good deal of time is wasted reading the same thing two and three times simply because it's on your desk. If you've read it once and haven't thrown it away, take a pen and mark the corner with a check or your initial to show you've already looked at it. Better yet, file or respond to it immediately.

Many offices are attempting to become paperless. This means the paper mountain is becoming an electronic mountain eating up computer memory. To free up precious memory space, trash unwanted E-mail. The same is true for computer files. Excess files on your hard drive or network will make it more difficult to keep track of everything and will slow your computer system. Think of your computer files as you would a regular filing cabinet. Place all documents of a certain type (e.g., letters, memos, contracts, reports) in the folders, and you will know exactly where everything is.

Always Back Up Your Work

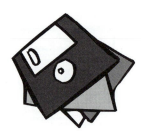

Have you ever typed a paper for two hours only to have your computer freeze on you? Nothing compares with that kind of panic, except when you do something similar in business where the stakes are even higher. Back up your work *while you are working on it.* Make an additional copy to be kept in another folder on your hard drive, and also make a copy on a floppy disk you can store elsewhere. The same goes for hard copies of documents. Make copies of anything that is very important or can't be replaced. Keep these duplicates in a safe place away from the originals.

Make Things Easy to Find

In school, it seemed as if you were always being asked for your student identification number, so you kept it handy. Some things you will use more frequently than others in the office as well. Certain phone numbers and addresses need to be kept on a sheet that is in front of you or can be found easily. Keep a list of the ten numbers or addresses you use the most on one sheet of paper, and post it in front of you in plain view. You might also want to laminate it so it stays neat looking.

Maintain a System

When it comes to filing, do whatever works for you. If you subscribe to the stack theory (everything organized in piles on your desk), designate each pile to mean something specific. You could have a pile to be filed, a pile to be read, and a pile to be handled immediately. The key is to be able to find everything. Some ideas include color-coding labels or folders by different tasks, departments, and types of documents.

Make Technology Work for You

Your college professor couldn't stress this point enough: Keeping abreast of technology is a must in the professional world. One way to do this is to read a trade magazine and attend technology trade shows. Another way is to take a beginners class that will immerse you in the world of technology. One of the best ways to stay on top of technology is simply to use some of its incredible products and make them work for you. To work smarter, invest in one of the time-saving gadgets listed below.

Microrecorders. With these, you can take notes, record ideas and memos, and draft letters. Many things happen in the course of the day, and things that cross your mind you can forget from one moment to the next, so why not be prepared?

Electronic rolodexes. These little gizmos—the size of a credit card and about a quarter-inch thick—have a little keypad for entering names, phone numbers, and addresses. Most also have a calculator feature. They run around $20 to $30 and can be found at discount stores (e.g., Wal-Mart, Best Buy, Target). These are great to keep in your pocket or purse.

Contact software. These programs combine the best of all worlds, such as a database, scheduler, organizer, and word processor. Keep a database with names, addresses, phone numbers, and critical information about clients and others. An additional great feature is that it keeps your schedule for you. If you need to call Fred to talk about a report due soon, schedule it; an alarm will go off and a screen will pop up to remind you. Some popular programs are ACT and Maximizer. They generally run from $100 to $250, but they can organize your entire life. If you spend most of your day on a computer or are very comfortable with one, this can save you time.

Money manager software. High-tech solutions to managing your finances are common software programs such as Quicken and Simply Money, both under $100. You can keep different accounts, such as savings, checking, and an IRA, and it allows you to track where your money goes.

HOW YOU ARE JUDGED: PERFORMANCE REVIEWS

Performance reviews are like report cards: they tell you whether you're measuring up to expectations. The same holds true with your job. You are entitled to evaluations. How else will you know if you're hitting the mark?

If you are going to play the game, you want to know the rules. Sometime prior to your first review, go to human resources and ask for a copy of the evaluation form to be used in your performance reviews. Some supervisors judge you solely by the numbers. Your performance and bottom line are all that matter. Others use more subjective criteria such as teamwork, effort, morale, and creativity. Rate yourself honestly. Where has the boss been critical? Where are you really doing a good job?

Prepare and Plan Well in Advance

Keep an ongoing file to document your performance. Make note of everything you've done that has helped the company, such as acquiring new clients, paring down expenses, successfully organizing events (and their results), and making money for the company. Prepare a full report highlighting the time frame under assessment (annual, semi-annual, or quarterly) with graphs, charts, examples, and rankings that document your achievements.

During Evaluations, Make Your Goals Clear

When you had one-on-one meetings with your school counselors, you probably discussed your future. Think of company management as a career advisor. Tell management your goals and find out what it would take to reach them. If you want to be promoted to account executive from assistant, find out specifically what you have to do to get there. Develop a game plan and discuss it with those who can help you achieve it.

KEEPING THE EDGE: STAYING SHARP AND MOVING AHEAD

Several weeks or months into your position you will begin to loosen up and adjust to the real world. You've learned the ropes and are quickly getting up to speed. Now you need to look at what will make you more valuable. Just because you understand what's going on doesn't mean you can coast from here. You must prove yourself every day. How do you keep the edge day in and day out throughout your career?

Be Self-Motivated

Manage your career the way you did your education—deliberately. You took courses with end results in mind, and it took initiative to attain the goals you set for yourself. Take this same purposeful initiative and apply it to your career. Don't wait for someone to tell you what to do. Think of your career as your own company. In essence, you are the manager of your career.

If you see a need, fill it. Carve out your own niche and become an expert at something. Consultant and author Richard Moran said, "The main function of a business is to produce and sell something. Get close to those activities." Make yourself valuable by being close to the front line so you can contribute to the bottom line.

See the Big Picture

Notice how one thing can affect many others. As you accept more responsibility, don't be as concerned about where it will get you in the short term. Consider what a decision or situation means down the road. To help you see the big picture, keep abreast of your industry. Subscribe to a magazine in your field and read it.

Make Good Decisions

Whatever the setting, professional or personal, you will be faced with choices and decisions that need to be made. The outcomes of those choices vary in importance. Although some might be as simple as where to go for lunch, others have major consequences. Several steps will simplify the process and help ensure a sound decision.

1. *Decide how to overcome obstacles.*   Consider the pros and cons. By looking at all sides of an issue, or the worst- and best-case scenarios, you can see what the consequences might be. This allows you to weigh the outcomes and consider the alternatives.
2. *Seek advice.*   Use other people as sounding boards, especially those who have faced similar decisions. Talk with your mentors. Wisdom often comes via a multitude of counselors. Use successful examples to fuel your decision.
3. *Follow your instincts.*   If it feels absolutely right and the data support it, go with it.
4. *Don't be too quick to answer.*   Take time to think about it. If other people will be affected by your decision, be sure and talk with them, especially your family! Don't let anyone pressure you into an impulsive decision.

THE *DON'TS* OF BUSINESS: WHAT TO AVOID

In the business world there are absolute taboos. Whatever your background or ethnic heritage, it's important to recognize these and other negative elements of the workplace so you can prevent them from happening to you or someone else.

Prejudice

Business is more global and the workplace more diverse than ever before. You have probably already experienced diversity on your campus. Mingling with people different from you is a tremendous advantage on the job. To be an effective employee today, you must open your mind and be tolerant of all heritages, ethnic backgrounds, religions, and sexual orientations.

If you are ever a victim of discrimination, don't tolerate it. You are protected legally. Don't accept the, "Oh, I was just kidding and didn't mean anything by it" excuse. This kind of insensitivity is inexcusable and mustn't continue. Let the person know you don't appreciate that kind of language or behavior.

Sexism

You may deal with sexist remarks, unwanted advances, and people doubting your abilities, especially if you are a woman. As with racism, some forms of sexism can be overt, while others are more subtle.

One of the most obvious examples of this is in the names women are called. Being called *honey, sugar,* or *darling* in the workplace is inappropriate. The only people who should call you by such terms are those to whom you are extremely close and who have your permission. If someone is being offensive, say matter of factly, "Please don't refer to me that way." If it persists, document everything, using a recorder if necessary, and tell a supervisor. If that doesn't work, you may want to seek legal action.

Gossip

Some things you will learn in the business setting are confidential and should be kept that way. If a client or coworker tells you something or you have special knowledge about him or her, maintain that trust and don't tell anyone. Spreading dirt about coworkers, or anyone for that matter, usually comes back to haunt you.

As a further precaution, be careful where you discuss business. Don't discuss delicate issues in the elevator after a meeting, in the lobby, or in the bathroom. Don't tell a coworker in the elevator what a schmuck your boss is; the person riding with you could be the boss's spouse. Use discretion anywhere there are other people.

CREATING A SUCCESSFUL LIFESTYLE

Working eight to five and often longer doesn't leave much time for those must-do activities such as going to the cleaners and grocery store, playing basketball, or shopping. What do you do? You still have to eat, sleep, and wear clean clothes. How do you make time for yourself and what needs to be done?

Most of the mundane tasks can be handled during the week. Going to the bank, dropping off laundry, and even grocery shopping can be done before or after work or during lunchtime. Try to find services and stores with locations close to work or home. In many urban areas, buildings are equipped with multiple on-site services. Look for these convenient services and put them to use.

Eat Healthy

Cooking at home is a lot healthier and cheaper than eating out. Even fast food meals now cost between $4 and $7, which means you may be spending from $80 to $140 a month. An efficient way to eat is to plan a menu. Figure out three or four dinners with rice or pasta as the base. Then cook a large bowl of rice or pasta on Sunday night and perhaps some chicken to reheat throughout the week. Keep lots of fresh fruits and vegetables on hand for healthy snacking. If your only choice is to eat fast food or starve, choose wisely.

Exercise

Your new work lifestyle may cause you to spend a minimum of eight hours a day sitting in an air-conditioned office. During this time, your only physical activity will consist of walking to another office or your car. Oddly enough, you will be tired and drained when you get home.

This new sedentary lifestyle, especially if combined with fast food, will result in several additional pounds and maybe the need for a new wardrobe. If you don't want to end up showing pictures of what you *used* to look like, eat right and get active. Try to work out, if possible; at least go for a walk during the day or take the stairs at work. Buy a bike or rollerblades. Perhaps you like to dance; put in a tape and go to it. The key to exercise is finding something you naturally enjoy and then making it part of your routine.

Widen Your Circle of Friends

Even if you have a group of friends from your hometown or college, it's good to branch out and make new ones. If you're asked to do something with a group of new people, don't hesitate even if you feel a little uncomfortable. Go just to expand your base of friends. If you say *no* too often, people will stop asking.

Plan group activities yourself. One idea is to have a dinner party. Ask each person to bring a dish: You provide the meat, while other guests bring the salad, side dishes, dessert, and wine. Put candies on the table and turn on some relaxing music. Or how about organizing a trip to a festival or a nearby town with a few friends?

Develop a Hobby

You can't think about work 24 hours a day, or at least you shouldn't. Learn a new skill or find something other than television and laundry to occupy your time. Keep yourself multidimensional by doing things completely unrelated to your work, something people wouldn't expect you to do. This makes you more interesting and fun to be around. Whatever you decide to do, choose something that will refresh you and enhance the quality of your life. A nice by-product of a hobby is that it helps you focus your full attention when you are at work.

Share the Wealth

Being young and just starting out, you probably can't support many activities simply by writing a check. If possible, however, give of yourself and your time. The best place to start is in your own backyard. Find a cause in your community you feel strongly about and contact a related organization. You may be an animal lover. The Humane Society often needs volunteer assistance. If your passion is saving the environment, spend a spring day helping clean up a river. Call your local chamber of commerce or Department of Human Services to learn about the organizations in your area.

Serving as a volunteer—giving back to your community—gives you immeasurable benefits and a different perspective. Too often we get wrapped up in our own lives and our own problems. Helping those less fortunate puts our own problems into perspective.

DEFINING SUCCESS

For some, success no longer means climbing the corporate ladder. All over the world, employees are transitioning out of business-related work and into a career culture that fits their values. To them a job isn't just about making money; it's about using their gifts and abilities to fulfill a life's mission. Think about your own definition of success and the transition it will take for you to achieve it. And along the way give a little bit of yourself to make a difference in someone else's life. That's one transition none of us can live without.

Applications & Exercises

1. From the Boss's Perspective

You are the boss of a small company with ten employees. Five employees have caused you a lot of trouble because they must be supervised constantly to ensure they work well. Two employees give you the bare minimum. The other three are excellent workers. Use what you have learned in this chapter and answer these questions.

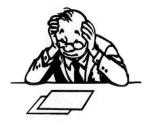

➤ What do you suppose sets the three excellent workers above the rest?

_____

_____

➤ Finish this thought: My company would be more successful if the five employees who constantly need supervision would just change their attitude about . . .

_____

_____

➤ When it comes time for me to reward employees, how can I best reward those who work hardest?

_____

_____

_____

2. Consider Your Own Work Habits . . .

➤ What made you successful in college? (Commitment? Perseverance?)

_____

_____

➤ Which of these positive attributes can you transfer from school to the workplace?

_____

_____

➤ What do you see as the main differences between school and work?

_____

_____

➤ Which attitudes do you need to change about yourself to make a smooth transition?

_____

_____

3. Your Career Tool Kit

You are going to bring tools to your first employer. You should use these to the best of your ability. As time goes on, more will be expected of you. Plan to increase your knowledge and skills to become a more valuable employee. Consider the following points:

➤ How good are you at setting realistic goals for yourself and assessing goals others set for you?

_____

➤ On a scale of one to ten, how adept are you at being taught?

_____

➤ Would you consider yourself more of a team player or an independent player?

_____

➤ How good are you at getting along with other people?

_____

➤ What is your strategy for people who are not easy to please? What about people you have to impress, but are not really fond of ?

_____

_____

➤ Would you be willing to learn from someone you resent?

_____

_____

➤ Name a characteristic you see in someone you respect that you wish you could add to your personality.

_____

➤ What are five aspects of a good communicator?

_____

_____

_____

_____

➤ Who are you when no one's looking? Finish these three phrases:
Ethics and integrity are important in the workplace because . . .

_____

_____

I can't wait to get on the job and broaden myself by learning how to . . .

_____

_____

No matter what it costs me on the job I will never . . .

_____

_____

4. Who Are You When You Are Not Working?

To be effective at a job, it is important to have a healthy and balanced life outside work. Work can be consuming; when the going gets tough, we all need an outlet.

➤ What are five things you like to do that cost very little?

_____

_____

_____

➤ Name three people you consider your friends.

_____

➤ What are the distinctive characteristics drawing you to these people?

_____

_____

➤ Finish this statement. I would like to volunteer once a month because it would help me to . . .

_____

5. E X P A N D Your Thinking

Life is full of opportunities to learn all kinds of exciting things. Unfortunately, our fear of the unknown keeps us from enjoying all life has to offer. Your life will be richer as a result of opening yourself up to the unfamiliar. In order to take these personal risks, first discover your fears and strategize the best way to overcome them. You become a more valuable employee when you learn to expand your thinking about yourself and the world of work.

➤ What do you anticipate as your greatest challenge in adjusting to the world of work?

_____

_____

➤ Take one of the things you dread and ask yourself, "How can I turn this dread into an opportunity for personal growth?" (Example: "I don't like to chat with people I don't know." Growth point: "I need to learn to be interested in new people. It makes life far more exciting, and I often learn something in the process.")

_____

_____

➤ Now go from a problem to an action. What are you going to do in the next couple of weeks to grow in this area? (Example: "Go to the library and read for two hours on something I know very little about." Or "Find out where there is a game, such as soccer, I know nothing about and let myself get caught up in the crowd's excitement.")

_____

_____

➤ Think about one such experience that has already happened where you had to step outside your comfort zone. How was the experience different from what you expected? How did you benefit from expanding yourself?

_____

_____

_____

_____

➤ Keep a journal and record similar stretching experiences. For example, at the end of each week or month, write about embarking on an unfamiliar experience and how you benefited from it.

5 CHANGING TECHNOLOGIES
How to Remain Current in an Ever-Changing World

In this chapter, you will explore answers to the following questions:

➤ What are some of the basic things I need to know about computers?

➤ What is the best computer for me?

➤ What are some of the security threats to my computer and myself when I use computers?

➤ What are some of the threats to my privacy through computer use?

➤ What are some of the emerging technologies that will keep me ahead of the game?

➤ How can I continue learning about new trends?

❓ Thinking It Through

Check those statements that currently apply to you:

❏ Although I realize that computers have many applications in everyday life, I am afraid to use them because I am unfamiliar with many of the technical terms.

❏ I am afraid that my computer will crash due to a virus on my computer.

❏ I fear my privacy is jeopardized whenever I use the Internet.

❏ My Internet connection is too slow, and I am tired of having to wait so long for Web pages to appear and to download files.

❏ I feel out of touch with some of the newer trends in technology.

❏ I need to find ways to stay current with new developments in technology.

A D V A N C E

5

CHANGING TECHNOLOGIES

How to Remain Current in an Ever-Changing World

In this—the Information Age—technological advancements are geared toward getting more information to people faster, cheaper, and more reliably. This is done primarily through the use of computers and vast computer networks. Thus to keep up with technological trends, it makes sense to focus attention on the developments in computers and the Internet. However, before peeking at how to keep up with technology, there must be a knowledge base in place to know what technology is being used. With this knowledge, you can stay current with the developing trends. Finally, although technology is always developing rapidly on the computer front, there are other emerging technologies to be aware of as well.

COMPUTERS 101

Computers can be scary. You just flip a switch, and with a couple clicks of the mouse, you can be "surfing the 'net," or writing the next great American novel, or perhaps learning a different language so that you can translate your great literary work. At any rate, there seems to be a lot of magic happening. Just the thought of all that computers can do may be so daunting that perhaps you don't want to deal with computers at all. However, computers are becoming so commonplace, it is almost necessary to know how to use them. In order to get over the initial hump, some of the jargon and magic needs to be lifted to reveal the smoke and mirrors. With some simple understanding, computers will lose their mystique.

The first task to having some useful knowledge about computers is to know the basics about the prefixes, memory, and timings of a computer. Some common terms heard around computers are *giga, mega, kilo, byte,* and *hertz.* The terms *giga, mega,* and *kilo* are all prefixes. Perhaps you are familiar with these prefixes from your chemistry or physics class. *Kilo* is short for multiplying a number by 1,000. Simply enough, 1 kilometer is equal to 1,000 meters. The less familiar terms *mega* and *giga* are simply larger multipliers. Mega is a multiplier by one million (1×10^6), and giga is a multiplier by one billion (1×10^9). (As you can see, each prefix multiplies by one thousand more than the previous one.) You may be familiar with the term *hertz* from your physics class as well. It is a unit of frequency per second. Thus 5 hertz is five times per second. The trickiest term is *byte,* which is strictly a computer term. One byte is equal to 8 bits. The word *byte* is more commonly used than *bits* because in the computing world a byte is the simplest logical memory unit. It is hard to qualify a byte, other than claiming that, with respect to personal computers, it is an extremely small piece of memory. For example, some of the newest software packages can take 50 megabytes (MB) of memory or more.

Some of these terms are commonly combined to give the specification of a computer. For example, take a recent ad for a computer, which has the following features:

1. 333 MHz Pentium II Processor
2. 128 MB SDRAM Memory
3. 8.4 GB Ultra ATA Hard Drive (9.5 ms)
4. 1600 HS 21" (19.9" v.i.s., .26dp) Triniton R Monitor
5. Diamond Permedia 2 8 MB AGP Video Card
6. 32X Max^ Variable CD-ROM Drive

A fairly good rule of thumb when comparing advertisements, like the one above, is to remember that generally bigger is better. The above ad describes one of the top-end personal computers. Next is a brief point by point summary.

The first item describes the processor or brain of the computer, called the *Central Processing Unit* (CPU). A "Pentium II" processor is the name of the latest processor produced by Intel, the most prolific computer processor manufacturer in the world. 333 MHz stands for 333 megahertz. This term describes how fast the "clock" of the processor is. Thus, there are 333 million "ticks" of the processor's "clock" per second. The faster the clock speed, the faster the computer processes information, which translates to faster overall performance.

The second item is "128 MB SDRAM Memory." Random access memory (RAM) is the temporary storage on your computer. When the computer is on, data is constantly being transferred in and out of RAM, making the memory temporary in one respect. The time it takes to access this memory is very quick. 128 MB stands for 128 megabytes, or 128 million bytes. Having more RAM can greatly increase a computer's performance because more memory from the hard drive can be stored in this fast memory. Since the computer has to access the slower hard drive less frequently, performance increases.

The third item tells about the hard drive. The hard drive is the permanent memory of the computer. When you install a program, or save a file, all of the information is stored there. The "8.4 GB" stands for 8.4 gigabytes or 8.4 billion bytes of memory. The 9.5 ms stands for 9.5 milliseconds or 9.5 thousandths of a second. This is referring to the amount of time it takes the computer to find anything on the hard drive. Here, a smaller number is better, since a faster seek time increases performance.

The fourth item describes the monitor. The important statistics here are the values 21", 19.9", and .26dp. The 21" stands for a 21-inch monitor. However, unlike the television industry, the computer industry does not have a standard for screen size. Thus a 21-inch monitor indicates only the size of the whole monitor. The important figure to look at is the 19.9" v.i.s., which is the actual viewable area that you can see. So, two different 21-inch monitors can have differing screen sizes. The .26dp stands for .26 dot pitch. This is the length between pixels, the dots on the screen that produce the image. Again, this is a case where smaller is better. A smaller dot pitch usually means a brighter screen, which makes viewing easier on your eyes.

The fifth item deals with video RAM. Many programs, especially games, have complex graphical content. As a result, graphics need to be displayed quickly. With more video RAM, graphics are brought to your screen faster and more smoothly. In this example, the video card has 8 MB (8 megabytes of RAM). Having more video RAM can also be helpful in playing video smoothly on a computer.

Finally, there is the CD-ROM (compact disc read only memory) drive. When CD-ROM drives were first released, the computer could read approximately 150 kilobytes per second. Thus the "32X" means this drive should theoretically read a CD 32 times faster than the original rate by spinning the CD faster. CDs currently have a 670 MB capacity.

Finding a Computer

Knowing how to find a computer to fit your needs can be a complicated task. All the bells and whistles are obviously nice to have, but do you really need them? This is a tough question because sometimes what you need and what you *will* need to keep up with technology are two different things. A typical college student may need only a couple of things from a computer, for example, word processing capability and means to get to the Internet. However, the newest Internet browsers require a fairly recent computer on which to run. So, newer computers are running on more complex operating systems, which hog a lot more memory than in the past. Even the simplest of word processors can take up a few megabytes of hard drive space. Therefore, while your needs don't require much memory or processing speed, you are virtually forced into buying a computer that was built fairly recently.

The computer in the sample ad isn't for the typical college student. The processor speed is lightning fast. Most people will not notice a difference between this speed and much lower speeds unless they are programming or playing games with intense graphics. Even with these games, having a good video card will probably do the trick. The amount of RAM is more than most students will need, unless you have several programs open at the same time or if the program you are using is particularly large. The hard drive space is plentiful as well. Even if you overcompensate and figure about 50 MB of space per program, this is still a lot of memory. In fact, it can be unmanageable. It would be difficult to use all of the hard drive space and consistently use all of the programs that are taking up the space.

One item worth spending extra money on is a good monitor. Fifteen-inch monitors are widely available, but having at least a 17-inch monitor is easier on your eyes. A fast CD-ROM drive is also not a must and is usually only necessary for playing games that have a lot of graphics. If a CD-ROM is used just to load software, to play music, or refer to an encyclopedia, then a CD-ROM drive of only a few times faster than the original should be enough.

Obviously, you need to buy something that fits your needs. If you only need to explore the Internet, then pour most of your money in a fast method of network communication, not on a mass of memory and quick processing times. In this instance, the network speed is the limiting factor, so having a fast processor and a large amount of RAM will not achieve noticeably better performance. When buying a computer, talk with the salesperson and be sure to tell her what you want from a computer. She will likely try to sell you a little more than you need, but hopefully she will be knowledgeable enough to fit your needs.

Security and Privacy

Even if you are not afraid of technology and are adept at using computers, you may still feel frightened about your own security and privacy while using them. Television commercials are currently running scare tactics about security. One commercial speaks about someone "hacking" into the network and bringing a company's whole network to a halt. Another commercial illustrates the perils of someone downloading a virus. As a result, no one in the office has the ability to print. News documentaries have sprung up saying how private investigators can find almost all of a person's information through the Internet. Many people are posting their unhappiness with the federal government's amassing a new database that will store information on every new hire in the United States, in order to find parents who are not paying child support. There are reasons for concern, but if you can learn to use computers responsibly, you can wipe your worries away.

Viruses

Viruses are frequently misunderstood by the typical computer user. It sometimes seems as though people think that their computer will actually explode if it gets a bad virus. Viruses are programs. These programs attach themselves to other programs in an inconspicuous way, so they go undetected. Some of the effects of viruses are not allowing a computer to start, erasing files from the hard disk, and not allowing certain types of files (a Microsoft Word document, for instance) to be opened. Some of these effects can be fairly violent, in computer terms. However, since viruses are not always understood, many people think that viruses can "magically" affect their own computer. It is important to remember that a virus is a program. Like any other program, nothing happens unless this program is run. A virus cannot run by itself. Therefore, unless a user runs a program to which a virus is attached, the computer will suffer no effects.

One word of warning: What is considered a program can sometimes be tricky. True, a word processor, a game, and a spreadsheet are all programs. However, many word processors and spreadsheets today have what is called a "macro" language. This language allows a user to do programming within their document. For example, you can use a macro language to calculate results for a certain spreadsheet you are working on. This calculation performed via the macro language is considered a program as well. Therefore, if you open a spreadsheet with a macro virus attached to it, then the virus can do its damage.

Keeping the definition of a virus in mind, there are a couple of myths about how a computer can get contaminated with a virus. More than once, I have received E-mail messages warning me that I should not open messages with certain subject headings. If I did, the messages warned, my computer would be infected with a virus. This is a complete hoax. Opening a text file from within an E-mail reader is not the same as running a program. However, if a file were attached to the E-mail and you were to run the attached file, then your computer is susceptible to infection. Another myth is that your computer can get a virus by downloading files from the Internet. Actually, this is partially true. There is a chance that a downloaded file has a virus attached to it. Unless this downloaded file is run, the virus will remain dormant. New versions of Internet browsers allow a user to run files directly from the browser itself. In other words, the file is downloaded and then run automatically by the browser. This can be dangerous because if a virus is attached to this file it can infect the computer. Thus, it is safest to only download files to the computer, and then check these files for viruses.

Checking for viruses is simple: You need to have a virus checker. They are readily available anywhere software is sold; a good virus checker is an absolute must. These programs are usually easy to install, and fairly easy to use. You can manually check for viruses as well as scheduling checks at certain intervals. Some virus checkers also have the capability to check for viruses while downloading files from the Internet. If you already have an infected machine, most virus checkers also have a "cleaning" process that can eliminate a virus from your machine. Finally, malicious people are always creating new viruses. Consequently, most virus checkers usually allow free upgrades for a certain period of time after you purchase a virus checker. The upgrades will include checks for new viruses.

Purchasing on the Internet

Viruses can cause some big headaches, but credit card fraud over the Internet has many people scared as well. Normal traffic across the Internet is not encrypted. If a person has the means to monitor what is being sent over a par-

ticular spot in the network, then this person can make sense of most of the data. Monitoring a spot on the network, however, is not a trivial task. Nonetheless, you need to be concerned when purchasing over a nonsecure connection. Many Web sites that sell merchandise or services over the Internet make use of a secure server. Thus data sent to and from your computer from these Web sites is heavily encrypted. There has been one reported case of a man in France who broke a single encrypted message. This message was secured by Netscape's 40-bit security. This might sound like cause for alarm, but it took this man eight days to decrypt the message, and he had to use approximately $10,000 of computing power to break a single message. As Netscape claims each encryption key is unique, a person would need eight days and $10,000 worth of computing power to break *each* successive message.

Therefore, it is not economical to try to decrypt messages, not to mention that it is quite difficult. In the United States, software can support a strong 128-bit security key. This means that decrypting a message is one trillion times more difficult than the French example we cited. Although it may seem a bit daunting to send your credit card number over the network, it is actually very safe.

Still, there are a couple of tips to use when purchasing items or services over the Internet. First, make sure the place you are purchasing from is secure. Both of the popular Netscape and Internet Explorer browsers have an icon, such as a key or a lock, to let you know that the transaction is secure. You also want to make sure you are buying from someone you trust. The company or person to whom you are sending your credit card information can see this information. Therefore, the possibility exists that it is some type of scam.

Cookies

There is no doubt that viruses and fraud are a gross breach of your security. However, Internet cookies are often debated as to whether or not they affect a person's privacy. Many people are not even familiar with the concept of a cookie. A cookie is a text string that is stored in your Internet browser's memory on your computer by a Web site that you are visiting. Since it is simply a text string, it cannot be used as a virus and it cannot read your hard drive. Not all Web sites make use of cookies.

Cookies, in fact, can be very useful tools. Some Web sites allow you to customize what information is presented to you when you visit that site. The only way a site can tell that you are visiting is by placing some identifier on your computer (usually some random ID) that can be uniquely recognized. When you visit the Web site again, the site reads the cookie or cookies and then customizes what is presented to you. Another use is for Web sites that have a wide array of merchandise to sell. When you visit a site like this, you can place items into a virtual "shopping cart." After leaving the Web site and then returning, you don't have to select the items you want to purchase again, because a cookie has been used to identify them. Cookies can even be used for keeping simple statistics. For example, they can be easily used to give an idea of how many different people have visited a particular Web site.

So far, it seems like cookies can do only good things. There does not seem to be any breach of privacy, but some people believe that the fact that information is being stored on their computer without their notification is a breach of privacy. The following situation gives a better scenario as to how cookies can be used to perceive a breach of privacy. Numerous companies exist that provide space and access for people or other companies to store their Web sites. Thus the Web site provider might store a cookie whenever someone visits a site that is on its server. The Web site provider is then able to trace the Web sites that a particular user visits, provided that these sites are stored on its server. A profile of this user can be built if a user visits enough of the Web provider's Web sites. Certain interests can then be ascertained. Consequently, when a user visits one of the sites that has an advertisement on it, the ad can be tailored to the user's interest. For example, if you were to visit a lot of sites pertaining to travel, then you might see an ad for a travel agency even if you were visiting an unrelated site. This seems a bit scary, but since no one company owns the whole World Wide Web, you will not be traced wherever you go. Unless you have given your name away, there is no way of identifying you directly. To the company, you are some random person who likes to travel.

Some methods of recourse do exist if you consider cookies a breach of your privacy. Internet browsers usually give users the option of being notified when a cookie is being sent, and then the user has the choice of whether or not to accept the cookie. This option can be toggled on or off through one of the menus. Also, there are programs you can download that will disallow cookies altogether.

Finally, users can delete cookies from their computers manually. Simply make sure your browser is not currently running, and then do a search on your computer for folders or files with the name "cookie" in them. Since cookies are text files, you can open and read them. Many times some of the information is cryptic, but you can then delete all of the cookies or only the ones that you wish.

Databases

You must remember that this is the Information Age. The Internet has made it easy for anyone and everyone to access a lot of information. A double-edged sword was formed with the widespread use of the Internet. Due to the ease of assessing information, companies are beginning to sell personal information to other parties. Some people are furious about the government's creating a database that tracks the information of all new hires. They complain that the government will be able to keep track of how much money a person makes. But as long as this person is filing his taxes correctly, the government likely already has access to this information. The point is, many people are in an understandable frenzy because they fear personal information like a person's name, address, income, phone number, and Social Security number is no longer private. Perhaps the biggest fear is that personal information is given out without a person's knowledge. Again, this is where the double-edged sword surfaces. People want to freely use the Internet, but want to keep their privacy intact. At any rate, personal information collected about you is supposed to be used only for your benefit.

Many people consider any access to this information by a company or person to be a breach of privacy. Companies can give or sell this information to others. Many Web sites require you to give some personal information before using their services. For example, if you want to buy a plane ticket, a few sites exist on the Internet that are convenient and easy to use; you can check for prices and schedules. However, sites like this usually require you to give them some personal information before trying to schedule a flight. As a result of entering personal information, you may find yourself getting some E-mail or postal mail from some travel agency, or maybe an airline. This information was obtained through the registration information you gave at the Web site. In response to this privacy scare, many Web sites that require you to register before using their services will tell you that they will not give or sell the information you provide to anyone else. If you do not see such a claim, then you run the risk of your information being traded.

In order to use a service, you may have to compromise some privacy; therefore, you must make a decision if the service is worth the potential compromise. As always, it is not advisable to give your Social Security number, and you should question anyone asking for it. There are very few services or transactions requiring such identification. The formula is quite simple: You are only as private as you want yourself to be. It may not seem fair that you have to compromise your privacy to take advantage of a service, but no one is forcing you to make use of the conveniences the Internet has to offer.

Staying informed on privacy and security issues is important. Without certain precautions, privacy and security can be compromised. Computers and the Internet do provide many conveniences. Yet, some inconveniences are present as well. With some research, you can take measures to keep personal information private and your computer virus-free. At the same time, if you do not mind people having certain generic information about you, then all of the conveniences of the Internet belong to you.

The Internet is not the only place where companies gather personal information. Signing up for a new credit card, subscribing to a magazine, or sending in a warranty registration are just a few examples of where personal information can be gathered away from the Internet.

EMERGING TRENDS IN COMPUTERS

Java

It is difficult to be around computers without hearing the term *Java,* especially associated with the World Wide Web. Java is a programming language, nothing more, nothing less. However, it offers certain advantages over other programming languages that make it extremely useful for the Web. There are two huge advantages. First, the language is secure. When Java was conceived, one of its requirements was to run securely over a network. One of the benefits from this is that programs written in Java are virus-free. The other advantage is platform independence. In other words, a program written in Java can run on personal computers with different operating systems, such as Windows 95® and Macintosh's operating system. Since Internet browsers are made for many different types of platforms, Java programmers do not need to worry whether or not their programs will run on different platforms.

There are a couple of other smaller advantages that Java has with its use on the World Wide Web. Java can be used to produce any type of graphics. This gives users the ability to interact with the Web much more easily. Also, the graphical capabilities give programmers a chance to provide a detailed graphical display that goes above and beyond the capabilities of HTML (HyperText Markup Language), the language used to program most Web pages.

Prior to Java, user interaction with Web sites was a long process. Information had to be sent across the network and processed at the Web site itself. This processing slowed down Web sites that were busy. Java programs are downloaded and run on your computer, eliminating much of the processing that the Web server previously needed to do. For these reasons, Java is mentioned many times in association with the Web. As you will see later, Java is starting to have other meaningful applications as well.

High-Speed Internet Connections

If you have access to the Internet at school or at work, then you are probably blessed with a very fast connection. If you like to get to the Internet from home, then you are likely victimized by slow transfer rates due to a slow modem. Trying to download a demo of the hottest new game takes forever. For example, if you want to download a 5-MB file with a 28.8-kbps modem, this would take approximately 25 minutes (kbps means kilobits per second; unfortunately, the computer industry has decided to measure transfer rates over the network in bits and not bytes, which causes some confusion). This is not productive, and you will have to tie up your phone line for that time as well. Fortunately, help is on the horizon. Typical modems are getting faster, with the fastest one having a transfer rate of 56 kbps. However, this is still not especially efficient. There are three other technologies that might give you the punch you want.

Integrated Services Digital Network (ISDN) is the most readily available, yet slowest, of the upcoming alternatives to a faster network connection. It can provide transfer rates of up to 128 kbps. Using ISDN, it would take only about 5 minutes to download a 5-MB file. The other advantage of ISDN is that it does not tie up your phone lines for incoming calls. Thus you can talk on the phone and surf the Internet at the same time. However, it is costly. It requires a fairly expensive installation, and monthly rates from the telephone company are fairly steep. Also, ISDN is not available in all areas.

Asymmetrical Digital Subscriber Line (ADSL) is a big step up from ISDN. This technology utilizes unused capacity over the existing copper wires that provide you with telephone service. ADSL has transfer rates of up to 8 megabits per second downstream—to you, the customer—and 800 kilobits per second upstream. If you downloaded a 5-MB file using ADSL, it would take only about 10 seconds. That is blazingly fast. This technology still ties up your phone lines, but with these speedy transfer rates, you are much less likely to miss a telephone call.

The reason for the discrepancy between the bandwidth to downstream and upstream is that ADSL was originally designed for interactive video. These include movies "on demand"; other video "on demand," such as delayed TV segments; video games; video catalogs; and video information retrieval. To send all this information to the user, a greater downstream bandwidth is required. ADSL is still in experimental stages, but it is slowly becoming available. However, since the technology uses existing phone lines, there is not too much work involved for phone companies to make it available. ADSL is a separate network, but it does not require as much work for the phone companies to provide this service as ISDN originally did. The best way to find out availability and cost information is to call your local telephone company or Internet service provider (ISP). They might even have information about ADSL on their Web site. ADSL is supposed to be as cost effective as ISDN, and even though it will require a special modem, no expensive installation is involved. Under these circumstances, it would be hard to pass up ADSL unless you really cannot tie up your phone lines.

A final alternative is the cable modem. It provides the quickest transfer rates. It allows for 10 megabits per second downstream and 2 megabits per second upstream (some with up to 10). Modems that have the capacity to transfer 30 megabits per second (mbps) are currently being developed. With a 10 mbps transfer rate, a 5-MB file would still take about 10 seconds to download, but there is more room to send information upstream. This capability makes videoconferencing much more feasible. Another big advantage is that since this is cable rather than telephone wires you do not tie up your phone line when using a cable modem. Also, there is no dialing in to an ISP, therefore, no busy signals. There is no need to worry about multiple cable connections for your cable modem and for your cable television. Simply use a splitter, and run one cable to the television and one to your computer. Again, cost and availability vary. The cost should be fairly comparable to some of the high-speed telephone modems. Cost-effectiveness might also be reached by the ability to rent a cable modem as part of your monthly service charge to your ISP. If it is available, the cable modem seems like a better choice than ADSL, but there is some debate over whether or not a cable modem can regularly supply the theoretical transfer rates that it is capable of. If the network is really busy, ADSL might be quicker since it is a dedicated line.

Recordable CD-ROM Drives

Compact discs seem to be a great way to store information. They can store up to 670 MB of information and only cost a few dollars. Given this, if a person could write or record to a CD, it would be a great benefit. For a few dollars you could have a fairly sizeable piece of memory to write to. CD recordable (CD-R) technology has actually been in existence for some time now, and all it takes is a CD recordable drive. You can then purchase recordable CDs and write information to them. This is a good way to back up large portions of information from your computer. While recordable drives can also be used like any other CD-ROM drive, having one regular CD-ROM drive and one CD-R drive allows you to copy CDs. Even audio CDs can be copied from one to another. Thus instead of making a custom tape for yourself, you could make a custom CD. However, when making copies of either audio CDs or CD-ROMs, be careful that you are not infringing on any copyright or licensing agreements.

Recently, rewritable CDs, also referred to as CD erasable or CD-E, have been introduced. With this technology you can write information to a CD, erase that information, and write new information. This technology is more expensive. Since CDs are inexpensive and can hold a lot of information, it may not be cost-effective to have the ability to rewrite.

Thin Client Applications

Finally, another new technology emerging in computers is thin client applications. The concept is fairly simple. The information that goes from your keyboard and mouse to the computer and from the computer to your monitor is small. Instead of needing a computer, you would need only a chunk of memory to hold your own files somewhere on the Internet.

Performance would not theoretically suffer even without a fast network connection because only the input from the keyboard and mouse would be coming from your terminal. In return, only information to your monitor would be coming back from the network. Thus, input and output are not great quantities of information. You can imagine that thin client technology would be like extending the cables coming from your keyboard, mouse, and monitor for numerous miles. One advantage is the availability of software that you would have at your fingertips. Currently, if you want to use a piece of software, you have to buy it, even if you want to use it only once. A great example is tax software. Every year tax laws change, yet there are many software packages you can buy to help you with the yearly event of computing your taxes. Unless the package you buy offers a discount on upgrades or free upgrades, you will have to shell out money each year. However, with your computer on the network, you could "rent" software as needed. So, during each new tax season, you might pay a simple low rate to use tax software for a few hours. If you are a game addict, you would not have to pay large sums of money to try the newest games. Simply rent whichever one you want for a while.

Currently, thin client technology is not readily available, but the concept has the potential to change the way we use computers. The most resistance to this may once again be privacy. There will likely be ways to track which software you rent, which would allow companies renting software to create a profile of your likes and dislikes. Also, if you were forced to keep personal files on the network, you would definitely be suspicious as to how secure they are. Your provider might claim that only you have access to your own files, but there is really no way to be certain. At any rate, you can be on the lookout for thin client technology in the years to come.

OTHER EMERGING TECHNOLOGIES

Smart Cards

An emerging technology that will likely change everyday life is the smart card. A smart card looks like a credit card, but it has a small integrated circuit, or processor, on the card itself. In other words, there is a tiny computer on board. The added security of the card makes it more advantageous than a credit card. First, it is nearly impossible to duplicate the processor—and the information inside—on a smart card. The magnetic strip that carries the information on a standard credit card can be replicated with relative ease compared to a smart card. Second, since there is a processor on a smart card, it is easy to store a personal identification number (PIN) on the card itself. The PIN can be used easily to verify any transaction since the PIN does not have to be transferred across a network to be verified. To use a smart card as a credit card for purchases at the

store, the purchase would be verified by a PIN rather than a signature, which could be forged easily; therefore, the consumer and the seller would be more protected against theft or damage.

While security is an added advantage and incentive for consumers, smart cards have almost unlimited applications as well. Smart cards can be used at pay phones that accept such cards. Many calling cards already exist, but the smart card is more secure. Smart cards can also be used to replace currency. Instead of going to an automated teller machine (ATM) to get cash, you would go to a machine and get money credited to your card. For this type of transaction, you would need a PIN, but to make purchases you would not. If the card was lost or stolen, someone else could use the remaining balance on the card. However, the same holds true if your cash were lost or stolen. In fact, the card would have the ability to be canceled if it was lost or stolen. Some laundromats use smart card technology. Instead of always needing loose change, a person can insert bills into a machine and get a smart card for the amount of money they put in. This person can then insert the smart card into readers on the washers and dryers, which will deduct the amount from the card. This is convenient for the user as well as the laundromat. It protects against theft, and rate increases are not limited to 25-cent increments.

Another possible application of smart cards exists in the health care industry. Instead of carrying a paper insurance card, you would be able to carry a smart card insurance card. When you enter a health care facility, all of your insurance information is already stored on the card, eliminating paperwork. Also, important personal medical information can be stored on the card, which could be lifesaving in an emergency situation.

Finally, smart cards have large applications for network usage. "Contactless" smart cards can be used to allow access into areas in your workplace. *Contactless* means that you would not have to insert your card into a reader. The reading is done by radio communications. It can also be used eventually to pay your bills from home. One final benefit that smart cards have is that all of these applications can be combined on the same card. The need to carry multiple cards is eliminated. Instead of sifting through your wallet to find the right card, you could use one smart card to make "cash" purchases, collect frequent flyer miles, make credit card purchases, rent videos, gain entrance to your dormitory, store insurance and medical information, and many other uses.

The advent of Java has actually helped the production of smart cards. Recall that smart cards have small processors on them. On these processors, some tiny programs can be run. One problem that is arising: different companies make different processors that fit on smart cards. This is the computer equivalent to having different platforms. Therefore, a program written in a language other than Java would have to be rewritten for each of the different processors. Java has the capability of writing these programs only once, and then they can be used on any processor. This capability shortens development time and diminishes the chances of one company creating a monopoly in the smart card industry. As a result of Java, smart cards will probably proliferate.

High Definition Television

High definition television (HDTV) is another new advancement, which the Federal Communications Commission (FCC) has already called the wave of TV in the future. Although digital satellite systems (DSS) use digital technology as well, HDTV will produce an even sharper image because it uses digital transmission instead of today's current analog transmission. With HDTV, the picture is as clear as 35-mm film, and the audio is enhanced as well. These new televisions will also feature wider screens, like those seen at movie theaters. Another advantage is that digital transmission uses a lot less bandwidth, producing room for many more channels to be sent through a cable. In much the same way that DSS can offer a broad package of channels, digital transmission would allow cable companies to do the same.

Legislation is being developed to make all broadcasts digital by the year 2006. Digital broadcasts render current analog televisions useless. This does not mean that you will have to spend the money to get a new HDTV by the year 2006. Converters will be available, so you can still use your current TV; however, you will not be able to take advantage of all the enhancements of owning an HDTV. The clarity will be the same of that associated with DSS, but that is still not nearly as crisp as viewed with a high definition TV. Also, the audio capabilities will not be enhanced either. Owning an HDTV is unnecessary if you plan on owning a 27-inch TV set or smaller. The clearer picture will be unnoticeable because most people sit far enough away from the set that it does not look "grainy." However, for large projection televisions, HDTV will show its worth by producing wonderful quality.

Digital Versatile Disc

If you want to watch a movie in the comfort of your own home, you have a few options. You can subscribe to a premium cable channel, order a pay-per-view movie, rent a movie on videocassette, or rent a movie on laser disc. All these methods have their merits, but the newest viewing medium for homes to hit the market gives the best quality picture and sound. This new technology is called digital versatile disc (DVD). These discs look like compact discs, but data is stored on them differently than CDs. Not only do DVDs have the capability to be used on both sides but they also have two layers on each side. Thus, by changing slightly the focus of the laser that is reading the disc, a layer below the surface layer can be read.

As for storing computer data, current DVD disks can store eight times more than a standard CD. Since the cost is not eight times higher for a DVD disc, they are much more cost-efficient. However, DVD technology is still new, so DVD drives for the computer are expensive.

Due to the increased storage space and the type of compression used to store video, DVD offers several advantages. First, the quality of picture is better than that of videocassettes and even laser discs. Each layer on a DVD disc can store up to 133 minutes of video. This means that different camera angles and different ratings (PG, R, etc.) of the same movie can be stored on one disc. DVD also has the capability to carry superior quality Dolby digital sound. Add these qualities to the qualities inherent with CDs (instant access to different tracks and quality that does not fade after time) and DVD seems to be a movie lover's paradise. This all sounds wonderful, but do not throw away your VCR yet. A recordable version of DVD will likely not be available until the year 2000. Although more and more movie titles are starting to be sold using DVD, and Blockbuster Entertainment Corporation has recently signed a deal to start the rental of DVD movies soon, finding the movie you want on a DVD disc is not a sure bet. Finally, you will need to make sure that your TV and audio equipment will be able to take advantage of DVD's superior audio and video capabilities.

KEEPING UP WITH THE TRENDS

You are now equipped with the knowledge of some technological trends. However, technology develops so fast, it can be difficult to keep up with it. The technologies presented here just scratch the surface of all sorts of emerging technologies. Trying to keep up with all emerging trends in technology can be a full-time job. Again, this is where the Internet can be very helpful. A plethora of information can usually be found about any subject on the Internet. If you hear of a new technology and want to know more, simply going to your favorite search engine and typing the new technology as the subject will likely provide you with more than enough information to get you up-to-date. In fact, Netscape's Navigator browser comes installed with a "Computer and Technology" bookmark section. Many of these bookmarks, or links, go to Web sites that give information on emerging technology. Magazines are also a good source of information. Numerous magazines exist for PC and Internet users. Check your local newsstand sometime; you might be amazed at the number of magazines devoted to computers and technology. Subscribing to one of these, or reading the magazine on-line, can keep you updated on current technologies. Newspapers and on-line news can also be used to stay in tune with the times. Many large newspapers devote part of the paper to technology nearly every day. There are also on-line news updates all the time. For example, the popular search tool Yahoo has a news service at http://dailynews.yahoo.com/headlines/. There you can find headlines under a few subject categories, including technology. Just by reading some of the technology headlines, you can keep yourself reasonably up-to-date on technological events. Finally, some cable channels offer shows dealing with new technology. With the advent of HDTV and the digital transmission that is needed to support it, there may even be entire channels dedicated to informing people of the latest trends in technology. As you can see, there are many sources that can be used for keeping up with the trends, yet only you can take the initiative to find out what the newest gadget will be.

SUMMARY

The technological explosion that has formed the Information Age has no end in sight. People can now access almost any amount of information from their own homes. The future will bring information to you more quickly, allow you to interact with others more freely, and store information more cheaply. It will be interesting to see whether or not the advancements in personal computers and massive storage devices, like DVD, will keep personal computers in everyone's home, or the progression in providing higher transfer rates across computer networks will lend itself toward people giving up their PCs and using thin client technology. If the latter is the case, it will also be interesting to note what actions will be taken to further protect the consumer's privacy. Technology is booming, so it is best to ride the wave and keep up with it; otherwise, you will be left in its wake.

Applications & Exercises

Key Into Your Life: Opportunities to Apply What You Learn

1. Reinforce Your Knowledge

Review the chapter for any new concepts that you have learned. Choose a couple of concepts that you would like to know more about or did not grasp completely. Use the Internet to find more information on these subjects.

What are the addresses of the Web sites you used to find the information?

_____

_____

_____

What information did you find?

_____

_____

_____

_____

2. Buy a Computer

Whether you are in the market for buying a computer or not, make a list of what you would want and need for your computer use. Next, go to at least two different stores that sell computers and ask a salesperson to assist you. Note which features come with each computer the salesperson suggests you buy. You may also try adding other requirements you want from a computer to see what different suggestions the salesperson makes.

Which stores did you go to?

_____

_____

List the features of each computer here (processor speed, amount of RAM, etc.).

_____

_____

_____

What were the prices for each computer system?

_____

_____

_____

List any terms that the salesperson used that you did not already know about.

_____

_____

_____

3. Buy a Virus Checker

Go to a store that sells computer software and seek information about the different kinds of virus checkers available. Usually, most of the needed information can be found on the box itself. Answer the following questions for each virus checker package that you look at:

What is the name of the virus checker?

_____

How many different viruses does the software claim to check for?

_____

_____

Does the software offer free upgrades to check for new viruses?

_____

_____

Does the software have the capability to clean, or eliminate, viruses that it finds?

_____

_____

Does the software offer any other utilities besides virus checking?

_____

_____

4. Find Out About Fast-Speed Internet Connections

Call a phone company or an ISP and find out if they offer ISDN or ADSL capabilities. Call a cable company or an ISP and ask if they offer cable modems. Compare the availability and the price of each of these technologies.

What were the results that you found?

_____

_____

5. Learn About a New Technology

Read the technology section from a newspaper or on-line news service for a few days. Choose a technology that interests you, and use the Internet to find more information about that subject.

What is the subject of interest?

_____

_____

What did you find?

_____

_____

Key to Cooperative Learning: Building Teamwork Skills

Get together with four friends and discuss what the future is going to be like. Each of you should choose an emerging technology discussed in this chapter or find one on your own. Then research the technology and think of different applications each technology will have in the future. Reconvene with your friends to discuss your ideas, and brainstorm about how these technologies can be used in conjunction with one another to get a global picture of what the future might have in store.

Key to Self Expression: Discovery Through Journal Writing

Talk about how current you think your technological knowledge is.

Do you feel overwhelmed by everything technology has to offer? What can you do to stay up on technology? How "in tune" with technology will you have to be to succeed at your career?

Key to Your Personal Portfolio: Your Paper Trail to Success

Apply what you have learned about technology and keeping up-to-date with changing technologies. Stay up-to-date using the following methods:

➤ Start a conversation with someone who knows a lot about technology. Get their perspective of what the future holds.

➤ Try explaining new technological concepts to a person who is not technologically inclined.

➤ Get into a routine to keep yourself current. Read a newspaper every morning, subscribe to a magazine, or choose any other method.

6 COMMUNITY SERVICE
A Foundation for Your Career

In this chapter, you will explore answers to the following questions:

➤ What are the differences among situational, long-term, and specialty volunteer service?

➤ What types of organizations need volunteers?

➤ Why volunteer?

➤ How do you go about volunteering?

➤ How do you document your efforts and create a portfolio reflecting your community service?

❓ Thinking It Through

Check those statements that apply to you right now:

❑ I'd like to volunteer but I don't really know how to go about it.

❑ I'm not certain if I have the necessary skills to be of use to an organization.

❑ I don't really know how other people find the time to volunteer, or the reasons why they do it.

❑ I need to know more about what I would gain from volunteer service.

S E R V

S E R V E

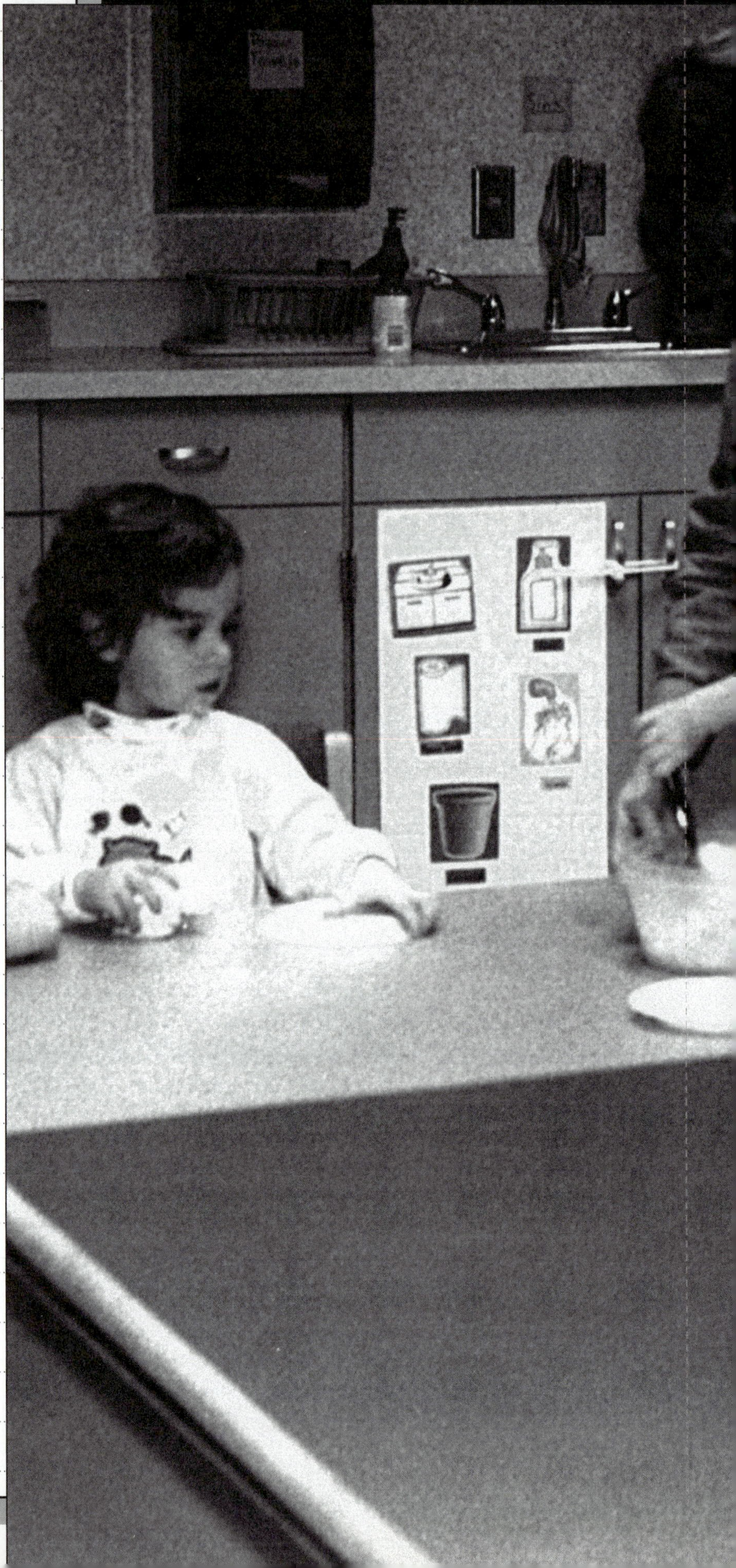

6

COMMUNITY SERVICE
A Foundation for Your Career

We live in an age where being a volunteer is a *good* thing. Many calls to action are made from churches, temples, and mosques to community centers, schools, and national organizations. Community service can be an opportunity to improve yourself, learn, and give back to the community.

First, let's define some terms. **Service** is the ability to help, work for, work with, or otherwise provide assistance (including skilled and non-skilled labor). Service requires the ability to take commands, fulfill wishes, and anticipate needs and desires. **Service learning** is a term used by many schools, colleges, and universities to classify courses requiring some form of community service. What is *community service?* **Community** is a group of people with common living interests in an area that includes economic, social, and political success. Now combine this with the definition of *service,* and you have the definition of **community service:** providing help, work, etc. to a group with common living interests. It seems simple enough. Let's discuss what it takes to volunteer, where you start, and what's in it for you.

YOUR VOLUNTEER SERVICE

Volunteers are people who offer their services by **free will.** It is free will that makes up the essence of a volunteer. Did you know there is usually a framework to being a volunteer? It depends on the organization, but a structure usually exists. Consider the three categories of service: **situational, long-term,** and **specialty.**

Situational Service

In situational service, an event or set of circumstances exists that requires volunteers until it is complete. (A Christmas toy drive is situational service—where the volunteer is usually needed for three to four weeks.) It may or may not require special training. Typically, in an orientation, a volunteer explains the system, answers most frequently asked questions, and discusses the schedule of work times. Then the volunteer jumps in and gets the job done. Gray areas exist, however. Do volunteers stay until their hours are completed or until the job/task is? Usually the volunteer gets "hooked" and stays until the job is over. The key to success is to get the volunteer committed to the project.

Let's look at a professional volunteer organization, the American Red Cross, which offers situational service opportunities. At most significant natural disasters, such as floods, earthquakes, and hurricanes, the American Red Cross is there. For every 45 volunteers there is one paid staff member. Volunteers come in all shapes and sizes, forming diverse and intergenerational workforces. Training will vary for the volunteer, based upon the job. For instance, health and safety instructors get a four-to-six hour course, with as many as 38 additional hours of training for special skills. (See the web site of the American Red Cross at www.redcross.org for more information.) Volunteers work throughout the disaster, and when the situation is over, the volunteering is also. Some of the volunteers, however, agree to stay involved on a long-term, as-needed basis.

KEEPING YOUR HAND IN . . .

Let's talk about George for a moment. George had completed his education and was staying at home with his small children, while his wife was the primary breadwinner. He wanted to keep himself active outside the home as much as possible, so he began volunteering at the homeless shelter for evening shifts when it would not disturb his family. Originally, he volunteered because several married couples from church had done so also, but all his friends dropped out by the end of the first year. George was an active volunteer, covering two evenings a month for well over two years. He felt he was providing a service and helping the paid professional staff, who were putting in many extra hours. He was also grateful for his own quality of life and was reminded of it every time he worked at the shelter. When the professional staff changed and he no longer felt valued or that he was making a difference, he resigned from the schedule. At the end of his service, he received a simple letter documenting his time, reliability, commitment to the community, and quality of work.

Two years later, George works successfully in the field of computer documentation. His career portfolio demonstrates his skills and abilities and includes a section called *community service,* in which he keeps the letter from the shelter. During the interview process, as well as during employment, he was told his organization valued volunteers. Having the volunteer experience also gave George an opportunity to improve his people skills and other skills that benefit his current employer.

Long-Term Service

Getting hooked on long-term service is something to watch out for . . . be careful, you might like it. Long-term service is a commitment past a specific situation. As in the case of the American Red Cross, what starts out as helping during a crisis can turn into a regular commitment. A person may be available on-call and consider nonemergency volunteering. Hospital auxiliary volunteers are another example of long-term service. The average person involved in the RIF (Reading Is Fundamental) campaign provides over 200 hours of service a year, with an average of three years' service.

Long-term service volunteers are put into information loops more than situational volunteers. Volunteer organizations also tend to invest more training and development in long-term volunteers. Additionally, long-term service volunteers have opportunities for leadership roles.

Specialty Service

In the first two types of service, you are more likely to fit into an existing structure; however, the rules change when you volunteer your services as an "expert" in a particular field. Specialty service is service in a specific skill area. For instance, a plumber may volunteer to put showers in a homeless shelter, or an accountant may offer to audit the books for an organization. Another example of expertise is when a "middle" person, such as a youth group coordinator, connects an organization with volunteers. Those with specialty services are often asked to place a cash value on their work. Specialty services may be difficult to grasp. An organization may know they need the service and often seek it out, but when the expert is on the scene the scope of the service may be redefined. If you want to volunteer a specialty service, be prepared to communicate what you have to offer, so the organization will be a better consumer of those services.

EXPERT VOLUNTEER . . .

For years, Francesca found little or no time for volunteering. After receiving a promotion from her company, she was called to do volunteer work in a nonprofit daycare center. She was told that after 40 to 50 hours she would be done, that all they needed was a quick fund-raising plan. She thought, "I can do this," and she went to meet the director of the center. After listening for 45 minutes, she discovered that what she had been asked to do and what the organization really needed were entirely different. Francesca was faced with a dilemma: should she do what they asked her to do, knowing it wouldn't solve the problem, or should she make a commitment for a much larger amount of time, using expertise and her additional resources to address the true problem?

Francesca went on to offer her services to recruit many other professionals in order to improve the health of the day-care organization. After being an active volunteer for over four years, Francesca has moved a thousand miles away from the day-care center, but she continues to support planning and fund-raising, as well as the morale of the organization. People with expertise in business functions have even saved the center from crisis. When asked why volunteers help, the reply is often the same: "We do it for the kids." It's interesting to see that what started as a small project has grown into a major commitment. Today Francesca continues this work both because she believes it reflects well on her business and she likes the kids.

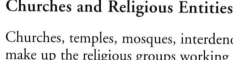

TYPES OF ORGANIZATIONS NEEDING VOLUNTEERS

It's difficult to find a group that would not benefit from a sincere, capable volunteer. But the question is "How do I succeed as a volunteer?" The best way to flourish is to understand the organization to which you are giving your time. A few specific nuances are noteworthy. For instance, some groups can provide you a meal while you work, and others cannot because of bylaws and governance. It is important to understand an organization's policies before problems arise. Some groups will pick up your expenses—some may not. Let's look at the type of organizations needing volunteers: churches and other religious entities, community associations, political groups, nonprofit organizations, and national charities and foundations, as well as regional and local charities.

Erma Bombeck, however, pointed out some commonalities among those who volunteer for these diverse organizations: "Volunteers are the only human beings on the face of the earth who reflect this nation's compassion, unselfish caring, patience, and just plain loving one another."

Churches and Religious Entities

Churches, temples, mosques, interdenominational youth centers, and more make up the religious groups working to improve communities. Activities and events can be as simple as holiday food drives or as long-term as running soup kitchens and homeless shelters. Many of this country's first volunteers came from these groups. It is also an easy way to network and socialize with people who have values similar to yours. Religious groups have tended to step in when the social system didn't have resources left. Many have as their efforts what others would consider "lost causes."

Community Associations

Alma Williams, a volunteer activist working to rebuild distressed Phoenix neighborhoods, said, "The best way to get something done is to find people who don't know it can't be done and do it." Community centers and groups run programs that range from shelters for battered women to soccer leagues. Causes range from social to youth-focused, including drug rehabilitation centers, halfway homes, sheltered workshops for the disabled, and senior citizen centers.

Organizations may need help staffing centers, fundraising, transporting clients, or any of a thousand other tasks.

Political Groups

Are you really a volunteer if you have a political agenda? Remember the definition of volunteering: one who freely gives of his/her services. The cause is not at issue. You might volunteer for the city. You may be involved in an environmental movement such as Greenpeace. You could volunteer for a specific political party during a campaign. If you volunteer for a political group, be aware of the political issues represented so your association is appropriate for *you*.

Nonprofit Organizations

This is a large category with many different concerns. A nonprofit can be as structured as a United Way agency or as career-specific as a volunteer professional organization. Each nonprofit group has a specific governing and tax structure. It exists to serve their cause. While the name implies something about profit, the opposite is true. A nonprofit can and should make a profit, but no individual may benefit; rather, the entire organization should. Nonprofit organizations always seem to be trying to stretch their financial, human, and physical resources. They remain some of the greatest sources for people who like to volunteer. These organizations maintain varying levels of formality. While always in great need, they tend not to have volunteer managers, as do community and religious groups.

National Charities

You're familiar with national charities, such as the Muscular Dystrophy Association, the American Cancer Society, the American Heart Association, Special Olympics, the American Lung Association, Make-A-Wish Foundation, and more. These are all nonprofit groups that want you to raise funds, provide gifts-in-kind (donations of items or services rather than money), or participate in special events. These groups usually seek out people with specialties to handle national management. Often these organizations have very specific volunteer criteria and volunteer management systems. In general, the national causes have an easier time getting people to volunteer because of their "public presence."

Regional and Local Charities and Organizations

Most national organizations have regional and local branches. Volunteers don't have to deal with a large group structure, only those in the local office. Other categories of charities exist, however, on a regional or local level, such as the Jimmy Fund in New England, a charity for handicapped children. Another example is a local arbor group promoting tree planting.

Support for the arts makes up a big chunk of the regional and local charities. Museums, symphonies, and school scholarships, for instance, support local causes: local groups investing in the local community.

Other Ways to Give

Philanthropy is defined as goodwill toward mankind, which includes the distribution of funds. Some charities may also fall under the category of philanthropic causes.

Volunteer firefighters represent another type of volunteer, usually long-term in service, yet specific in skill. Often an employer will need to be supportive of a worker who is a firefighter, because of the dependence communities have on volunteers.

Neighborhood watches are formal volunteer groups that neither raise funds nor operate with permanent staff.

Humanities and the arts represent activities embracing music, museums, and other forms of community culture.

WHY VOLUNTEER?

What motivates people to volunteer? The question must be asked if you will be involved in management or providing leadership to other volunteers. When asked why they volunteer, most people give similar answers.

They have special skills.   An example of someone with special skills is a school bus driver who operates the community shuttle because he has the appropriate driver's license. Others are the chef who prepares and serves the food at fund-raisers and the doctor who serves as a day-care physician. These people use their specialized skills to help others.

They have fun doing it.   Fund-raisers know if people can have fun they are more likely to volunteer and participate in special events. People enjoy participating in walks, sport events, bicycling, dancing, marathons, and more. They do so for fun, to keep in shape, be seen, and get a T-shirt. Others may work the Little League food concessions for a chance to see the games. Volunteers serve in booths at fairs, for instance, to participate in social events.

They feel it's their duty.   Some people feel an obligation (e.g., patriotic) to do a job, to pay back society for a benefit received. Entertainer Danny Thomas prayed to St. Jude early in his life and pledged that, in return for guidance, he would build a shrine to St. Jude. Several years later, he founded the world-famous St. Jude Children's Research Hospital. He also helped to found the American Lebanese Syrian Associated Charities (ALSAC) to raise money for the hospital. He held a deep belief that Arabic-speaking Americans should, as a group, thank the United States for the gifts of freedom given their parents. Thomas also believed that supporting St. Jude Hospital would honor his immigrant ancestors.

They learn from the experience.   Volunteering is always more rewarding when you can take something from the experience. Many people volunteer in order to learn from others, or to learn new skills that can be used in other areas. First-year culinary students gladly volunteer to work at gala dinners for the experience of working with professional chefs. Youth centers are often built around the concept of volunteerism as a means of teaching kids new skills, as well as keeping them out of trouble.

Their friends are doing it.   Volunteering often has a social component. Some people come with the logic that "I was going to spend time with my friends anyway; why not support a cause at the same time?" One of the best strategies for a nonprofit organization is to find a ringleader to recruit her friends. It is a great way to pull together a group of people who work well together, and their commitment to the cause is usually made stronger by their commitment to each other.

They want to make a difference.   Many people have a true desire to help others. Some take in an exchange student so they can make a difference in his life. Others volunteer in hospitals because they can make someone smile. It makes you feel good when you can help a person walk again. It makes you feel good to achieve something and give something back to others. Each of us can make a difference in the quality of another's life.

They have the needed time and resources.   Many people are brought up to waste little. Instead of discarding used items, they donate them to Goodwill Industries or the Salvation Army. One man would take 20 dozen eggs to a homeless shelter every week. Share what you have.

They are told to volunteer.   More and more people are required to volunteer for community service by schools, professional organizations, and businesses or to qualify for certain scholarships. These organizations want to show they're giving back to the community.

The community as a whole is supported.   Youth organizations, including 4-H Clubs, Boy Scouts, and Girl Scouts, teach the value of service to the community and the importance of citizenship. When you recycle cans, conduct paper drives, or sing carols at nursing homes, you're supporting your community.

The sole purpose of some service organizations *is* community service. Groups such as the Lions Club, Jaycees, and Rotary provide people with a venue for serving. People also join these organizations to be part of a social group and gain leadership skills, and they sometimes do so because it's expected and rewarded in the workplace.

Corporate volunteerism is required.   Many people are required by their companies to participate. One hotel chain in the Midwest expects all employees to complete between eight and ten hours of community service a week. Companies want people to focus on giving back to the community that supports them. It's also good business.

No one else will do it.   It's a dirty job, but someone has to do it. AIDS babies may get proper medical care, but who is going to hold them and show them love? Some people volunteer to do so because they feel no one else will. In Baltimore, an organ tuner goes to a poor church (one for every two paying jobs) and tunes their organ for free. Some veterinarians donate their time to animal shelters.

They want to gain or refine skills.   **Strategic volunteerism** is a trade-off. A volunteer gets to practice new skills, and the organization receives donated time and energy. One PR person lost her job when she didn't have the needed skills. She approached a nonprofit organization about developing their marketing plan and materials as a volunteer if they would allow her to document her skills, abilities, and time. She volunteered 20 hours a week for six months and then returned to her old company and even received a promotion. Be very clear about requesting up-front documentation of your skills, abilities, and time when done.

If you can get good at dialing into others' needs, you'll be able to satisfy your own needs and motivate others in the process.

HOW TO VOLUNTEER

Suppose you are told by a teacher or employer to clock 40 hours of community service in the next two months in order to meet an education or job requirement. What are you going to do? Where are you going to start? If you belong to an organization where volunteering is an integral component, you have no problem. If, on the other hand, you're clueless, here are a few guidelines to help you out.

Step 1: Look at causes you already support or would like to support. If you could do anything you wanted, what would you like to do? Which organizations do you know of now that you would like to help? Keep in mind it could be a national charity organization, a local Little League, or anything else. You may want to think about an organization whose needs complement you professionally.

Step 2: Where can you best use your abilities and talents?   Take a look at what you can do and what abilities you have. Or you may want to volunteer for an organization where you can pick up specific skills.

Step 3: Make a list of the times you are available.

Step 4: Decide if you want to volunteer for a one-time event or over an extended period of time.

Step 5: Contact the group.   It's time to contact the organization of your choice. Either pick up the phone and call, or start networking with your friends. It's easy to volunteer. Most organizations need only your name and a way to contact you. On the other hand, *you* need to know what you will be doing and what kind of training is involved. You may be asked to take a skills test. If you are volunteering to be a lifeguard or CPR instructor, expect to prove your skills before they give you the job!

If you're still not sure where to look for volunteer opportunities, check these resources:

➤ Religious groups
➤ Community centers
➤ Local public schools
➤ Local branches of national organizations such as the American Red Cross, American Heart Association, Special Olympics, Ronald McDonald House, and Big Brothers/Big Sisters
➤ Local hospitals and nursing homes

Keep in mind that these are not the only places to look. Many organizations are just waiting for your help.

You *will* get the opportunity to volunteer somewhere. There are never enough volunteers to fill the demands. Just decide what you want to do, and then take a few friends with you!

TRANSFERABLE SKILLS AND OTHER PERKS

Besides knowing you're doing good things for the world, other perks to volunteering exist, such as acquiring needed skills and refining others that will transfer to many jobs or careers. In addition, volunteer work is impressive on a resume. Several large service employers in the hospitality industry look for people with volunteer experience because of the character they believe it represents. A leading regional recruiter for McDonald's Corporation said, "I would rather have a volunteer with 'C' grades than an 'A' student who has never volunteered. If you see that a person has volunteered, you can more than likely always count on that person for help. I don't care where they have volunteered, just that they care enough to help."

Transferable skills are a combination of universal skills and skills unique to you. So what is this skill stuff? Skills are the ability to do certain activities. Knowledge is basically information about a subject or topic. A transferable skill is a skill or knowledge that can be taken from one area and used in a different field. A manager moving from banking to a manufacturing firm would be able to use the same management skills in both fields. She may need to learn a new way of doing things and new regulations affecting the industry, but the skills used to manage people are similar.

Here is a shopping list of skills that tend to be transferable, depending on the particular field:

➤ Ability to delegate
➤ Ability to implement
➤ Ability to plan
➤ Ability to train
➤ Communication skills
➤ Computer skills
➤ Conceptual ability
➤ Creativity
➤ Customer oriented
➤ Flexibility
➤ Ethical
➤ Follow though

➤ Leadership
➤ Organizational skills
➤ Phone etiquette
➤ Problem-solving
➤ Public speaking
➤ Self-managing
➤ Setting priorities
➤ Takes initiative
➤ Team building
➤ Team leader
➤ Team player

Sometimes unique opportunities present themselves, for instance, training in CPR, roofing a house, or singing and dancing at a fund-raiser. It is possible to get (1) training beyond what you started with and (2) a chance to work with talented experts.

EXCUSE ME, PLEASE, COULD YOU HELP ME DOCUMENT MY EFFORTS?

All it takes is a plan for getting the most out of your time. Do you have a plan for what you will learn and do? Do you have a direct supervisor or volunteer coordinator? What can you do to succeed?

➤ Keep a journal of your activities, including a skill list and log of hours.
➤ Keep a contact list.
➤ Keep an equipment list (it may be significant that you can operate specific machinery).
➤ Before you finish the job, request documentation in writing. Offer to share your notes. Be specific as to the skills and talents you want your supervisor to address. If you are a long-term volunteer, do this each year on the anniversary of your start date.
➤ Collect work samples, such as programs, advertisements, recipes, and anything else you created for the cause. Keep the samples in your career portfolio to document your transferable skills.

CREATING A CAREER PORTFOLIO REFLECTING YOUR COMMUNITY SERVICE

The career portfolio is a tool you use to help you get a new job or improve your current position. It can be a zippered, three-ring binder containing information about your beliefs, experiences, and education. It will contain samples of your work—those completed on the job, as a volunteer, and in a classroom setting. The portfolio may also include lists of your skills and competencies.

It is designed by you to help present the best of yourself to others. As a tool in an interview or job review, it can be used to generate conversation about your abilities and interests, demonstrate things you've accomplished, and, more importantly, provide proof of what you've done. It can distinguish you from the competition and give you an edge. Remember that people tend to believe more readily what they can see.

The portfolio can be a powerful tool, but much of its power comes from the process behind it. Developing your career portfolio doesn't happen overnight. It takes time to accumulate work samples. It takes time to verbalize your beliefs and determine your short- and long-term goals. It is a process of seeing what is good in yourself and incorporating it into the portfolio. Document awards, memberships, and involvement in community service. It is proof of your abilities.

For more information on how to put together your career portfolio, see *Creating Your Career Portfolio: At a Glance Guide* (1997), Anna Graf Williams, Ph.D., and Karen J. Hall, Prentice Hall. This book guides you through the process and even gives you three-hour emergency instructions.

Consider what volunteering can do for you. Good luck in your career!

Applications & Exercises

1. The Experience of Volunteering

➤ List the community service activities in which you and/or members of your family have been involved. Rank each by classification: situational service, long-term service, or specialty service. Briefly, describe what you gained from each experience, or what family members may have gained.

_____

_____

_____

_____

_____

_____

_____

➤ Get yourself ready to volunteer. Write the steps you will go through. Be specific and include time lines.

_____

_____

_____

_____

_____

➤ Make a list of your current transferable skills and those you would like to learn through volunteering.

_____

_____

_____

_____

2. Cooperative Learning

➤ With three or four people, use the following search engines to look up volunteer opportunities for yourselves.
www.yahoo.com
www.dogpile.com
www.altavista.com

List all the terms you searched. What key terms would you recommend to narrow the search?

_____

_____

_____

_____

_____

_____

_____

_____

_____

_____

➤ As a group, write a letter to request documentation for volunteer work. Include skills, time, and information about the organization.

7 ATTENDING U.S. SCHOOLS AS A FOREIGN STUDENT
Keys to Success

In this chapter, you will explore answers to the following questions:

➤ What do you need to know about college in the United States, and how is it different from your country's educational system?

➤ What are the two key ingredients you will need to succeed as a foreign student?

➤ What activities can you take part in to help you adjust to your new college life?

➤ How can you structure your studying so you will succeed?

? Thinking It Through

Check those statements that currently apply to you:

❏ I really don't know what is different culturally and educationally in the United States.

❏ Sometimes I feel lonely and lost in this new place and in my new role.

❏ Even though I am motivated to succeed in college, I am not sure exactly what to do to succeed.

❏ I have worked hard to get to college, but I need to learn to study for my courses in the United States.

❏ I believe I know enough to succeed as a student, but I need to learn about the new activities here.

A D A P

A D A P T

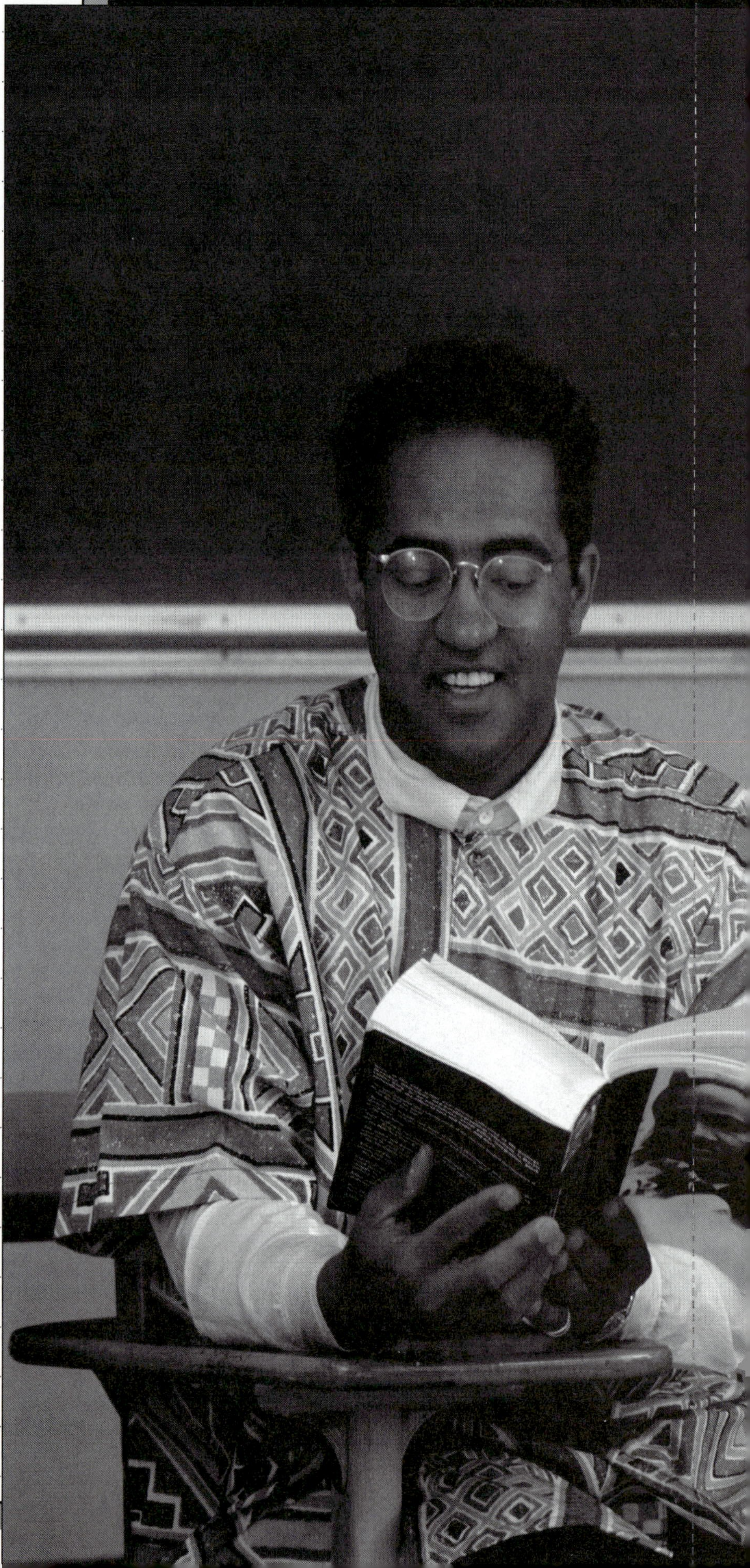

ATTENDING U. S. SCHOOLS AS A FOREIGN STUDENT

Keys to Success

GENERAL DIFFERENCES BETWEEN EDUCATIONAL SYSTEMS

Going to college in the United States means many different ways of doing things. Adjusting to these new ways is a challenge. You will succeed if you know what is different and expect changes.

Registration and Class Selection

When you register to take classes at a college or university in the United States, you will choose the courses you want to take. You will have an advisor, who may suggest some classes. There is also usually a guide to course selection for different majors in the college catalog. It is a good idea to ask for help in deciding which classes to take, but the final decision is yours.

You are also the person who decides what your major will be. You have probably already decided which area you are going to study, such as math, engineering, psychology, or sociology. This gives you a good start, but as you choose and take courses, you may find that you want to try other areas. In American colleges, you can try courses from different areas.

Most colleges and universities allow you to make some changes to your list of classes (which is also called a schedule). You are usually allowed to add or drop classes in the first few weeks of school. Usually, you have to make changes in the beginning of the semester, or term, before a certain date. Sometimes it will cost extra to make changes. It is OK to make changes, especially if a class is too difficult or very different from what you thought it would be. Still, try to plan carefully so there are not too many changes.

Responsibility

One more area that is difficult for some students is the lack of supervision. You have probably studied on your own to get to college, but most often you had someone to check your progress. For some students, this was parents; for others, advisors, counselors, or teachers at school that kept track. At a U. S. college, you are responsible for your own success and good grades. This means that you have to be sure you know what grades you are getting during the semester. Check with your professors if you are not sure how you are doing. If you need help, get it as early as possible. Remember, it is not wrong to ask for help from professors, assistants, and other students.

The Social Scene

One difference you will encounter is the social ways of the United States. Relationships are informal here. Your professors will talk to you on an informal basis. The classroom atmosphere will be relaxed. You may even feel that the work is not as hard and that not as much is expected of you as in your country's schools. You may feel that you can be more relaxed as well, but you must be careful. The academic standards are still high. Even though you may speak in class and speak to your professor, all of your work must still be done and turned in on time. You should speak up in class and offer your opinions and answers about school work. You must still respect your professors.

Professors at U. S. colleges and universities also teach in many different ways. Some of them give lectures and expect you to take notes. However, some professors, especially in smaller classes, want students to actively participate in the learning process. Sometimes they will use questions to start a discussion in class. It can be difficult for speakers of English as a second or foreign language to feel comfortable in these classes. Try to speak in class and answer questions even if you are not sure of the answers. It is not a problem to be wrong. Professors like their students to try to figure out answers, and you will not get in trouble for giving wrong answers in new subjects. If it is very hard for you to understand what the professor is trying to teach, you should talk to the professor during her office hours.

ACADEMIC REQUIREMENTS

Your professors will give you many assignments in the next few months. The first important point to remember is to plan for deadlines. Assignments always have a time when they must be turned in. Professors will often lower grades for work turned in after the appointed deadline. Sometimes they will not even accept the work if it is late. Plan ahead so that you can do all your work on time. If you do fall behind, go meet with the professor to arrange a new due date if possible.

> **Assignment:** Get a notebook or calendar ready for the first semester or term at school. Choose something with spaces big enough to write in. As soon as you get your assignments, write them all in so you know when assignments are due.

Next, you must know what format the professor wants the assignment to be in. Before the first assignment is due, be sure to check on the format:

➤ Should it be typed or computer printed?
➤ Can you write on both sides of the paper?
➤ For written answers, do the answers need to be in complete sentences?
➤ For math or science classes, do you need to show all the work for each problem?
➤ Are there any special requirements, such as a specific notebook or color of materials?

GRADING SYSTEMS

Your work will be graded according to the professor's system. Most professors tell their classes at the beginning of the semester how that system works. If yours don't, you need to ask. Here is a typical grading system:

Daily homework assignments	= 25%
Weekly lab assignments	= 15%
Quizzes	= 15%
Tests	= 25%
Final exam	= 20%

Also, you need to understand U. S. grading policies. Most colleges and universities give letter grades. Professors may use different scales, but here is a common scale:

A = 90–100%
B = 80–89%
C = 70–79%
D = 60–69%
F = 59% or lower

Some schools also give other grades, such as:

P   = Pass (generally, a grade of C or above)
NP = Not Pass (generally, a grade of D or F)
S   = Satisfactory
I   = Incomplete (the class work is not finished and must be completed in a later semester)

Remember that you must earn good grades to continue to go to college. Every college or university is different, but each one has a standard that you must uphold. Low grades will mean that you will have to leave.

ATTENDANCE

Attendance is another problem area for some students. You are not actually required to attend classes, but it is not a good idea to miss them. Most professors expect you to attend all classes. You may miss something very important if you do not attend. There will not be anyone to tell you to go to class; you must do this yourself. Not attending classes is the first step toward getting bad grades.

CULTURAL DIFFERENCES THAT AFFECT YOUR ROLE AS A STUDENT

Going to college is a new and exciting event in anyone's life. It is a time that offers you new opportunities and new challenges. For a student who will be studying as a speaker of English as a second or foreign language, it is even more challenging. You must meet the requirements for success as a college student, and you must do this as well in another language. Also, you may be surrounded by a new culture and country, and you must adjust to these new conditions. Everyone wonders and worries about succeeding in a new situation.

You want to do well in your new "job," so it will help if you can learn about your new situation and get help before it is too late. Some of the most important parts of higher education in the United States have to do with getting adjusted to a new way of life.

Getting Adjusted to a New Way of Life

You may have come to the United States just recently. Already you are beginning to make adjustments. You are living in a different place where even your house or apartment is different. You have begun getting used to eating

American food, talking to people in English, and seeing new sights. You probably expected many things to be different. In the beginning these changes can be fun and exciting. Later, you may realize that having everything different can also be upsetting. After the first weeks or months, you may begin to feel homesick or a little lonely or sad. This part of your adjustment is normal. Almost everyone feels this way. Even American college students feel this way. When this begins to happen, there are several things you can do that will help.

1. Keep busy. Try to find activities to do with or without other people. Even if you don't feel like doing things, it is good to go out.

2. Visit the foreign students' office or club. Try to find someone from your country or someone who speaks your language to talk to. Maybe there is even a group for you to join. Talking with other people who are doing well helps.

3. Talk to a counselor if you really feel bad. Ask your advisor to help you find someone to talk to if things are not going well. Don't wait too long. It is not a bad custom to ask for help in the United States. Your status in college will not be affected.

Getting Adjusted to New Social Ways

Your classmates will soon become your friends. Making new friends is one of the most exciting parts of a new situation. You will meet many new people on campus: professors, assistants, students, advisors, and others. Your new friends may be men or women. If this is the first time you have been allowed to make your own friends, enjoy—but be careful. Try not to develop serious relationships too soon. Don't allow friendships to distract you from studying and doing well.

Also, you may find that friends in the United States do not have the same expectations of their friends as you do. You may expect your friends to give you more help and attention than American students are used to giving. You might also find that the opposite is true; that is, you may feel American friends take too much of your time and energy. Talk to your new friends about your expectations, and try to compromise so that everyone feels comfortable.

Adjusting to a New Look

The way you dress may be different from the way U. S. students dress. You may see American students dressed for class very casually; however, this does not mean that you have to look the same. It may be fun to try out American fashions, but remember to always try to feel comfortable with what you are wearing. There may be different standards of dress in America than you are used to. Try to look around you and discover what is acceptable and what is unacceptable. Then dress accordingly.

You may also have to adjust to different standards of personal hygiene. Whatever your rituals at home, consider taking a bath or a shower daily. Using deodorant is also important.

Asking for Help

You will need advice on academic and school-related problems. You will probably be assigned an academic advisor. You may also have an international student advisor or counselor. Go talk to these helpful people when there is something you don't understand. Don't be afraid to ask even if the question does not seem too important.

Also, do not be afraid to go to talk with your professors and assistants. Most professors have office hours. They will tell you when these office hours are at the beginning of the semester. Office hours are a time when the professors are available to answer your questions and give you advice. Try to go to your professor's office often and get the help that you need.

Knowing What to Do If You Are Ill

You may become sick or ill at some time during the school year. Before this happens, you need to find out what medical care is available to you. Most schools have student health services. You need to know where these services are and when they are open. You also should have health insurance. At the beginning of the year, you need to find out how to get insurance and where you can use it if you become ill.

Absences are allowed because of sickness, but you are responsible for any work you may miss. As soon as you are well enough, call or see the professor to ask what work you need to do. If you are sick for a long time, you should ask your doctor for a written excuse. Also, you should try to have someone contact your professors to let them know that you are sick and will be absent. Perhaps there is some work you can do while you are away from school. It also really helps if there is another student in the class who you may ask about work and activities in the class.

> **Assignment:** Try to make contact with other students in each of your classes. If possible, get their phone numbers so that you can trade information and advice with each other.

TWO KEY INGREDIENTS: AVOIDING CHEATING AND PLAGIARISM

One of the most difficult and important problems for students coming to the U. S. from other countries may be inadvertent cheating. American schools do not allow students to help each other on tests. Each student must do his or her own work and not get answers or ideas from other students. Your culture may have a different point of view on students sharing information and claiming it as their own. It may be all right to share answers or help other students at certain times in your culture. However, you must understand this is not an accepted practice, and in fact is illegal, in the United States. Students caught cheating on a test may be given an F for the test and also for the entire class. Professors may also take disciplinary action and make the student leave the college. Don't even try to cheat. It is not worth it.

Another key to success is understanding another form of "cheating" that is not allowed. This is called *plagiarism.* Plagiarism is when you copy someone else's words and put them into your own essay or paper without giving credit to the source of the information. You may get into trouble with your professors and the college if you plagiarize, and you may have to leave. You must learn how to do research for your papers and projects, and how to write using your own words.

You can use other authors' words in a paper *if* you give them credit for writing the words. When you read something in a book, magazine, journal, or even on the Internet, that sounds like what you want to say in a paper or project, you may use short pieces of it and give credit to the original author. That is, you are going to tell people that these are not your words, but someone else's. To do this you must put the words in quotes (e.g., "these words are in quotes"). Then you must also put the author's name and the title of the book or article in your paper. You can learn how to do this in a class or from a book. It is very important that you learn to do this correctly.

Here is an example of a quote used within a paragraph:

I am happy to take on new challenges. I like to try new things and take risks. After all, as President Franklin Roosevelt said, "The only thing we have to fear is fear itself."

At the end of the paper or project that has this quote in it, you will make a list of all the books and other materials, or sources, that you used to prepare your work. Therefore, at the end of the paper with the quote from Roosevelt you would see: Roosevelt, Franklin D. "First Inaugural Address," Washington, D.C., March 4, 1933. Even if you do not quote words directly from someone but use their ideas, called paraphrasing, you still must list them, along with all the other books and materials that you used. This list at the end of your paper is called a bibliography.

HINTS FOR SUCCESSFUL STUDYING

You have already completed much school work successfully, so you have developed some good study habits. Here are some hints to help you continue your good work.

Take notes every time you are in class. Sometimes the English may be difficult to understand. If it is, then you must get help from your professors. If you ask, some professors will allow you to tape-record the class so that you can listen to the discussion again later. Try to take notes in an outline form or in some other organized form. Learn some abbreviations so that you can write more quickly. For example, you could write AH for American history, ch for chemical, or int for integer.

Make your own flash cards and study sheets to organize your material. For example, if you have many new vocabulary words to learn, you may want to put each word on a separate index card (3" by 5"). On one side put the word, on the other side put the definition. Then you can review and quiz yourself with the cards. Study sheets are similar, but you put all the information on one or more pieces of paper. An example of a study sheet would be to put all the scientific formulas that you need to memorize for a test on one piece of paper.

Again, you can review or quiz yourself using the paper. Remember, these cards and sheets cannot be used during a test unless the professor says so.

Sometimes your professor will assign you to do a group project. This means that you will work with some of your classmates to get something done. You will meet with your group, and each of you will do one part of the work. When the professor tells you to do this, it is not cheating but cooperative work. Be sure you understand your part of the project and get it done on time. The whole group will get the same grade, so it is important to do your part.

Another time that it is appropriate to work with others is in study groups. You may want to work with classmates or friends. It can be very helpful to discuss assignments and study together, sharing ideas and understanding with each other. Just be sure that everyone does their own work.

ACTIVITIES TO HELP YOU ADJUST

There are many activities that can help make life as a college student more fun and comfortable. One of these is making new friends. You will share many interests and values with other students in your classes. Making friends with them will be easy.

Joining clubs can be helpful and fun. On campus there are clubs of many kinds. There are clubs that meet to work on certain problems, for example, an environmental club or a peace group. Since everyone shares the same concerns, this is a good place to feel welcome and meet friends. There are also activity clubs, such as a hiking club. This club meets to plan and take hikes. There are also social clubs, such as an international students' club.

Sports are also good activities. Most colleges have official sports programs with teams that represent the school. They also have intramural or less formal sports programs for students who just want to play and have fun. These informal sports can be fun and good exercise. If you want to play volleyball, basketball, baseball, or many other sports, you will probably find a group you can join.

WORKING

You may need or want to work while you are a student at college. If you don't have to work, it is really best not to. Working takes a lot of your time and energy. You are going to need much time to study. If you must work, be sure that your visa allows you to work legally. If you are having financial trouble, you should check with the student financial assistance office for help and counseling.

GETTING AROUND

Transportation can be difficult at some colleges. Whenever you can, it is good to take public transportation such as buses or subways. Walking or riding a bicycle is also good. If you have a car, be sure to take care of the legal requirements. You must have a driver's license and car insurance. Don't think that because you are not a citizen, it's all right not to have these. It isn't! Also, be sure to find out where to park and get a parking permit, if needed. Parking tickets can be very expensive, so be careful. In fact, if you do not pay your fines, getting your grades can be delayed as can enrolling for the new term, and you could even get arrested!

As you begin to adjust to the differences and challenges of being a student in the United States, remember that change is always part of your life: You are learning valuable lessons that you will use in the future.

Applications & Exercises

Key into Your Life: Opportunities to Apply What You Learn

1. Discover Yourself

Define a clear picture of yourself and your goals. Answer the following questions to help "see" yourself.

What area or major do you want to study? What made you choose this area?

_____

_____

Why did you choose to come to the United States for college?

_____

_____

What are two values or ideals that are very strong in your country that will help you as a student in the United States?

_____

_____

What is the most exciting part of your new life in the United States so far?

_____

_____

2. Discovering Others

Get together with a student in your class. Try to work with someone who is not from the same country as you are. Take turns asking each other the following questions and writing down the answers. Try to understand how your partner is different from you and how he or she is the same as you.

What is your favorite or most interesting subject to study?

_____

_____

Who decided what college you would go to? Was it you, your parents, your teachers, or others?

_____

_____

Are you the first person in your family to go to college in the United States?

_____

_____

How important is it to you to get good grades and to graduate from college?

_____

_____

3. Study Skills

Briefly describe what you need to know about each course you take at college and then list the ways you can study for that course.

	Course	Study Ideas
1.	_____	_____
2.	_____	_____
3.	_____	_____
4.	_____	_____
5.	_____	_____
6.	_____	_____
7.	_____	_____
8.	_____	_____
9.	_____	_____
10.	_____	_____

Keys to Cooperative Learning: Building Teamwork Skills

As a class, make a list of the problems that new students face when they enter college. Try to find two positive actions to take for each problem. Include names, addresses, and phone numbers of people and places that can offer help. When finished, make copies to share with everyone.

Keys to Self-Expression: Discovery Through Journal Writing

To record your thoughts, use a separate journal.

Imagine that you are going to change your major. What is another area of study that is interesting to you? Why would it be fun or interesting to study? How would other people see you differently if you changed your major?

Key to Your Personal Portfolio: Your Paper Trail to Success

On a separate piece of paper, make a list of the high school courses you took. Divide the courses into the areas of Language, Mathematics, Science, Social Studies or History, Business, Art, Music, Physical Education, and Other. If you don't have a transcript (an official record) of your courses, try to remember all of your courses. Keep this list to compare your courses to prerequisites for college courses. Prerequisites are courses that must be taken before you can take the college course. Also, if you don't have a high school transcript, write to your high school to see if you can get your own copy. As you take courses in college, be sure to get copies of your college transcript as well.

PART II

Success Across the Disciplines

8 KEYS TO SUCCESS IN BUSINESS

In this chapter, you will explore answers to the following questions:

➤ Who is working in the field of business today?

➤ What skills can you learn while pursuing a degree in business?

➤ What fields of study are there in business?

➤ How can you increase your chances of success in the business world?

❓ Thinking It Through

Check those statements that currently apply to you:

☐ I think that business is only for people interested in managing money.

☐ I want a career that uses skills that I'm good at—or want to be good at.

☐ A good way to get a really great job after graduation is to know people.

☐ I'd like to know how to organize my time better.

☐ I'd love to be more of a leader so that people use my good ideas!

D I S C O V E

DISCOVER

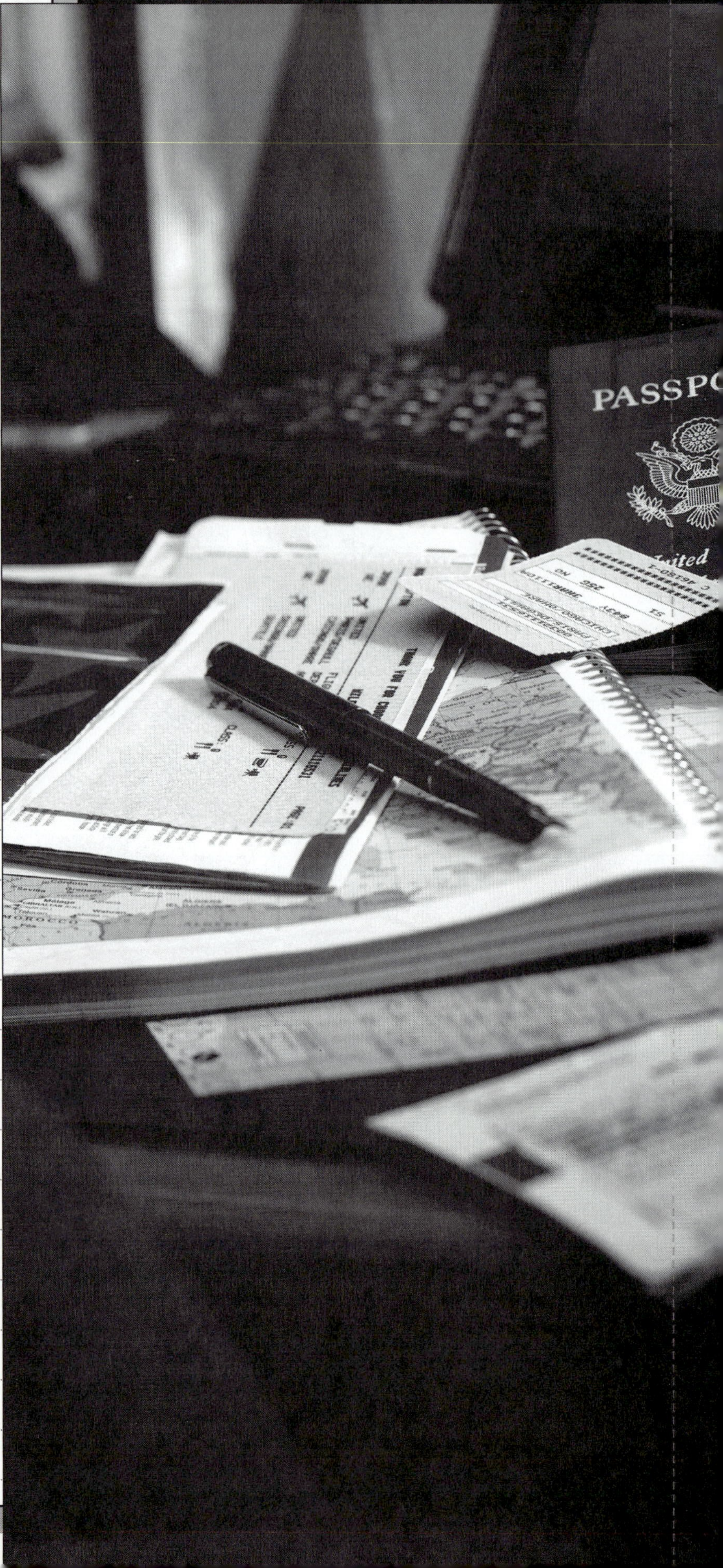

KEYS TO SUCCESS IN BUSINESS

Welcome to the world of business! Whether you are creative or analytical or interested in human relations or technical components, you can be an integral part of a company. You may even have an interest in management—in coordinating people with different skills, much as a conductor leads an orchestra. As a reflection of society, a company is composed of many different types of people with different interests and strengths. Together, a company's total performance can be worth more than the sum of its individual parts. Organizations help drive the world—producing products to satisfy people's needs and desires and providing a range of employment opportunities to develop our individual potentials.

WHO IS WORKING IN BUSINESS TODAY?

We have seen organizations become much more diverse in recent years—in culture, education, age, and gender. Women represented 40 percent of the workforce in 1976, but that number is estimated to grow to 47 percent by the year 2000. In addition, there are increasing opportunities for women. The percentage of women in managerial positions in the United States has increased from 15 percent in 1966 to 40 percent in 1990. Minorities are expected to account for more than 30 percent of the new entrants in the U.S. workforce by the year 2000. The average employee is also getting older. In the United States, the median age for employees was 27 in 1970, but it is projected to reach age 39 by the year 2000. These changes present many opportunities for people as well as challenges in managing the diversity.

WHERE ARE THE JOBS?

In 1997–1998, almost one-half of positions offered to graduating seniors were in the key areas of business: marketing, finance, economics, accounting, and management (see Figure 8.1).

Figure 8.1. *Jobs offered to graduating college seniors, 1998.*

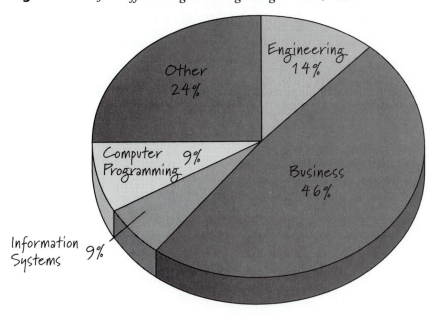

Source: *Salary Survey,* April 1998 (figures from September 1997 to March 1998).

More jobs in accounting were offered than for any other business field, and sales and marketing job offers accounted for 25 percent of the total in business (see Figure 8.2).

Figure 8.2.   *Jobs offered in business to graduating college seniors, 1998.*

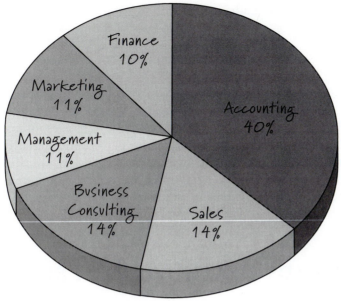

Source: *Salary Survey,* April 1998 (figures from September 1997 to March 1998).

WHAT SKILLS CAN YOU LEARN WHILE PURSUING A DEGREE IN BUSINESS?

Leadership

A business education allows you to learn from the examples of others. Through case studies of companies and managers, you can evaluate many leadership styles. You can see successes and failures and be able to evaluate techniques that can help you succeed. Through group projects, you'll be able to work with other people, developing your interpersonal and group communication skills—the tools of leadership.

Finance Management

In business courses, you will learn the basics of finance and budgeting, which can help in your personal life, whether you're buying a car, financing your education, or planning for a vacation. Understanding business helps us to manage our own lives by developing strategies and goals—critical building blocks for success.

Communication

There are many ways to communicate with others. We now have e-mail, faxes, letters, memos, and telephones, to name a few methods. We can communicate one-on-one or in groups. We are able to use technology to present

our ideas in many new ways and to gather information. Using these methods of communication effectively requires strategic thinking. Studying business can give insight into the advantages and disadvantages of each method and develop our skills for making all methods of communication the most effective they can be.

Ability to Analyze Complex Business and Economic Issues

Quite often, we hear news stories on major policy changes taking place, and the effects of these changes can be far-reaching. To understand, for example, how a standard European currency will affect Americans, we need a basic understanding of business and economics. We will be able to make better decisions for our own lives if we learn about the factors that compose our economy.

WHAT FIELDS OF STUDY ARE IN BUSINESS?

Accounting

What is it?   Accounting is the system that measures business activities, processes that information into reports, and communicates the results to decision makers. For this reason it is called "the language of business." What grammar is to English composition, accounting is to business. There is much more to accounting than bookkeeping. Bookkeeping is the procedural element (much as arithmetic is a procedural element of mathematics). Accounting is much more than procedures—it is a process that begins and ends with decision making. It is an important function of a successful business because it provides vital information that enables managers in production, marketing, and personnel to make informed decisions.

Accounting has a long history. Some scholars claim that the skill of writing first arose in order to record accounting information. Indeed, accounting records date back to the ancient civilizations of China, Babylonia, Greece, and Egypt. The rulers of these civilizations used accounting to keep track of the costs of labor and materials used in building structures such as the great pyramids. The need for accounting has existed as long as there has been business activity.

In the nineteenth century, the growth of corporations spurred the development of accounting. Corporation owners (stockholders) were no longer the managers of their businesses but still needed to know how well their companies were doing. With records and an accounting system, managers could report this information to the owners. And because managers naturally want their performance to look good, there needed to be a way to ensure that the reported business information was accurate.

In the United States, the Financial Accounting Standards Board (FASB) determines how accounting is practiced. The FASB works with the Securities and Exchange Commission (SEC) and the American Institute of Certified Public Accountants (AICPA), the largest professional organization of accountants. Accounting practices must follow certain guidelines. The rules that govern how accountants measure, process, and communicate financial information fall under the heading GAAP, which stands for *generally accepted accounting principles.* The FASB wrote the framework for GAAP. In the United States we also have certified public accountants (CPAs), who are licensed to serve the general public rather than one particular company.

Computers have revolutionized accounting in the late twentieth century. Tasks that are time-consuming when done by hand are handled quickly and easily by computers. Computer programs today also assist with the financial applications of accounting, making decision making easier.

Sometimes the accounting procedures used will depend on the type of business or organization: proprietorship, partnership, or corporation. A proprietorship has a single owner who is generally also the manager. These organizations tend to be small retail establishments or individual professional businesses. Partnerships join two or more people together as owners. Most partnerships are small or medium-size, but some are huge, exceeding 2,000 partners. A corporation is a business owned by stockholders—people who own shares in the business. A business becomes a corporation when the state approves its articles of incorporation. It becomes a legal entity, an "artificial person" that conducts its business in its own name. From a legal standpoint, corporations differ significantly from proprietorships and partnerships, both of which are legally obligated for the business's debts. If corporations go bankrupt, its lenders cannot take the personal assets of the stockholders.

What are my career options?   Accountants are needed in almost every industry. Specifically, you could be a cost, managerial, or systems and procedures accountant. Tax, budget, and forecast accountants and auditors are also needed. You can use an accounting degree in a number of other careers. For example, with some additional training, you could be an actuary or an underwriter in the insurance industry. You could work in the banking industry as an administrator. In financial services, people with accounting degrees are needed as financial analysts, planners, and stockbrokers. In many industries, cost estimators and compensation analysts have an accounting background.

A master of business administration (MBA) degree helps in certain careers, such as business and public administration. By passing an inclusive exam, you could also be a certified public accountant (CPA).

Marketing

What is it?   Basically, marketing is learning what customers want and need and providing products or services to meet those wants and needs. Boiled down to a few words: Marketing satisfies needs! It sounds simple, but in today's business environment companies must perform many marketing functions in order to succeed.

Behind the scenes, businesses must analyze the environment, looking at external factors, such as the economy, competition, and trends, and evaluating consumers' needs and characteristics before they begin planning their products. Any product that reaches the market has gone through a number of modifications; decisions have been made on everything from the image and brand name to packaging and optional features.

Communicating with customers and the public through advertising, public relations, personal selling, and sales promotions is another important part of the marketing process. The price and distribution process must also be determined. Marketing managers coordinate all of these functions in order to make a product or service successful.

As marketers determine the best way to present a good or service for consumers' consideration, they have a number of decisions to make. The marketer's strategic toolbox is called the marketing mix, which consists of the factors that can be manipulated and used together to create a desired response in the marketplace. These factors are the product itself, the price of the product, the place where it is made available, and the promotion that makes it known to consumers.

What are my career options? Because marketing is an essential part of business today, a great number of career opportunities in many industries are open to graduating students with marketing degrees. Entry-level sales representative positions exist in many industries, including advertising sales, direct sales, business-to-business sales, retail sales, and sales management. Besides sales, marketing majors can seek careers as brand, marketing, promotion, and product managers. Other positions that can be obtained by marketing majors in advertising include advertising copywriter and media director. Public relations is another career path for which a marketing degree can very beneficial. Research can also be conducted as a marketing research analyst or at the university level with a higher degree.

Management

What is it? Management is the process of accomplishing goals or sets of goals with and through other people. There are many different levels of managers: first-line managers (supervisors), middle managers, and top managers, but they all perform the following four basic functions:

1. **Planning.** Planning is setting goals and deciding on courses of action, developing rules and procedures, developing plans, and forecasting what the future will likely be for the company.
2. **Organizing.** Organizing entails identifying jobs to be done, hiring people to do them, establishing departments, delegating authority to subordinates, establishing a chain of command, and coordinating the work of subordinates.
3. **Leading.** Leading means motivating other people to get the job done, maintaining morale, molding company culture, and managing conflicts and communication.
4. **Controlling.** Controlling is setting standards (such as sales quotas or quality standards), comparing actual performance with these standards, and then taking corrective action as needed.

Managers don't spend an equal amount of time on each function. Usually, top managers will spend more of their time planning, while first-line managers use most of their time leading and controlling. Through an understanding of general management principles, individual and group behavior, organizational change and design, and human resources management, managers can make an impact on the success of an organization.

Early hunting civilizations used management when people banded into tribes for protection, the Egyptians used it to build pyramids, and the Romans to control their empire. Management theory as we know it today began with an effort to study the management process with scientific rigor. This began in the mid-1700s with the birth of the Industrial Revolution. The division and specialization of work led to enormous increases in productivity and output. Frank Taylor developed a set of principles that became known as *scientific management;* its basic theme was that managers should study work scientifically to determine the best way to get the job done.

Scientific management became very popular but eventually scrutinized every detail of the work process in so much depth that individual needs were ignored. In 1927 in Chicago, researchers at the Hawthorne Plant of Western Electric Company conducted what became known as the Hawthorne Studies. The original study focused on the working conditions of employees. They looked at the effect that lighting had on productivity—they studied how low light, medium light, and bright light affected the amount of work performed. What they found surprised everyone at the time—no matter what they did, productivity increased. They concluded that the researchers' interaction with the employees during the study made them feel special and resulted in the productivity increase. And so began the *human relations movement* and *behavioral approach to management.*

Behavioral scientists, such as Douglas McGregor and Rensis Likert, translated their ideas into methodologies that became the basis for participative management and management by objectives (MBO), where subordinates set their goals with their supervisors and are measured on the accomplishment of those goals.

After World War II, a trend of applying quantitative techniques to a wide range of managerial problems developed. This movement, management science, like scientific management, uses the scientific method to find the best solution to industrial problems. This approach is closely associated with the systems approach, which views an organization as a system made up of different interrelated parts. Since the 1960s, organizations have started using the contingency approach to management—changing the management principles and organizational structure based on the rate of change in an organization's environment and technology.

What are my career options?   A degree in business administration prepares you for a wide range of jobs in accounting, sales, production, and management. Although recent graduates don't usually go into high-level management positions immediately, a variety of paths will lead to these positions. Many industries look for graduates with management degrees for supervisory positions. (If you have knowledge of the particular industry, it will help.) If you choose to go into the banking or financial services industries, you can also begin your career as an administrator, bank loan officer, or investor relations manager. Financial analysts and planners, management consultants, purchasing agents, salespeople, and information specialists are needed in many industries. With additional training, you can also go into hotel, airport, city, or hospital management. An MBA degree in conjunction with work experience can sometimes help move your career into upper-level management.

Finance

What is it? Finance is the study of how to create and maintain wealth. It is the art of administering and managing money, which is crucial to the success of every business. Although you learn and use many calculations, financial management is really concerned with the logic behind the techniques. For instance, you come to understand what factors determine interest rates and the effects of those rates on future earnings. You learn the valuation and characteristics of stocks and bonds and how to evaluate a firm's financial performance. You also examine the functions and purposes of monetary systems, credit, prices, money markets, and financial institutions.

Before money existed, people produced much of what they needed to live and traded with others for items they could not produce themselves. When only real, or tangible, assets existed, people could save only those items. This was inconvenient, at best, and in this case, there was no mechanism to transfer the savings for value.

When paper money, or cash, came into being, we could then store our savings in the form of money. This was better, but it was not perfect because there was still no mechanism for transferring money. Very few people will just hand over their cash! The concept of a receipt that represents the transfer of savings from one economic unit to another moved the system further along. Receipts enabled a person or company that had surplus savings to lend those savings and earn a rate of return, which the borrower paid.

Once loan brokers came into existence, they could help locate pools of excess savings and channel them to people needing funds. Sometimes, people will purchase the financial claims of the borrowers and sell them at a higher price to other investors. This process is called *underwriting*. In addition, *secondary markets* developed, which represent trading in already existing financial claims. For example, if you buy your parents' General Motors common stock, you have made a secondary market transaction. In advanced financial market systems, financial intermediaries come into existence. These are the major financial institutions such as banks, savings and loan associations, credit unions, life insurance companies, and mutual funds. They all offer their own financial claims, called *indirect securities,* for entities with excess savings. The proceeds from selling these indirect securities are used to purchase the financial claims of others, the *direct securities.* For example, a mutual fund company sells their own shares (indirect securities) and buys common stock from other corporations (direct securities). A developed financial market system provides for a greater level of wealth in the economy.

The field of finance has changed over the past decade because of the wave of acquisitions, mergers, and divestitures. The U. S. Department of Labor Statistics estimates that financial services will grow at a faster rate than services as a whole. Along with this growth, controversy and debates regarding the system's alterations have developed. Since late 1986, there has been a renewal of public interest in the regulation of the country's financial markets. The key event was a massive insider trading scandal. Much debate also followed the collapse of the equity markets on October 19, 1987, when the Dow Jones Industrial Average fell by an unprecedented 508 points. And, in early 1990, the investing community became increasingly concerned over a weakening in the junk bond market. With all of this new awareness has come an appreciation of the crucial role that regulation plays in the financial system.

What are my career options?   There are four basic areas for careers in finance: banking, consumer credit, corporate finance, and securities.

In the banking sector, positions for finance majors include commercial loan officer, consumer bank officer, trust administrator and bank manager. There are also opportunities with the Federal Reserve banks as bank examiner or operations analyst.

In consumer credit, jobs related to installment cash, sales, and mortgage credit are available as well as consumer credit counselors, credit officers, and managers.

The chief financial officer is at the top of the ladder in corporate finance. Other positions include treasurer, controller, pension fund manager, and financial analyst, or a person could be employed in financial public relations.

Securities sales and trading companies, as well as those in financial planning and underwriting, need finance majors. The SEC also hires people with finance degrees as investigators.

Becoming a CPA or earning an MBA could help when you're looking for a job in some of these fields. In addition, there are increasing opportunites for positions in international finance.

Economics

What is it?   The field of economics studies how people make choices when faced with scarcity. Because we don't have an unlimited amount of money (or time, land, etc.), we must make difficult choices about how we will spend it. If you buy a less expensive car, you might be able to afford a needed computer, for example. Economics is the study of choices on individual, national, and global levels. Economists apply the principles of economics to weigh alternatives to many decisions that will affect the well-being of people around the world. With the help of economics, we can understand the world and make better decisions for our lives.

Early economic theories were based on the principle that governments should regulate economic activities because only governments could ensure that trade was conducted fairly. In the 1700s, the idea emerged that government should participate less in economic life. Adam Smith (1723–1790) advocated free competition and free trade as a way to promote economic growth. His book, *An Inquiry into the Nature and Causes of the Wealth of Nations* (1776), provided the foundation for the free enterprise system and contained insights that still guide modern economic analysis.

Smith argued that human progress is possible in a society where individuals follow their own self-interests and that this individualism leads to social order and progress. In order to make money, people produce things that other people are willing to buy. Buyers spend money for things they need or want most. When buyers and sellers meet in the market, a natural pattern of production develops that produces social harmony. Smith also believed that national income grows when profits are used to expand production, which creates more jobs and national prosperity. He advocated that governments stay out of business and provide only social needs not met by the market.

In the early 1900s, economists began to apply scientific methods to the study of economic problems. They discovered relationships between different aspects of the economy and studied the booms and depressions associated with free enterprise.

Today, the field of economics is studied from two perspectives: microeconomics and macroeconomics. Microeconomics is the study of the choices made by individuals, companies, and government and how these choices affect the markets for all sorts of goods and services. Macroeconomics, on the other hand, is the study of the nation's economy as a whole. It is a policy-oriented subject that was developed during the 1930s when the entire world suffered from massive unemployment.

What are my career options?   Economists are needed in many industries and can apply their knowledge in a number of careers. In the insurance industry, economic majors are hired to be actuaries and underwriters. Because they understand the interactions of many economic variables and policies, economists are needed in the financial industry as bank administrators, financial analysts, and investor relations managers.

Economists working for other businesses and public utilities spend much of their time applying economic theory to analyze issues that are important to their employers. They may analyze the effects of economic activity, in the United States and the world, on the demand for the company's product, conduct a cost-benefit analysis of the projects that the company is considering, or determine the effects of government regulations on the company. Careers in these areas include compensation analyst, business administrator, market researcher, and cost estimator.

Economists in government agencies forecast the effects of various policy proposals on the economy and study the impacts of government regulations and taxes on industries. Today, economists in international development and trade are especially needed. They may also be hired as regional planners, demographers, and statisticians.

Research and teaching at a university are open to individuals with master's and doctoral degrees. Economics also provides a very good base for students going on to law school.

HOW CAN I INCREASE MY CHANCES FOR SUCCESS IN THE BUSINESS WORLD?

There are many things you can do while in school that can help to prepare you for your career. College is the best time to analyze your skills and learn about different careers to determine the best possible match. Make the most of this time—set a good, solid foundation for the rest of your life. Internships, contact development, skill analysis, and research can help give you an edge and enable you to make a smooth transition from school to work.

Internships

Any kind of work experience related to your field that you can get while in school will greatly increase your chances of employment in that field after graduation. This work experience can come in several forms: part-time job, paid internship, unpaid internship, co-op program, and volunteer work.

To make the most of your work experience, you should concentrate on learning new skills, taking initiative, and meeting as many people as possible. It is very important that the work experience you undertake during your college years is directly related to the field in which you think you may be interested. Even in an unpaid internship, the experience you gain will be worth more in the long run than the wages you can earn in the short term.

Contact Development

Throughout your education, try to meet as many people as you can who are in careers you find interesting. You can start with alumni from your university who are working in your area of interest. The career office can help locate alumni. Or take the initiative yourself and call people in the human resource departments of companies for which you might like to work. They can arrange informational interviews—many managers are very willing to spend time helping students; they were students themselves not so long ago! Always ask the people you meet for names of other people you should speak with. Keep a log of all the contacts you make and develop your network.

Business Skills Assessment

From the classes that you take and the work experience you get, keep a journal of skills that you learn. Note what you do that you really like—and what you don't. This will help to formulate a base of skills that you enjoy using. Then you will be able to better determine what kind of position and career you might prefer. Everybody is different. Some people really like people—talking to them, understanding them, leading them—while others might really enjoy analyzing numbers and putting them together to tell a story. You are unique. The key is to find what you—alone—want to do. One way to do that is to constantly analyze what you are doing and what skills you are using and developing.

Researching Industries and Companies

If you think you might want to work for a certain company or in a particular industry or field, you'll want to do a lot of research. Talk to as many people as possible who are currently working for the type of company you're interested in—again, use informational interviews. Research the Internet (use a general search by name). Also use Lexis-Nexis or the Wall Street Journal Index, for example, to get more detailed information on particular companies. Look in the library or call the company and order their annual report (if they publish one). Read trade journals for the industry.

Advanced Degrees

Advanced degrees can sometimes increase your chances for getting a position. Sometimes they can also increase your starting salary. However, they are the most valuable to you, in the long term, if you have some work experience in between degrees. Many recruiters and managers recommend working for a couple of years after obtaining a bachelor's degree before going back for a graduate degree. You can get more out of an advanced, or graduate, program if you have some real-world experience and specific goals that you want to achieve. With experience and goals, an advanced degree can ultimately help your career and long-term salary.

Applications & Exercises

Key Into Your Life: Opportunities to Apply What You Learn

1. Skills Analysis

1. Think about a class that you really enjoyed. Take a few minutes to write down what you enjoyed about the class and what you were required to do in the class. Be as specific as possible. What skills did you use? Did you analyze information? Work with people? Use mechanical ability? Make a list of five skills you used. Now rank them according to how much you like to use them (number one being your favorite).

_____

_____

_____

_____

2. Think about something you accomplished in your life that made you really proud. Write a story about it. Now go over the story and analyze what you had to do to make that happen. What skills did you use? Make a list of five skills you used and rank them as you did in question 1.

_____

_____

_____

_____

2. Leadership

1. Describe a person who you really admire. What makes that person unique? How can you develop the qualities that you admire?

_____

_____

2. Compare and contrast two world leaders. Research their lives and leadership styles. Do you consider them good leaders? Why or why not? What do you think has contributed to their success?

_____

_____

_____

3. What are the differences between a leader and a manager?

_____

_____

3. Researching Careers

Choose three careers you think are interesting.

1._____

2._____

3._____

Now, identify one person in each career with whom you could speak. Interview the people and have them answer the questions from the table below. Make extra copies of the questionnaire.

_____

Career:_____

Name of the interviewee:_____

What is the most interesting part of your job?

_____

_____

_____

_____

What do you like least about your job?

_____

_____

_____

_____

What advice would you give to students who are interested in pursuing this career?

_____

_____

_____

_____

What skills should one have in order to do a good job in your field?

_____

_____

_____

_____

How can I find out more information about this field?

_____

_____

_____

_____

_____

Key to Cooperative Learning: Building Teamwork Skills

After everyone has completed Exercise 3, gather in small groups. Discuss the skills that are needed in each career. Are there any similarities in the skills needed among the careers? Choose four skills and write down specific ways that students can begin to develop those skills.

Activity to Help Develop Skill	Skill 1	Skill 2	Skill 3
1. _____	_____	_____	_____
_____	_____	_____	_____
2. _____	_____	_____	_____
_____	_____	_____	_____
3. _____	_____	_____	_____
_____	_____	_____	_____
4. _____	_____	_____	_____
_____	_____	_____	_____

Key to Self-Expression: Discovery Through Journal Writing

Describe the perfect job. What would you be doing? What would you want to accomplish the first year on the job? Where would the job be? What would the people you work with be like?

Key to Your Personal Portfolio: Your Paper Trail to Success

Contact Development

Create a table to keep track of all of the people with whom you will speak regarding career choices. You may want to include the following:

Name _____

Company _____

Address _____

Email address _____

Phone number _____

Position _____

Comments/Suggestions _____

_____

_____

Additional people to contact _____

_____

Add any other categories you think are important, and fill in the information you gathered from Exercise 3.

9 KEYS TO SUCCESS IN ENGINEERING

In this chapter, you will explore answers to the following questions:

➤ How well do you know yourself and where you want to go within the engineering field?

➤ What are key ingredients you need to succeed as an engineer?

➤ What should you do to build your marketability throughout your educational experience?

➤ What are the challenges you must face in the twenty-first century to succeed in engineering?

? Thinking It Through

Check those statements that currently apply to you:

❏ I really can't explain why, but I want to be an engineer.

❏ I am not sure of the kinds of engineering opportunities open to me. I would like to better understand what types of engineering careers are available.

❏ Even though I want to learn about opportunities in the engineering field, I can't seem to get any real-world experience.

❏ I have worked in other fields but am new to engineering, and I don't know what the field will demand of me.

❏ I don't see the point of learning other subjects not pertaining to engineering.

B U I L D

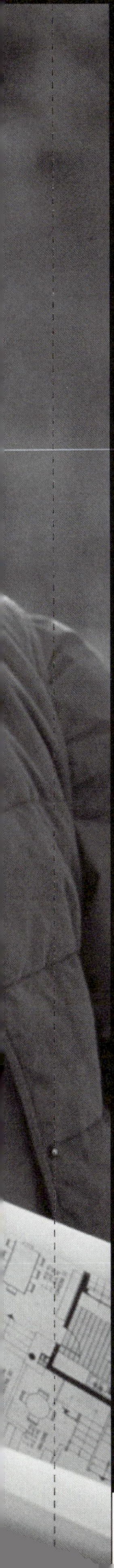

9

KEYS TO SUCCESS IN ENGINEERING

HOW WELL DO YOU KNOW YOURSELF?

When you think about becoming an engineer, what does such an endeavor involve? Hopefully, influential people have given you some advice and guidance in choosing a career, but regardless of others' help, what steps can you take to give yourself more direction? As technologies change and develop, becoming an engineer opens up new possibilities and unlimited opportunities. But you need to know how to prepare for the challenges ahead of you in college and beyond. Knowing these challenges, and creating options for yourself with the right strategies, can boost your chances to open doors to success in your engineering career.

Knowing yourself and your motivations for becoming an engineer will make you more effective not only as an engineer but also in your ability to influence and lead others in your company and community at large. To illustrate the importance of self-assessment, consider Mary's story:

> A woman named Mary came to visit career counselor David Campbell, author of *If You Don't Know Where You're Going, You'll Probably End Up Somewhere Else*. A financial analyst, Mary had earned undergraduate and graduate degrees in finance and had worked in a bank for the last five years, advancing quickly in the organization. Campbell said he led Mary through several self-assessment activities. Mary remembered that as a small child she loved building and drawing things like castles, houses, and towns and the roads that led to them, using sand, paper, or wood to build them. Another particularly important recollection was her most valuable gift as a child: An old, used set of Lincoln Logs that belonged to her father as a boy.
>
> Through continued exercises on her values and skills, and by interviewing some real-world professionals who worked in areas she thought she might like, Mary decided to pursue additional education and training in civil engineering. Today Mary is a designer and builder of custom homes and is nationally recognized as an urban planning consultant.

REFLECTING ON YOUR ENGINEERING GOALS

What can reflection on goals and self do for you during your engineering training? It can increase your awareness of market demands and goal setting. It can also help you know yourself so you can make better choices about engineering fields and specialties while remaining focused as to how your studies can be applied to a broader range of engineering applications. A key to giving yourself direction is to find opportunities to strengthen your versatility in the engineering market. Be prepared to change with transitions in your life and fluctuations in the job market.

Private career consultant Betsy McGee defines reflection as insights gained by deliberately taking time to think about recent and past experiences. For aspiring engineers, strategically reflecting on those times that inspired you to go into the field of engineering could give you more insight into your goals. McGee says that such an exercise has a great impact on how you develop professionally and personally.

A lack of reflection means a lack of self-awareness, or possibly denial of what you're really thinking and feeling. Neglecting to spend time reflecting about what you're learning about yourself and things around you could lead you into a field or specialty in engineering that doesn't truly fit you. And finding a field and specialty is only part of the purpose of reflection. Understanding what skills you need to become more versatile within the major you choose holds tremendous importance as well.

Broad Range of Engineering Options

As you think about engineering and its different applications, reconsider the definition of engineering. According to the Engineers Council for Professional Development in the United States, engineering is "the creative application of scientific principles to design or develop products, structures, machines, apparatus, or manufacturing processes, or works utilizing them singly or in combination." Engineers have several functions. Some may be involved in research and development, while others may design structures or products. Many engineers may perform management duties, such as analyzing customer requirements and resolving related problems.

Engineering functions encompass a broad range of work, such as refining or designing machinery, products, systems and processes, buildings, highways, rapid transit systems, and systems for automation and control (manufacturing, business, and management processes). Consider the four main engineering disciplines, their related descriptions, and some selected specializations in the table below.

ENGINEERING DISCIPLINES	DESCRIPTIONS	SELECTED SPECIALIZED BRANCHES
Civil Engineering	Oldest of the disciplines, civil engineering involves the design, site preparation, and construction of all types of structures and facilities, such as bridges, roads, tunnels, harbors, and airfields. Most projects in this discipline are in the public sector, concerning the development of urban, regional, and national infrastructures.	Structural engineering, foundation engineering, public health and sanitation engineering, irrigation engineering, systems engineering, municipal and traffic engineering (most recent).
Chemical Engineering	Developed over the last 50 years, this discipline is concerned with the design of processes and equipment for large-scale conversion of petroleum components by means of chemical reactions. This discipline adds chemistry as a third science to the foundations of mathematics and physics required in the other three disciplines.	Process engineering, petroleum engineering

(continued)

Electrical Engineering	This discipline covers the design and installation of main electrical systems.	Electrical systems engineering, electronics engineering, communication engineering, instrument engineering, medical engineering, computer engineering
Mechanical Engineering	Starting with the impact of the Industrial Revolution, this discipline distinctly concerns the design, development, and testing of all types of industrial machinery and engines.	Automotive, aeronautical, and marine engineering, precision engineering, production engineering, mechanical systems engineering, agricultural engineering

Description based on *Encyclopedia Britannica* from Britannica Online (www.eb.com).

Do a search on the Internet for more information regarding engineering specialties and related resources. Recommended topics to explore include *WWW Virtual Library: Engineering* and *Women in the Engineering Industry.*

Asking Self-Analysis Questions

Having just started your studies and possibly gathered a few hands-on experiences in the engineering profession, do any of these engineering professions interest you in a new way? As you study, allow yourself to be constantly open and aware of your developing interests, which naturally emerge with growing knowledge and skills. In the diverse field of engineering, it is important for you to think about the type of working conditions and responsibilities you will feel most comfortable with. There are many environments you could find yourself in, depending on your preferences, so knowing these aspects of yourself may help you to narrow your choices.

1. What kinds of working conditions would I like?
2. Do I like to sit behind a desk or get out and get my hands dirty?
3. After I receive my engineering training, what are the lowest and highest levels of responsibility I would feel most comfortable accepting?
4. Do I want to work with others or independently?
5. What kinds of characteristics would I like to see in the people I work with?

The above questions center on values that play a key role in your choosing the kind of engineering work where you will find satisfaction and happiness; they have been adapted from Richard Knowdell's *Career Value Card Sort.*

Education, Strategy, and Experience

Since most beginning engineering jobs require a bachelor's degree from an accredited college or university and a strong foundation in math and physics, it is imperative that you study the offered curricula from different colleges.

According to *Occupational Outlook Handbook,* about 340 colleges and universities in the United States offer a bachelor's degree in engineering, and 300 colleges offer a bachelor's or associate's degree in engineering technology for a more production- or design-oriented career track. The main specialization branches of engineering (electrical, mechanical, civil, industrial, aeronautical, chemical, materials, petroleum, and mining) accounted for more than one-quarter of all engineers in 1994, according to the *Occupational Outlook Handbook, 1997.*

In addition to the nine specializations mentioned above and in the preceding table, numerous other choices exist in the field of engineering. For example, architectural engineering, biomedical engineering, environmental, and marine engineering are all established college programs.

According to the *Occupational Outlook Handbook, 1997,* 25 engineering specialties exist and the many subdivisions of those specialties present additional opportunities for you. For example, as outlined above, specialties of structural, environmental, and transportation fit within civil engineering. In addition, the industries where you could apply your skills are innumerable: Computer, medical, missile guidance, and power distribution industries are just a few that could present possibilities.

Industries present one possible specialty, while different technologies, such as propulsion or guidance systems present more options. Choosing a specialty involves experience and strategy, which will be best determined once you get your first job. However, brainstorming what kinds of experience you would enjoy the most during your educational experience would help you get a head start on pursuing more direction. An interview with a senior civil engineering student gives a real-world perspective on his quest for direction.

REAL-WORLD PERSPECTIVE

Edward Stafford, Senior,
Colorado School of Mines, Civil Engineering

My motivation to be an engineer first started when I was a sophomore in high school. I participated in a job-shadow program for the City of Thorton in Colorado. I experienced site surveying and control point maintenance, and I liked the wide variety and challenges, and how I could go in and out of the office. Civil engineering is great for that kind of flexibility. This hands-on experience inspired me to look into college programs for civil engineering. I chose Colorado School of Mines because of its small site and quality reputation. My main purposes in my career are personal enjoyment and the challenge of learning and having an influence on each new project I'm involved in. I hope to advance into project management—I like putting all the pieces together and not just working on one specialized part.

Advice

My advice to others is to go out and "shadow" engineers in the areas you're interested in. Check your municipal governments to see if they have a youth and government program. My last words of advice are simple: Pursue something you're truly interested in and have fun. If you're just trying to get great pay or please your family or friends, you won't be as successful.

WHAT ARE THE KEY INGREDIENTS FOR SUCCESS AS AN ENGINEER?

The Demand to Think and Perform as an Engineer

As you grow in your level of classes, experience, and knowledge, working on essential engineering abilities on your own time will help you perform more successfully in the profession (see Figure 9.1).

Figure 9.1. *Engineering abilities and descriptions.*

ABILITIES	DESCRIPTIONS
Creative thinking	Engineering is a creative process that involves making and refining many things like structures (playground equipment), processes (the luggage system at the airport), and commercial products.
Critical thinking	An essential ability to question all aspects of an engineering situation or problem and to astutely figure out the pros and cons involved is needed in engineering. For example, engineers need to see the pros and cons of material quality versus cost whether they are building a bridge or devising a security system for an office building.
Analysis	Engineers need to see an entire engineering design or structure and break it up into its various components. For example, engineers analyze the scope of a project and break tasks into milestones to be completed by certain dates.
Evaluation	Evaluation skills are needed in engineering to determine the value and appraise the worth of a work problem, process, or product. For instance, engineers need to perform cost analyses and evaluate the effectiveness and durability of their work whether it's a bridge or a solar oven.
Synthesis	Combining individual products or parts to make a whole is a process involved in the engineering applications for machinery, structures, systems, products, or processes. For example, computer engineers will not simply work on one component within a computer but will know how the whole computer works, and ultimately, how that computer fits within the computer network system at an organization.
Communication	Engineers need to convey information or knowledge through various electronic, verbal, and written channels about engineering. Engineers must perform many communications tasks, such as writing a technical proposal or making a verbal presentation to clients.

Source: From the Colorado School of Mines' Engineering Department course materials.

A Need for Multidimensional Skills

Your pursuit of competence in engineering should include attaining versatility in a number of important skills. You need to look at your chosen major and your repertoire of skills and be able to transfer those qualifications to a broad spectrum of engineering professions. Some versatile skills include draftsmanship, management, sales, leadership, and problem solving within the general design process.

Draftsmanship, or sketching, skills cannot be overemphasized in the field of engineering, especially for civil, mechanical, or electrical engineering majors. Try to take as many technical drawing courses as possible, and if needed, take courses in drawing at a nearby community college if your university does not offer what you need.

Take any opportunity available to gain experience in the management of people and projects, including the organization of time for project milestones. Another versatile skill includes selling yourself to others, such as peers, upper management, and customers. Proving you can handle leadership positions and be flexible enhances your marketability to prospective employers.

Pay attention to opportunities to gain better understanding and experience in the general engineering design process (or problem-solving process) by (1) identifying the need or problem; (2) defining the project requirements; (3) gathering data; (4) defining the options for possible solutions; and (5) preparing a plan to accomplish the final design choice. An illustration of the general design process can be seen by briefly describing the construction of an industrial robot: The design process involves planning the functions it needs to perform *(identifying the problem, defining the project requirements, and gathering data)* and designing components *(defining optimal solutions and preparing a plan).*

A later phase in the engineering design process involves testing and maintaining components and fitting them together into a unified whole. For example, this phase of engineering requires skills in supervising the production in factories, determining causes of a breakdown, and testing products to ensure quality.

Be multidimensional when thinking about yourself and what you can do. You will surprise yourself with the large range of options you can create for yourself.

When building your marketability, a multifaceted approach is one of the best ways to ensure your versatility in the job market. For example, Information Systems Development Manager Dan Kesselring explains that recruiters will look for evidence that you can sell yourself to others, including peers, upper management, and customers. You should have a strong base of technical competence, hands-on experience, communications skills, leadership skills, teamwork abilities, and flexibility *(Job Choices in Science and Engineering, 1998).*

Design and development encompass a broad range of tasks: machinery, products, systems and processes, buildings, highways, rapid transit systems, and systems for automation and control (manufacturing, business, and management processes). In addition, Frederick Giesecke, a technical graphic designer, emphasizes the need for young engineers to know graphic language and design:

The engineer or designer must be able to create idea sketches, calculate stresses, analyze motions, size the parts, specify materials and production methods, make design layouts, and supervise the preparation of drawings and specifications that will control the numerous details of production, assembly, and maintenance of the product.

In order to perform or supervise these many tasks, the engineer makes liberal use of freehand sketches, and the ability to work with computer controlled drawing techniques (Giesecke, Frederick E., *Technical Drawing*, New York, NY: Macmillan Publishing Company).

An Emphasis on Creative Thinking

The new technological advances that are occurring rapidly everywhere, such as national defense technology, communications, and radio and television media, illustrate the serious demand for creativity in engineering—whether it's applied to research, structures, processes, or product development.

Creativity, a highly rated quality of any professional, may be easily overlooked in engineering because of the many technical skills required. However, experts in nearly every field and walk of life realize that creativity—the ingenious making of a new twist on an idea—is the "key to success in every endeavor," assert creative communications specialists Craig Johnson and Michael Hackman.

Some of the most creative inventions have been products, systems, or structures designed or introduced by engineers. Such inventions show the importance of creativity in engineering. Increasing your own creativity is an important factor in succeeding as an engineer. As you think about this important quality, ask yourself some questions:

➤ What social and environmental factors would encourage your creative skills as you prepare to be an engineer?
➤ What characteristics do creative thinkers in engineering have in common?
➤ What steps can you take to improve your own creative thinking skills in engineering? To improve the creative skills of others around you in your classes and activities? (Questions adapted from Hackman and Johnson's *Creative Communication*)

Examining Your Competencies as a Technical Communicator

A broad perspective. Accountability and specialization, two new trends in the engineering profession, impact the need for communication skills. Increasingly, engineers and their companies are being held accountable to the public, and those who are specialists have to communicate their expertise to the public clearly. Engineering concepts must be made more understandable to laypeople. For example, people want to know why a space shuttle exploded, especially since their tax money pays for the damage. Or people want to know if it really is safe to live near a nuclear reactor or power lines.

According to George Heilmeier, corporate executive of Bellcore, "Communications skills are extremely important. Unfortunately, both written and oral skills are often ignored in engineering schools, so today we have many engineers with excellent ideas and a strong case to make, but they don't know how to make that case. If you can't make the case, no matter how good the science and technology may be, you're not going to see your ideas reach fruition" (Educating Tomorrow's Engineers, *ASEE Prism,* May/June 1995, p. 12). Excellent written and oral communication involves the ability to persuade, sell, manage people and projects, and function well in groups.

Effective teamwork. Although as humans we have come to solve many complex scientific problems and have advanced technological methods, the successful collaboration between two people still confounds us. In engineering, the growing complexity of problems as the technology quickly advances demands that people work together. "Solving these problems demands the integration of many divergent points of view and the effective collaboration of many individuals" (Larson and LaFesto, *Teamwork: What Must Go Right, What Can Go Wrong,* Newbury Park, CA: Sage).

Written and oral communications. As an engineer, you will rarely be judged for your technical work alone. The way you convince others of your ideas orally and in writing will also impact the opinion others form of you. Getting extra training and experience in making verbal and written presentations will prepare you for this challenge in your engineering career.

SOME VERBAL PRESENTATIONS YOU MAY ENCOUNTER

➤ Recommendation reports
➤ Product information
➤ Tutorials
➤ Status or progress reports
➤ Technical proposals
➤ Sales presentations
➤ Technical seminar papers
➤ Project result reports

SOME WRITTEN PRESENTATIONS YOU MAY ENCOUNTER

➤ Project memo/reports
➤ Design packages
➤ Design analysis documents
➤ Technical proposals
➤ Contracts
➤ Project management proposals
➤ Inspection reports
➤ Recommendation proposals

As you consider your competencies as a technical communicator, consider how you could expand your experiences in verbal and written skills by asking yourself the following questions: What kind of speaking opportunities could I volunteer to do? How can I improve my writing skills?

PURSUING CAREER DEVELOPMENT OPPORTUNITIES

Take advantage of your career services office on campus to keep up with the latest trends in resume writing. In the process of gaining additional experience, knowledge, and training, you can record professional growth in many areas that will help to develop your resume.

As you develop sample resumes, consider two main types that will be useful. Know how to succinctly describe yourself in a biographical form so you will be prepared to write project team profiles, which are used by engineering firms when they are bidding for a contract. The second type of resume is the common one, requiring one to two pages that concisely—yet thoroughly—describes your work experience.

As you work on developing resumes and biographies, take advantage of the opportunities in front of you. Contact professional associations and do research on various branches of career development in your particular areas of interest. The following informative Web page on the Internet can link you to a multitude of other helpful pages pertaining to engineering:

http://www.mse.arizona.edu/faculty/birnie/196HelpPage.htm.

Don't Waste Time in Your Current Circumstances

People tend to forget that their course work provides plenty of opportunities to build an experience base. Check off any actions you have accomplished in the list below:

_____ 1. Documenting client-based projects for classes

More than a few college classes will have real-world client projects. Keep track of the company's name, and keep clips showing your work and the results. When graduation looms near and you remember your interest in the client, contact the professor of the class project and ask for a recommendation. In addition, keep a record of the client's name, phone number, and address. If you're really interested, assert yourself to the client by offering to do more project work there and negotiate possibilities for an internship.

_____ 2. Taking advantage of classes and extracurricular activities

Classes and extracurricular activities offer innumerable opportunities for you to build your resume. Any successful team you are a part of, whether it's a student government team or a class project team, would be excellent experience to list on your resume, since teamwork is a valued commodity in the workplace. In addition, papers that you write in class can be developed into publications for student engineering organizations, especially with the support and guidance of your professors. Getting published will enhance your resume and highlight the diversity of your skills in the eyes of prospective employers.

_____ 3. Professional engineering licensure

Getting your professional engineering license (P.E.) provides you with many benefits, and as Steven Schenk, P.E., advised, it's important that you begin the licensing process now while you're still in school or a recent graduate. According to Schenk, licensing "of engineers is provided by the law in order to safeguard the health, welfare, and safety of the public" *(Job Choices in Science and Engineering, 1998).* Although in most states graduates who work in industry, government, or education do not need a license, those who work with consulting engineering firms cannot call themselves engineers or sign and seal drawings until they complete the licensing process. In addition, many industries allow only licensed engineers to obtain certain job levels and titles.

Because each state has its own laws that govern licensing, you should check with your state board to gain more information on the steps you need to take to get licensed.

_____ 4. Extracurricular activities and professional associations

Leadership positions in various campus associations offer you an opportunity to show your ability to manage projects and relate to different people outside of your engineering interests. You can also broaden your experience by getting involved in the student chapters of professional associations. Becoming an officer in such an organization would widen your networking circle tremendously, and it will increase your contacts for landing future jobs.

SUMMING UP

Pursuing excellence in engineering involves much work, persistence, and versatility as you work to attain a broad base of important skills. As you continue to advance in your course work, do not neglect to continually improve your competencies in ethical behavior, technical communication, and cognitive ability. As you reach your goals academically, regularly check your career development progress and record your efforts diligently. Soon—maybe sooner than you think—you will be in your first engineering job.

Applications & Exercises

Key into Your Life: Opportunities to Apply What You Learn

1. Career Office

Visit your career center on campus regularly. Make an appointment with a counselor, and tell him or her of your current interests. Make sure to accomplish the following tasks during your visits to the career center:

1. Have someone in the career center show you their library.
2. Write down at least three possibilities of industries and/or companies you would like to investigate for engineering career opportunities.
3. See if your career office provides a list of alumni engineers who have volunteered to talk to interested students about career development. Other sources include friends and relatives who may know someone you can contact. Pick up information on how to conduct effective informational interviews from the career center.
4. Contact at least two engineers through your research and set up appointments for informational interviews at their companies.
5. Keep a record of what you do during each visit:

_____

_____

_____

_____

_____

_____

_____

2. Research

Do some extra research before you talk to people or conduct informational interviews. Find and summarize two articles on specialty areas or industry applications that you are considering. List the titles of articles you find:

_____

_____

_____

_____

_____

_____

3. Technical Communication

Try to communicate technical information coherently. Describe a technical problem from one of your current classes to a nontechnical person and ask for feedback on what was confusing or hard to follow. Then correct your vagueness and see how much it helps your nontechnical listener to understand what you're saying.

4. Sketching and Design

Sketch a design of your idea of a fun piece of playground equipment that is different than traditional types. Write down what you would need to do or research in order for a manufacturing company to make it. Talk about the engineering design process with others in your class.

_____

_____

_____

_____

_____

Key to Cooperative Learning: Building Teamwork Skills

Management Decisions

In teams, assign roles and solve a crisis engineering management problem. For example, look in your local paper for a general engineering problem and act out what you think might have to be discussed in a management meeting. Role-play decision makers and subordinates in a board meeting.

Key to Self-Expression: Discovery Through Journal Writing

Engineering Curiosities

Write down anything that you remember that triggered your interest in engineering, and explain why such events are significant to you.

Key to Your Personal Portfolio: Your Paper Trail to Success

Your Engineering Log

Keep copies of notes from informational interviews, with an analysis of what you gained from each one, in a notebook. Now that you have completed this chapter on the keys to success for engineers, summarize your goals on the pathway to success:

➤ Research goals: Discuss library research and interviews with professionals.
➤ Professional goals: Summarize the hands-on work experience and on-campus nonengineering leadership goals you plan to perform.
➤ Personal goals: Describe what professional goals you want to reach that will enable you to attain personal satisfaction from your career.

10 KEYS TO SUCCESS IN THE LIBERAL ARTS

In this chapter, you will explore answers to the following questions:

➤ What is a liberal arts education?

➤ What is the value of a liberal arts education?

➤ What majors are available within the liberal arts discipline?

➤ What real-world skills does a liberal arts education build?

➤ What support is available for liberal arts majors?

➤ What careers are accessible to liberal arts majors?

➤ What schools offer liberal arts degrees?

? Thinking It Through

Check those statements that currently apply to you:

❑ I am an undeclared first-year student who has not quite figured out what to do with my life.

❑ I am looking for life skills.

❑ I may be interested in trying several careers.

❑ Some of my goals are to know how to think, to learn, and to create.

❑ I want to broaden my understanding of the world and my place in it.

❑ I plan to attend graduate school.

If you checked one or more of the questions, then you might want to explore the possibilities of a liberal arts education.

ACHIEVE

10

KEYS TO SUCCESS IN THE LIBERAL ARTS

Undoubtedly, the question you will hear most often through your college career is "What is your major?" At most colleges and universities, a major means a discipline that you will explore and study through a series of courses designed to give you a foundation of knowledge in that discipline. This chapter is designed to give you information about the liberal arts major.

WHAT IS A LIBERAL ARTS EDUCATION?

A standard meaning of a liberal arts education is a form of education that develops *general* knowledge and *general* intellectual capabilities, as opposed to professional, vocational, or technical studies.

Another view of a liberal arts education is that it is a program of courses that equips you with knowledge about how humans work in the world. It is a curriculum intended to draw together the usually separate worlds of technical scientists and humanists, or social scientists. This curriculum serves as a mediating factor among the disciplines to help the student uncover the essential *unity of knowledge*. This view subscribes to the idea that the main goal of a liberal arts education is the development of a *wise* person.

The principal reason for embracing the liberal arts is to develop the knowledge, skills, and understanding essential for the pursuit of wisdom. Combining the two views of what constitutes a liberal arts education brings us to the view that the liberal arts curriculum teaches students how to *think,* how to *learn,* and how to *create.*

WHAT IS THE VALUE OF A LIBERAL ARTS EDUCATION?

"The mind is not a vessel to be filled, but a lamp to be lighted."

UNKNOWN

Building on our definition of a liberal arts education, the main value of a liberal arts education is to illuminate the mind, providing a foundation of wisdom that will allow you to live knowledgeably, responsibly, and humanely.

The broad educational foundation of a liberal arts degree allows you to begin or change careers, to pursue advanced study in a discipline, or to study for a professional career, such as law or medicine, and, in general, to lead a rewarding and productive life.

The liberal arts curriculum helps students increase substantive knowledge, learn such skills as logical argument and clear expression, gain insights about relationships in nature and society, develop critical thought and interpretive ability, solve complex problems rationally, and heighten aesthetic appreciation.

"Over the years liberal education has been thought of as an education having great value, indeed an education having greater value than any other."

JANE ROLAND MARTIN

Many believe that the main value of a liberal arts education may lie in the potential for growth that it affords students. The liberal arts are thought to uncover and encourage your thinking and creativity, allowing you to "actualize" your human potential. In other words, a liberal arts education can help you become a better "you."

WHAT MAJORS ARE AVAILABLE WITHIN THE LIBERAL ARTS DISCIPLINE?

One of the biggest decisions you will make as a college student is choosing a major—an area of specialization. While it is true that we have been speaking generally about liberal arts and that we have established that one of the values of a liberal arts education is that it gives you knowledge in general areas, the liberal arts also gives students many discipline areas from which to choose a major. Some possible majors include psychology, sociology, English, communications, history, and philosophy. See the box on the following page for a more complete list.

The choice of a major might depend on your interests, your talents, your values, or your plans for a future career. In addition to this personal inventory, take advantage of the resources your campus offers to assist you in choosing a major:

1. Carefully read your school course catalog descriptions.
2. Avail yourself of any personality or interest indicator tests your school's counseling center might have.
3. Talk to your academic advisor.
4. Talk to students who are getting ready to receive a degree in a discipline that interests you.
5. Take classes in a wide range of disciplines to test the waters.

Check your school's course catalog for possible majors, double majors, and major/minor combinations. Some schools allow you to "design" your own major by combining courses from several disciplines that are related in some way. If this interests you, check with your advisor about the opportunities for self-designed majors. To get you started in the thought process, on the following page is a partial list of typical liberal arts disciplines along with a generic description of the knowledge you will acquire in that discipline.

WHAT REAL-WORLD SKILLS DOES A LIBERAL ARTS EDUCATION BUILD?

"Man ultimately decides for himself, and in the end, education must be education toward the ability to decide."

VIKTOR FRANKL

One of the most frequently asked questions from college students is "But what does this have to do with the *real world*? Good news! Liberal arts majors are bombarded with real-world skills in the courses they take—skills that help prepare you for both the personal and professional realms of your life. Following is a partial discussion of some of the real-world skills a liberal arts major acquires.

Ability to Conduct Research and Assimilate Ideas

Most liberal arts courses are a blend of lecture and discussion—students *participate* in class. Students are expected to assimilate information and connect gathered

Major	A student with this major will generally possess knowledge of:
Anthropology	Human origins and evolution, present conditions of human life, and future prospects of human life
Communication	Theory and application of interpersonal, group, organizational, and public communication
Economics	The science of decision making in a public arena, such as government, finance, trade, etc.
English	Literature: An understanding and appreciation of literary heritage and a foundation to evaluate contemporary writing
	Writing: An ability to express ideas in a clear, succinct, and capable manner
Fine Arts	History and technique of various media in the visual arts, such as painting, photography, drawing, sculpture, etc.
Geography	Economic, physical, and social background to investigate environmental issues, socioeconomic problems, planning, etc.
History	Process of change in the human condition over time in order to identify social trends and analyze critical causal factors
Music	Music theory, literature, and performance
Philosophy	Transmission and evaluation of basic beliefs and values
Political Science	Who has the power, where it comes from, how it is used, how the public good is defined, etc.
Psychology	Human development and behavior, learning and adjustment, etc.
Sociology	Theories and methods of the analysis of social behavior
Theater	Diversified theater areas, such as production, direction, performance, designing, teaching, etc.

data to other relevant study areas. Most courses require some sort of research-gathering paper or project, where students note historical information, develop a thesis, and make connections between established research and their own ideas.

This research or integration, skill is used every day in personal and professional circumstances. In personal situations, you need to gather information and correlate it to your needs and present situation in order to make decisions about your life. Consider these basic life questions: *Where should I live? How do I determine a career? Why should I marry (or not marry) this person?* A liberal arts education prepares you to become a considering decision maker.

In professional situations, you will be expected to generate research and write reports as you do in school. Many positions require a compare–contrast way of formulating business proposals. A liberal arts education prepares you for the assimilation of ideas and information required for this type of analysis.

Communication Skills

The best idea, if it cannot be communicated, is worthless.

A liberal arts education emphasizes the ability to express well-formed thoughts. In addition to the class discussion aspect, most liberal arts programs require individual courses in speech, interpersonal communication, and the fundamentals or psychology of communication.

In its broadest sense, the term *communication* includes all methods of conveying any kind of thought or feeling between persons. This simple definition becomes enormously important when you consider that studies estimate that we spend up to 80 percent of our waking hours engaged in some form of human communication. A liberal arts education can improve and enhance the communication in our daily lives.

On a personal level, consider where better communication skills would improve your quality of life. Do you find it easy to introduce yourself to someone new? Would you like to express your feelings better to your friends and family? Do you have frequent areas of "miscommunication"?

On a professional level, consider the importance of good communication skills. Many articles in the business sections of local newspapers contain the view that corporations are looking for people who can organize effective presentations; write concise, clear reports; facilitate group discussions; and so forth.

Critical Thinking

Critical thinking basically means that you examine, analyze, and question information you are receiving, rather than just "storing it away." Critical thinking is important thinking that involves asking questions. It is important to question established ideas as well as create new ideas and to turn information into tools to solve problems and make decisions.

A liberal arts education doesn't just give you knowledge; it can help you develop the critical thinking skills that will help you apply that knowledge. *The Importance of a Liberal Arts Education* page on the Web (http://www.winona.msus.edu) states that, perhaps, the most important value of a liberal arts education is that it helps the student explore, develop, and articulate the questions necessary for critical thinking. It also states, "Questions of why? and why not? are considered along with those of How? where? and when? Additionally, questions of what if . . . ? and suppose . . . ? are encouraged—questions that lead to some of life's most important answers." As one liberal arts professor put it, "if everything is done right, a liberal arts major will graduate from college with more questions than answers. Answers are a short-term fix, but questions equip you for life."

In personal circumstances, critical thinking helps you decide what your life goals and values are. Remember when you were a kid and your mother said to you, "If all your friends jumped off a bridge, would you do it just because they did?" Critical thinking helps you decide whether jumping off that bridge really is a good idea for you. Critical thinking helps you formulate the answer to "Where do you see yourself in five years?"

In professional circumstances, critical thinking helps you to *produce* knowledge, rather than just to *re*produce it. Employees who can ask "How can we work smarter? Produce more? Be more efficient?" are very valuable indeed.

Problem Solving

We should rejoice at the existence of a problem. The mere existence of a problem proves that we are participating in life—not simply watching it pass by.

One of the goals of a liberal arts education is to remind us that problems exist, and also that we should embrace the mere notion of a problem arising; a problem can signal growth and awareness instead of mere complacency regarding the status quo. Once again, *The Importance of a Liberal Arts Education* Web page emphasizes how a liberal arts education can prepare you to embrace problems and to acquire the skills to handle them: "Primary characteristics of a liberal arts education are its breadth and its emphasis on multi- and interdisciplinary perspectives in problem-solving. The problems in today's and tomorrow's worlds are increasingly complex, and to make appropriate choices we must be able to approach decisions from wide and multiple perspectives. . . . No other form of education provides such characteristics and preparation for living."

Think of the problems that arise in your personal life. Two of the core courses you need are scheduled at the same time—*what* will you do? Your financial aid is denied—*where* else will you go for help? Your boyfriend or girlfriend broke up with you—*how* will you handle this? The multi- and interdisciplinary approaches used in a liberal arts education will help provide you with a repertoire of steps to use to reach a solution.

What about your professional life? Many corporations today are divided into self-directed work teams. These teams are expected to develop, test, and troubleshoot products, services, and/or ideas within their own groups. The skills you learn within a liberal arts curriculum will make you a valuable member of the team.

With a liberal arts education you will be well equipped to handle the "real world." Consider how well the liberal arts students below applied their research abilities, critical thinking, and problem-solving skills in the following liberal arts anecdote currently making the campus rounds:

THREE DEGREES OF THOUGHT

A student convention was being held. Traveling on the train to the convention were math majors, engineering majors, and liberal arts majors. Each of the liberal arts majors and engineering majors had his or her own train ticket. But the math majors had only ONE ticket for all of them.

The engineering majors started laughing and snickering. The math majors ignored their laughter. Then, one of the engineers said, "Here comes the conductor!" All of the math majors piled into a bathroom. The engineering majors and liberal arts majors were puzzled. The conductor came aboard and collected tickets from all the engineering majors and liberal arts majors. He went to the bathroom, knocked on the door, and said, "Ticket, please." A math major stuck their only ticket out under the door. The conductor took the ticket and left. A few minutes later, the math majors emerged from the bathroom. The engineering students gathered and whispered.

On the way back from the convention, the group of liberal arts majors again had tickets for each member of their group, the math majors again had one ticket, but the engineering majors had NO tickets. When the math majors snickered at them, the engineers just smiled. When an engineer major shouted, "Conductor coming," all the math majors again piled into a bathroom, and all but one engineering major piled into the other bathroom. Then, before the conductor came on board, the remaining engineering major knocked on the math majors' bathroom door and said, "Ticket, please!"

He turned to the liberal arts majors and said, "If you had a major that made you use your brain, like I do, you wouldn't have to be paying for this trip." One of the liberal arts majors replied, "Well, we ran down a list of questions and options and found that your solution wasn't feasible."

Snickering at this answer, the engineering major turned around to find the same conductor from the previous trip, only this time the suspicious conductor had with him a railroad security person. The math majors and engineering majors were kicked off the train and had to walk home.

The moral of the story is that in life, being able to add two and two is important, and the ingenuity to improve a plan can take you in the right direction, but it may be the critical thinking and simple logic that you learn as a liberal arts major that will make the ride a little more pleasant.

WHAT SUPPORT IS AVAILABLE FOR LIBERAL ARTS MAJORS?

"The purpose of education is to nurture thoughtfulness. The lesser function of thinking is to solve problems or puzzles. The essential purpose is to decide for oneself what is of genuine value in life. And then to find the courage to take your own thoughts seriously."

ALBERT EINSTEIN

One way to nurture thoughtfulness and learn how to solve problems is to foster the feelings of cooperation that Einstein is talking about—to take advantage of available resources on and off campus. The resources on your campus can be divided into three sections: people, organizations, and campus publications. Within these three sections, what resources are available to a liberal arts major on campus?

People

Familiarize yourself with the people connected with your school's liberal arts program. These people may include instructors, administrative personnel, advisors and counselors, and fellow students.

Instructors can be a valuable resource for you. They can give you a clear sense of course content and requirements. Often instructors can also direct you to student organizations that will provide support and assistance in your college career.

Administrative personnel, such as department chairs, deans, bursars, and financial aid officers, may be able to help you tailor your liberal arts degree or provide information about how the school may provide assistance to you as you pursue your degree.

Advisors and counselors can assist you with both the educational and the personal aspects of pursuing a liberal arts degree. Academic advisors can help with timing and scheduling of courses, providing information about how liberal arts courses intertwine, and explaining how to develop a sequential course load toward your major. Counselors may offer personality or vocational testing to help you determine the best major for you within the liberal arts arena.

Fellow students are the ones who will give you the "real scoop." Students who have experience in the liberal arts program can offer opinions on professors, courses, study habits, test-taking strategies, clubs, etc. If you elicit opinions from fellow students, be sure to talk to several students to ensure a well-rounded picture. Check with your campus tutoring center, mentoring office, or major discipline department to obtain names of students with some experience on campus.

Campus Organizations

Your school has many organizations within the liberal arts arena that can offer many forms of support as you pursue your education. Consult your advisor, your school activities office or bulletin board, the department for your major, or your school's Web page for the possibilities at your school. Some organizations are school-sponsored, others are student-run organizations, and still others are campus branches of local or national organizations. Look for interest clubs related to your major, such as the Anthropology Club, History Club, or Philosophy Club. Look for scholastic or fraternal societies such as Psi Chi (psychology), Phi Alpha Theta (history), as so forth.

Professional Organizations

In her book, *How To Choose a College Major,* Linda L. Andrews advises students to obtain information from professional organizations. "Professional organizations have a vested interest in providing information to students. Informing students about the benefits and particulars of their profession ensures a continuing supply of people in the next generations to carry on their work, and pay dues" (p. 215).

The book specifically advises asking associations for the following kinds of information:

1. People in your geographic area who are willing to give informational interviews

2. Internship and volunteer opportunities for finding out more about the profession

3. Scholarships available for students studying in the association's field

4. Packets of information on the variety of jobs held in this profession

Many professional organizations would be appropriate for the liberal arts major. How can you find out about these organizations? You could ask your advisor, check your school bulletin boards for student branches of the organizations, and browse the Web.

The box below offers a partial list of organizations to get you started.

Professional Organizations

Interest	Organization
Anthropology	American Anthropological Assoc. 4350 N. Fairfax Dr., Suite 640 Arlington, VA 22203 (703)528-1902 www.ameranthassn.org
Art	American Artists Professional League c/o Salmagundi Club 47 Fifth Ave. New York, NY 10003 (212)645-1345
Writing	National Writer's Assoc. 1450 S. Havana, Suite 424 Aurora, CO 80012 (303)751-7844
Communication	National Communication Assoc. 16 E. 34th St., 15th floor New York, NY 10016 (212)683-8585
Economics	American Economic Assoc. 2014 Broadway, Suite 305 Nashville, TN 37203-2418 (615)322-2595 www.vanderbilt.edu/AEA
Geography	American Geographical Society 156 Fifth Ave., Suite 600 New York, NY 10010-7002 (212)422-5456
History	American Historical Assoc. 400 A St. SW Washington, DC 20003 (202)544-2422
Music	National Assoc. of Schools of Music 11250 Roger Bacon Dr., Suite 21 Reston, VA 22090 www.nasm.org

(continued)

Philosophy	American Philosophical Society 104 S. Fifth St. Philadelphia, PA 19106-3387 (215)440-3400
Political Science	American Political Science Assoc. 1527 New Hampshire Ave. NW Washington, DC 20002-4242 (202)336-5500 www.apa.org
Sociology	American Sociological Assoc. 1722 N St. NW Washington, DC 20036 (202)833-3410
Theater	American Alliance for Theatre & Educ. PO Box 873411 Dept. of Theatre Arizona State University Tempe, AZ 85287-3411 (602)965-6064

Campus Publications

Most colleges and universities have Web sites containing useful information, and these can be a good beginning resource for you. A complete listing of college/university Web sites can be obtained through the Web search service, Yahoo! Use the path http://www.yahoo.com, then type in the name of the college or university. However, you should be aware that most Web sites have disclaimers about the accuracy of the information, such as "Remember, this electronic message is not the official policy of this college." For official policy you'll want to consult the specific college course catalog or their student handbook.

A specific course catalog will explain the school's position toward a liberal arts education—how that particular school views the composition and end goals of a liberal arts degree. Each department lists their own objectives for a degree in that discipline as well as course requirements and course descriptions.

Your student handbook will usually contain contact names and phone numbers for some of the other resources we've discussed (such as counselors, clubs, organizations, etc.).

WHAT CAREERS ARE ACCESSIBLE TO LIBERAL ARTS MAJORS?

The goals and values surrounding the philosophy of a liberal arts education sound lofty indeed, but you might be asking yourself, "but will this degree help me get a job?" The answer is a resounding *yes*. According to a recent survey conducted by Hobart and William Smith College, 90 percent of the business leaders surveyed feel that a liberal arts education is essential to the development of critical thinking skills, 77 percent feel that it is essential to problem-solving skills. Boston University conducted a survey that revealed that 50 percent of the Fortune 1000 companies that recruit on campuses seek out liberal arts majors.

The U.S. Department of Labor, Bureau of Labor Statistics states that the growing trend in the job market is jobs involving *services,* not goods. A liberal arts education is viewed as an entirely appropriate preparation for careers in many firms, and, for some starting positions, it is even viewed as giving the graduate an edge.

The Purdue University home page (http://www.purdue.edu) claims that liberal arts majors are in demand. Sylvia Howell, coordinator for placement in the School of Liberal Arts at Purdue University, states: "Employers find that liberal arts students have an ability to learn, they communicate well, they have decision-making skills and do well in many areas. . . . Already this year, 75 employers have been on campus looking for liberal arts majors. That's an increase of about 35 percent over two years ago."

The Liberal Arts Major and Business

"Liberally educated managers—especially managers with excellent . . . communication skills are increasingly recognized as critical to the successful corporation."

JOSEPH H. WYMAN, CEO, CBS, INC.

"If I could choose one degree for the people I hire it would be English . . . you can teach a group of Cub Scouts to do portfolio analysis."

SENIOR VICE-PRESIDENT OF A LARGE FINANCIAL INSTITUTION

We've already established that the skills acquired by a liberal arts major are valuable in both the personal and professional arenas. However, can liberal arts majors compete with business majors for positions in the business world? The book *Educating Managers: Executive Effectiveness Through Liberal Learning,* written by a team of scholars, business executives, and academic administrators, says they definitely can. The book's foreword, in particular, points to the broad perspective a liberal arts major acquires as a particular asset in the changing climate of today's business world: "We live and work in an increasingly complex world characterized by dramatic change and accelerating rates of change. Business decisions affect, and are affected by, many parts of society. With such a premium placed on thoughtful, sensitive, creative, and flexible management there is no place for leadership with a limited perspective. . . . Liberally educated managers, especially managers with excellent written and verbal communication skills, are increasingly recognized as critical to the successful corporation" (p. ix).

The Liberal Arts Major and the "High-Tech" World

The Stanford University home page (http://daily.stanford.org) affirms that liberal arts majors are in demand in the job market, even in technical fields. Lance Choy, associate director of the Career Planning and Placement Center at Stanford, reminds us that "There is an image that only engineers get hired by

technology firms. A lot of liberal arts majors go to career fairs and get frustrated because they see companies swarming after computer science and engineering majors. The opportunities are there (for liberal arts majors); you just have to work harder to find them."

Julie Davisson, a recent English major from Stanford, secured a position at Trilogy, a major software company. She says that "of my recruiting class, 21 of us come from Stanford, and five are non-technical." Ben Zaniello, with a double major—urban studies and German—from Stanford, also works at Trilogy. He says, "Often the best marketing team comes out on top, regardless of the quality of software, so slowly, but surely, software companies have realized the need for clarity of prose in their releases and documentation, the necessity of strong leadership for running trade shows, and the benefit of a quick mind in marketing strategy."

Both Davisson and Zaniello recommend being diligent in pursuit of a career. Davisson advises that the liberal arts major should submit a resume to any company desired, regardless of outward technical appearances. Zaniello takes this approach a step farther. "Go talk to them, learn what they do and how they do it. If you think there's a match, don't hold back—demand an interview, and tell them why. Enthusiasm, motivation, and good communication—those can be your tickets into the high-tech world."

Some Famous People and Their Liberal Arts Degrees

➤ Warren Littlefield, President, NBC Entertainment; English
➤ Bill Watterson, cartoonist (Calvin & Hobbes); Political Science
➤ Robert Harlan, President, Green Bay Packers; Journalism
➤ Richard Gephart, U.S. Congressman; Speech Communication
➤ Saul Bellow, Novelist; Sociology
➤ Richard Nixon, U.S. President; History
➤ Alice Rivlin, Assistant Director of the Federal Reserve; Economics
➤ John Cougar Mellencamp, Singer/Songwriter; Broadcasting

Where to Go For Information on Possible Careers

Your school may have a career services center, a co-operative education placement office, or an internship program in place. Check your catalog, or ask your advisor if any of these services are available.

Another resource on campus is your school library. The following are just a few of the titles found in a typical university library that could assist you in your job search:

➤ *Aside From Teaching, What in the World Can You Do?*, Dorothy K. Bestor
➤ *For Your Action—A Practical Job Search Guide for the Liberal Arts Student*, Wayne Wallace

➤ *Jobs For English Majors and Other Smart People,* John Munschaver
➤ *High-Tech Jobs for Non-Tech Majors,* Mark O'Brien
➤ *Great Jobs for Communications, English, Foreign Language, History, and Psychology Majors,* Julie Degalan and Stephen Lambert
➤ *150 Best Companies for Liberal Arts Graduates,* Woodruff and Ptacek
➤ *Liberal Arts and the Corporation,* Useem

Another excellent resource in considering career opportunities is *Commission for Career Development VI: Liberal Arts Committee.* This national organization is comprised of career specialists from colleges and the community. The committee identifies career resources available to the liberal arts student, maintains informational newsletters, and produces conventions/career fairs for liberal arts majors. For information, contact:

Jo Ann Cornell
Liberal Arts Career Counselor
Colorado State University
jcornell@vines.colostate.edu
(970)491-5707

WHAT SCHOOLS OFFER LIBERAL ARTS DEGREES?

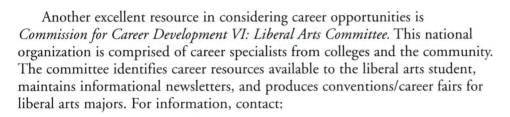

If a liberal arts education sounds good to you, you might be wondering about which schools offer a liberal arts education. Start by investigating what is available on your own campus in the liberal arts. Then gather information about other schools and compare and contrast, using the critical thinking skills that we talked about earlier.

Browse the Web and check your campus library or bookstore for publications that provide information about colleges and universities. Some publications merely list the institutions; others try to provide an assessment of life on campus, tuition, school values, etc. Still others attempt to "rate" the colleges in some manner. Some titles to get you started:

➤ *Barron's Profiles of American Colleges*
➤ *Cass & Birnbaum's Guide to American Colleges*
➤ *The College Handbook*
➤ *The Fiske Guide to Colleges*
➤ *The Insider's Guide to the Colleges*
➤ *U.S. News and World Report—"America's Best Colleges,"* published annually

WHAT'S NEXT?

Now that you have more information on a liberal arts major, go back to the first page and think it through again. A liberal arts education will give you a broad foundation to examine life, to begin a variety of careers, and to prepare you for graduate school. What do you think? Is it for you?

Applications & Exercises

Key Into Your Life: Opportunities to Apply What You Learn

"Real life is not wished, it is lived."

1. Identify Yourself

Take a piece of paper, write the numbers 1 to 20 down the left side, and at the top of the paper write: I am . . . Now finish the "I am" statement with 20 one-word descriptive answers (such as *I am smart, I am creative*). Just write the first answers that come to your mind, but be sure to complete all 20.

Now look at your list carefully. Close your eyes, take a few moments to relax, and try to construct a mental image of the person described in this list. Try to paint a picture that not only captures your physical characteristics but also reflects the attitudes, aptitudes, feelings, and beliefs included on your list. Who are you? After reading this chapter, do you think the person identified in this list would be happy as a liberal arts major?

2. Identify Your Values

Each of us maintains a set of values—moral or ethical judgments of things we consider important. Values are fairly enduring conceptions of the nature of good and bad, of the *relative worth* you attribute to the things, people, and events of your life. Your values should guide your decision when choosing a major. Your major should be compatible with your general values to avoid conflict and stress in your life.

To help you uncover your values, answer the following questions:

a. What do you value in other people?

_____

_____

_____

b. What does your family value (e.g., getting ahead, social conscience)?

_____

_____

_____

c. Do you agree with your family's values?

_____

_____

_____

d. If you had all the money you needed and were working just for the satisfaction, what would you be doing?

_____

_____

_____

3. Identify Your Skills and Interests

Two factors you should take into consideration when choosing a major are what are you already good at and what do you want to learn to be good at? Check with your school's counseling or career center—they may have some vocational interest tests you could take to determine your aptitude toward certain careers (such as the *Strong Interest Inventory®,* or the *Myers-Briggs Type Indicator®*). But for now, just take an inventory yourself. Look at the following list of typical skill areas examined by a liberal arts major and put a check under "Already Have" for the skill areas in which you already possess a degree of proficiency. Now go back and put an "X" in the right column for the ones you'd be interested in acquiring. Do they fit the profile of a liberal arts major?

Already Have	Skill Areas	Want to Acquire
_____	Artistic	_____
_____	Brainstorming	_____
_____	Communication	_____
_____	Creativity	_____
_____	Critical thinking	_____
_____	Decision-making	_____
_____	Discussion	_____
_____	Ethics	_____
_____	Language	_____
_____	Performance	_____
_____	Philosophical issues	_____
_____	Problem solving	_____
_____	Reading	_____
_____	Research	_____
_____	Social issues	_____
_____	Writing	_____

Key to Cooperative Learning: Building Teamwork Skills

If you're considering liberal arts as a major, but still haven't made up your mind, then you need to consider three possible teams to help you. In order to utilize your teams successfully, arrange a meeting place ahead of time and let the team know what the discussion will be about, so that they can do some thinking before the meeting. You will also want to do some thinking, and you need to bring your answers to the first three exercises.

The first team is your *family*. Your family probably knows you better than anyone, so take advantage of that knowledge. First, ask yourself, "What do I really know about my *parents'* occupations? Do you *really* know what it is they do, and *why* they chose that career, or why they continue in it? Ask your parents and your siblings to complete the first three exercises, answering with their perceptions of how they see you. Now compare their answers with your answers. Do they see you differently? Is their view valid?

The second team is your *friends.* Your close friends have a different view of you than your family. Sometimes friends will be a little more objective about your strengths and areas of improvement. Also, your friends might have information about you that your family does not. Did you share "fantasy" thoughts with your friends about what you'd like to do when you "grew up" that you were too embarrassed to tell your family? Perhaps your friends are aware of your favorite excuses, or "cop-outs." Ask them to complete the first three exercises, answering with their perceptions of how they see you. Compare their answers with your answers and with your family's answers.

The third team is your academic *advisor* and/or school *counselor.* Before your appointment, be sure to write a list of questions. These questions could pertain to liberal arts in general, specific majors, or about possible career opportunities for liberal arts majors. At your appointment be sure to inquire about possible vocational interest tests and about other resources available on campus.

Key to Self-Expression: Discovery Through Journal Writing

To record your thoughts, use a separate journal.

You have some information about a liberal arts education. Now is the time to do some deliberating. Divide your page and do some "pro/con" thinking. What are the pros and cons as far as personal interest, financial concerns, and careers?

Now write descriptions of how you picture yourself one year from now, and in ten years. What will you be doing? What will you enjoy most about your life? What contributions will you be making to your family and to society? What is the one thing that will give you the greatest feeling of pride? The major you choose should be pointing you in the direction you've just described.

Key to Your Personal Portfolio: Your Paper Trail to Success

The first table that you'll want to construct is one that reflects possible majors/careers within the liberal arts arena that reflects your personal interests. Using all of the resources discussed in this chapter, narrow your list to the possibilities you'll want to pursue further. Your table might look something like this:

Major	Reason Why Interested	Possible Careers
Psychology	I'm interested in what makes people tick	counselor, mediator, advertising consultant

Another table you might want to construct is a list of possible resources. Your table might look something like this:

Name	Affiliation	Address/Phone Number
Jane Doe	President, Psi Chi (psychology honor society)	On campus (building A-24) 555-1515

Your portfolio should be changing as you receive new information, so don't forget to update it on a regular basis.

11 KEYS TO SUCCESS IN THE RESEARCH SCIENCES

In this chapter, you will explore answers to the following questions:

➤ How much do you know about the different branches of science, and why do you think you would fit best in one particular field?

➤ How can you get the necessary exposure to a research job before you decide to go to graduate school?

➤ How can you become competitive in the field of scientific research?

➤ What skill areas beyond your major should you develop to become successful in scientific research?

? Thinking It Through

Check those statements that currently apply to you:

❑ I need help determining whether I would be good at research, especially as an undergraduate.

❑ I'm not sure how to use my school training to help me become more adept at scientific research.

❑ Even though I'm interested in the sciences, I haven't ever sat down and asked myself why.

❑ I've thought about choosing research science as a major, but I feel unsure of that choice.

❑ I love to read and study the sciences, but I wonder where my interest is leading me.

D I S C O V E R

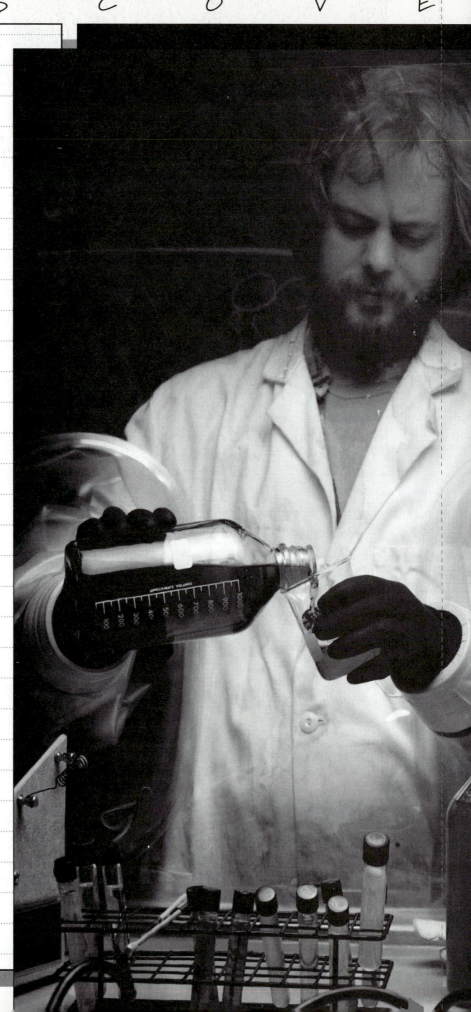

11

KEYS TO SUCCESS IN THE RESEARCH SCIENCES

◆ INTRODUCTION

Whether you are coming back to college after working for a while or are entering right after high school, if you are there to study one of the scientific fields, you may discover you have an aptitude for scientific research. Ask yourself an important question: "Do I want to come up with a discovery that could further the field of science, improve the environment, or help humankind?" If the answer is yes, and you have an inclination toward continual, persistent efforts to make new theories come alive, perhaps your ideal career path would be to become a research scientist. Research is a rigorous activity that requires creativity, excellent critical thinking skills, and determination. Although it requires precision and analysis, it is not a cold, unfeeling occupation. Research science can open a new world of beauty, joy, and discovery to you and to others who may benefit from your work.

As you consider pursuing the path of a scientist, recall the meaning of the word science: It comes from the Latin word *scientia,* meaning knowledge. Are you a person who loves to gather new information about a subject? Scientific knowledge focuses on the gathering of observable facts and the relationships between those facts. Scientists search for discoveries in a vast array of areas, such as searching for clues to the origin of the universe or for uncharted molecular structures in living organisms.

Understanding the various jobs of research scientists in different fields holds tremendous importance for you as you complete your undergraduate studies. One way scientists are categorized is as pure, or basic, and applied, or practical. Pure scientists focus on new discoveries that may not have any immediate application to everyday life. For example, a pure scientist in the field of mathematics may discover a new theorem in the field of topology; whereas an applied scientist would take the new theorem in topology from the pure scientist and use it to develop new methods of manufacturing on a microscopic scale. Applied scientists take the basic research from pure scientists to develop new drugs or medical treatments, increase crop yields, or protect and clean up the environment. The distinction between pure science (theoretical) and applied (practical) science can easily become blurred; the two categories often overlap.

Advances in scientific research present many exciting possibilities. Scientific research in the branches of mathematics, physical sciences, and life sciences offers a wide expanse of choices for you. As you read about each area, you will answer questions designed to help you reflect on whether a future in a certain branch of scientific research is for you. Hopefully, you will gain more insight into what you need to do during your undergraduate training to give yourself more knowledge of what the road to success will involve.

One thought to keep in mind is that scientific research does not easily lead to amazing discoveries. Scientific breakthroughs are rare, but a great deal of satisfaction can still be gained from making small advances in a field that you enjoy working in. Discoveries of theories or major advances in knowledge may come from years and years of persistent hard work or a sudden spark of ingenuity. One sudden discovery can illustrate how unpredictable scientific research can be: Sir Alexander Fleming, a British bacteriologist, discovered penicillin unexpectedly in 1928 when he saw that a smudge of the mold *Penicillium* had contaminated a laboratory plate that had bacteria on it. Fleming noticed that the bacteria around the mold had been destroyed (*World Book,* "Science," p. 195).

WHAT SKILLS ARE NEEDED FOR SUCCESS IN SCIENTIFIC RESEARCH?

Understanding the skills that any scientist should have when conducting research is helpful in determining whether or not you would be a good research scientist. The following table describes some of the most important skills and qualities for success in the research sciences.

SKILLS AND/OR QUALITIES	DESCRIPTION
Creativity	To be open-minded and have knowledge of a wide variety of subjects such as art, history, and politics. To use the skills of problem solving, asking questions, looking for answers, and evaluating references.
Math	To use quantitative skills and statistics, and to work with numbers.
Grant Writing	To be able to find money to fund research; includes good communication skills of persuasion and writing.
Diligence	To stick with a project despite initial or repeated problems, paying careful attention to details.
Observation	To study nature and statistical patterns, seeing things others may not notice, or seeing things in a new way.

Understanding the Research Process

You cannot be expected to jump into any scientific research method without having developed skills in the overall research process. The research process is quite involved and the familiarity and experience you can receive as an undergraduate will help you to know whether scientific research truly suits your interests. To gain more knowledge and insight about the scientific research process, visit some informational Web sites pertaining to this topic listed at the end of this chapter.

Finding a mentor. The most important step you can take toward success in learning the research process is to have a mentor. A mentor will help you understand and gain experience in research. You must get involved in some hands-on experience. To find a mentor, you can volunteer to assist someone doing research. If you do not already have someone in mind, talk to a professor in science, a science graduate student, or those in industry, medicine, or technology and ask them for recommendations of someone who would be interested in having a volunteer to assist them.

Alertness to scientific research in real life. An important attribute of success is being alert to current scientific research progress. As you go to your classes and gain the academic background to become a scientist, take time to pay attention to current occurrences reported in the media.

Examples of Current Scientific Research

Biological research. As described by Jerome Groopman (*The New Yorker*, 6/15/88), Philip Needleman is an industry science researcher for Monsanto Company. He was doing basic research to understand more about the inflammation process that causes pain in arthritis and in joint injuries. From his

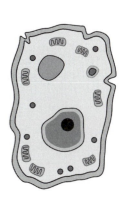

observations of the activity of inflamed cells, he generated a hypothesis that the cells contained two different types of receptors for prostaglandin, a key hormone in the inflammation process. He had not actually seen the second receptor, but his tests and subsequent observations made him predict that one existed.

Needleman presented his research at an international conference, and shortly thereafter other scientists did the work to confirm his idea: They found the second cell receptor for the inflammation process. From this point on, Needleman's work became directed toward finding a drug that could inhibit the second receptor, and thus offer a much-needed treatment for arthritis (the potential economic benefit for the drug companies ensured funding for additional studies). Thus his initial basic research to understand inflamed cell physiology turned to applied research to find a drug to inhibit the inflammation. Additional applied research carried out by others involved tests showing that the inhibition of the second receptor site could possibly be used to treat Alzheimer's disease.

Gene mapping. There is an international effort to map the entire human genome by the year 2000 called the Human Genome Project. Mapping the human genome involves making discoveries about all of our millions of genes, which determine not only things like eye color but predisposition to diseases such as diabetes and heart disease. Many ethical issues attend this kind of research. For instance, what if you could have a test at birth that would tell you what illnesses you were destined to have later on in life? How would this affect your psychological state or your family? Privacy issues also become important. Who would have access to the information? Perhaps prospective employers or insurance companies would gain access. And what kinds of decisions would they make based on this information? Will couples have genetic testing on their unborn children and make pregnancy termination decisions based on the results?

On the other hand, tremendous advances in genetics have led to the identification of the gene, or genes, for many congenital diseases, such as cystic fibrosis. Other genetic research is working on a technique known as gene therapy to replace deficient genes with new, efficient ones. Research areas in genetics also include genetic engineering, which is used in the production of foods and medicines.

Physics and astronomy. Constant observation of the universe is a pursuit that often involves working throughout the night, using complex technology and requiring a great deal of patience. Recently, scientists have used images from the Hubble Space Telescope to discover that much of what we see in the telescope's visible light images conceal star formations in more distant galaxies. To solve this problem, work is being done using infrared telescopes. Researchers anticipate that by the year 2001, two infrared observatories will be in operation. The telescopes will be in orbit above the earth's atmosphere to provide clearer pictures of the stars (Ron Cowen, "Unveiling the Hidden Universe," *Science News,* vol. 153, no. 21, pp. 328–330, 1998).

Life sciences. The first known case of chlorophyll use in the physiology of animals was recently discovered by researchers from Finland and England while they were studying the rare red glow and vision of the loose-jaw fish *Malacosteus niger.* They found that the light spectrum of the pigments in the fish's eyes contained modified chlorophyll. This type of research is an example of basic research, and while it is primarily conducted to better our knowledge and understanding of a species, it may be the first step to preserving life on the planet and to finding possible uses for the discoveries. Ethnobotanists do applied research by studying plants to discover useful medicines. For example, Tamoxifen, which is used to treat cancer, is derived from the yew tree.

To get a better idea of the wide variety of research going on—from the practical to the seemingly outlandish—go to the library, or subscribe to the weekly magazine *Science News.* Additionally, visit the *Science News* Web site (listed at the end of this chapter).

WHICH SCIENTIFIC AREA DO YOU WANT TO RESEARCH?

Understanding the broad range of studies available in science influences the type of advanced educational and training programs you choose. Scientists are usually trained in one area within physical science, biological and medical sciences, or mathematics. As you consider your research interests, the following descriptions of the educational and training requirements should help you to clarify your interests. Keep in mind that you do not need to decide what specific research area you will pursue while you are an undergraduate. Simply realizing which area you are interested in and acquiring a strong background in that area will prepare you for choosing a specialty for graduate school and beyond.

Mathematics

As in all the branches of science, mathematics has two main classes: pure, or theoretical, and applied. Theoretical mathematicians develop new principles as well as distinguish relationships between existing principles. While their work adds to the body of mathematical knowledge, it does not include any practical applications. Applied mathematicians use theoretical and computational methods and mathematical models to formulate and solve practical problems in government, business, engineering, physics, and myriad other fields. Both theoretical and applied mathematicians are vital to the production and advancement of science and engineering, and the large number of successful applications would not have been possible without the contributions of theoretical mathematicians.

Training. A four-year degree is the minimum requirement for mathematicians. According to the *Occupational Outlook Handbook, 1998, (OOH)* most colleges and universities in the United States offer an undergraduate degree in mathematics; 240 offer a master's degree, and 195 offer a doctoral degree. For a job in the federal government, a four-year degree is acceptable if the 24 semester hours required in mathematics studies have been completed. In private industry, a master's degree or Ph.D. is required to work in research and development labs with technical teams where pure or basic mathematics research takes place. If you are planning on going to graduate school, expect to conduct research, take advanced courses, and specialize in a subfield of math such as algebra, number theory, real or complex analysis, geometry, topology, logic, or applied mathematics.

Reflection on your interests. If you are interested in mathematics, answer the following questions:

➤ What are some mathematical areas of study mentioned here that interest you?

➤ Why are you intrigued about mathematics as a research area?

➤ What about the study of mathematics may relate to your previously identified interests?

➤ What are some action steps you can take to further investigate your interests, such as finding a mentor, locating updated science news, or working on some of the key skills for success?

Physical Sciences

The physical sciences examine the nature of the physical universe, and include four main branches: (1) physics and astronomy, (2) chemistry, (3) geology, and (4) meteorology. Study in these branches covers the structure and properties of non-living matter, from microscopic atoms to vast galaxies. The following chart shows the description of scientific branches and the associated field training expectations.

SPECIALTY	DESCRIPTION	FIELD TRAINING AND EXPERIENCE
Physics and Astronomy	Physics is the study of energy and matter. Astronomy, a sub-field of physics, uses the principles of mathematics and physics to study the sun, moon, and galaxies.	Doctoral degrees usually required because most jobs are in basic research and development. A master's degree can be helpful in applied research and development and manufacturing.
Chemistry	Chemistry involves research to gain new knowledge about chemicals. Applying chemical research has led to the discovery and development of new and improved synthetic fibers, paints, adhesives, drugs, cosmetics, electronic components, lubricants, and thousands of other products.	Minimum requirement is a bachelor's degree. Many research jobs require a doctorate.
Geology	Geologists or geophysicists, otherwise known as geoscientists, study the physical aspects and history of the earth; they study rocks, analyze information collected by remote sensing instruments in satellites, conduct geological surveys, construct field maps, and use instruments to measure the earth's gravity and magnetic field.	Bachelor's degrees are required for beginning jobs. Geologists and geophysicists often start their careers in field exploration or as research assistants in labs or offices and then advance to management and even research positions.

(continued)

Meteorology	Meteorology is the study of the atmosphere—the blanket of air covering the earth; the atmosphere's physical characteristics, motions, and processes, and the way it affects the rest of our environment.	A bachelor's degree, majoring in meteorology, for beginning jobs is required. A master's degree is the minimum for research and development, and a Ph.D. is required for most basic research jobs. Those planning to go into research should get a bachelor's degree in mathematics, physics, or engineering for preparation.

Job Outlook and Educational Programs for the Physical Sciences (adapted from the *Occupational Outlook Handbook, 1998*).

Physics and astronomy. Physics research jobs are highly competitive. Grant money is limited to research projects that are often defense-related research. There are 500 college and university programs in the United States that offer a Bachelor of Science in physics, while 180 colleges and universities have a Ph.D. program in physics that follows the bachelor's degree programs.

Studying astronomy offers intriguing research possibilities as well. For instance, you may want to study what research in cosmology would entail. An excellent video for those interested in astronomy is "A Brief History of Time," about the life and work of renowned physicist Stephen Hawking.

Chemistry. Most job growth will be in drug manufacturing and research, development, and testing services firms, according to the *OOH, 1998*. Because the chemical industry faces demands for better pharmaceuticals and personal care products, firms will devote money to research and development, which will spur an increase in the number of job opportunities. Firms providing research, development, and testing services are expected to be good sources of jobs through 2006. Several hundred colleges and universities offer advanced degree programs in chemistry; around 320 offer master's programs, and about 190 doctoral programs are approved by the American Chemical Society.

Geophysics. A growing demand for oil and gas and new exploration and discovery techniques have returned stability to the petroleum industry. The demand for geologists and geophysicists has increased, and job opportunities are expected to be good. Hundreds of colleges and universities in the United States offer a bachelor's degree in geology, but for the other geosciences, such as geophysics and oceanography, there are fewer programs available.

Meteorology. The federal government is the largest employer of civilian meteorologists; nearly 90 percent of them work in the National Weather Service's stations throughout the United States. The remaining 10 percent work in research. Relatively few colleges offer degrees in meteorology or atmospheric sciences, although many departments of physics, earth science, geography, and geophysics offer atmospheric science and related courses. If you want to be a meteorologist, make sure your school offers the courses required by the National Weather Service.

Life Sciences (Biological Sciences)

Life sciences, or biological sciences, involve the study of living organisms. The primary life sciences are genetics; botany, dealing with plants; zoology, involving the study of animals; and health, the study of human physiology and anatomy, disease, and response to disease.

Biological and medical scientists generally work in research and development. They conduct research to further the knowledge of living organisms, including viruses, bacteria, and other infectious agents. Colleges and universities, private industry, and federal government agencies, such as the National Institutes of Health and the National Science Foundation, all contribute financial support for feasible research proposals from scientists who have the potential to develop new ideas or processes.

Most biological scientists are classified by the type of organism they study. Some broad classifications of biologists include aquatic biologists, biochemists, botanists, geneticists, microbiologists, physiologists, zoologists, ecologists, agricultural scientists, and health scientists.

Field training and education for many life science researchers are doctoral degrees. Many with a bachelor's degree in biology enter nursing, medical, dental, veterinary, or other health profession schools and are classified as applied scientists.

Depending on the field, biological scientists may face intense competition in the upcoming years for coveted basic research positions *(OOH, 1998)*. Unfortunately, even though average job growth has occurred in the past few years, recent federal budget tightening has led to little increase in funding for research and development. This, once again, emphasizes the need to have excellent communication and grant writing skills.

WHAT CAREER DEVELOPMENT GOALS SHOULD YOU PURSUE?

Developing yourself as a whole person, not just a scientist, will make you a better research scientist. As you think about what will help you attain success, keep striving to broaden your repertoire of abilities and interests within the context of career development so that you can increase your main skill areas for success: creative thinking, mathematical skills, grant writing ability, diligent habits, and observational acuity.

PREPARING A RESUME AND CURRICULUM VITAE

Take advantage of your career services office on campus to keep up with the latest trends in resume writing. In addition to this initial step, start the process of writing a vitae. A vitae is a longer description of your experience in preparation for research positions, and it requires publishing and specific evidence of involvement in research. In the process of gaining additional experience, knowledge, and training, learn how to record professional growth with the format and marketing language important for an effective resume and vitae. Go to the career services office on campus, and participate in career search activities available to you.

Enhancing your resume and vitae can be accomplished through several methods. An interview with a recent physics major gives a real-world perspective on his quest for direction, his search for a mentor, and some strategies he recommends.

REAL-WORLD PERSPECTIVE

from Brian Roy, a first year graduate student,
Colorado School of Mines, Physics Major

I wanted to have a job where I wouldn't be doing the same tasks every day, where I could discover new things, ideas, and concepts. One person who helped guide and motivate me along the way was a professor here who encouraged me to study physics for my undergraduate degree and then enter a one-year master's program in material science. In general, I like how all the professors here have an open door policy so you can come and talk to them at any time. Although I like physics, going to one year of graduate school in materials science provides a larger job market for me. Physics is pretty limited with a master's degree. What really helped me to decide on my course of study and industry direction was to talk to everyone. I talked to people in different departments, to professors who would give me a five-minute take on life.

Advice

I think that being a scientist, a pure scientist, requires an open mind in every sense, so you are always questioning things. You should also try doing what I'm doing now, that is, working in a physics lab analyzing samples and getting exposure to research scientists like I'm experiencing here at a university. Also, I think people studying science should value working in groups. I'm against it usually, but lately I've been appreciating teamwork. You learn a lot more, and have to explain and talk to someone else.

GETTING ORGANIZED

To be successful, a major part of your pursuit should be to organize your future goals. Whether you have been in the workforce or are just coming out of high school, you will have your own style of organization. No matter what your style is, augment it by taking advantage of useful tools available on your campus. Again, go to the career center at your school. They are waiting to help you.

Ask yourself the following questions:

➤ What activities help you organize yourself? (Use your own experience such as organizing an event, a party, cleaning your room, studying for a test.)

➤ Using the skills you already have, how can you better organize your future goals? What tools, seminars, or people are available on your college campus to help with organization?

USING YOUR PRESENT CIRCUMSTANCES TO YOUR ADVANTAGE

People tend to forget that their course work provides plenty of opportunity to build an experience base. More than a few classes will require research projects, and by enthusiastically pursuing those kinds of projects, you could enhance your vitae greatly. During college you have exposure to expert researchers in the various scientific research areas, and gaining experience under their leadership is essential and could even lead to future graduate school opportunities. An excellent step to take for success: Ask your professor how you can go beyond the usual class requirements for the research projects in order to document your class project on a resume or vitae.

Beyond talking with your professors, a class team project is an excellent experience to list on your resume because teamwork is a highly valued commodity in research science. In addition, papers that you write in class can be developed into publications for student scientific organizations, especially with the support of your professors.

USING EXTRACURRICULAR ACTIVITIES AND NONSCIENTIFIC INVOLVEMENT

Any successful teams you are a part of, whether a student government team or a leadership team in campus ministry, can help you develop skills for success. Leadership positions in various campus associations offer you an opportunity to show your ability to manage projects and communicate with people outside of your scientific interests. A multifaceted approach is one of the best ways to demonstrate your versatility in the scientific research job market and improve your chances for success. For example, Information Systems Development Manager Dan Kesselring explains that recruiters will look for evidence that you can sell yourself to others, including peers, upper management, and customers. The repertoire of activities in your résumé and vitae should have a good indication of technical skills, hands-on experience, communications skills, leadership skills, teamwork abilities, and flexibility *(Job Choices in Science and Engineering, 1998)*.

ASKING QUALITY QUESTIONS

As a research scientist, you are a theorist, a developer of hypotheses, a formulator of ideas, and a classifier of knowledge. You are constantly asking "Why?" and looking for new twists on old information. Increasing your own investigative abilities by asking appropriate questions is an important factor in succeeding as a scientist. Developing the skill of asking questions in your classes about the information you assimilate helps you develop essential critical thinking skills.

LEARNING ABOUT RESEARCH GRANTS

Most scientific research jobs are funded by research grants through the federal government or private foundations. Your ability to write persuasive research proposals could determine whether you gain work as a research scientist. Traditional undergraduate and graduate training in the sciences rarely covers this topic, so you will have to find where you can learn how to write research grants.

Although you may have an excellent idea that could influence a scientific field, if you cannot persuade others to support your idea with an effective, persuasive, and logical research proposal, your brilliant idea will remain just that—a brilliant idea that is stuck where it cannot be used. To find more information on grant writing, visit the Web pages listed at the end of this chapter.

SUMMING UP

As you think about your research interests in the sciences, remain broad and open to new possibilities and concentrate on getting a strong academic base of knowledge in mathematical, physical, and biological sciences and the liberal arts. No matter what degree of certainty you have concerning a research specialty, follow these steps: Gain experience in the research process by finding a mentor, volunteering, and doing class research projects. Begin to learn about grant writing and science by visiting research sites on the Web, which are listed at the end of this chapter. Follow the steps in this chapter to reflect on your interests and strengths and to gain a better appreciation of the many exciting research areas available. Finally, read as much as you can by visiting your college bookstore or library's science shelves. You will find many fascinating materials to read.

RESOURCES FOR FURTHER INFORMATION

These references are not exhaustive by any means, but are meant to give you a taste of what is out there for your discovery as a research scientist. Hopefully, these Web sites and readings will spark your interest and inspire your dreams.

Web Sites

http://www.sciencenews.org   The magazine *Science News* produces this site, which features special reports on a variety of research and references, including mathematics.

http://www.ana.org   The American Nurses Association provides information on nursing science, education, and legislative issues; an online journal; and links to research sites.

http://www.ama-assn.org   American Medical Association news, ethical issues in medicine and research, an online journal, and links to other medical and health science sites can be found here.

http://www.science.org Includes links to multiple pages concerning every kind of science from physics to photons, quasars to quarks, and everything in between. Features pages just for students, too.

http://www.naturalhistory.org The Natural History Science Museum's site with book listings and education opportunities in the natural sciences.

http://www.ncbi.nlm.nih.gov National Center for Biotechnical Information: Gives a great deal about genetic research, and offers PubMed (online search of most all health-related journals) and other science links.

http://www.grantwriters.com The Grant Writers Home Page will lead you to grant writing guides and some free information on grant writing, workshops, and sources for grants. For other grant writing information, simply go to the library and ask the reference librarian. They are often called on to provide information in this area and will have abundant resources for you.

Books

Authors to look for in the library or bookstore include:

➤ *Stephen Jay Gould,* Harvard professor of natural history. For an overall look at science and its place in our world today, no one can expound on science like Gould. He is extremely literate, connecting ideas into logical sequences that you would have never thought possible.

➤ *Stephen Hawking,* physicist and cosmologist. Hawking wrote the book *A Brief History of Time,* which was also made into a video. It is fascinating to watch as an illustration of how a scientist's mind works, and it is inspiring material for your daily life.

➤ *William H. Calvin.* Calvin writes extensively about neuroscience and avant garde brain research. His work is extremely thought-provoking for those who are curious about the way the mind works.

Other scientists to read about:

➤ *Charles Darwin,* Naturalist. Read about Darwin to discover the patience it takes to reach greatness. He spent many years studying carefully collected specimens before writing anything of his theories.

➤ *Barbara McClintock,* Geneticist. McClintock was a pioneer in the field of genetics, and her reward was at least 20 years in the making. In the 1950s, people thought her ideas quirky and far out; today she is a recognized genius.

Applications & Exercises

Keys for Your Key Chain: Skills Worth Keeping

List here the five most important keys, or skills, you have learned from reading this chapter.

1. _____
2. _____
3. _____
4. _____
5. _____

Key into Your Life: Opportunities to Apply What You Learn

1. Locating Professors Who Can Guide You

Start finding out who's who in scientific research at your college or university. Find a professor who is involved in research you're interested in. Then branch out of your immediate interests and talk to professors who are engaged in research across campus. Go and talk to those professors about who else they would recommend you talk to, and what actions they would recommend you take. Make sure to thank them and visit them periodically to tell them of your progress. Begin making a list of professors you will contact below:

_____
_____
_____
_____
_____

2. Trying Out Field Observation

Do some primary research in the form of field observation. Through industry research and your campus career office, find a local firm that has a scientific research and development department. Contact an authority at the company to see if you can observe the department at work for a few days.

3. Getting Familiar with the Campus Career Office

Visit your career development, or services office and make an appointment to talk with someone who has helped others with goals to continue on to graduate school. Plan follow-up visits. Record whom you talked with and their suggestions.

Key to Cooperative Learning: Building Teamwork Skills

Review the chapter's main emphasis on information concerning key competencies, the research process, and qualitative and quantitative inquiry with others, in groups. Each group of four or five should consider itself a team of researchers which has been assigned to complete an educational/informational sign program

concerning water quality within a nearby state park. Project requirements include sign engineering, cost analysis, and scale model production.

Discuss the following topics:

➤ How would you divide responsibilities to work on a particular research problem in a team? Who would do what and why in completing the research process and final presentation to the client?

➤ Why are assignments of responsibility and roles so important in a team?

➤ How would effective teamwork help advance scientific research?

➤ Have each team member talk about his or her strengths as a team member through past experiences and, if they are comfortable, describe a teamwork attribute they would like to improve.

Key to Self-Expression: Discovery Through Journal Writing

Take a few moments to write about what sparks the most questions in your head about the world around you, about humans, animals, plants, or the galaxies and stars. Don't concern yourself with grammar, writing style, or organization; simply write freely the thoughts that come to mind.

Key to Your Personal Portfolio: Your Paper Trail to Success

Now that you have completed this chapter on the keys to success for research scientists, summarize your goals on the pathway to success in the following three areas:

➤ Learning the research process and gaining key competencies: How do you plan to gain experience as an undergraduate?

➤ Investigating your particular scientific branch of interest: Keep track of whom you talk to and what they say. Record what you have done and what you plan to look into further.

➤ Widening your scope of practical skill areas: What are your goals in gaining grant writing skills, developing your résumé and vitae, and improving ability to work in teams?

12 KEYS TO SUCCESS IN THE HEALTH SCIENCES

In this chapter, you will explore answers to the following questions:

➤ What areas of study are there in the health sciences?

➤ Are your interests and skills compatible with studying the health sciences?

➤ What are the career opportunities in the health sciences?

➤ How can you increase your chances for success in the health sciences?

❔ Thinking It Through

Check those statements that currently apply to you:

☐ I think I have to be a people person to work in the health sciences.

☐ I love science and am good at it.

☐ I want a career that offers lifelong learning and opportunity for growth.

☐ I want to get a job as soon as possible.

☐ I want to study as long as it takes to get the kind of work I want.

☐ I'd like a plan for exploring my options in the health sciences.

NURTURE

12

KEYS TO SUCCESS IN THE HEALTH SCIENCES

If you are reading this because you are interested in both health and science, then congratulations are in order because opportunities for careers in this area have never been better. Together, medical and health care make up the health sciences to create the largest and most varied occupational area, employing eight million people in an amazing assortment of jobs. As an industry, health science is the fastest-growing sector of the economy and is expected to produce 4.5 million new jobs by the year 2005. The good news for you is that as long as you want to work in a science field and are interested in health, you will likely find an area to pursue as a career goal.

In this chapter, you will look at what the health sciences have in common as well as how they differ. Furthermore, reading this chapter will give you practical steps that you can take to make your own plan for success. An entire book could be written to do justice to this widely diverse field, but, for now, highlighting each of the major areas will help you decide if the health sciences are for you or not.

WHAT'S THE OUTLOOK FOR HEALTH SCIENCES?

There are myriad reasons for growth in the health sciences, but they mainly come down to these three:

➤ The U. S. population is aging.
➤ New technology is continually being developed.
➤ Health promotion and disease prevention are in demand.

A closer look reveals why these three reasons are producing a growth in careers for those interested in health.

Aging population. Not only is the population getting older but people are living longer. This means more people with chronic illnesses who require health care and a growing demand for professionals who can manage their illnesses, working in long-term care facilities and in-home health care. The area of geriatrics is one of the fastest growing in health care today. The aging population is also demanding to be fit and healthy so they can enjoy activities such as snowboarding, kayaking, and globe-trotting.

New technology. Gallbladder surgery used to require a week in the hospital, but with new technology, it is now performed in one day with no overnight hospital stay necessary. The same is true of many other surgeries and procedures. New drugs, therapies, and machines for tests and monitoring come onto the market nearly every day, and people are needed to discover, produce, service, and use this technology. And, don't forget, computers are becoming increasingly important in health care to track data and evaluate services.

Healthy living. Health care is focusing on healthy living for two reasons. First, people are demanding it, and second, it costs less than illness. Keeping people healthy saves the health care system millions of dollars because it costs less to monitor and screen for problems than to treat those problems in an emergency department or hospital after they occur. Jobs include teaching patients and families about health through efforts such as diet and exercise, screening exams for problems like breast cancer, and immunizations to prevent childhood diseases.

WHAT DO YOU NEED TO SUCCEED IN THE HEALTH SCIENCES?

Science Ability

First of all, science is a must, although the number and depth of courses vary tremendously depending on the area you choose. For instance, you can become a radiology technician in one year, a nurse midwife in six years, and a cardiac surgeon in ten to twelve years. Science, however, is the common thread that runs through all the varied careers you can choose from, so be prepared to study it. If you already love science and are good at it, you have it made. If you like science and are fair at it, you also have it made, although perhaps you'll need to work extra and be determined. If you are afraid of science, have a hard time with science, or it's been so long since you took a science class you don't remember it anymore, don't give up. Two things can help you succeed: determination and a tutor.

Determination is your job and a tutor is your school's job. Tutors are available at your school, usually at no cost, because almost all graduate students work in this role as part of their education and training.

Interest in Health

Health is a part of the health sciences package, and, generally—except in veterinary science—you are interested in the health of the human mind, body, or soul. Health is a broad term and a fascinating concept with many definitions. Often, health is defined as a continuum with illness on one end and a disease-free condition on the other. A person can be anywhere on this continuum.

Another view of health is holistic; health is not dependent on the presence or absence of disease, but rather on how a person perceives her health in a total, or holistic, way. Holistic is a term that simply means the whole person, that is, as a combination of mind and body. At this point you might be thinking that although you are interested in both health and science, you really don't care to work with people. Wait—don't give up! There are a surprising number of areas in the health sciences that don't involve working with people. You can work with machines instead, or chemicals, or, if you prefer, just parts of people, such as tissue samples and cells; medical engineering, pathology and lab work, and clinical chemistry are examples. On the other hand, if you are a people person, there are abundant opportunities for you to pursue.

SKILLS FOR SUCCESS IN THE HEALTH SCIENCES

Science Skills

Creativity. Problem solving is at the heart of the scientific process, and creativity is essential to problem solving because it includes careful and innovative analysis. This involves the ability to look at problems from multiple views and find new ways to do things.

Critical thinking. Critical thinking means being able to analyze information, make appropriate connections, and most importantly, continuously ask questions. Critical thinking is a skill you may have already begun to develop, and it must be polished and perfected as you go.

Observation powers. Are you the first to notice that an old building in your neighborhood was torn down, that an acquaintance has a new haircut, that there are tiny red spiders on the leaf of a tree? Good observation skills are critical in science in order to assess objective information, evaluate, and work on solving problems.

Oh, Say, Can You "C" Your People Skills?

Caring. Entire books have been written on this topic, but basically caring means that you know how to put yourself in the shoes of another person and, as they say, walk a mile in them. It means having empathy, not sympathy or feeling sorry for them; it means taking their best interests to heart and advocating for them; and it means working hard to do the best job you can.

Communication. Sure, everyone can communicate in one way or another, but are you good at it? Are you an effective writer and a good speaker? Do you have computer skills? Can you persuade others, without coercion, but through logical presentation of relevant data and organization of thoughts, to see things your way? If you have done any reading about career skills, you know that communication tops everyone's list. As science and technology increase in complexity, the skill of articulating your thoughts, as well as listening to and understanding others, is vital to your success.

Collaboration. Collaboration means teamwork. So many problems related to the health and well-being of humans are worked on by a team of professionals—all with different ways of doing things and different professional principles guiding them. You must be able to get along with others by negotiating effectively and by learning to reach a consensus.

WHAT DIFFERENCES ARE THERE IN THE HEALTH SCIENCES?

Differences in obtaining a health science career are primarily related to the following:

➤ Length of education
➤ Salary
➤ Professional growth and opportunity for advancement
➤ Independence and autonomy
➤ Work setting

Overall, you will find that these five things go hand in hand. The longer the requirement for training, the better the salary and the more independent you will likely be with perhaps the exception of physicians, who, due to the inflated status of medicine in the United States, tend to earn disproportional salaries compared to others with similar amounts of education. For instance, a family practice doctor working in a clinic may have ten years of schooling and earn $160,000 a year; a pharmacist or nurse with a Ph.D. teaching at a university may have ten years of education and earn around $60,000 a year. But this rule of thumb usually applies: The more you invest in your education, the better opportunities you will have, remembering, of course, that positions that are more highly valued in our society—that is, a physician versus a teacher—will have the best opportunities of all.

Another difference is the setting of your work. Again, the more education, the more flexible you'll be. An RN with a college degree can work anywhere in the world—a hospital, a clinic, an office, or from home. It is the same for nurse practitioners and physicians. Some careers are limited to laboratories, like medical technicians; hospitals, like respiratory therapists; or testing facilities, like nuclear medicine technologists. Setting may be a consideration in making a career decision if your workplace is especially important to you.

More than a few nurses chose the profession of nursing so they could have a great deal of mobility and flexibility. As with setting, hours of work will vary. Some health science careers require working at all hours, such as physicians and surgical technicians. Many require work on weekends and holidays, such as nurses and those physicians employed by a hospital. Any facility that is open 24 hours a day, 365 days a year will need you to work odd hours. If you are adverse to this, look for an area where workers work the day shift, Monday through Friday.

WHAT AREAS OF STUDY EXIST IN THE HEALTH SCIENCES?

There are many ways to divide and categorize areas of study in the health sciences, but there are some distinctions you may not be aware of. They include differences between two of the largest areas, medicine and nursing. These areas are often confused even though nurses and doctors have distinct principles that guide their professions. For instance, medicine is primarily concerned with disease, whereas nursing is concerned with disease prevention and health promotion. As in all things, however, the boundaries blur because many physicians teach patients about health and many nurses prescribe medication to cure diseases.

Category 1: Disease Prevention, Health Assessment, and Promotion

Registered nurses, nurse practitioners, physician assistants, and therapists (physical, respiratory, occupational, and speech) are in this category. Most require four years of college, and some, like nurse practitioners and speech therapists require a master's degree. Salary averages range from $32,000 for a respiratory therapist to $59,000 for a pharmacist to $90,000 for a nurse anesthetist. The job outlook for these areas is excellent; they are the fastest-growing careers that you will find (except for respiratory therapists and pharmacists which is average).

Category 2: Disease Diagnosis and Cure

Chiropractors, dentists, optometrists, physicians, doctors of osteopathy, podiatrists, and veterinarians fall best into this category. (Remember, all categories overlap somewhat.) The job outlook for these areas is better than average, except for dentists and optometrists, which have average growth. Don't let predictions stop you, though, because they can change depending on unforeseen economic circumstances. Health care has been buffeted around by gusts and gales in the past few years, and it is not likely that the storm will let up anytime soon, so expect change. Most of the areas in this category require at least four years of college. Salaries average from $57,500 for a veterinarian to $80,000 for an optometrist to $238,000 for a physician.

Category 3: Technologists and Technicians

Technology is an area of health care that is expanding by leaps and bounds. From genetic engineering to new diagnostic tests to health screening exams, all fields related to technology are in a growth phase. Technicians and technologists include those used in cardiology, radiology, neurology, emergency medicine (EMTs), medical records, engineering, and other specialty areas. They work in pathology laboratories, hospitals, clinics, home health care, and dental offices. Most require a two-year associate's degree, although some, like opticians and electroneurology technicians, may be trained on the job. Salary averages range from $25,000 for an EMT to $39,400 for a nuclear medicine technologist.

Category 4: Alternative or Integrated Health

This is a fast-growing section of health care as people are reportedly turning to acupuncture, homeopathy, naturopathic medicine, herbal cures, and massage in record numbers. Many insurance companies are even beginning to reimburse the practitioners of these services. For more information on practitioner organizations, schools, degrees, and licensing, visit the Alternative Medicine Homepage: http://www.pit.edu/~cbw/altm.htm.

The box on the next several pages offers descriptions of more than 30 occupations in the health sciences field.

HOW CAN I INCREASE MY CHANCES FOR SUCCESS IN THE HEALTH SCIENCES?

The best thing you can do to succeed is to take the time to find out if you want to go into the health sciences. Sounds easy, doesn't it? The more certain you are that you want a specific health science career, the better off you'll be because you will know beforehand how to plan your course of action for getting into school, financing school, and eventually finding work. So, the first step is to decide what area you are most interested in, and hopefully, this chapter is helping you in that process.

Volunteer, Observe, Join

These three words sum it all up because success means doing what you want or are interested in, and what you have an aptitude for. Success also means creating paths for yourself that lead to a good school and good job. First, knowing

Descriptions of Occupations

Biomedical Equipment Technician Installs, maintains, repairs, calibrates, and modifies electronic, electrical, mechanical, hydraulic, and pneumatic instruments and equipment which are used in medical therapy, diagnosis, and research. May be involved in the operation, supervision and control of equipment.

Dental Assistant Receives and prepares dental patients and assists the dentist during treatment. Tasks include chair side assistance to the dentist and may include, maintaining and sterilizing instruments, taking and processing x-rays and preparing dental compounds. May include some clerical duties.

Dental Hygienist Performs patient examination procedures, notes conditions of decay and deviation, administers local anesthetic, places temporary and permanent restorations, takes and develops x-rays, and educates patient about proper dental health habits. Works with the supervision of a dentist.

Dental Laboratory Technician Creates dental prostheses replacement for natural teeth from the specifications of a dentist.

Dentist Diagnoses and treats diseases of the teeth, gums, bone and soft tissue of the mouth. Helps patients prevent dental problems through education and treatment.

Dietitian Provides expertise on food and nutrition in relation to health; sometimes called a nutritionist. May work in a variety of settings including medical facilities. **Dietetic Technologist** works under the supervision of a Dietitian in handling routine duties of the food service team.

Electrocardiograph (EKG) Technician Operates a specialized machine to obtain readings of the electrical activities of a patient's heart.

Electroencephalogram Technician (EEG) Operates instruments that measure and record electrical activities of the brain. Records are used to diagnose and assess disorders of the brain.

Emergency Medical Technician (EMT) Provides immediate emergency care to critically ill and injured patients and may drive the ambulance. Determines the nature and extent of the illness or injury and establishes priorities for emergency care.

Licensed Practical Nurse (LPN) Works under the direct supervision of physicians or RNs to administer medications, monitor equipment, maintain patient charts, and take vital signs. May work as a private duty nurse in home or hospital.

Medical Assistant Performs office, laboratory and treatment functions to assist physician in caring for patients. Work is generally front office (administrative tasks of reception/secretarial, medical machine transcription, bookkeeping and medical insurance) or back office (sterilization of equipment, supply readiness and may include patient history gathering, blood pressure, temperature, respiration, pulse and routine tests).

Medical Laboratory Technician/Medical Technologist Performs complex chemical analyses and routine chemical and biological tests on blood and body fluids using a variety of laboratory techniques and instruments; these tests are used in the prevention, detection, and diagnosis of disease.

Medical Social Worker Helps patients and their families with problems that accompany illness or inhibit recovery and rehabilitation. Collects patient information to assist other health professionals understand the social, emotional and environmental issues underlying a patient's illness. Provides emotional support, makes referral to other helping agencies, and often makes discharge plans.

Nurse Practitioner Has additional nursing training. May perform physical examinations and diagnostic tests, develop and carry out treatment plans and counsel patients about their health. Some work in specialty areas and some work independently with a consulting physician.

Nursing Assistant Certified (NAC) Provides patient care with the direction of a nurse. Duties often include daily patient hygiene; feeding; admitting and discharging; taking and charting vital signs; may work in a hospital, nursing home, or doing home care.

Occupational Therapist Plans and organizes activities to improve the functioning of patients who are physically, mentally, or emotionally disabled. Plans and directs educational, vocational and recreational activities to help patients become sufficient in self care and daily living.

Occupational Therapy Assistant Works under the direction of a licensed OT to plan and carry out individualized therapy programs. Reports progress, prepares materials, makes repair or adjustment to therapeutic machines. May instruct skill building and craft activities.

Optician Prepares and dispenses contact lenses, eyeglasses and other eyewear according to the written prescription of an ophthalmologist (MD) or optometrist (DO).

Ophthalmic Technologist Assists Ophthalmologist by using sophisticated equipment/techniques to gather information during eye exams. Also, assists with eye surgery, using microscopic and intricate instruments. Instructs patients about diagnosis/treatment.

Orthotist/Prosthetist Designs, writes specifications for and fits artificial appliances for disorders following the prescription of a physician. Appliances include artificial arms, legs, and back braces and surgical supports. **Orthotic Technician** makes and repairs orthotic devices such as surgical corsets and corrective shoes. **Orthotic Assistant** provides care to patients with disabling conditions of the limbs and spine. **Prosthetics Technician** makes and finishes artificial limbs. **Prosthetic Assistant** provides care to patients with partial or total loss of limbs.

Patient Representative* Works with hospital patients and their families to address any special needs that may arise.

*no related course work

Pharmacist Provides drug information to physicians, nurses, and other health care practitioners to assure optimal uses of drugs in patient care. Prepares compounds and dispenses medicine. Provides information and educates consumers about medicines, its storage and use. Works with pharmaceutical industry to develop and sell new drug products.

Pharmacist Assistant Level A, under the direct supervision of the pharmacist, may fill prescriptions, make routine mixtures to be verified by the pharmacist; Level B, under the supervision of the pharmacist, types prescription labels, does filing, bookkeeping, and pricing, and stocks medicine.

Physical Therapist Assistant Works under the direction of a licensed physical therapist to plan and carry out the individualized treatment program. May teach exercises and instruct patients and their families in the care and use of equipment.

Physical Therapist Evaluates, plans and administers treatment to patients with problems related to muscular and skeletal systems. Long and short term problems are generally the result of injury, disease or surgery. Administers and interprets tests for muscle strength, coordination, range of motion, respiratory and circulatory efficiency. Educates patients and their families about the use and care of treatment equipment.

Physician Diagnoses and treats human disease with medicines and other treatment. Works to maintain and improve the health of their patients. Some specialize in one field of practice, others teach or do research.

Physician Assistant Is a highly skilled professional, who under the supervision of a licensed physician, performs many of the routine duties usually done by a doctor. Some states allow independent practice with coordination of a physician.

Radiologic Technologist Works with a diverse group of professionals to perform a variety of diagnostic studies using ionizing radiation. X-ray technicians use radiation to make images of the internal organs and bones of the body, develop x-ray film, prepare records of findings, and make minor adjustment to equipment. **Nuclear Medicine Technician** uses radioactive materials to form images of organ systems to determine the presence of disease. **Diagnostic Ultrasound Technician** creates diagnosis images using high frequency sound. **Radiation Therapy Technician** uses various forms of radiation to treat cancer and other diseases. Other technician fields include **MRI**, **CT** and **Special Procedures**, each uses specialized equipment to diagnose and treat disease.

Recreational Therapist Is a specialist within the recreation profession and is involved in organizing, administering and presenting therapeutic recreational activities for patients that make a definite contribution to the recovery of or adjustment to an illness, disability, or specific social problem.

Registered Nurse Works to promotes health and wellness and prevent disease using substantial, specialized knowledge, judgment and skill based on the principles of the biological, physiological, behavioral and sociological

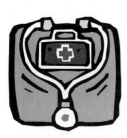

sciences. Increasingly, nurses specialized in one area of practice, provide education and training or work in the administration of healthcare programs.

Rehabilitation Counselor Assists clients with physical, mental, emotional, and social handicaps to adjust to their handicaps and find suitable employment. Develops a service plan which may call for occupational training, medical therapy, psychotherapy or counseling. Works with employers to redesign jobs to fit the capabilities of the client.

Respiratory Therapist Treats patients with heart/lung disorders under the direction of a physician. May give temporary relief to patients with chronic breathing problems, emergent problems of heart failure, stroke, drowning, and shock. May instruct patients on the use of equipment and conduct educational sessions on disease treatment and prevention.

Speech Pathologist and Audiologist Specializes in communication disorders. A speech-language pathologist is primarily concerned with language problems, while an audiologist is concerned with hearing disorders. These specialists test, evaluate and plan therapy to restore as much normal functioning as possible. Works closely with teachers, rehabilitation counselors, and medical professionals.

Surgery Technician Shares the responsibilities of the operating room team before, during and after surgery. Assists surgery team to scrub, arranges sterile instruments, prepares the patient, passes instruments to the surgeon and the assistants, maintains supplies, transports the patient after surgery, and performs related duties.

Veterinarian DVM/Veterinarian Technician Veterinarians assisted by technicians treat and prevent illnesses in pets, livestock and marine animals.

From Washington State Healthcare Human Resources Association.

what you want can best be achieved by watching others doing the job (not on TV, of course!). For instance, one student was working with a doctor for the summer to learn something of that profession, but as he spent time in the hospital, he realized that the work the nurses were doing was what interested him the most. He saw how nurses spent a lot of their time talking to the patients and families and teaching them about health. He switched his major in the fall when he returned to school.

The second way to success is getting to know people. This cannot be recommended or encouraged highly enough. Making contacts is the best way to help you get what you want. By observing or helping those in the area of your interest, your enthusiasm and ability to work with others will become known. When it comes time to apply to school, you will know people in the field to recommend you, and when it comes time to get a job, you will have an insider's knowledge of the market. Every health professional will tell you the same thing: Get into the area of your interest either by volunteering to help, observing, or by joining local professional organizations and attending their meetings and educational offerings. Join a community group of concerned and involved citizens and professionals. For example, local managed care organizations often use health care consumers for advisory purposes. Volunteers are almost always needed and accepted in hospitals and clinics (including veterinary). If the area you are interested in does not include any of these, call the office or lab where the work takes place and talk with the director. Tell the director that you are interested in pursuing a career in her field and would like to do some observation to get a better idea of what the work involves.

Getting a realistic picture of the career you're interested in will save you time and money and even heartache. Who wants to choose a field of study and get into it only to find it is not the right one? Of course, even if you follow the steps we mentioned above, this still might happen, but at least you will have done all you could to clarify your choice. Mistakes happen to everyone, and they will happen to you; don't try to hide them or think they are not useful. In fact, mistakes, or others' ideas of your mistakes, can turn into something good. For example, Patti Krafft was told by more than one nursing instructor that she was not cut out to be a nurse, yet she persevered in her alleged "mistake" and today is a success in the fields of diabetes teaching and cardiac rehabilitation exercise. Another student made it a quarter of the way through preveterinary classes and decided she didn't like animals very much. She went on to become a nurse.

The Final Word

In case you haven't already noticed, you will need to do a fair amount of communicating with others to explore your options and to enhance your chances for success. If you are painfully, or even moderately, shy, it is time to work on that, too. Remember, it is all about learning communication skills, and these skills are necessary even if you work all by yourself in a small laboratory at night in the Arctic Circle. (If you end up there, you will still need to write grants, order supplies, and send e-mail or messages to your psychiatrist!)

Take one step at a time to avoid getting overwhelmed. Start at the library or on the Internet and work your way up to human beings, preferably starting with ones you already know. From there you can start talking to total strangers on the phone and move to meeting them in person. You will have a notebook and pencil with you to take notes, and in case of emergency, you can hide behind that for a second or two to regain your composure.

Really, though, even if it is hard for you, people who agree to talk to you will be loving every minute of the meeting. Everyone loves to talk about themselves, and although you might think they are doing you a gigantic favor by taking their important time to talk to insignificant you, it is really the other way around. You are the one doing them the favor by asking them questions about themselves and about what is hopefully their life's work full of excitement and interest. They want talented and motivated people to enter and enhance their profession, and perhaps you will be that talented and motivated person.

Applications & Exercises

1. Skills Analysis or "I'll never forget the time . . . "

One way to find out what skills and important interests you already possess is through the telling of a life story, especially one that was significant and memorable to you. Think of a time you did something that was interesting—of an event that was very memorable, of a "I'll never forget the time I . . ." and then fill in the blank.

_____

_____

_____

     Ask yourself: What was so important to you about this event? What were your underlying feelings and thoughts associated with this event? What skills did you bring to the situation?

2. Career Analysis or "My three top careers would be . . . "

First, list one career that absolutely fascinates you, then one that is of great interest, and finally, one that is definitely worth considering. Next, list one person you know in each position. If you can't think of anyone, think of someone who can help you find someone, such as parents, a mentor, a teacher, or a reference librarian. Set up an appointment to talk with each of the people in the positions, either in person, on the phone, or by e-mail. Ask them the following questions and add additional questions of your own:

What is the most interesting part of your work? The least interesting?

If I wanted to pursue this area, what advice would you give me?

What skills should I have?

How can I get more information?

_____

_____

_____

_____

_____

_____

_____

Keys to Cooperative Learning: Building Teamwork Skills

Get together with a group of friends or science classmates and identify the skills needed to succeed in science. Talk and listen to each other (these are good communication skills, too) and try to find common threads in the discussion. At the end of the discussion have everyone write down three ways that they can develop each skill and then share these with each other to get new, fresh ideas for developing your skills and pursuing your goals.

Keys to Self-Expression: Discovery Through Journal Writing

Writing in a journal requires reflection, and reflection is an essential element of both scientific and critical thinking. The ability to observe and record your thoughts and feelings is a valuable key to learning how to observe the world around you. Thinking about the events that occur each day will assist you in developing better critical thinking skills.

Start your journal process by writing a detailed description of your dream job. Let this exercise take as long as you need: several days or weeks if that helps you to get all the details as precise as possible. Questions to help you with this exercise include the following:

What are you doing in the job?

Who do you know of, living or dead, who has done this work and what do you admire about them?

What do you see yourself accomplishing?

Where are you working? Internationally, locally, in space?

Keys to Your Personal Portfolio: Your Paper Trail to Success

From the work you did in Exercise 2, make a list of the people you need to communicate with. List each one along with their address and phone number. Designate a specific date and time you will begin trying to contact them to make an appointment to speak with them or to e-mail them.

Resources: Visit Web sites relevant to health sciences (start with www.kaplan.com or nursingworld.org) and especially to your area of interest. Keep a running list of Chat Rooms or people to contact. If you do not have access to the Internet, go to the library and ask the reference librarian for help.

Read books and take notes in your journal to give you ideas about your interests and skills. Again, visit the library and ask for help, and go to a bookstore and ask for books related to your area of interest. Fiction, nonfiction, and biographies can all be useful.

13 KEYS TO SUCCESS IN MATH

In this chapter, you will explore answers to the following questions:

➤ Why do you need math skills?

➤ How can you master math basics?

➤ How can you overcome math anxiety?

➤ What techniques will help your performance on math exams?

❓ Thinking It Through

Check those statements that currently apply to you:

☐ I'm not sure why I need math skills.

☐ I know I need to learn basic math, but I don't know how to do it.

☐ At this point, I'm not sure even how to distinguish among arithmetic, algebra, geometry, and the other types of math.

CALCULATE

KEYS TO SUCCESS IN MATH

When asked about math, many students reply by saying—often with a sense of pride—"I hate math," or "I was never any good at math." In today's world, however, a basic knowledge of and ability in math are as necessary and critical as the abilities to read and write.

This chapter will look at the need for mathematics in today's highly competitive and technologically changing world. You will explore two of the most common problem areas in mathematics: word problems and math anxiety. You will also examine several problem-solving strategies linked to doing well in mathematics.

WHY DO YOU NEED MATH SKILLS?

Math is much more than a course to be dealt with in school and then put aside. Math is an integral part of the modern world. Consider the following:

➤ You make $2000 per month in your job. How do you determine how you allocate your money to pay your bills?

➤ You want to carpet your house. However, many of the rooms and hallways are not regularly shaped. How do you determine the amount of carpet you need to buy?

➤ You are trying to schedule your classes for next semester. Each of your classes is offered only at certain times. How do you go about making the best possible schedule?

➤ In Canada, the rate at which the spruce budworm can defoliate balsam firs is a major problem. The budworm population is affected by its birth rate, its death rate, and predations by birds, while the balsam fir population is affected by such factors as seed pollination, weather, fire, and budworm defoliation. How would you study this problem, taking into account the growth of the budworm population and the growth of the balsam fir?

These are just a few examples of problems involving mathematics that you might encounter in your personal life, school, and career. Fill in your answers to the brief questionnaire in Figure 13.1—it will help you explore whether your beliefs about mathematics are based in reality.

Here's the truth: Upon examination, *none* of these statements is universally true and the last one is true—more often than you would expect. Surprisingly, mathematics *can* be fun. You can find out only if you try.

TYPES OF MATH SKILLS YOU MIGHT NEED

Math skills are becoming more important in this world of increasingly complicated technology. Your level of math knowledge will affect all areas of your life. The level of competency you need will vary depending on your specific career goals and objectives, but everyone will need some minimum amount of skill. These skills can be broadly broken down into the following areas: thinking logically and reasoning, arithmetic, algebra, geometry, probability and statistics, calculus and differential equations, and higher math.

Thinking Logically and Reasoning

The single most important skill that math teaches you is the ability to think logically and critically. Math is, at heart, a problem-solving discipline. The ability to think logically and to solve problems is crucial to everyday life. You need to think logically in deciding how to plan your day, where to eat, what to eat, how you will drive your car, and so on. Logical thinking involves two types of reasoning: **inductive reasoning** and **deductive reasoning**. Although mathematics seems to develop skill primarily in deductive reasoning, it is actually created through a process of both deductive and inductive reasoning.

Figure 13.1   *Mathematical beliefs and myths.*

Mark the following statements true (T) or false (F) according to your opinion about the validity of the statements.

_____   1.   Men are better at doing mathematics than women.

_____   2.   Mathematics completely relies on logic, disregarding intuition.

_____   3.   Mathematicians are more intelligent than other people.

_____   4.   People are born with an ability to do mathematics.

_____   5.   Mathematics is a rigid subject.

_____   6.   Mathematicians are able to solve problems quickly, in their heads.

_____   7.   Mathematicians rarely make mistakes.

_____   8.   Very few people are any good at mathematics.

_____   9.   Counting on your fingers is wrong.

_____ 10.   Mathematics is not creative.

_____ 11.   Mathematicians are eccentric.

_____ 12.   There is a lot of memorization in mathematics.

_____ 13.   Most people don't need to know mathematics for daily living.

_____ 14.   It is always important to get the exact answer in mathematics.

_____ 15.   There is always only one best way of solving a problem.

_____ 16.   You must always know how you arrived at an answer.

_____ 17.   Math can be fun.

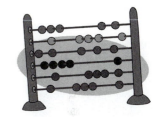

Inductive reasoning, or induction, means determining a generalization from a list of specific events (example-to-idea thinking). For example, if you see thirty men in a row wearing red shirts, you might conclude that all men wear red shirts. In mathematics, induction is often used in determining what a statement or theorem might be. However, it requires a proof of some sort before an induction is considered valid. In the instance above, you would need proof before concluding that all men wear red shirts.

Deductive reasoning means applying a general statement to a specific instance (idea-to-example thinking). For example, if you were told that all fish were goldfish, and you had a fish in a tank, you could conclude it must be a goldfish. Using deduction requires caution, however, because when applying any generalization you need to know whether the generalization is in fact true (which, in the above instance, it is not). This is especially necessary in such fields as sociology and psychology.

Another factor in reasoning is the ability to **estimate.** In 1989, the National Council of Teachers of Mathematics recognized the importance of estimation skills in its publication, *Curriculum and Evaluation Standards for School Mathematics.* In these standards, the NCTM notes the use of exploring estimation strategies, recognizing when estimation is important, using estimation to determine the reasonableness of results, and applying it in working with quantities, measurement, computation, and problem solving. Estimation involves both inductive and deductive processes. The ability to use estimation effectively will save you time and effort in solving many real-world problems.

Arithmetic

Many of your everyday tasks require **arithmetic.** Arithmetic consists of numerical computations such as addition, subtraction, multiplication, and division. It also includes handling decimals, fractions, ratios, and proportions. Examples of where these skills are used are:

➤ Paying the correct amount on a bill and seeing that you received the correct change
➤ Calculating tips in restaurants
➤ Balancing your checkbook
➤ Comparison shopping at grocery stores, clothing stores, and so on.

Algebra

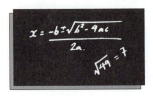

A knowledge of **algebra** is needed almost as frequently as arithmetic. Many times you figure out problems without consciously realizing that you are using algebra. Some places where algebra shows up are:

➤ Computing interest on credit cards, loans, and so on
➤ Figuring your GPA
➤ Cutting or enlarging cooking recipes
➤ Solving problems in areas such as geology, biology, anthropology, chemistry, nursing, physics, and astronomy
➤ Determining efficient travel plans

Algebra involves determining an unknown value using known values. For example, if you wanted to make 100 cookies and had enough flour for only three batches, you might use algebra to figure out how many cookies would have to be in each batch: $3(X) = 100$, where 3 is the number of batches, X is how many cookies, and 100 is the number of cookies desired. Through algebra you can find that X = 100 divided by 3, or approximately 33. Therefore, you need a cookie recipe that makes about three dozen cookies.

Geometry

Along with algebra, **geometry** is the most-needed math skill in everyday life. The most important uses of geometry occur in determining areas and volumes. However, geometric ideas occur in many other forms. Examples of places geometry is found in your life are:

➤ Determining the amount of paint needed to paint a room or a house
➤ Determining what size heater or air conditioner is needed for a room or house
➤ Determining how much punch you should make for a party
➤ Determining how closely you can pass a car
➤ Buying and arranging furniture and appliances
➤ Packing luggage

For example, when you pack up a suitcase for a trip, in your head you are calculating the size of the different items you will put in the suitcase, adding

them up, and determining whether they will fit inside the space determined by the size of the suitcase sides.

Probability and Statistics

A knowledge of basic **probability and statistics** is needed to understand the relevance and importance (or lack thereof) of the overwhelming amount of statistical information we are deluged with from the media. Without some knowledge in these areas, you are unable to evaluate the usefulness of such information. For example, if a woman reads breast cancer statistics, her statistical and probability knowledge can help her determine what her chances are of contracting breast cancer, and how certain precautions can improve those chances.

For some careers, such as actuarial or genetic science, a strong background in probability and statistics is crucial. Some areas of business, economics, and engineering also require such skills. In fact, even journalism majors are required to take courses in statistics.

Calculus and Differential Equations

Calculus and differential equations are needed for most engineering fields, business and economics, physics, and astronomy. Any problem in which a rate of change is needed involves calculus and differential equations. Many problems that involve work, water pressure, areas, and volumes also use calculus.

Higher Math

There are some fields and careers in which a high level of mathematics is required. Linear algebra occurs in some business areas and industrial engineering. Abstract algebra appears in computer science and physics. Other careers that require even further mathematics are theoretical physics, economic research, and, of course, mathematics itself.

Certainly not every student will need to master calculus or linear algebra. The basics, however, will be of use to everyone.

HOW CAN YOU MASTER MATH BASICS?

Learning mathematics is essentially the same as learning any other skill. General learning strategies that apply to all subjects will be useful in learning math as well. Certain specific strategies, however, will help improve your math learning. Mastering math basics involves your approach to the classroom, the textbook, studying, homework, and word problems.

The Classroom

In taking a math class, as with any other class, attendance is the single most important factor in your performance. Nothing can replace the learning experience of your presence each day in class. Go to class alert and prepared. Be aware of the topic being covered that day. Be prepared to ask questions on the previous topic and homework. In taking notes, follow general note-taking guidelines: Note examples, focus on the central ideas, and connect supporting examples to those ideas. Pay special attention to things the instructor emphasizes.

The Textbook

Math textbooks seem to add an extra level of difficulty for many students. The ability to read a math textbook is a skill that must be developed. Do not expect to read mathematics in the same way that you would read literature, history, psychology, and so on.

Reading math is often a time-consuming process. When reading a math book, try keeping a pad of paper with you. As you read, slowly, take special note of the examples. If steps are left out, as they often are, work them out on your pad. Draw sketches to help visualize the material as you read. Do not move on until you understand the example and how it relates to the reading. The examples provide keys in working the homework.

Also, note what formulas are given. Consider whether these formulas are important; recall whether the instructor emphasized them. Be aware that in some classes you are responsible for all formulas, while in others, the instructors will provide them to you. Look over your lecture notes and see how they compare with the text. After you read the section(s), then you are ready to attempt the homework.

Studying and Homework

Following class, try to review your notes as quickly as possible. This is as crucial in mathematics as it is in other classes, if not more so. It's especially important to fill in missing steps in the instructor's examples before you forget them. In reviewing your notes, have the book alongside and match lecture information to the book. Then work on the homework.

Since math is a problem-solving course, doing a lot of problems is critical. Do not expect to just sit down and do every problem without effort. Often the effort required is quite challenging—and the realization of how much effort is needed often provokes students to quit. The frustration factor can be quite high. To fight frustration, stay flexible. If you are stuck on a problem, go on to another one. Sometimes you need to take a break to clear your head.

If you have done the assigned homework but still aren't sure about the method, do some of the other problems. Doing a lot of problems is the only way to really learn how the concepts and the formulas work. Try a few problems under test conditions—that is, in a time-constraint situation with no cues.

Math is an area where study groups can be extremely useful. Other people's perspectives can often break a thought logjam. Even if your math classes have smaller lab sessions, try to set up study groups outside of class. Plan to do as much of your homework as you can and then meet to discuss the homework and work through additional problems. Be open to other students' ways of thinking, and don't hesitate to ask them to explain their thought processes in detail.

WORD PROBLEMS

In math, the single largest stumbling block is word problems. There is a famous *Far Side* cartoon titled "Hell's Library," which shows a shelf filled with books entitled *Story Problems, More Story Problems,* and so on. Word problems represent the number one fear of students of math. The bottom line is that word problems will be the most common way you will encounter mathematics throughout your life. Therefore, the ability to solve word problems is a necessary skill.

Why do people have so many difficulties with word problems? The reason lies with the fact that word problems force you to translate between two languages, English and mathematics. Math is a language in and of itself, and an extremely precise one. English and other living languages, however, are not precise. Although this lack of precision helps such languages achieve their richness in poetry and literature, it makes the process of translating more difficult.

Steps to Solving Word Problems

Translating from English or any other language to math takes a lot of practice. George Polya, in his 1945 classic, *How to Solve It,* devised a four-step method for attacking word problems. This procedure has been adopted in one form or another in nearly every math textbook. The basic steps are as follows:

1. *Understand the problem.* This means reading the problem carefully. Understand what it is asking. Know what information you have. Know what information is missing. Draw a picture, if possible.
2. *Devise a plan.* Try to decide how you want to solve the problem. Think about similar problems. Try to relate the given information. This is the translation step, where you need to develop and use your problem-solving strategies.
3. *Carry out your plan.* Solve the problem. Check each of your steps.
4. *Review your result.* Check your answer, if possible. Make sure you've answered the question the problem is asking. Does your result make sense in the context of the problem? Are there other ways to do the problem?

The best way to develop your skills in solving word problems is by doing a lot of them. Do extra problems. Practice a lot. The following section lays out several problem-solving strategies by working through different types of word problem examples.

Problem-Solving Strategies

Strategy 1: Look for a pattern. G. H. Hardy (1877–1947), an eminent British mathematician, described mathematicians as makers of patterns and ideas. The search for patterns is one of the best strategies in problem solving. This process is used in police work as well as in mathematics.

EXAMPLE 1: Find the next three entries in the following sequences:

   a.   1, 2, 4, ____ , ____ , ____

    b. O, T, T, F, F, S, S, ____ , ____ , ____

    c. 1, 1, 2, 3, 5, 8, 13, ____ , ____ , ____

Solutions to Example 1:

  a. One important thing to remember about trying to identify patterns is that you may very well make connections and find a different pattern than someone else. This doesn't mean yours is wrong. In example 1a, there are actually several possible answers. Here are two:

    1. First, you might recognize that each succeeding term of the sequence is twice the previous term. In that case, the next three values would be 8, 16, 32.

    2. Another possibility is that you might notice the second term is 1 more than the first term and the third term is 2 more than the second. This might lead you to guess the fourth term is 3 more than the third term, the fifth term is 4 more than the fourth term, and so on. In that case, the next three terms are 7, 11, 16.

  b. Example 1b is a famous pattern that often appears in puzzle magazines. The key to it is that O is the first letter of one, T is the first letter of two, and so on. Therefore, the next three terms would be E, N, and T for eight, nine, and ten.

  c. Example 1c is another famous sequence called the Fibonacci sequence. It's named after Leonardo of Pisa (c.1170–1250), an Italian mathematician who was also called Fibonacci. In 1202, he wrote a book about algebra called *Liber Abaci* in which he introduced this sequence. You determine each succeeding term by adding the two immediately preceding terms together, so term three is $1 + 1 = 2$, term four is $1 + 2 = 3$, and so on. This means the next three terms are $21 = 8 + 13$, $34 = 13 + 21$, and $55 = 21 + 34$. The Fibonacci sequence occurs frequently in nature. The seeds of a sunflower spiral out from the center in a Fibonacci number of rows, for example, and the scales of a pineapple spiral in a Fibonacci number of rows as well.

Strategy 2: Make a table. A table can be used to help organize and summarize information. This then may enable you to see a pattern that lets you solve a problem.

EXAMPLE 2: How many ways can you make change for a half dollar using only quarters, dimes, nickels, and pennies?

Solution to Example 2: To attack the half-dollar problem, you might construct several tables and go through every possible case. You could start by seeing how many ways you can make change for a half dollar without using a quarter, which would produce the results shown in Tables A and B on the following page. There are 36 ways to make change for a half dollar without using a quarter.

    Using one quarter results in the options shown in Table C on the following page. Using one quarter, you get twelve different ways to make change for a half dollar.

    Lastly, using two quarters, there's only one way to make change for a half dollar. Therefore, the solution to the problem is that there are $36 + 12 + 1 = 49$ ways to make change for a half dollar using only quarters, dimes, nickels, and pennies.

Table A.

Quarters	0	0	0	0	0	0	0	0	0	0	0	0	0	0	0	0	0	0
Dimes	0	0	0	0	0	0	0	0	0	0	0	1	1	1	1	1	1	1
Nickels	0	1	2	3	4	5	6	7	8	9	10	0	1	2	3	4	5	6
Pennies	50	45	40	35	30	25	20	15	10	5	0	40	35	30	25	20	15	10

Table B.

Quarters	0	0	0	0	0	0	0	0	0	0	0	0	0	0	0	0	0	0
Dimes	1	1	2	2	2	2	2	2	2	3	3	3	3	3	4	4	4	5
Nickels	7	8	0	1	2	3	4	5	6	0	1	2	3	4	0	1	2	0
Pennies	5	0	30	25	20	15	10	5	0	20	15	10	5	0	10	5	0	0

Table C.

Quarters	1	1	1	1	1	1	1	1	1	1	1	1
Dimes	0	0	0	0	0	0	1	1	1	1	2	2
Nickels	0	1	2	3	4	5	0	1	2	3	0	1
Pennies	25	20	15	10	5	0	15	10	5	0	5	0

Strategy 3: Examine a simpler case. Often patterns can be found to help solve a problem by looking at a simpler case.

EXAMPLE 3: In a portion of a city, the streets divide the city into square blocks of equal size, as seen in the following picture. Sam drives his bus daily from the bus terminal (B) to the train station (T). One day, he drove due west from the bus depot to the courthouse (C) along Ash Street, and then due south to the train depot on Seventh Street, covering a distance of eleven blocks in all. To relieve the monotony of the drive, Sam varies his route, but to conserve fuel, he doesn't travel any unnecessary distance. How many possible routes are there from the bus depot to the train station?

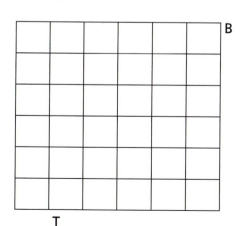

Solution to Example 3: By starting at the bus depot (B), you can look at simpler cases of this problem to attempt to determine a pattern. Looking at the following diagram, you are able to find the number of ways to get to each point from B.

	C					
	1	1	1	1	1	
	6	5	4	3	2	B 1
	21	15	10	6	3	1
	56	35	20	10	4	1
	126	70	35	15	5	1
	252	126	56	21	6	1
	462	210	84	28	7	1
T						

The numbers in the lower left corners of each cell represent the number of ways to go from the bus depot (B) to that corner. In looking at the pattern, notice, after checking the first few for yourself, that each corner number can be derived by adding the numbers in the corners directly above and to the right of the corner where you are. In other words, add the two numbers for the two corners closest to B that directly connect to your corner. In doing this, you will find there are 462 possible routes from the bus depot (B) to the train station (T).

Strategy 4: Identify a sub-goal. Breaking the original problem into smaller and possibly easier problems may lead to a solution to the original problem. This is often the case in writing a computer program.

EXAMPLE 4: Arrange the nine numbers 1, 2, 3, . . . , 9 into a square subdivided into nine sections in such a way that the sum of every row, column, and main diagonal is the same. This is what is called a *magic square.*

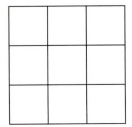

Solution to Example 4: Since each number will go into one of the squares, the sum of all the numbers will end up being three times the sum of any given row, column, or main diagonal. The sum of $1 + 2 + 3 + 4 + 5 + 6 + 7 + 8 + 9 = 45$. Therefore, each row, column, and main diagonal needs to sum to $45/3 = 15$. Now you need to see how many ways you can add three of the numbers from 1 to 9 and get 15. In doing this, you should get:

$$9 + 1 + 5 = 15 \qquad 8 + 3 + 4 = 15$$
$$9 + 2 + 4 = 15 \qquad 7 + 2 + 6 = 15$$
$$8 + 1 + 6 = 15 \qquad 7 + 3 + 5 = 15$$
$$8 + 2 + 5 = 15 \qquad 6 + 4 + 5 = 15$$

Now, looking at your magic square, notice that the center position will be part of four sums (a row, a column, and the two main diagonals). Looking back at your sums, you see that 5 appears in four different sums; therefore 5 is in the center square.

	5	

The number in each corner appears in 3 sums (row, column, and a diagonal). Looking through your sums, you find that 2, 4, 6, and 8 each appear in three sums. Now you need to place them in the corners in such a way that your diagonals add up to 15.

2		6
	5	
4		8

To finish, all you need to do is fill in the remaining squares to get the needed sum of 15 for each row, column, and main diagonal. The completed square is as follows:

2	7	6
9	5	1
4	3	8

Strategy 5: Examine a related problem. Sometimes a problem you are working on is similar to a previous problem. In that case, it is often possible to use a similar approach to solve the new problem.

EXAMPLE 5: Find a magic square using the numbers 3, 5, 7, 9, 11, 13, 15, 17, and 19.

Solution to Example 5: This problem is very similar to Example 4. Approaching it in the same fashion, you find that the needed row, column, and main diagonal sum is 33. Writing down all the possible sums of three numbers to get 33, you find that 11 is the number that appears four times, so it is in the center.

	11	

The numbers that appear three times in the sums and will go in the corners are 5, 9, 13, and 17. This now gives you:

13		17
	11	
5		9

Finally, completing the magic square gives you:

13	3	17
15	11	7
5	19	9

Strategy 6: Work backwards. With some problems, you may find it easier to start with the perceived final result and work backwards.

EXAMPLE 6: In the game of "Life," Carol had to pay $1500 when she was married. Then she lost half the money she had left. Next she paid half the money she had for a house. Then the game ended and she had $3000 left. With how much money did she start?

Solution to Example 6: Carol ended up with $3000. Right before that she paid half her money to buy a house. Since her $3000 was half of what she had before her purchase, she had 2($3000) = $6000 before buying the house. Prior to buying the house, Carol lost half her money. This means that the $6000 is the half she didn't lose. So, before losing half her money, Carol had 2($6000) = $12,000. Prior to losing half her money, Carol had to pay $1500 to get married. This means she had $12,000 + $1500 = $13,500 before getting married. Since this was the start of the game, Carol began with $13,500.

Strategy 7: Draw a diagram. Drawing a picture is often an aid to solving problems. Pictures are especially useful in gaining insight into geometrical problems. However, the use of pictures and drawings can be helpful in many other types of problems.

EXAMPLE 7: There were twenty people at a round table for dinner. Each person shook hands with the person to his or her immediate right and left. At the end of the dinner, each person got up and shook hands with everybody except the people who sat on his or her immediate right and left. How many handshakes took place after dinner?

Solution to Example 7: To solve this with a diagram, it might be a good idea to examine several simpler cases to see if you can determine a pattern of any kind that might help. Starting with two or three people, you can see there are no handshakes after dinner, since everyone is adjacent to everyone else.

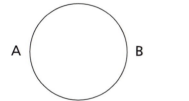
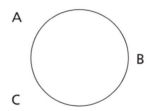

In the case of four people, we get the following diagram, connecting those people who shake hands after dinner:

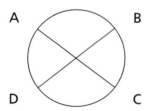

In this situation, you see there are two handshakes after dinner, AC and BD. In the case of five people, you get this picture:

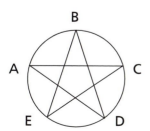

In this case, you have five after-dinner handshakes: AC, AD, BD, BE, and CE. Looking at one further case of six people seated around a circle gives the following diagram:

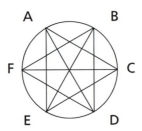

In this diagram, there are now a total of nine after-dinner handshakes: AC, AD, AE, BD, BE, BF, CE, CF, and DF. In noticing from the diagrams what is happening, you realize that if there are N people, each person would shake N − 3 people's hands after dinner (they don't shake their own hands or the hands of the two people adjacent to them). Since there are N people, that would lead to N(N − 3) after-dinner handshakes. However, this would double-count every handshake, since AD would also be counted as DA. Therefore, this is twice as many handshakes as actually took place. So, the correct number of handshakes is [N(N − 3)]/2. So finally, if there are twenty people, there would be 20(17)/2 = 170 after-dinner handshakes.

Strategy 8: Write an equation. This is the most often used strategy in algebra.

Example 8: A farmer needs to fence a rectangular piece of land. He wants the length of the field to be 80 feet longer than the width. If he has 1080 feet of fencing available, what should the length and width of the field be?

Solution to Example 8: The best way to start this problem is to draw a picture of the situation and label the sides.

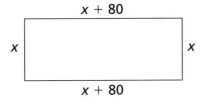

Let x represent the width of the field and $x + 80$ represent the length of the field. The farmer has 1080 feet of fencing and he will need $2x + 2(x + 80)$ feet of fencing to fence his field. This gives you the equation:

$$2x + 2(x + 80) = 1080$$

Multiplying out:	$2x + 2x + 160 = 1080$
Simplifying and subtracting 160:	$4x = 920$
Dividing by 4:	$x = 230$
Therefore,	$x + 80 = 310$

As a check, you find that

2(230) + 2(310) = 1080

Strategy 9: Guess and check. Once discouraged in favor of algebraic or other methods, it is now recognized that guess and check is an integral way many people solve everyday problems. The strategy involves making an initial guess, checking to see if it is correct, and then using that information to make another guess.

Example 9: Looking out in the backyard one day, Sue saw an assortment of cats and birds. Counting heads, she got a total of 22. Counting the feet, she got a total of 68. How many cats and birds were in the yard?

Solution to Example 9: Since Sue saw a total of 22 cats and birds (assuming none had more than one head), a good first guess might be that there are 11 cats and 11 birds. Checking the number of legs then gives:

11(4) + 11(2) = 44 + 22 = 66 legs.

Since Sue counted 68 legs, this isn't quite correct, but it is close. Since you need more legs, and cats have more legs than birds, there need to be more cats and fewer birds. Suppose then there are 12 cats and 10 birds. This would give you

12(4) + 10(2) = 48 + 20 = 68 legs

which is exactly what you wanted. Therefore, Sue sees 12 cats and 10 birds in the backyard.

These sample problems are designed to help you understand some of the basic math strategies you will use in your classes. If they have made you feel anxious, however, you will benefit from some information about math anxiety.

HOW CAN YOU OVERCOME MATH ANXIETY?

Math anxiety is a term used to describe any of several high-stress, uncomfortable feelings that appear in relation to math. One of the most common—often caused by a failure on an exam or failure to learn a topic—is a student's belief that he or she can't do any math at all. As a result of this feeling, students sometimes just give up, feeling the subject is impossible. Additionally, students often won't ask for help because they don't want others to think that they're stupid. A sense of personal embarrassment often occurs.

This sensation of incompetence is very common. If a student has understood the subject up to that point, however, the immediate leap to "It's impossible" on the next topic is usually not a rational response, but an *emotional* one. For this reason, the student might be able to relieve this anxiety by taking the subject a little slower and not hesitating to ask questions. If a student feels uncomfortable asking questions in class, he or she should seek out an instructor during office hours, a fellow classmate, or a tutor. The key is to avoid letting your anxiety have power over you. Work hard not to let an anxiety attack paralyze you and prevent you from seeking the help you need.

"Minds are like parachutes. They only function when they are open."

SIR JAMES DEWAR

Gender Issues and Math Anxiety

In the United States, there is evidence that women, more than men, are afflicted with math anxiety. This has resulted in the inaccurate perception that women aren't as adept at math as men are. Recent research has sought to determine whether there are some key gender issues involved in learning and teaching mathematics and the sciences. Another misperception in the United States is that people are born with or without an ability to do mathematics. This misperception implies that if you can't do a math problem, then you will never be able to do mathematics. In contrast, in a similar study done in Asia, people indicated that what was needed to be good at mathematics was simply hard work.

Use the questionnaire in Figure 13.2 to get a basic idea of your math anxiety level.

Before and During Exams

Math anxiety occurs most often right before or during an exam. The sense of not knowing anything or of being a failure looms large as a person gets ready to take a test or suddenly happens in reading a problem on a test. At this point, a student often describes what happens next as completely "blanking out." This can happen also on exams for other subjects, but there seems to be an especially high incidence of it in math exams.

Figure 13.2 *Explore your math anxiety.*

Answer the following statements by marking a number from 1 (Disagree) to 5 (Agree).

_____ 1. I don't like math classes, and haven't since high school.

_____ 2. I do okay at the beginning of a math class, but I always feel it will get to the point where it is impossible to understand.

_____ 3. I can't seem to concentrate in math classes. I try, but I get nervous and distracted and think about other things.

_____ 4. I don't like asking questions in math class. I'm afraid that the teachers and/or other students will think I'm stupid.

_____ 5. I stress out when I'm called on in math class. I seem to forget even the easiest answers.

_____ 6. Math exams scare me far more than any of my other exams.

_____ 7. I can't wait to finish my math requirement so that I'll never have to do any math again.

Scoring Key
28–35: You suffer from full-blown math anxiety.
21–27: You are coping, but you're not happy about mathematics.
14–20: You're doing okay.
7–13: So what's the big deal about math? You have very little problem with anxiety.

The best way to overcome test-time anxiety is through positive reinforcement. You must put yourself in the situation often enough to become comfortable with it. Keeping up with your homework is a major step. Understanding the concepts and preparing well in advance will help you feel confident. Taking timed practice exams will give you a sense of the time factor. Doing your homework or taking practice exams in the exam location will ease the sense of disorientation that occurs when you're in an unfamiliar environment. These are all strategies that will help you become more familiar, and especially more comfortable, with the subject and your surroundings. Figure 13.3 shows additional ways to reduce math anxiety.

Even though math anxiety is a real and potentially paralyzing problem, students need to realize that they must also take responsibility for their math anxiety. Personal responsibility is a key to becoming successful in college and in life. Figure 13.4 lists responsibilities that students should be aware of and accept regarding mathematics and math anxiety.

Finally, along with being a responsible student, you also have rights regarding your mathematical learning. Sandra Davis has written a list of these rights, among which are the following:

➤ The right to learn at your own pace.
➤ The right to ask any questions you have.
➤ The right to need, and seek, extra help.
➤ The right not to understand.
➤ The right to view yourself as capable of learning math.
➤ The right to be treated as a competent person.
➤ The right to dislike math.
➤ The right to define success in your own terms.

Beyond working to control your math anxiety, several other techniques will help you do your very best when you are tested on your math skills.

Figure 13.3 *Ten ways to reduce math anxiety.*

1. Overcome your negative self-image about math.
2. Ask questions of your teachers and your friends, and seek outside assistance.
3. Math is a foreign language—you need to practice it often.
4. Don't study mathematics by trying to memorize information and formulas.
5. READ your math textbook.
6. Study math according to your personal learning style.
7. Get help the same day you don't understand something.
8. Be relaxed and comfortable while studying math.
9. "Talk" mathematics. Discuss it with people in your class. Form a study group.
10. Develop a sense of responsibility for your own successes and failures.

Figure 13.4 *Mathematics code of responsibilities.*

It is my responsibility to:

1. Attend all math classes and do all assigned homework.
2. Acknowledge the rights of others to learn at their own pace.
3. Seek extra help when I need it.
4. Visit the teacher during office hours or schedule an appointment for help.
5. Come to class prepared with my homework done and any questions I have ready to ask.
6. Speak up in class when I don't understand.
7. Put forth at least the same effort for my math classes that I give to other subjects.
8. Begin with math study at my current skill level, and be honest with myself about what that level is.
9. Maintain a realistic attitude about my abilities.
10. Research instructors prior to registering for class.
11. Learn, and use, stress-reduction skills.
12. Act as a competent adult.
13. Approach math with an open mind rather than assuming it will be a nightmare.
14. Establish realistic goals and expectations.
15. Face failure if it happens, learn from it, pick myself up, and move ahead.

WHAT TECHNIQUES WILL HELP IMPROVE YOUR PERFORMANCE ON MATH TESTS?

In addition to the general strategies for test taking that you have explored, there are several other techniques that can help you achieve better results on math exams. These include reading through the exam first, doing "easy" problems first, using objective exam strategies, and checking answers.

Read Through the Exam First

It's important when you first get an exam to read through every problem quickly. As you read through the exam, make notes on how you might attempt to solve the problem, if something occurs to you immediately. If possible, categorize the problems according to what type of problem they are.

Do "Easy" Problems First

Doing "easy" problems first means that if you read a problem and know immediately how to do it without thinking too hard about the method, then do that problem. Go through the exam doing all of the problems that come most easily to you. In general, it is not a good idea to start with the first problem, then move to the second problem, and so forth, following the exam order exactly. Although some tests start with easier problems and increase in difficulty, this logic will not always apply—other tests may list problems in random order.

There are two major reasons for starting with the easiest problems. First, the goal of any exam is to achieve the highest score possible. On many math exams, all problems are worth the same number of points. You are much better off earning the points for the problems you know how to do than spending twenty minutes on a really hard problem, not getting it, and then having very little time to do the problems you know how to do. Even if the problems have different point values, you are still better off doing the problems you know how to do and ensuring that you earn those points.

The second reason is that as you do the "easy" problems, you begin to think more positively about the exam. This eases some of the tension and stress that cause math anxiety. As your anxiety eases, you gain in confidence. Suddenly, problems that you weren't sure how to solve when you first read them become easier.

Even if you don't get through some of the harder problems, your confidence will help you earn as many points as possible. You are always better off missing points on problems you didn't know how to do than missing points on the problems you knew how to do.

Use Particular Objective Exam Strategies

If your math exams are objective in nature, there are several helpful strategies to use. First, if the questions are multiple choice or matching, hide the answer choices. Work out the problem without looking at the answers. Carefully check your work, making sure you've answered the question accurately and completely. Finally, look at the choices and see if your answer is one of them. If not, you may be able to immediately eliminate some of the choices. Mark out any eliminated choices so that you will not keep looking at them. Examine your work and the remaining choices. If possible, put the remaining answers into the problem and see if they work. If not, go to another problem and come back to this one later. See Chapter 8 for more details.

Check Answers

One of the most beneficial strategies, and one of the hardest to train yourself to do, is to check your work carefully. Once students have finished a problem, they tend to not want to look at it again. If you have finished an exam early, it is always a good idea to look back over your work, especially if you were unsure of some problems. This doesn't mean you should automatically begin changing answers, however. Keep track of which answers you change; see if changing them helped or hurt you. Be aware of your own tendencies. For example, if you often lose points for careless mistakes, checking your work can help you catch these. The more of this you can learn to do, the better you will do on the exam.

All the strategies you are learning aren't useful just in your math classes. Many science classes have a mathematical element that will require you to use your math knowledge.

Applications & Exercises

Key Into Your Life: Opportunities to Apply What You Learn

1. Where Are You When It Comes to Math?

Math anxiety seems to afflict many people in today's world. As everyday life, society, and business become more technological, anxiety can become a serious problem. The severity of math anxiety is causing critical shortages of people who are qualified to handle this emerging technology. How do you deal with the challenges of mathematics? Respond to the following statements as accurately as possible in light of your own experiences and the information provided in the chapter.

1. When I make an error on a math problem, I _____

   _____

2. When I get embarrassed about doing math, I _____

   _____

3. When I'm unable to solve a particular problem, I _____

   _____

4. If I were able to do mathematics, I would _____

   _____

5. When I'm able to solve a problem that was difficult, I feel _____

   _____

6. One thing I enjoy about doing math is _____

   _____

7. Working on mathematics makes me feel _____

   _____

2. The Math Autobiography

For the following exercise, choose a math class you are taking (if you have none, choose one you took as recently as possible). With regard to that class, write an autobiography of your experiences in the subject. Examine both where you've come from and where you would like to go. Use the information from the chapter to help you.

1. My major reason for taking this class is _____

   _____

2. Before this class, the last math course I took was _____

   _____

14

CARËËR SH

You Can Do Anyt

In this chapter, you

following questions:

➤ Is it a job or a c

➤ Why is career sh
these days?

➤ Why do people sh

➤ What are the ste
shifting?

➤ How can you gain

⊘ Thinking

Check those statements

☐ I don't understand why ca

☐ I anticipate undergoing a
I'm unprepared.

☐ I have a dream for shifting

☐ I understand that I will ne
careers.

☐ I want to assess my skills t
another field.

☐ I have considered the risks

3. An early experience I recall from a math class was _____

_____

4. I remember one particular math teacher because _____

_____

5. I feel _____ was the most difficult topic to learn because _____

_____

6. I feel _____ was the easiest topic to learn because _____

_____

7. I believe I learned my current attitudes about math when _____

_____

8. To improve my attitudes about math, I expect to do the following for myself:

_____

_____

9. To improve my performance in math, I expect to do the following for myself:

_____

3. Which Strategies Did You Use?

Using a math book, copy down three questions from the text. For each question, name a problem-solving strategy or strategies from this chapter that will help you solve the problem. Solve the problem on a separate piece of paper.

Afterwards, state here why you chose the strategies you did. Are there other ways to solve the same problem?

Problem 1: _____

_____

Strategies: _____

_____

Problem 2: _____

_____

Strategies: _____

_____

Problem 3: _____

_____

Strategies: _____

_____

A S P I R

ASPIRE

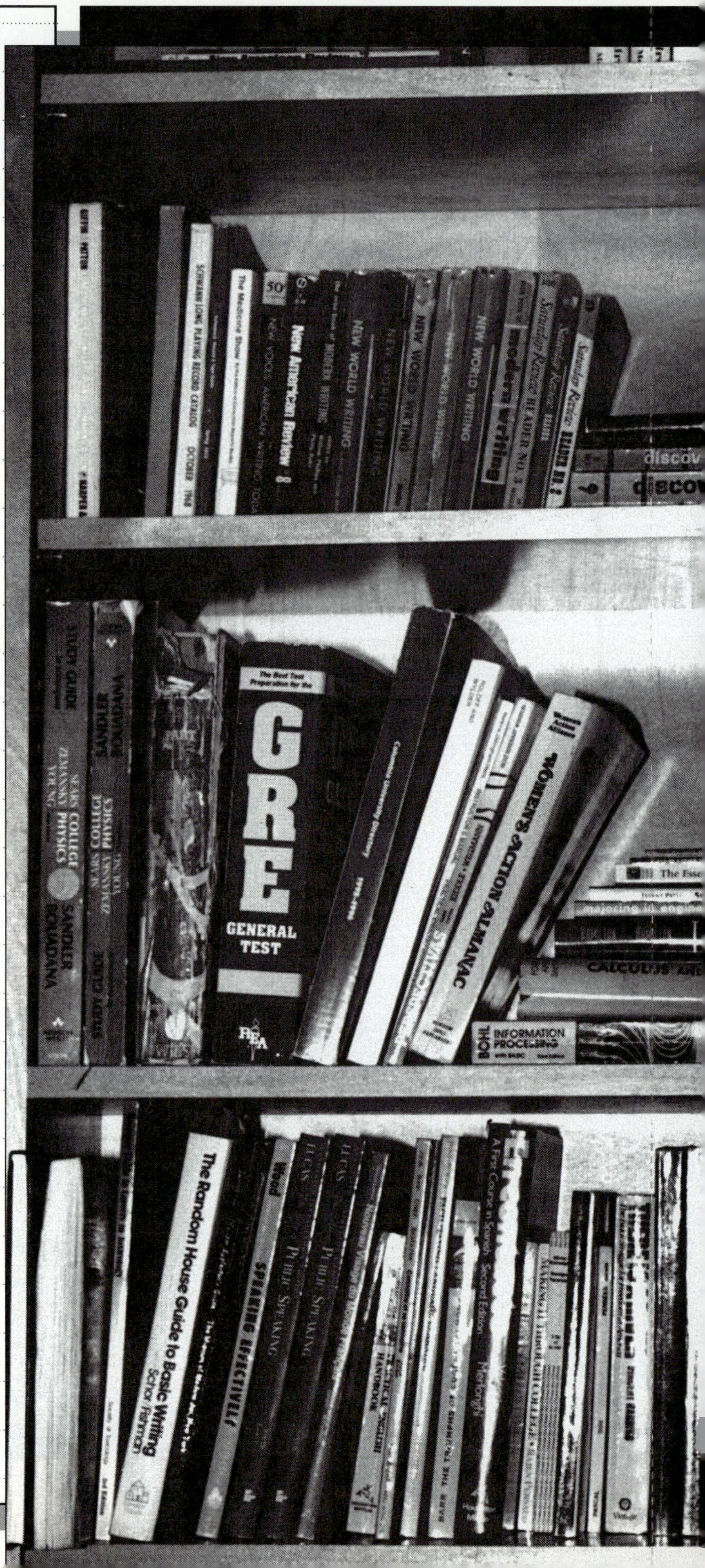

14

CAREER SHIFTING
You Can Do Anything with Your Life

Think about the jobs you've had. How often have you taken a position just to get the money to do something else? Have you been plugging away through a series of jobs, feeling trapped in a career or position you don't really enjoy? Perhaps you've reached the top in one field and are ready for new challenges in another. All are good reasons for considering a career shift.

In this chapter we will be looking at:

➤ Job shifts, career shifts, and the differences between them
➤ Why people career shift
➤ How to plan for a career shift
➤ Where to get the skills you need to career shift

IS IT A JOB OR A CAREER?

In this chapter we define a **job** as work you do for money so you can do something else. You could be working to support your education, family, car, or shopping habit. A **career** is a job or series of jobs *in a particular field* and usually involves the opportunity for promotion within the field. For example, both doctors and nurse's aides have careers in the field of medicine. If a nurse's aide goes to medical school to become a doctor, he is advancing his career in the field of medicine.

A **job shift** occurs when a person moves from one job to another. A **career shift** occurs when a person moves from one field of interest to a different field. If a doctor retires from medicine and joins the pro golf tour, she is making a career shift.

Are you looking for a career shift? If you're unhappy in your current job and unexcited about the field you're in, you may want to look for alternatives. If you feel trapped in your job because you need to support your family or don't feel you can take time for more education, career shifting may seem like a dream. Or you may be currently employed in an industry undergoing major technological changes. This may lead to corporate downsizing or restructuring, and you may find yourself out of a job. You may be trying to figure out how to turn your interests and hobbies into a career. All these are good reasons for career shifting.

WHY IS CAREER SHIFTING A BIG ISSUE THESE DAYS?

Current labor statistics show that most people will shift jobs 7 to 13 times in their lives. A major career shift will occur one or two times. These statistics are changing even as economic and social changes occur in the workplace. Alterations in values and work ethics are also leading people away from traditional work paths. It's important to note that career and job shifting are not seen as negatively as they used to be. People today are seeking more money, better benefits, and a good corporate culture.

ELEANOR & MARION: CAREERS IN MOTION

In the Beginning—Eleanor wanted to be a baker. She had grown up on a farm and enjoyed working with food. When she graduated from high school in the late 1940s, she applied for entry-level bakery jobs and to bakery schools in the Midwest. She was turned down for the jobs because women weren't bakers; that was a man's job. She wanted more education, so she looked at her alternatives: In those days women were teachers, nurses, or clerical staff. She earned a teaching certificate in home economics and then got a teaching position with a high school.

Marion grew up on a farm and always had an interest in machinery. He inherited a strong work ethic from his parents and after high school got a job washing cars. From there he worked his way up to grinding valves and installing engines. He worked at his brother's service station where he serviced cars and pumped gas.

One day he went with his brother to check out a used car. When Marion told him it had been wrecked and repainted, the salesman alerted the shop's owner. The next week the owner offered Marion a job as a mechanic. He took it. He enjoyed his work and was good at it.

Transition—Marion and Eleanor were married in the early 1950s. Eleanor taught, though she didn't really enjoy it. She did some substitute teaching when her children were very small, but she went back to full-time teaching as they got older. Marion got a promotion from mechanic to service manager, in charge of the operations of the garage.

In the late 1960s, both Eleanor and Marion were ready for a change. They decided to go to Arizona and start fresh. Marion would get a job and Eleanor would find something later. They sold their house and were getting ready to move when Marion was injured on the job. He was hospitalized for several weeks. Since he needed a secure job with benefits, they felt they had to stay where they were. They had to find a house quickly, so they bought one in town.

Marion stayed at his job, while Eleanor got a new teaching position. She was fired when the school board sided with a parent over a grade dispute. In retrospect, it was probably the best thing that could have happened to Eleanor; after 11 years of teaching, she applied for a management position in the local university's food service. Nothing was open at the time, but a few months later a cook's position became available. When the personnel department saw her background and experience, she got the job, with the assumption she would take a management position when available.

Adjustments—Eleanor worked as a cook for two years in different food centers on campus until she disagreed with the union over a labor dispute.

A few months later, the position of manager of the university president's kitchen opened. For two years, she worked independently, cooking and managing dinner functions for the president. She became a supervisor and was assigned to a food service unit. Eleanor worked as supervisor of various units for 17 years.

Meanwhile, Marion was still hard at work as the service manager of the garage. He worked for the dealership for 35 years until the owner died and new management came into the shop. After several disagreements over how the shop should be managed, he received an offer he couldn't refuse by a rival dealership, so he moved down the road, taking many customers with him. He worked there another 10 years until his retirement in the early 1990s. Marion's career spanned 45 years in the auto business.

In the 1980s Eleanor's new boss encouraged her to take the manager's test. After passing it she managed one of the units for three years, then offered to step down to a supervisor's position (keeping the same salary) to allow a younger person to be promoted to manager. Three years later she retired. She had spent 11 years as a teacher and 25 years in the university food service.

Now that you've read the story, here's the quiz:

1. How many job and career shifts occurred in Marion's career? Did he have a career?

2. How many job and career shifts occurred in Eleanor's career? Did she have a career?

Answers:

1. Yes, he had a career. His jobs all fell within a specific field: automobile repair. He had approximately seven job shifts:

   Car washer → Mechanic → Gas station attendant/mechanic → Mechanic → Mechanic → Service Manager

   Did he have a career shift? No, all his work was in the field of auto repair.

2. Eleanor had one career in education and another in food service. Moving from teaching to a civil service job in management is a career shift.

   Eleanor had several job shifts as well:

   Substitute and full-time teacher in different school systems and different subjects (having once taught French and mathematics!)

   Teaching career shift to food service:

   Cook → Supervisor in president's kitchen → Supervisor in five different units → Manager → Supervisor

EMPLOYMENT SHIFTS IN THE LAST CENTURY

Job and career shifting are normal occurrences today, but that hasn't always been the case. People who grew up during the 1930s through World War II lived through experiences of hardship and widespread unemployment. In those days if you had a job, you kept it. If you kept changing jobs, you were perceived as shifty. If you couldn't hold a steady job, there was something wrong with you. The work ethic of the time said you worked to make money, provide for your family, and prepare for retirement. You found a good job that paid well and stuck with it. The ideal plan was to work your way up through the ranks of one company. It was not unusual for men and women to work in the same company for 30 or 40 years and retire comfortably, with a gold watch.

Downsizing. That work ethic remained in place until the 1970s when the increase in corporate mergers and takeovers led to the era of downsizing. Companies were laying off employees to save labor costs, and the loyalty of long-time employees began to lose its value. Even employees of 20 years were let go. The introduction of the personal computer in the 1980s also led to shifts in job functions. Many secretarial positions were eliminated, and people were forced to learn new skills to provide their own office support.

Industry changes. As more jobs shifted from industry to information and service organizations, more people were left with specific skills that had lost their value. This was true in the case of steel mill workers in the late 1970s when 80 percent of the steel mills in the country downsized or closed. The increased use of plastic, the decreased need for steel for military purposes, and the introduction of automation and robotics led to the death of a once-booming industry. People who were let go had to find jobs in related fields or retool their skills.

Outsourcing. In the late 1980s we saw the emergence of contracting and outsourcing. In order to control costs, companies were moving some processes outside the company to specialized services. Businesses got rid of bookkeeping departments and outsourced their payroll process to payroll services. In-house cafeterias were no longer run by the company but were contracted out.

Changing workforce.   The 1990s have brought a continuation of downsizing and corporate mergers. Job shifting has become commonplace, and people are continually looking for jobs that provide good money, benefits, and corporate culture. The work ethic is also changing. People in the baby boom generation have grown up in an era of plenty, with more time to dedicate to leisure pursuits. They question the reasons for working. In addition to providing for their family and retirement, they want to make a difference. (Enjoying what you do is part of the new work philosophy.)

At the end of the 1990s there is more confidence in the economy. The baby boomers are getting older and beginning to reach retirement age. Many are within five to ten years of retirement. They're looking for positions that will provide pensions, retirement benefits, and better medical benefits. As they reach retirement, many workers will consider part-time employment or career shifts.

Growth of small business.   Another critical factor in employment today is the growth of small business. These businesses typically employ 5 to 25 people and are multiplying at a great rate. More people will be employed by small businesses than ever before. Small companies usually provide more interesting corporate cultures, but they struggle to offer the benefits provided by big corporations.

WHY DO PEOPLE SHIFT CAREERS?

Economic and Industry Changes

As we saw earlier, changes in technology and automation, as well as a decline in the growth of an industry, can lead to changes in a field. When people believe they're in a dying field or potential for advancement and growth is limited, they begin to consider career shifts.

> Tom was a middle- to upper-management supervisor in a steel mill. When his plant closed due to lack of demand, he received a good severance package, which allowed him to look around for other jobs or retraining. He went back to school for a management degree. With the degree and his previous skills, he shifted to a middle-management career in banking.

If you're in a dying or constantly changing industry, be consistently looking at opportunities for retraining. This is certainly true of those in computer programming and other highly technical and quickly evolving fields.

The state of the economy is always a factor in the frequency of job and career shifting. If the economy is good, people feel more freedom to explore other jobs and/or careers. If the economy is slow, people tend to stay where they are, safe in a job providing security.

Changing Interests and a Need for Challenge

If you are unhappy with or unexcited about your current job—or you don't feel you make a difference—consider a career shift. People's interests continually change as they grow, and their experiences and desires will often lead them to new careers. The key question is "How much do you want it?"

Some people need to be challenged in a job in order to enjoy their work. In some companies, two kinds of tasks exist: "maintenance work" and "creative work." Many people hate to do maintenance tasks such as balancing the checkbook, sending out packages, typing notes, finding proposals, and engaging in repetitive tasks. On the other hand, many love to be creative: writing; giving seminars and presentations; and developing proposals, brochures, and slide presentations. They enjoy doing things that make them think and offer chances to be creative. They only tolerate the maintenance tasks. Some people would not survive well in an all-maintenance job. Consider this example:

> Anna chose to leave the field of academics to open her own business. One reason was because she had achieved the rank of professor by the time she was 33. She had reached the top of the field and didn't want to wait in the same position to retire for 20 to 30 years . Anna needed the kind of challenges being her own boss could bring.

Family Shifts

Career changes can also be made due to shifts in the family, such as a spouse who is asked to relocate, or making a decision to have children and remain at home while they're small. When people have the opportunity to think about new possibilities, they often take new, previously unconsidered avenues.

> Seven years ago, Carol was a training manager in a bank. When she had a baby, she decided to be a stay-at-home mom. After a year or two, she began to sell kitchen products in a home-party atmosphere to work at her own pace in her spare time. Today, she is a district manager with the company and supervises 75 to 100 people. She's changed careers from corporate training to direct marketing sales and management, and she loves it. Carol has already surpassed her previous income and would never consider going back. Her career shift would never have occurred if she hadn't chosen to stay home with her children.

You Get an Offer You Can't Refuse

You may shift careers when you're offered a great opportunity, something too good to turn down. It may be a promotion to a different area of the company, a chance to head a family business, or the opportunity to combine your talents with others to form a new business. A hair stylist may decide to sell his business and join a friend running a costume shop. It could be a great opportunity for him, a chance to work with his friend doing something totally different. There can be all kinds of opportunities you can't turn down.

> Dean was a recreational education teacher with a university. He volunteered to be part of the coordination committee for the Extreme Games on CNN, which were taking place in his city. He did such a great job volunteering that CNN offered him the job of managing the games. It was such a good offer that he felt he had to take it. Before he left, he did have a backup plan to reenter the university if things didn't work out.

Significant Life Events

Marriage, death, accidents, changes in health, and retirement are all significant life events that can bring about career shifts. Imagine going from schoolteacher to princess by marriage, as Diana Spencer did. Talk about a major career shift!

Accidents.   Accidents and changes in a person's health may force a person to shift careers when they are no longer physically able to do the job. Kay was a factory worker for many years until she was injured on the job. While on disability, she chose to go back to school to pursue a degree in hotel restaurant management. Her disability gave her the opportunity to do something she had always wanted to do.

Retirement.   Retirement is also a reason for career shifting. With more free time available, many people choose to volunteer or pursue a lifelong hobby or dream that can become a second or third career. They may volunteer or choose to become a consultant, spreading their expertise to new organizations.

> Raymond was manager of a large chemical company. When he took early retirement in his fifties, he took courses and studied to be a financial planner. He had no formal training in financial planning, but did have a lifelong interest in the process. He is now very successful and makes almost as much as he did in upper management in the chemical company.

Gradual Shifts

Sometimes career shifts occur gradually, and unconsciously. Many times we start our careers in one field, picking up a little knowledge here and there to make our jobs easier. Sometimes we find the added experiences in jobs often lead us in new, unexpected directions.

> Cara was a customer service representative who specialized in technical software testing. She worked on the testing team for several years and took training classes with the programmers when they received new software packages. She began doing minor programming and was better able to communicate the tester's needs to the programmers. During the next year, she continued to expand her programming abilities and experience, and after a year she was officially promoted to programmer. Her career change occurred gradually as one job led into another.

KEYS TO SHIFTING CAREERS

Now that you know why people change careers, how do you go about making the change? There are several steps to follow to make the change a reality. Here's a look at a planned career shift.

> When John was young, his father had been a steel mill worker for 44 years and taught him that you got a job to make money, support your family, and plan for retirement. John took this philosophy with him to college and got a degree in accounting because the field paid well. He got married and took a

job as a CPA. John worked for several years as an accountant, but didn't enjoy the work—even though he made a good living.

Four years later he realized wanted to make a difference helping people, and he didn't feel he could do that as an accountant. He began to dream about shifting to a career where he could help people, and then he started talking about it with his family. John had always had an interest in medicine, and he wanted a top profession.

After spending 18 months exploring possible careers, his interest in his own body and his discipline as a runner led him to consider physical therapy as a career. At the library, he read magazines and newspaper articles on different professions, scoured the Internet weekly—looking at specific sites dedicated to medicine and physical therapy—and went to seminars to meet people in the profession. He joined all the associations in the field he could. He wrote to organizations for information about the profession. After he had thoroughly researched the field, John asked to "job shadow" people for a day to see what they did. He also volunteered on Saturdays at the hospital for six months to determine if he liked working in that atmosphere.

At the same time he was researching the field, John was also calculating the risks of switching careers:

➤ He would have to take one full-time year of prerequisite courses before he would be accepted into a four-year program.
➤ He and his wife would have to live off her salary all that time.
➤ He might not be accepted into the program after taking the prerequisite courses.
➤ He was concerned he might not be able to get a position after graduating.
➤ He worried that he would be 32 years old when he graduated.
➤ He had to consider the impact of switching careers on his marriage, as well as what might happen if his wife were relocated.

John decided to make the commitment to the career change. He has turned his volunteer work into a part-time job and is finishing up the year of prerequisite courses with straight As. Members of the selection committee for the program assure him he will get in. His wife and family have been tremendously supportive and adjusted their lifestyles to accommodate his need for study time. His alternate plans are ready in case things don't work out.

John thinks one of the key skills from his years as an accountant is his professional attitude. In addition, his experience in accounting will give him the background he needs if he ever wants to be an administrator or own a physical therapy business. He made a decision to make a major career shift and has done an incredible job preparing for it.

Seven Steps for Successful Career Shifting

Career changes seldom happen without major thought and consideration. Consider these seven steps when shifting careers.

1. Have a dream—an idea of what you want to do
2. Explore and investigate your desired field
3. Determine what skills and attitudes you need to succeed

4. Consider the risks of change

5. Decide how you are going to get there (e.g., education, job, training, self-study)

6. Determine additional activities to help you gain experience (e.g., community service, a second job, education, training, networking)

7. Search out the job and shift your career

Step 1: It All Starts with a Dream

What do you want to do? What would you be doing right now if you could do anything, regardless of your level of education, experience, background, or income? The first part of making a career change is giving yourself permission to think about changing. If you love your job, you probably aren't thinking about shifting careers. Instead, you're thinking about how to advance in your current career. It takes some dissatisfaction with the current situation to bring about a desire for change.

Step 2: Exploring Your Potential Career

Career shifts are rarely made on the spur of the moment. Changing careers takes serious thought and support from other people. When considering a specific occupation, look at it from all angles. Take a look at some of the following resources:

Libraries.   Check out books, magazines, and newspaper articles on your desired field.

The Internet.   Search for job opportunities and career information on the Web. Using a browser or search engine, enter key terms for your field and look for matches. Look at web sites of companies and organizations for information. Check out the following web sites for career and job information:

➤ Online Career Center: www.occ.com/
➤ America's Job Bank: www.ajb.dni.us/
➤ Career Mosaic: www.career mosaic.com/
➤ College Grad Job Hunter: www.collegegrad.com/
➤ E-Span: www.espan.com/
➤ Job Web: www.jobweb.org/

Talk with people in the industry.   People in the field can give you viewpoints and information you won't get from reading. They can tell you true-life stories and both sides of the profession, good and bad. Networking with people in the industry is also a strategic way to get placement in the field. It's easier to find jobs when you know the people who are hiring. See if you can job shadow them for a day to see what they do.

Check out professional organizations.   Become familiar with the field's professional associations and organizations. They can be a rich resource to jobs, career information, education, training sources, and networking resources.

Volunteer work. Consider volunteering for positions to help you gain experience and exposure to your field of interest. Opportunities exist in all work areas, which can give you a feel of the career choices you're considering.

Step 3: Determine the Skills and Attitudes You Need to Succeed

As part of the career exploration phase in Step 2, you'll discover the qualifications needed by a professional in your desired field. Take a look at the experiences, skills, and knowledge you already have and decide what additional skills you will need. Usually you will have some skills in the related field simply because of your interest. Most mechanics don't become hair stylists unless they already have a great interest in and love for working with people.

Professional skills can be divided into two types: **field-specific** and **transferable.** Frequently, you will pick up on field-specific skills when you read job descriptions and talk to people as you research the field.

Transferable skills are a combination of skills that are universal and those that are unique to you. **Skills** are abilities to perform certain activities. **Knowledge** is information about a subject. A **transferable skill** is a skill or knowledge that can be taken from one area and used in a different field. A manager moving from banking to manufacturing would use similar management skills in both fields. She may need to learn a new way of doing things and regulations affecting the new industry, but the skills to manage people are the same.

Here is a shopping list of skills that tend to be transferable, depending on the particular field:

➤ Ability to delegate	➤ Leadership
➤ Ability to plan and implement	➤ Organizational skills
➤ Ability to train	➤ Problem solving
➤ Communication and computer skills	➤ Public speaking
➤ Conceptual ability	➤ Self-management
➤ Creativity	➤ Setting priorities
➤ Decision-making	➤ Taking initiative
➤ Flexibility	➤ Team building/leading
➤ Follow-through	➤ Team play

Step 4: Consider the Risks

Calculating risk is one of the key steps to making any career shift. Is a shift the best thing for you? What is really important to you? This is where you really decide if you want to do this or not. Fear of the unknown and fear of change are two of the biggest obstacles to making the decision to career shift. Many people look at the risks and decide the shift isn't worth the time and effort. Others look at the risks and decide on ways to minimize them. Here are some of the factors to consider when pondering a career shift:

➤ Is the career you want feasible?
➤ Is employment available anywhere or only in certain geographic locations?

➤ What training or education do you need to do the job?

➤ How will you get this training?

➤ Can you afford to make the switch?

➤ Are you established in an area? Can you afford to leave friends and family?

➤ Do you have support from your family, spouse, or significant other?

➤ Do you need to find alternative sources for health insurance or benefits?

➤ Can you gain the skills you need through a part-time job or volunteer work?

➤ Are there any educational options provided in your current job?

➤ What skills do you already have that will be useful in your new career?

➤ Will all the time and effort be worth it? Will this be a profession for the rest of your life?

➤ *Am I certain this is really what I want to do?*

If you're not sure what you want to do, consider using interest inventories and career-counseling opportunities offered through local colleges and universities, as well as the Internet. They offer several types of tests to help you focus on your interests and can map them out to specific career fields.

Step 5: How Will You Get There?

Overcoming obstacles.   This step is about removing the barriers to a career change. When John decided to pursue a degree in physical therapy, he worried about getting into the program. He decided that to get accepted he needed to take the prerequisite courses and ace them. He also strategically networked with the program's decision makers through his volunteer and part-time work with the staff. Before committing to the program, John did waffle a bit. The fact that he would be 32 by the time he graduated concerned him until a relative pointed out that in five years he would be 32 anyway. (You're never too old to do what you want to do.)

Look at your risks for career shifting and figure out how to minimize them. If money is a problem, see the financial aid department of your local college. Check out scholarships based on specific careers, regional location, financial need, and merit. Of the local and specific scholarships available, almost 40 percent are not used because no one has applied for them.

Map out a plan.   Before you can reach your new career goal, you must be able to visualize it. Once you see it, make a list itemizing everything you need to do. Determine the costs associated with each step. This means you need to be dialed into your personal budget and financial needs. You must also look into the future and predict expenses that might interfere with your career shift (e.g., family needs, new cars, living expenses). Keep 15 percent of your income aside for emergencies.

Don't forget to include your family and significant others in the decision-making process. It's much easier to shift careers when those around you provide support. Look at their needs and the impact your shift will have on them.

Step 6: What Else Can You Do to Gain Experience?

Once you are set on your course, including gaining the skills you need to succeed in your new profession, see if there are other ways to achieve experience and exposure to the field. Education, experience, part-time jobs in the field, and volunteer efforts are some of the ways.

> Allison always wanted to be a doctor. In high school she volunteered for the American Red Cross, served as a CPR instructor, and gained her lifeguard certification. She also took a job at a local nursing home as a nurse's aide. In college, she took premed courses while continuing her volunteer efforts. Allison attended the National Youth Red Cross convention in Europe as a representative. She was accepted into medical school and earned her medical degree. Everything she did helped her focus on her goal of becoming a doctor. Her employment, education, and community service all involved a health focus.

Education.   Additional education may involve going back to school part-time, perhaps in the evening, looking for educational opportunities at work, or going to school full-time to pursue a career. Depending on the field you are entering, you may not need additional education. In some cases, the skills you gain on the job provide enough background for you to switch directly into a new career. Regardless of the level of education you pursue, your interest in the field and determination to switch careers will help in your education process. You'll find the classes more interesting and more related to your interests. It may take years to determine what you really want to do in life. It's important to remember that you're never too old or too deeply into a career to switch. Sometimes you just need to try out several different jobs before you realize what you are good at and enjoy doing.

Professional memberships and networking.   Membership in a professional organization is a great way to keep up-to-date in the field and make connections with new people. It can also be a great opportunity to network with people who have interests similar to yours. They may be able to lead you to others who will help you find positions and opportunities in a different career. If you're trying to gain management skills in preparation for a career shift, consider volunteering for a leadership position within the organization.

Retraining programs.   It's important to take advantage of educational opportunities at your current job. If your company offers you opportunities to attend seminars on management, training, and educational issues, which would give you transferable skills, take advantage of them. Not only can they give you valuable information, but they also look impressive on a resume. Pursuing additional training shows people you're willing to learn and pursue your own professional growth.

You may also want to investigate continuing education classes available in most junior colleges and universities around the country. Most are offered in the evenings and won't interfere with your current job, and many focus on acquiring basic skills, such as in business.

Community service.   Community service with a nonprofit organization can teach you to work in teams, develop people skills, and perform crisis management. They will also help you in planning, training, and managing people, as well as in developing specific skills.

Job shifts to gain special skills.   You may also need to change jobs in order to gain special skills. This may involve taking a position with lower pay or status. Stockbrokers often start their careers as runners on the floor of the stock exchange. Look for opportunities for a second job that will allow you to gain experience while holding your current job.

Learning on your own time.   If appropriate classes are not available, find books or tutorials to complete at home. This is especially feasible for learning computer software programs. Check out your local public library. Many companies also have libraries with tapes and books available for checkout that can help you gain management, sales, and administration skills.

Step 7: Search Out the Job

Much of your original research work will come in handy here. Ponder two questions while preparing for a new job:

➤ Are you willing to relocate?
➤ Do you have any special requirements in taking a job (e.g., benefits, location)

Consider these questions when looking for a job because the answers will affect your search strategy. If relocation is not an issue, search out web sites listing national job leads and opportunities. If you are restricted by geography, your search should start with the local paper and network. Use memberships in organizations to network with people. You can use the Internet, but restrict your search by location.

Timelines.   Start your job search four to six months before you need the job. Because the average process for hiring new employees requires 30 days, you may not get to an interview for a month or more. (This may vary, depending on how hungry your field is for new employees.) It's important to be truthful about when you will be available to take the position. It should come out by the end of the first interview. You want to be certain your education or retraining is completed before taking a new job; it's a matter of ethical behavior. When national unemployment is low, it is truly an employees' market. In other words, you can tell the truth and set the timelines you need.

Documenting your work.   Employers are always trying to find ways to distinguish between applicants. When they want to see proof of your skills and abilities, a portfolio of your work is the answer. As you complete training and education to prepare for your new career, keep samples of projects, papers, and other materials you produce that will show what you can do. Organize this portfolio by skill areas. It can make a difference in your interview.

Scannable resume.   The resume of the '90s has changed from those of the '70s and '80s. Today many resumes are not reviewed by people, but are scanned into a database of applicants. The customized formatting and look of the document are not as important as the contents and language used.
Here are some guidelines for writing and formatting a scannable resume:

Writing a scannable resume:

➤ Use industry terms and vocabulary in your resume. These may be used for keyword searches (e.g., *supervised, managed, training, production*)
➤ Quantify things at every opportunity (e.g., dollar-volume served, number of trainings completed)
➤ Include common words that accurately describe your skills, experiences, abilities, and interests (e.g., *detail-oriented, ability to delegate, team leader, willing to travel, ability to train, college graduate*). Computers search for these words in matching your résumé to job vacancies.
➤ Use understandable abbreviations and acronyms

Formatting a scannable resume:

➤ Place your name at the top
➤ Use white paper and black ink
➤ Use 12- to 14-pitch fonts for body text
➤ Use 16- to 18-pitch fonts for headings
➤ Avoid italics, script, boldface, underlined passages, bullets, photos, graphics, and shading
➤ Use simple, popular, common typefaces such as Arial, Courier, or Times New Roman
➤ Use serif instead of sans serif fonts. They're easier for software to read.
➤ Use one-inch margins around the document
➤ Put your name and the page number in a header or footer
➤ If faxing, use the "fine mode" setting.

WRAP-UP

Career shifting requires soul-searching. It can be one of the best things that ever happens to you—an opportunity to start fresh and create your destiny all over again. Look at your abilities and interests, and if you can find a niche in the forecasted job future, you will be tremendously successful. It does take a plan, tenacity, and knowing who you are.

Success in your career!

Applications & Exercises

1. Learning from Other Career Changers

Do you know anyone who has shifted jobs? How long did they prepare for this change? Did they use the seven steps for successful career shifting? List your observations for each step.

(1) Have a dream

_____

_____

(2) Explore and investigate

_____

_____

(3) Determine the skills and attitudes needed

_____

_____

(4) Consider the risk factors

_____

_____

(5) Map out a plan

_____

_____

(6) Additional activities

_____

_____

(7) Search out the job

_____

_____

2. Discovering a Pattern

➤ List all the jobs you have held. Do you have a career path? What is it?

_____

_____

_____

_____

➤ In order of priority, make a list of the transferable skills for your chosen career.

_____

_____

_____

_____

3. Cooperative Learning

In a small group, make a list of transferable skills to seek out in any field you pursue.

_____

_____

_____

_____

4. Exploring the WWW

On the Internet, check out the following job-search web pages. What do you notice? Are there links to other pages?

➤ http://www.jobweb.org

_____

➤ http://www.careerpath.com

_____

➤ http://www.jobbankusa.com

_____

➤ http://www.job-fest.com

_____

➤ http://www.monster.com/

_____

15 CORPORATE CULTURE
Do Their Goals Meet Yours?

In this chapter, you will explore answers to the following questions:

➤ How can we connect American culture to corporate culture?

➤ Why is corporate culture distinguished from all other cultures?

➤ How has corporate culture changed throughout history?

➤ How can you discover what kind of corporate culture suits your needs?

➤ How can you stay true to yourself while still advancing in business?

❓ Thinking It Through

Check those statements that currently apply to you:

❏ I thought culture was something that pertained to communities, not corporations.

❏ I am not sure how to determine what kind of corporate culture will be best for me.

❏ I don't see the difference between the way corporations interact and the way the rest of the world does.

❏ I don't want to subordinate my own ethics and values to the overall corporate culture of my company.

SYNCHRONIZE

15

CORPORATE CULTURE
Do Their Goals Meet Yours?

Do you ever think about what makes you happy? What is important to you in your life? What is your purpose? We spend most of our days working, either for ourselves or for others. Does your work make you happy? Is it a means to an end or the end itself? Whatever your life looks like, is it the way you want it?

Many of us let life happen to us instead of taking control and designing how we want our lives to look. We need to set goals for all the areas of our lives and take action to see that our goals are met. How do the goals we create for ourselves fit with the mission and goals of our employers?

WHAT IS CORPORATE CULTURE?

Culture is the behavior typical of a group that shares a particular set of intellectual and moral codes. These codes, or values, are products of beliefs that the group holds as important. Because the cultural group shares these values, their behavior with respect to one another is shared and largely predictable. The individuals within the cultural group also have values. People are driven by their values; they make choices and conduct themselves based on those values. Values are the spirit and soul of people and cultures.

Corporate cultural values are the spirit and soul of a corporation. They reflect the organization's beliefs, which are the philosophies behind how it conducts its business. Corporate culture is the context of how a corporation projects itself both outwardly, to the public, and inwardly, to its employees. As we approach the year 2000, traditional corporate culture in America is changing. The graduation-to-retirement careers that sustained your parents and grandparents are rare. Most people in the workforce today will change careers every 10 years, and today's college graduate will have 10 different jobs before retiring. Those entering the job market, as well as those already working, will benefit by understanding where we were, where we are, and where we are going as a culture and in business. Examining your own values and targeting goals and understanding your employer's values and goals are important steps in taking control of your life and future. Let's see where we've been.

WHAT ARE VALUES?

A value is a judgment that we either knowingly or unknowingly have toward that about which we have feelings. For example, you rarely give thought to the floor you walk on. However, if the particular floor under consideration is hardwood, freshly refinished by hours of your own labor and at great expense, and someone walks on it with mud and gravel on his shoes, you will have some feelings about that. You *value* your time, money, labor, the floor's beauty, the infringing person's lack of respect, and the injustice of having to clean it. Your feelings are engaged and you have a judgment about the situation. Think of any aspect of your life that engages your feelings and you begin to know what your values are.

Values are deeply held beliefs that come from your conditioning, the moral concepts you absorb from birth by observing your environment and families, and later your schools, churches, and society. They are concepts of good and desirable traits that motivate human behavior and serve as criteria for the choices you make about your behavior. Values include concepts like fairness, respect for others, thrift, material success, individualism, freedom, courage, honesty, hard work, patriotism, and compromise. You use these standards to make judgments about what is acceptable in your life experience.

Cultural values are the morals and concepts that a society holds important. When the people and groups with which you associate share your values, you feel comfortable because you know their behavior is in harmony with your own. You seek the comfort of fitting in with others who share your beliefs. As a child, you experimented, evaluated, and modified your behavior to fit into the world around you. By the time you left high school, your values were locked in. Your attitudes and behaviors may change on the surface, but without dramatic change in your life, your internal processes and judgments, based on the values you've established, are set. You take values for granted; they influence and guide your behavior and the actions you take. Without values to serve as an internal compass, you lack vision and direction to act responsibly in your life.

AMERICAN CULTURE/CORPORATE CULTURE—WHAT'S THE CONNECTION?

In order to understand corporate culture, we need to look at the history of American cultural values because the values expressed in traditional corporate culture reflect those of traditional American culture in general. (This overview of American cultural values is from a general perspective without economic or ethnic considerations.) Where did American values come from?

Since this country was founded in 1776, each generation has worked hard and experienced a life of greater prosperity and opportunity than the generation before. America, the land of opportunity, possessed seemingly unlimited resources, and the American dream grew to represent "bigger and better" for all who applied themselves. People valued hard work, honesty, family, and community.

This bigger-and-better-through-hard-work philosophy is the foundation for the traditional American value system. People took responsibility for themselves through hard work and community spirit. There was respect for authority; there was right and wrong. Prior to World War II, the slow-paced, low-tech consistency of life reinforced these beliefs. Based on these values, this became the American Dream—a better life and lifestyle for the next generation.

After World War II, this materialistic trend intensified with unimagined prosperity. Companies already operating grew; new companies were formed that would grow to become economic giants. Technology mushroomed, creating new jobs and new companies. People moved to the cities to work in factories. The goal for the new military–industrial complex and burgeoning technology was the bottom line. People valued success, and success was measured in dollars.

The American Dream knew no bounds. Within this framework, corporate culture grew to reflect general American beliefs—resources are unlimited and prosperity and abundance is available to all who will work hard. In order to control growth and wealth, corporations created and implemented a hierarchical, top-down philosophy of management. Decisions were made at the top and carried out with no questions asked; after all, everyone in the system was making money, so why rock the boat? The goal was to beat the competition and get to the bottom line. Money and position meant power. Employees were encouraged to follow the leader. Money and success were valued over relationships and experience. Everyone was on the same fast track: employees complied with the system, did what they were told, and collected a paycheck; customers did what they were told, consumed products, and enriched their lifestyles. This kind of management overlooks quality and satisfaction in all areas, but for a while no one noticed because, collectively, this demonstrated the bigger-is-better and success-equals-materialism values that drove the American business culture and American culture in general.

SOMETHING'S GOTTA GIVE— AT HOME AND AT WORK

In the 1960s, our culture began to change. Throughout that decade and into the 1970s, Americans experienced many events and conditions that made us question our traditional values. As a nation, we were involved in a war in Vietnam that many citizens did not support. We experienced civil unrest, political assassinations, government scandal, a feminist and sexual revolution, and skyrocketing divorce rates. As a society, we began to question our leaders in particular and authority in general. Americans became frustrated—the authorities that they had always looked up to were breaking down. People became isolated and mistrustful and began to look inward to redefine their priorities because looking outward and believing in the traditional American values were no longer sources of security. During this time of transition, there has been a shift in these values.

Many experts believe we are experiencing a crisis in our personal and cultural values today. A *Newsweek* survey asked its readers: "How much do you blame the following for problems that make you dissatisfied?" Of the people who responded, 80 percent indicated that the "moral decline of people in general" is the number one problem. Americans see each other as having no values, no strong moral guidelines.

How do you see yourself? When you consider the relationships and associations in your life, what values are represented? Do you share these values with others?

It may seem that we have come pretty far afield from our original mission to look at corporate culture. But have we? The values of a company are the principles, standards, and actions that people in that organization represent, that is, the things they consider inherently worthwhile and important, for example, how to treat people, how people, organizations and groups conduct business, and what's important to them. Personal values provide the same guidance for individuals. A company's values are critical to its success, and personal values are critical to the success of an individual. Looking at the values and culture of one aspect of your life without considering the effect that other aspects have on it doesn't make any sense. For the past 30 years, the status quo has been changing in this country, people have been reexamining what is important to them and what makes their lives valuable. How does this impact corporate culture?

CORPORATION AND EMPLOYEE: TWO POINTS OF VIEW

Traditional corporate culture is changing in response to the changes in society. The reason is the need for improved productivity and quality, and the demand by employees for more satisfactory working conditions. The low-tech age of mass production and its accompanying hierarchical management is being replaced by the high-tech age of information, where global communication is possible in an instant. Global competition requires management competence and puts pressure on companies to find more creative ways to compete. In a world with shrinking resources and tremendous personal unrest, material considerations are becoming secondary to a sense of self-worth and fulfillment. Corporations are beginning to value individuals for their ideas and participation. And individuals, recognizing that today's career positions are not the permanent, lifelong situations that they were in the past, no longer seek to "sell their souls" to the company and disregard personal satisfaction with their jobs. Considering this issue from different points of view is a good way to understand employer–employee relationships. Let's look at corporate culture today from the point of view of both employer and employee.

The Employee—Looking for Satisfaction

Generally, workers today do not share traditional American work values because they grew up in a world much different than any previous generation. Remember that children absorb their values from their environments from birth forward. The bulk of today's workforce grew up knowing about aspects of adult life that never before influenced a generation of children. The media, primarily television, exposed them to graphic, real-life depictions of war deaths, poverty, racism, sexism, murder, drugs, child abuse, crime, abortion, suicide, pollution, energy shortages, and, probably the most affecting to children, skyrocketing divorce—issues that are difficult enough for adults to absorb, let alone small children. In response to this, children saw, and still see, adults pointing fingers at each other, looking for someone or something to blame for the mess. Is it not difficult to understand why many adults today, raised on images of the negativity in the world and little feeling of protection and security, place more value on an every-person-for-himself perspective rather than trusting outside entities, such as government, community, and parents, to protect them. If traditional American values are not evident in the behaviors of people today, what *is* of value anymore? Life has never held any guarantees, but where does one turn today for firm footing? The intention here is not to join in with the negative, finger-pointing state of values and morality but to emphasize the importance of the role that values play in determining the direction of our lives, our careers, and our families.

For past generations of the American workforce, the only place to go with careers was up. Living standards improved with each generation. This trend soared with job promotions and economic prosperity. Job security came from the company, and as long as the company was successful, it could ensure employment. But the economy has changed. Today, U.S. manufacturers are responding to economic pressures and global competition by downsizing through attrition—many corporate contracts protect the benefits and salaries of older workers, and there simply isn't enough to go around for new hires. Many entry-level jobs are low-paying with no future. Fringe benefits have largely disappeared. Employees are asked to do more for less pay.

Workers are reevaluating what makes them happy in a job. They are no longer equating success with money at the cost of responsibility to friends and family. Workers today want their lives to reflect what they didn't experience as children—security and satisfaction not only from career but from family and personal interests as well. They are looking for companies that will communicate, be honest, encourage involvement, and help employees develop both personally and professionally. Workers today want to be valued for their creativity and contributions. Not all corporations can accommodate these demands, but many are trying.

The Employer—What Corporations Are Facing Today

The rules of the traditional corporate game were that bigger and faster is better; knowledge is to be kept and not shared; money and position are all-powerful; and focus is not as much on quality and employee/customer satisfaction as on the bottom line. A paternalistic attitude existed to encourage blind faith and dependency among employees. The good worker gets a paycheck for loyalty. When greater emphasis was placed on making money than on caring about people, consideration for what was truly valuable was lost.

For corporations as well as individuals, the scene has changed. Companies can no longer offer the benefits and salaries of the past. Employees and customers are demanding satisfaction. But how do employers get more quality work from employees to whom they are offering less in compensation and who now feel no particular loyalty to the corporation? How do corporations meet both employees' and customers' demands for satisfaction while keeping their heads above the surface in today's treacherous economic waters?

Corporations still want to find and keep top-level professionals who work hard for salary and benefits, and they are realizing that they need to help these people develop by providing education and training. The workforce itself has changed. Many qualified women—many of them sole providers for their families—and minorities are bringing cultural diversity and its challenges and opportunities to the workplace. In order to inspire and motivate employees, companies are realizing that they need values clarification and mission statements that can inspire and keep people.

Many corporations realize that management of the future is collaborative and inclusive: Motivated teams participate in decision making rather than looking to the person above them to make a decision that they then carry out. If employers give employees the ability to direct and discipline their own performance through feedback from colleagues and customers, corporations will move toward creating an environment where people can work together to get the job done well.

In summary, American corporations are facing many challenges today. Among them are:

1. Managers and leaders must have the skills to help the firm and its employees deal in the world economy. International business consultant Lawrence Miller says that problem-solving, communication, and team building are among the most important of these skills.

2. Today more than ever, effective employees require motivation beyond financial rewards. Companies must anticipate and meet changing employee needs.

3. It works to the advantage of both the employees and the corporation when employees are encouraged to think creatively, to be self managers, and to retrain when necessary to help accomplish corporate goals.

IT ALL COMES BACK TO VALUES

At the core of the human soul is the search for meaning. Given the frustrating and turbulent past 30 years, people today want meaning and significance in their lives. Do corporations provide meaningful environments? Do they act consistently with a statement of values so that employees feel their efforts on behalf of the organization are personally meaningful and significant? Today, more and more companies—and the people who identify with these companies—care about more than the bottom line. Corporate leaders who want to succeed in today's economy are taking a hard look at values and what their company stands for, and they are communicating these intentions with creative mission statements. Corporate mission statements today are reflecting values different from the past. General Electric's CEO, Jack Welch, took a bold step when he included the following in the company's annual report to stockholders, Wall Street analysts, and potential investors:

> . . . a company where people come to work every day in a rush to try something they woke up thinking about the night before. We want them to go home from work wanting to talk about what they did that day, rather than trying to forget about it. We want factories where the whistle blows and everyone wonders where the time went, and someone suddenly wonders aloud why we need a whistle. We want a company where people find a better way, every day, of doing things; and where by shaping their own work experience, they make their lives better and your company best.

Companies that want to grow encourage workers to participate and take risks, and they motivate employees to broaden consumer choices and encourage business teams to think and act big. But responsibility for making these changes cannot be the sole burden of the company. Employees today must participate in the process. William J. Morin, CEO of an organizational and individual consulting firm, believes that employees share in the responsibility for the value shift in business today. From his book *Silent Sabotage:*

> While management holds many of the cards, employees play a big part. For example, as an employee you must realize that the only way to secure your job in the future is to perform better and more efficiently, rather than blaming every problem on everyone else or on the inefficiency of the organization. You must really see yourself as a leader as well. In the future, employees will essentially become the experts in their jobs or solely responsible for some portion of the process of creating goods and services. (p. 48)

Morin notes that some business leaders do not believe that employees will step up to the challenge of increased responsibility even if they are given the right conditions and tools to do their jobs. These leaders are viewing workers through the worn-out perspective that they are a force with limited potential, rather than a source of untapped strength. The time is right to try a new approach, and Morin adds, "We know what happens when nobody cares. What happens when we do care?"

WHERE DO YOU GO FROM HERE?

This chapter promised to look at personal and corporate goals, and how you, as an individual evaluating your present situation with regard to work, could determine if your personal goals were supported by your workplace. This in-depth look at values is important because individuals and organizations rarely achieve goals that do not fit with their values. Later in this chapter, you will have a chance to think about and list your personal values and, from that, create a list of achievable goals.

If everyone valued the same concepts, harmony and cooperation would be easier, but diversity exists and it is important to prioritize and clarify what you stand for as an individual and as a member of an organization. Just as many corporations are reevaluating their values and policies in order to meet the demands of the changing workforce and the global economy, as an individual, you need to clarify your values and focus on your mission in life so that you can be happy with the work that you do. This includes setting short-term and long-term goals based on what is important to you in your life. Let's look at the process of goal setting.

GOALS

Goal setting is one of the most important tools for gaining control of and focusing your life. According to author and motivator Anthony Robbins: "Human beings are goal-setting individuals. It gives purpose to all human activity. When we aren't seeking goals and making progress in the direction we desire, we stagnate." The process of achieving the goals is as important as the goals themselves. In our journey to fulfill our desires, we create energy and inspiration that impact many others along the way.

There are many things to consider when creating and prioritizing goals. For example, people rarely achieve goals that do not fit with their values. Reaching your goals can impact the lives of your family and friends, so others in your life need to be considered as well. Some goals are long term, and some are short term, so be realistic about the time it will take to achieve your goals. Another important consideration is your motivation, or your reason to succeed: Your success will only be as great as your motivation.

Robbins, in his audiocassette series *Unlimited Power,* offers these five steps to consider when setting goals:

1. State your goal in positive terms. Rather than saying "I will stop smoking," say "I am now a nonsmoker."

2. Be specific. Imagine it, see it. How does it look, feel, smell, taste? In your imagination, experience your goal as being a reality.

3. Have an evidence procedure. What will tell you that your goal has been reached? Many people reach their goals and don't realize it. How will you know when you have achieved it?

4. Be in control. You need to initiate and maintain your goals and not make them contingent upon changes in other people.

5. Be sure that the goal is something you want. What are the consequences? What is the cost of the goal? Imagine it already achieved and see how it affects you, your family, your career.

When setting goals, let go of any limitations you might have in your thinking. If you were guaranteed success, what would you pursue? Be passionate and enthusiastic. Put your heart and soul into the process—after all, you are designing your future!

Linking Personal and Corporate Goals

Your values guide you in the actions you take and define you as a person. You will be more effective if your values and the values of the culture of your life are aligned. You act not just to meet your personal needs but out of a sense of what is important and meaningful to the larger picture of your life. Values motivate and inspire you to move forward to greater achievement, and you are more effective if they align with the work that you do.

Many of the values that are behind the rules by which we live and work are unconscious. People often don't take time to discuss them, but they are the foundation of the rules nonetheless. Think about the rules under which you work. Think about these rules from the point of view of values: What underlying value is represented? For example, if the company has a no-smoking policy, the values represented are respect for others and promotion of good health. If the company has generous policies about parents being absent to stay home with ill children, the value is the importance of family life.

For some companies, expressing commitment to good values is merely window dressing because policies that are in the interest of employees are often not in the immediate interest of the bottom line. Does your company stand behind its rules? For example, if the company has a policy of flexible parent absenteeism, does it then penalize an employee for staying home with a sick child? Or does the organization have a no-smoking policy and then take a large, lucrative contract from a tobacco company?

Believe in Your Vision

In order to be serious about setting and obtaining goals that you want for your life, you must take time to examine your life, define your purpose, and create a vision for your future. In a perfect world, you could define and implement your plan, work toward the desired end, and achieve perfect results. The world, however, often seems to conspire against us, more so in these fast-paced and uncertain times than perhaps ever before. Though frustration and dissatisfaction often motivate you to make changes in the first place, you can waste the creativity and intelligence you need to implement changes if you don't have the positive attitude necessary to believe that the changes you desire are attainable. Once your active, conscious mind designs a concrete plan for reaching goals, engaging your creative, unconscious mind for support is a helpful thing to do.

Once you are clear about where you are going, be positive. Believe your dreams are coming true. Speak as if they are; act as if they are. Envision your success and the positive effect it has on your family, your friends, and you. Positive vision is essential to having your dreams come true.

SUMMARY

Where work was once the consuming aspect of many people's lives in their quest to succeed, for most people entering the workforce today, it is just one aspect. People want to feel satisfied—with a sense of self-worth—at home, at play, and at work. They want to balance their careers and personal lives and are no longer committed just to jobs, professional standards, and company goals. Family life, personal interests, and other work activities are considered.

We have looked at the ways in which American corporate culture is changing and why. Traditional corporate culture that considered only the bottom line is declining and making way for a more enlightened approach to success for companies and individuals. The decline of the traditional business approach is about internal as well as external concerns. Companies recognize that the market is changing from industrialized, mass-production to an electronic market fueled by information that connects us globally in an instant. Companies need improved productivity and quality and are looking for better ways to compete in the global economy. They recognize that the workforce and its motivation is changing from an emphasis on personal material gain to one of personal satisfaction. Companies with existing business structures that do not allow employee participation are changing to accommodate the needs of a workforce with different values than past workers. They are embracing values that understand and promote the new definition of success and values that can inspire and keep good employees.

By thinking about what you have learned in this chapter and working through the exercises that follow, you will have looked at your values, your goals, and your definition of success. How you implement your plan for achieving the future of your dreams is limited only by your vision and determination. Go for it!

Applications & Exercises

Key into Your Life: Opportunity to Apply What You Learn

What Are Your Values?

1.   There's a country-and-western song that states "You've got to stand for somethin' or you'll fall for anything." Your personal values are the qualities that you feel passionate about; they are the principles that guide your behavior so you don't fall for situations or behaviors you will regret. The first step is to take a few minutes and list the things in your life that are most important to you. Consider all the aspects of your life—family, friends, community, work. When you are finished with your list, put a star by the five most important ones and list them below.

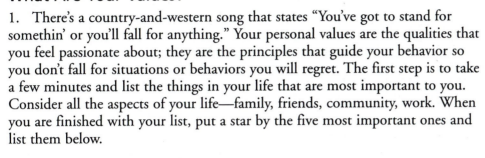

     What values do the top five areas represent? Write the value next to the starred item. Remember, values are concepts, such as honesty, courage, hard work, fairness, and thrift. Values are traits that influence our behavior. If you are committed to having a savings account, you value thrift, which motivates you to be careful with your money. If you consider spending time with your children an important priority, you value family and relationships and are motivated to arrange your schedule to accommodate them.

2.   Personal values are critical to success. What does success mean to you? List four things that make you feel successful, both in your personal life and at work. Consider money/financial stability, material possessions, health, family, and career. Remember to consider that life goes on after we are gone. How does your success contribute to making life better for others?

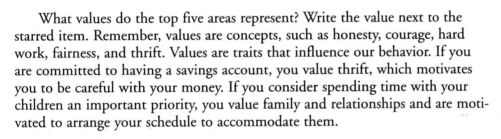

3.   To get started with goal setting, begin by listing your dreams. What are your dreams? Dreams are the desires from which goals are developed. If you can express your dreams, no matter how big and unreachable they seem at this moment, you can work backward and design a plan for achieving them.

     Let's say your dream is to have a home overlooking the ocean on the rugged northwest coast, containing an artist's studio where you produce your widely successful sculptures for the galleries in San Francisco. That may seem like a remote possibility if you are sitting in a two-room apartment working for a low

wage while you complete your education. But if you have your mind on the destination, you can plan the journey from where you are. What can you do now? Continue to perfect your craft? Find places to show your work so it begins to be recognized? Find income resources and develop a financial plan that projects to your desired future? Move to a location that supports what you do? If you want to be an Olympic medalist in running and you now run in the park after work and on weekends, what can you do now to start a path in the direction of your goal? Join a running club? Obtain coaching? Change your daily priorities in order to have more time to train? What goal can you set and reach this week, this month, this year that will bring you one, two, three steps closer to your dream? Consider family, your home environment and the people you live with, where you want to live, finances, career, emotions, health, spirituality, spare time, and creative self-expression. Take a few minutes now to list your dreams on the lines below.

_____

_____

_____

_____

_____

_____

_____

_____

4.   Why do you want your dreams to come true? People need compelling reasons to pursue their goals. *Why* you want something is more important than *how* you do it. The "how" will fall into place if your reason "why" is great enough and inspires enough passion in you. Write a paragraph about why it is important to you for these dreams to come true.

_____

_____

_____

_____

5.   What action steps can you take? Do you need education? discipline? time management? Who do you know that can help you? What resources do you have, both internal and external? Who is doing, or has achieved, what you want that you can learn from and emulate along your path to success? Be realistic and honest about the steps you are willing to take. Arrange them in priority on the blanks below.

_____

_____

_____

_____

Now that we have defined values, goals, and priorities, how do we get a picture of the way all this fits into our work environment?

_____

_____

_____

_____

_____

Key Into Your Life: Opportunities to Apply What You Learn

Earlier in these exercises, you defined what success means to you. Think about your current work environment. Based on your definition of success, can you be successful where you are? In groups, discuss the companies where you work. Does the company offer you the support and opportunity to feel that you are going in the direction you desire, both personally and professionally? If you are not currently working, what working conditions would be required for you to feel successful and realize your goals?

_____

_____

_____

_____

_____

What kind of corporate mission would rally your support? Earlier in the chapter, you considered the rules of your workplace and the values that those rules represented. What values do you want in the place where you work? How do these values compare with those of your classmates?

_____

_____

_____

_____

If you enjoy your work, but question the values of the workplace and corporate goals, what can you do to participate in the company's reexamination of its mission? Far from being presumptuous, taking an active interest in company life is appreciated by many corporations today because it is exactly the kind of involvement they want to encourage from their employees. Finding and keeping good employees is a challenge. Company leaders with vision want to hear from employees about ways to improve productivity and satisfaction. Certainly, you cannot change company policy by yourself, but you might help implement change for an organization that does value its employees and their participation. Who can you talk to—your manager or your coworkers? This is not meant to encourage you to vent or complain about your working conditions—if you're not part of the solution, you're part of the problem! Have a clear idea about how you would like to voice your concerns and some suggestions to offer. Go back to the list of resources that you made earlier and determine if there is anyone who can help.

Key to Self-Expression: Discovery Through Journal Writing

Journal writing is an excellent way to keep track of your progress, for example, the day-to-day successes and challenges you encounter on your journey to a balanced life. Begin a journal by creating an agreement with yourself. What are you willing to do to achieve your ends? Success is often disguised as hard work. Be realistic about your ability to take responsibility for your goals and the actions they will require. What is your motivation, discipline, and perseverance? Write a paragraph about the commitment you intend to make to yourself as part of the process of reaching your goals. As you continue on your journey, review your agreement and determine how well you are keeping it.

Key into Your Personal Portfolio: Your Paper Trail to Success

Along with using your journal to keep track of your personal journey to success, you can keep a file of important articles and documents pertaining to your company and its policies. Keep articles about progress your company and other companies are making with regard to employee relations and corporate policies. These are interesting from a personal perspective and can also serve as resources to support the changes you implement in your life.

References

Goman, Carol K. (1991). *Managing for Commitment.* Crisp Publications, Los Altos, CA.

Miller, Lawrence M. (1985). *American Spirit: Visions of a New Corporate Culture.* William Morrow and Company, New York.

Morin, William J. (1995). *Silent Sabotage.* AMACOM (American Management Association), New York.

Robbins, Anthony (1986). *Unlimited Power.* Simon & Schuster, New York.

Scott, Cynthia D., Jaffe, Dennis T., and Tobe, Glenn R. (1993). *Organizational Vision, Values, and Mission.* Crisp Publications, Menlo Park, CA.

16

BECOMING INDISPENSABLE IN A DISPOSABLE WORLD

How to Become and Remain Marketable

In this chapter, you will explore answers to the following questions:

➤ How can you, as an employee, meet world-class standards?

➤ How do you become "indispensable"?

➤ Can you believe in your talents and work to develop them?

➤ Can you stay abreast of technology?

➤ How can you make sure that you and the job fit each other?

➤ What does it mean to "insure" your career?

? Thinking It Through

Check those statements that apply to you right now:

❑ The world is changing so quickly that I'm not sure I can keep up.

❑ I don't feel as valuable to my employer as I would like—I'm not sure I have the right workplace know-how.

❑ My life isn't as balanced as it needs to be; my leisure time is often compromised by school work or long work hours.

TRANSFORM

16

BECOMING INDISPENSABLE IN A DISPOSABLE WORLD

How to Become and Remain Marketable

Our world is changing. Consider a few of the transformations that have taken place in just the past forty years: Men and women in the 1990s are now tested for drugs at the workplace; advised to learn Japanese to enhance their careers; prohibited from smoking on the job; successfully suing former employers for having been fired or given a bad reference; choosing doctors and lawyers from newspaper ads; going to jail for misusing insider information; failing to advance because of a lack of basic computer skills; having children through surrogate mothers; choosing from hundreds of TV channels; donating eyes and hearts to organ banks (or receiving them); jogging five miles a day; stopping to grab a bite at one of three dozen fast food outlets in the neighborhood; transmitting memos instantaneously all over the world via fax machines; and routinely making telephone calls from cars.

As we head toward the millennium, jobs as we once knew them continue to change. In some companies, titles, corner offices, and clear hierarchies no longer exist. Today's world is one where mergers and technology have rewritten old rules about counting on lifetime employment with a firm. You are required to be not only an individual contributor, but also a team member and innovator. Yet it's also a world where virtues such as loyalty, honesty, and hard work are still keys to advancement. It's a world where how you dress, how you write the English language, how you behave, and how you treat others—both above and below you in an organization—vitally affect how far up the ladder you go. It's a world where little things can make huge differences.

WORLD-CLASS STANDARDS

For most of this century, as this nation took its goods and know-how to the world, America did not have to worry about competition from abroad. At home, the technology of mass production emphasized discipline to the assembly line. Today, the demands on businesses and workers are different. Firms must meet world-class standards, and so must workers.

The qualities of high performance that characterize our most competitive companies must become the standard for the vast majority of businesses, large and small, local and global. By "high performance" we mean work settings relentlessly committed to excellence, product quality, and customer satisfaction. These goals are pursued by combining technology and people in new ways. Decisions must be made closer to the front line, drawing upon the abilities of workers to think creatively and solve problems. Above all, these goals depend on people: managers committed to high performance and the competence of their workforce and responsible employees who are comfortable with technology and complex systems, skilled as members of teams, and have a passion for continuous learning.

The Bad News First

"Fired? It can't happen to me." Statistics say it can. One of every four people will be fired at some point in their lives (based on a nationwide survey of personnel directors and top executives published by ADECCO Placement Services in Oakbrook, Illinois). This statistic is not referring to the loss of jobs while in high school and college. It's talking about *you*—an educated, skilled, and valuable employee. Even worse, of the 25 percent of American men and women who will be fired at some point, 20 percent will not deserve to lose their jobs. Why is this happening?

Bankruptcies, Mergers, and Takeovers

Not long ago, companies chose bankruptcy as a last resort, a legal remedy to crushing debt, and through restructuring, a chance to pull themselves out of a financial mess and continue in business. During the same era, bankruptcy carried with it a stigma; those who were forced to seek it as a shelter—businesses and individuals alike—felt shame and frustration at ending up in that position.

Today, however, bankruptcy has become a management tool. Stalemates in union negotiations are broken by the company's entry into Chapter 11, which forces unions to lower their demands on the company when it emerges from protective bankruptcy as a "new" company.

Mergers are another popular trend that can cost you your job and cut down on the number of opportunities for better jobs in your future. The value of mergers and acquisitions has reached an all-time high in recent years. When two companies merge, instantly resulting in two vice-presidents of sales, two controllers, and two of just about everything else, it doesn't take a genius to realize some people have to go. This tumultuous atmosphere raises a number of obvious questions:

1. How can I protect my job if my company is taken over?
2. How can I read the signals regarding my future with a company that has been acquired?
3. How am I preparing myself in the event I lose my job?
4. What are some advantages I might exploit in a merger or takeover?

The Good News

One good thing has come out of the chaos of our merger mania: being unemployed no longer automatically carries a stigma. It's expected that people will hold a variety of positions throughout their professional lives, not only because they choose to move more often, but because they will be laid off more than once. Today, it is estimated nine out of ten executives fired are victims of company mergers, acquisitions, or workforce reductions. Being out of work is no longer something to be ashamed of. You're in good company.

How can you turn this situation to your advantage? Remember the old saying "Necessity is the mother of invention"? That's probably true philosophically, but women and men who live by it in their working lives are headed for trouble. When your company is acquired—and you're fired—is not the time to begin thinking about getting another job. People expecting success in this world need to start operating from the basic assumption that they will have to look for another job at some point in their careers, whether they want to or not. In other words, be ready to be fired, even in the best days of your job. Robert Half suggests keeping a *personal personnel file*. Don't rely on your memory after years on your present job. Write down every achievement in your present job and file it: how you contributed to the efficiency of your department, cut costs, increased profits, or brought in a new client.

Continually develop your knowledge base and skills to increase your marketability. At any time, you should know of three or four other jobs you could do should you lose your present one. This may sound like a daunting task, but if you prepare yourself for change as you go along, you'll be ready for the unexpected. Being laid off or fired isn't the end of the world; in fact, it may be the very thing that propels you into a job you love.

TODAY'S EMPLOYEE-FRIENDLY WORK ENVIRONMENT

Although you may feel anxious about the lack of security in today's job market, there's probably never been a better time for you to deepen your career roots. That's because companies have never been as "employee friendly" as they are today. Workers are no longer viewed as just cogs in the wheel. Your creativity and ideas are welcome, even expected.

Human resource departments and executive officers are deliberately fashioning work environments that promote employee happiness and satisfaction. They are taking into account that employees aren't mechanical robots but human beings with thoughts, feelings, and aspirations about their roles in the workforce.

Today's competitive workplace, however, can also cause significant pressures on family and personal life. The management of stress has become a priority in the business world. Enlightened organizations offer support services to ease the tension and strain of modern life. You are encouraged to take advantage of counseling and crisis intervention services because employers have finally learned a very simple yet profound concept: if the employee is happy, the customer will be, too. It's the ultimate trickle-down effect.

With these newfangled perks also come greater employee responsibility and accountability. Employers expect performance. Today more than ever, employees are being paid to think. "We look at people as more than a pair of hands," said Don Soderquist, Chief Operating Officer and Vice Chairman of Wal-Mart, the nation's largest private employer, with 687,000 employees. "We look to them as a source of new ideas." For example, an employee in Crowley, Louisiana came up with the idea of "people greeters" at the entrance to the store, which is now implemented nationwide.

BECOMING INDISPENSABLE

With so much change and fierce competition, how can you make yourself indispensable on the job? First, recognize that change is constant. You may have escaped downsizing, but now you work overtime to compensate for all those bodies that are no longer there. You may have relied on your college degree to get you to retirement, but now you realize your skills need a major overhaul. You may even be thinking about switching careers to find work you love. Regardless of your situation, there are some steps you can take to become truly indispensable.

Make Sure the Job Fits

To be truly effective (and thus indispensable), you must love what you do. If you're in a job that doesn't fit your values, temperament, and skills, it will be an uphill battle. People who find working with numbers boring shouldn't become accountants. If they are accountants, they should use their background as a path to something else—such as selling tax services to the accounting profession.

This sounds simple, but countless people choose professions and occupations because they're "glamorous" or offer big money, without regard for whether they're equipped for that field. Define what success means to you. Many executives are jumping off the corporate ladder and into less lucrative jobs because of their desire for meaningful work. Don't let yourself get stuck in a career rut. Think creatively about your options. Ask yourself, "In what other job arena could I use my skills?"

Avail yourself of guidance and career counseling services in your area. Many offer testing services to give you a more focused and unbiased analysis of your true career potential in any given profession or job area. There are a number of books that accurately describe jobs and fields of work; a careful reading will give you a pretty good indication of what's demanded of individuals seeking success in those fields.

Most people have to feel that what they do makes some difference in the world. Few things are as rewarding as the knowledge that our gifts are benefiting society, even if indirectly. If you can answer *yes* to the following questions, you have a great job: Do I like it? Am I good at it? Does the world need it? If you answer *no* to any of them, you'll probably be unhappy in your work and therefore less effective.

Sometimes the problem is not that you're unsuited to the work, but that you're in a company culture that doesn't fit your style or values. In that case, your task is to find the culture that fits you. Throughout your career, you must continually ask yourself the above questions, because the answers may change as you mature. Analyze your real motives and the real you, then get moving. Eventually, you'll find work you love.

Believe in Your Talents and Develop Them

You may think, "Lots of people can do what I do." You're right. A lot of people can type a letter, drive a truck, write a memo, install a phone line. *But no one can do it the exact same way you can.* All the things that make you unique—your voice inflection, the grip of your handshake, your facial gestures, your personality, your life's perspective—are unlike anyone else's in the world. Your skills are valuable and worthy, not because they stand alone, but because the bearer of these talents is a human being. You carry out functions, which we call a *job,* differently than anyone else. You are valuable, you are needed, and, in the purest meaning of the word, you are truly indispensable.

Secondly, to become and remain marketable, you must invest time and energy in developing your talents. The biblical parable in the book of Matthew, Chapter 25, reveals an important truth about the cultivation of our talents: If you don't *use* them you will *lose* them. "The major purpose in life should be the exploration and development of all your talents," says Kawanza Kunjufu, educational consultant for *African-American Images* of Chicago. If you think only a select few in this world are gifted with talents and you're not included, you're sorely mistaken. Make the most of yourself; everyone benefits when you do.

Stay Abreast of Technology

Most of us seem to fall on one side of the fence or the other when it comes to technology: We either love it and are excited about the possibilities, or we hate it and wish we could go back to "simpler" days. To the latter group, technology looms like a monstrous mountain. Regardless of your technical inclinations, keeping abreast of this pervasive industry is vital to career success. And although you may not be able to tame the wild beast of technological advancement, it can be harnessed to serve your purposes. In the process, you may even discover talents you didn't know you had.

"Human beings are capable of doing things we never thought of before, especially our capacity to think logically," explains Donald R. Ingram, senior professor at DeVry Institute of Technology in Chicago. "You might be a great programmer but never thought of it; or a great commercial artist, but you've only done art for beauty. An auto mechanic can become a technician repairman or vice versa. My advice to today's worker is be *open-minded.* Look into areas of technology you've never considered." Here are several practical steps you can take to do just that.

1. Go to your local bookstore and peruse the technical magazines on the racks. Find one that interests you. Do the same at public and college libraries. Subscribe to one and read it. They provide a wealth of information.

2. Attend technology shows, which are usually advertised in trade publications.

3. Take a beginners' technology course at a local college. This will immerse you in the environment of technical learning, helping you become familiar with terminology and concepts.

4. If you haven't already done so, purchase a minimal home computer from *one* retail source; that way, if you need technical assistance you call only one telephone number. To find a good computer package, browse a computer outlet and write down the names and prices of the ones that interest you. Take your list home and look up the same computers in the index section of a computer sales magazine. Compare prices. Select one that fits your budget and meets your needs.

5. Learn basic computer skills, which means you should become familiar with the following (in order of complexity):
   ➤ Word processing
   ➤ The creation of a spreadsheet
   ➤ A drawing/graphics program
   ➤ Programming. The hot languages are JAVA, related to the Internet, user-friendly; C++, difficult to learn but opens doors to many technical jobs; and Visual Basic, whose name is self-explanatory.

6. Purchase a subscription to the Internet. You will need a modem of 28,800 bps or faster. Cruising the Internet will help keep you up-to-date and give you access to a vast array of information.

"Don't be discouraged if you're going to school late in life. Some of my best students are mature, seasoned employees," says Ingram. "They have two things that the young whipper-snappers don't have: experience and discipline. The ability to learn diminishes very slowly. Sixty-year-old men and women have 90% of the same ability to learn as they did at age twenty. You're never too old to learn," he says.

Behave Like an Entrepreneur

No matter how big the company you work for is, the only way to navigate the inevitable upheavals is to act as if you were in business for yourself. Make sure you know your value to the organization. Business leaders have trouble finding workers who'll take responsibility for making good things happen. Too many people have become institutionally dependent, blaming others, looking for someone else to take responsibility.

The first step in becoming a "career entrepreneur" is to look objectively at your skills and figure out what is missing. For instance, go to the personnel department and ask recruiters what skills they seek in new hires. That will give you a clue as to which skills your employer currently values. Also, check your newspaper and make a list of the skills and qualities businesses seek. Study this list and choose at least one skill and one qualification that you can either hone or add to your professional repertoire. Find a way to improve your skills and learn new ones. If your company does not offer training, find courses at local colleges and attend seminars in your field.

Another way to increase your value to a company is to make yourself so visible that managers in search of new staff might consider you, rather than look outside. Is there an internal employee publication? If so, seek out the chance to write for it. Also, continue to sharpen your writing skills and submit material to trade magazines in your industry or profession.

Third, know your industry. Attend conferences, join associations, and maintain a network of colleagues outside and inside your company. The idea is to expand your knowledge to become more effective.

Seek Feedback

Job forecasters predict that within five years everyone will have to do a "360-degree" review. Here's how it works: You get feedback on your performance from everyone you work with: colleagues, those in other departments, subordinates, superiors, customers, and suppliers. You don't get a promotion just because your boss thinks you're great—you get one only if your peers, your boss, and those who report to you give you good marks. The more this happens, the more it will drive the democratization of the workplace. Everyone will have a vote on you. And if you don't get good votes, you won't get ahead.

If your company hasn't instituted 360-degree reviews, you can do your own, informally. Use three words: *continue, stop,* and *start.* Ask people face-to-face or send a memo they can return anonymously. Say, "I'm trying to become more effective, and I'd appreciate your feedback. What should I continue to do? What should I stop doing? What would you suggest I start doing?" Do that every six months, or at least once a year, and you will be amazed how powerful it is.

Move Beyond Mentors

In the old, hierarchical organization, you needed a mentor to get ahead. Someone taught you the ropes and championed you to the "right" people. Often, mentors—invariably white men—chose people in their own image, bypassing women and minorities.

The rules have changed. Now every employee must not only do his or her job, but must also expend extra effort and drive to help the company compete globally. Your company is interested in your development, but it won't have a tutor standing by.

Instead, you can take responsibility for setting up your own mentoring process. Today this is called "modeling." A model is someone you identify with, someone you admire. Find a good team player who takes initiative and study how he or she behaves. Or set up study groups. Choose 20 people in the same business who are not your direct competitors, and set up meetings quarterly or monthly to share what's happening in your industry.

Think Teams

More and more companies are moving to teams to gain a competitive edge. Working on a team adds another dimension to work. Not only must you be competent as an individual contributor; you must also be able to work with others to produce a desired result. When teams work well together, they can accomplish more than the sum of their parts.

The most important skill needed for teamwork is empathy. You must really listen to others and be able to put yourself in their shoes. Solicit everyone's input, and be sure to give yours. Back up your position with data and pertinent information. When looking for solutions to problems, the ideal is win/win: Everyone is happy with the result. But sometimes you have to go for win/lose, or find a compromise where you meet halfway.

Take Risks

We live in a world of uncertainty. You may feel victimized by external forces, but don't buy into the victim mentality. Be willing to foster change and reject the status quo. It's up to you to shape your future. In your company, find a need, then take initiative to fill that need. Do not look to the business for direction. Build good relationships with others instead of focusing on others' weaknesses. If you do these things, your world will offer opportunity, increasing responsibility, and increasing financial and emotional rewards.

Be A Problem Solver

In the new work environment, you will have to tackle problems outside your immediate area. At Ritz-Carlton Hotels, for example, a waiter who gets a complaint from a guest about a broken TV calls engineering and then follows up to be sure the repair has been completed. "An employee who does whatever is necessary for the guest's well-being is truly exceptional. They will benefit from taking this initiative," says President Horst Schultze.

Learn to Be Literate

Our ability to communicate clearly and quickly these days is facilitated by technology that was only science-fiction speculation forty years ago. Yet so many of our young adults in the workforce, including those who seem to aspire to much better jobs, are woefully undereducated in such things as international and domestic geography, economics, history, writing, and even reading.

We've become an age of specialists, which, despite its advantages in many situations, breeds groups of people whose focus is upon their specialty only, without any understanding of how what they do fits into the much larger and complex puzzle of business and fife.

Consider this: It's estimated by the U. S. Department of Education (DOE) that 25 million American adults—one in seven—are functional illiterates, who can't read, write, calculate, or solve problems even at a level allowing them to accomplish simple tasks. The DOE indicates that 45 million adults working today are either functionally or marginally illiterate. Functionally illiterate adults account for about 30 percent of unskilled workers, 29 percent of semiskilled workers, and 11 percent of all managers, professionals, and technicians. That's scary. Estimates vary, but a median figure, based on government statistics, would be that adult illiteracy costs this country an estimated $225 billion annually in lost productivity, lost tax revenues, prison support, crime, and other related social ills.

If you happen to be a highly literate person, particularly in verbal and written communication, good for you, but don't be smug: You might have a way with words but, at the same time, be an *innumerate*. Innumerates are people illiterate in mathematics. The Educational Testing Service conducted an extensive survey of how "math-smart" our high school students are. The results were appalling—and they were dealing with *basic* math.

We seem to be no better at teaching geography. The majority of students in another survey could not point to the United States on a world map.

Obviously, the problems of illiteracy, innumeracy, and geographical ignorance are pervasive in our work world. Imagine your edge if you're able to communicate verbally and in writing and have a basic understanding of practical mathematics and simple economics.

To distill this chapter to one suggestion for becoming an indispensable employee . . .*get smart*. And don't stop learning as long as you're breathing.

Let Your Conscience Be Your Guide

If you meticulously carry out the above ten suggestions, but fail to do the same with this one, you taint all other good intentions. If you're seeking to become an indispensable employee, the word *ethics* could be the most important word in your vocabulary, rivaled only perhaps by *loyalty*.

In the workplace, unethical behavior can take many forms. Workers are unethical when they fail to work hard, dishonestly account for their time and expenses, and steal an employer's time. They are clearly unethical when they reveal trade secrets to competitors or create resumes that do not honestly represent their background and skills.

Employers—on the other side of the ethical coin—may practice unethical business behavior because of unabashed greed and a lack of social responsibility. The fact is that an employer's pattern of doing business will often affect the conduct of employees throughout their work lives, for better or worse. Nothing lowers office morale more than a boss who treats workers unfairly. The reverse is also true. Fair and ethical treatment of workers creates an atmosphere of trust and a sense that "we're in this together."

As we learn from the Bible's Golden Rule, it's a good idea to treat others the way you want to be treated. Those are words to live by both in and out of the office setting. As you groom yourself for greatness, remember, ethical behavior is always in style. You cannot become an indispensable employee without it.

BALANCE YOUR LIFE

Author Stephen C. Covey, in his book *The 7 Habits of Highly Successful People*, advises people to write a personal mission statement outlining their priorities in life. Usually, this includes some combination of work, family, and community. "It's essential to know what's important to you and that you can organize your life so you say *'yes'* to what's most important and *'no'* to what's unimportant or not as important," writes Covey.

Always being the last to leave the office does not make you an indispensable employee. In fact, those who work long hours for extended periods are prone to burnout. The trick is to develop clear priorities, honor your commitments, and keep a balance in life.

Make the Most of Leisure

One way to ensure balance is by making the most of your leisure time. How does leisure pertain to becoming an indispensable employee? At first, the idea of leisure enhancing your work may sound contradictory. Nothing could be further from the truth. There are two good reasons to make the most of your nonworking hours. First, engaging in an avocation opens up windows to the world. You are therefore more interesting and, consequently, more marketable than a person who is one-dimensional. Second, in case you haven't discovered this nugget of truth already, it is often during leisure activities that your mind is free to roam and some of your best ideas pop to the surface. And here's an added bonus: Perhaps your boss or coworkers have similar extracurricular interests and hobbies. In fact, become familiar with their outside recreations and develop at least enough knowledge of them to become conversant on the subject.

If you have small children, much of your off time will be spent with your family. However, you still need time for yourself to reflect, exercise, and develop friendships. Your free time should consist of activities that refresh you. This sounds easy, but it can be difficult considering how many things clamor for our attention.

Dr. John Oswald, an ordained minister in the United Methodist Church and author of the book *The Leisure Crisis,* believes we in the Western world face a dilemma about what to do with our free time. He writes:

> If we are to have any hope of making leisure a more humanizing experience rather than a dehumanizing one, we must come to some healthy understanding of the concept. Primarily, the idea is a negative one today. It is not doing something. To an alarming extent it is caught up in passivity. The growth of spectator sports is one manifestation of this. A much more detrimental manifestation is the voyeurism that accounts for the stellar increase in pornography in this country. But leisure at its heart is not negative. Leisure is the freedom to pursue an art or a skill that is not a means to an end. . . . Human beings alone have decorated their tools and have sought pleasing forms for their vessels. They alone have made songs and poems for the sheer joy of it. We have the opportunity to amplify our uniqueness by leaps and bounds through leisure.

As a first step toward thinking for yourself about this issue, take a couple of minutes now to answer some questions. Don't worry; you can't flunk! Be perfectly honest with yourself.

1. How do you define the word *leisure?*
2. How do you feel about leisure? Why?
3. What causes you to feel creative? Why?
4. Who are the most leisured people you know? Why?

5. If you had five free days and could go anywhere you wanted and do anything you wanted, where would you go and what would you do? Why?

6. On a scale of 1 to 10, with 10 being highest, rate the importance of leisure in your life. Why did you choose that particular rating?

7. What do you think would help you enjoy your leisure time more?

Your "Dream" Job

Successful, happy people are those who seek and find positive aspects of their present jobs. They are also people who extend grace when others make mistakes. These people know that no job is perfect no boss an ideal human being and manager. They practice loyalty to their current employers by working hard and giving it their all, while looking to the future and preparing for their next move.

Abraham Maslow, the pioneering psychologist, studied people who were happy and well adjusted, rather than focusing on those who weren't. He found that happy people enjoy "peak experiences" in their everyday lives. They take pleasure in the task at hand, no matter how far removed it might be from the dream job they hope to get one day. When your work life is viewed in this positive light, a more realistic evaluation of how successful you really are emerges. For well-adjusted, realistic people, your dream job is often the one you're doing right now. You just have to open yourself up to that possibility. When you do, you move closer to becoming an indispensable employee.

WORKPLACE KNOW-HOW

Recently, the U. S. Department of Labor and Secretary's Commission spent 12 months talking to business owners, public employers, union officials, and workers on the lines and at their desks. The message conveyed to us by these individuals was the same across the country and in every kind of job: Good jobs depend on people who can put knowledge to work. New workers must be creative, responsible problem solvers and have skills and attitudes on which employers can build.

Traditional jobs are changing and new jobs are created every day. In fact, the U. S. Department of Labor says almost half the jobs we are presently doing will no longer exist 20 years from now. They predict technology will usher in new jobs to replace many old ones. High-paying, unskilled jobs are disappearing. Employers and employees share the belief that all workplaces must "work smarter."

From these conversations, the U. S. Department of Labor identified five competencies and three foundational skills and personal qualities needed for solid job performance. These are the following:

Competencies—Effective workers can productively use:

1. Resources—allocating time, money, materials, space, and staff.

2. Interpersonal Skills—working in teams, teaching others, serving customers, leading, negotiating, and working well with people from culturally-diverse backgrounds.

3. Information—acquiring and evaluating data, organizing and maintaining files, interpreting and communicating, and using computers to process information.

4. Systems—understanding social, organizational, and technological systems; monitoring and correcting performance; and designing or improving systems.
5. Technology—selecting equipment and tools, applying technology to specific tasks, and maintaining and troubleshooting technologies.

The Foundation—Competence requires:

1. Basic Skills—reading, writing, arithmetic and mathematics, speaking, and listening.
2. Thinking Skills—thinking creatively, making decisions, solving problems, seeing things in the mind's eye, knowing how to learn and reason.
3. Personal Qualities—individual responsibility, self-esteem, sociability, self-management, and integrity.

Real Life

Today's jobs require even the basic skills—the old "3 Rs"—to take on a new meaning. First, you have to read well enough to understand and interpret diagrams, directories, correspondence, manuals, records, charts, graphs, tables and specifications. Without the ability to read a diverse set of materials, workers cannot locate the descriptive and quantitative information needed to make decisions or recommend courses of action. What do these reading requirements mean on the job? They might involve:

➤ interpreting blueprints and materials catalogs
➤ dealing with letters and written policy on complaints
➤ reading patients' medical records and medication instructions
➤ reading text of technical manuals from equipment vendors.

At the same time, most jobs call for writing skills to prepare correspondence, instructions, charts, graphs, and proposals, in order to make requests, explain, illustrate, and convince. On the job this might require:

➤ writing memoranda to justify resources or explain plans
➤ preparing instructions for operating simple machines
➤ developing a narrative to explain graphs or tables
➤ drafting modifications in company procedures.

Mathematics and computational skills are also essential. Many employees are required to maintain records, estimate results, use spreadsheets, or apply statistical process controls as they negotiate, identify trends, and suggest new courses of action. Most of us do not leave mathematics behind in school. Instead, we find ourselves using it on the job, for example, for:

➤ reconciling differences between inventory and financial records
➤ estimating discounts on the spot, while negotiating sales
➤ using spreadsheet programs to monitor expenditures
➤ employing statistical process control procedures to check quality
➤ projecting resource needs for the next planning period.

Finally, very few of you will work totally by yourselves. More and more, work involves listening carefully to clients and coworkers and clearly articulating your own point of view. Today's worker has to listen and speak well enough to explain schedules and procedures, communicate with customers, work in teams, understand customer concerns, describe complex systems and procedures, probe for hidden meanings, teach others, and solve problems. On the job these skills may translate readily into:

- ➤ training new workers or explaining new schedules to work teams
- ➤ describing plans to supervisors or clients
- ➤ questioning customers to diagnose malfunctions
- ➤ answering questions from customers about post-sales service

"INSURING" YOUR CAREER

Every technique in this chapter can be summed up under the concept of "career insurance." We're all comfortable with the idea of insurance for our homes, health, cars, and lives, but is it possible to buy career insurance?

Yes, and it is even more important in this tumultuous day and age than ever before. The premiums you have to pay to insure your career aren't expensive in terms of dollars and cents. Money does have to be spent on a decent wardrobe; business, trade, and professional subscriptions; an answering machine; good stationery; and other tangible assets every indispensable employee must possess. But the real cost is paid through your hard work.

Here is a recap of what your indispensable insurance portfolio should include: The more extensive and up-to-date your network of contacts, the more job insurance you own. If you've created the *personal personnel file* cataloging your contributions to the workplace, the amount of job insurance is even higher. It takes effort to seek out and obtain those publications that will give you greater visibility within your company and industry, but it's worth it. Although continuing your education will cost you both time and money, the value of your job insurance portfolio continues to grow. If you've taken the time and effort to learn to communicate better as a speaker and in writing, that adds to your coverage, too. Keeping abreast of technology is another essential component to carrying adequate career insurance.

Most importantly, when looking to insure your career, view your work life not in terms of one job after another or one job for a long period of time. Rather, the maximum amount of career insurance is obtained when you view your work life as a continuous progression, a series of steps carefully considered, prepared for, and taken. Then you will have developed a firm grounding and understanding of the principles for building a successful lifetime career.

SUMMING UP

The world has always been challenging. For most professionals, the world is becoming more complicated and the changes so profound it's hard for any of us to keep up with it. Those who cope best, however, become most successful and are better able to improve their current jobs or locate better ones elsewhere. These days you remain marketable by anticipating change and seizing the opportunities it awards. You become indispensable when you do those things well.

Application & Exercises

1. How Have Successful People or Companies Stayed on Top?

Think for a moment about a person or big name company that has existed in the public eye for many years (examples Coca-Cola, McDonald's, Madonna). Ask yourself why they have survived and others have faded through the years. Jot down some of your thoughts.

Questions to consider:

➤ How have they adapted to changing circumstances?

_____

_____

➤ How have they stayed in touch with their audience or consumer?

_____

_____

➤ What personal changes might the individuals have had to overcome?

_____

_____

Think about people you know who have successfully evolved with the workaday world.

➤ What character traits stand out in them?

_____

_____

➤ What do people say about them?

_____

_____

➤ How do they spend their time?

_____

_____

➤ What are their work habits?

_____

_____

If possible, take one or more of these individuals out to lunch and pick their brains about these issues.

2. The Pluses and Minuses of Progress

Having read this chapter, list five traits about yourself that make you indispensable on the job.

1. _____
2. _____
3. _____
4. _____
5. _____

Now list five traits that have caused you problems in the workplace and keep you from being indispensable on the job.

1. _____
2. _____
3. _____
4. _____
5. _____

Accurately assess your weaknesses and ask yourself:

➤ Do I want to grow in these areas?

_____

➤ Have I read any books or materials to help me improve?

_____

➤ Do I know someone at my office who does these things well?

_____

➤ Is this person or someone else available to give me some pointers?

_____

Key Question: Am I willing to change?

_____

3. Finding a Balance

Take a few moments and answer these questions:

➤ What motivates me at work?

_____

_____

➤ How do I respond to negative feedback?

_____

_____

➤ What is the purpose for leisure in my life?

_____

_____

➤ What do I really want from work?

_____

_____

Complete these statements:

➤ My "dream job" is . . .

_____

_____

➤ I want to grow in the marketplace so I can . . .

_____

_____

➤ To broaden my skill base starting today, I would need to take these five steps:

1. _____

2. _____

3. _____

4. _____

5. _____

➤ When I have trouble keeping my focus and reaching my goals, I follow these steps to help me:

1. _____

2. _____

3. _____

4. _____

5. _____

➤ Leisure helps me to . . .

_____

_____

➤ Ten words to keep in mind to get where I want to be are (example: commitment):

1. _____   6. _____

2. _____   7. _____

3. _____   8. _____

4. _____   9. _____

5. _____   10. _____

4. How Can I Put Shoes on My Feet of Progress?

➤ Ask yourself this question, "What keeps me from taking a chance and moving on?" (Examples: Fear of change, procrastination, feeling overwhelmed.) Be honest with yourself.

_____

_____

➤ Sometimes career and personal growth seems overwhelming. The goal is manageable, however, if we break it down into smaller tasks. Start by doing one or two activities to move you in the right direction. Fight the urge to solve problems overnight. Take your time and plan logical "baby" steps.

Now list five practical activities you are not already doing. (Example: Take a computer class.)

1. _____
2. _____
3. _____
4. _____
5. _____

➤ Now select one of these and decide to take action. (Example: Spend one hour checking on how to enroll in a computer class at a local community college. The first step is to obtain a listing of college courses from the campus of your choice. Start the process by calling the registration office.)

Complete this statement: This week I am going to . . .

_____

_____

➤ Set aside a day and time of the week to do this.

On _____ at _____ I will accomplish this task.

➤ Decide what your reward will be for accomplishing each activity on your list. (Example: when I complete a four-week computer course, I will take a weekend vacation at the beach.)

1. _____
2. _____
3. _____
4. _____
5. _____

➤ Sit down and write a personal contract with yourself to complete the above steps. Have someone you know hold you accountable for them.

_____

_____

_____

_____

_____

17 DRESS FOR SUCCESS
Making a Professional Impression

In this chapter, you will explore answers to the following questions:

➤ Why is your appearance so important at work?

➤ What does your appearance say about you?

➤ What should you wear to a job interview?

➤ How do you know what to wear to your new job?

➤ What should you wear on "casual Friday"?

? Thinking It Through

Check those statements that currently apply to you:

❑ I think my appearance reflects who I am.

❑ If I had a job interview tomorrow, I know exactly what I'd wear.

❑ I try hard to look my best most of the time.

❑ I do wardrobe maintenance weekly.

❑ I like my wardrobe and feel confident in my work clothes.

❑ I know and use a good tailor.

❑ I watch for store sales on things I need for my work wardrobe.

I M P R E S

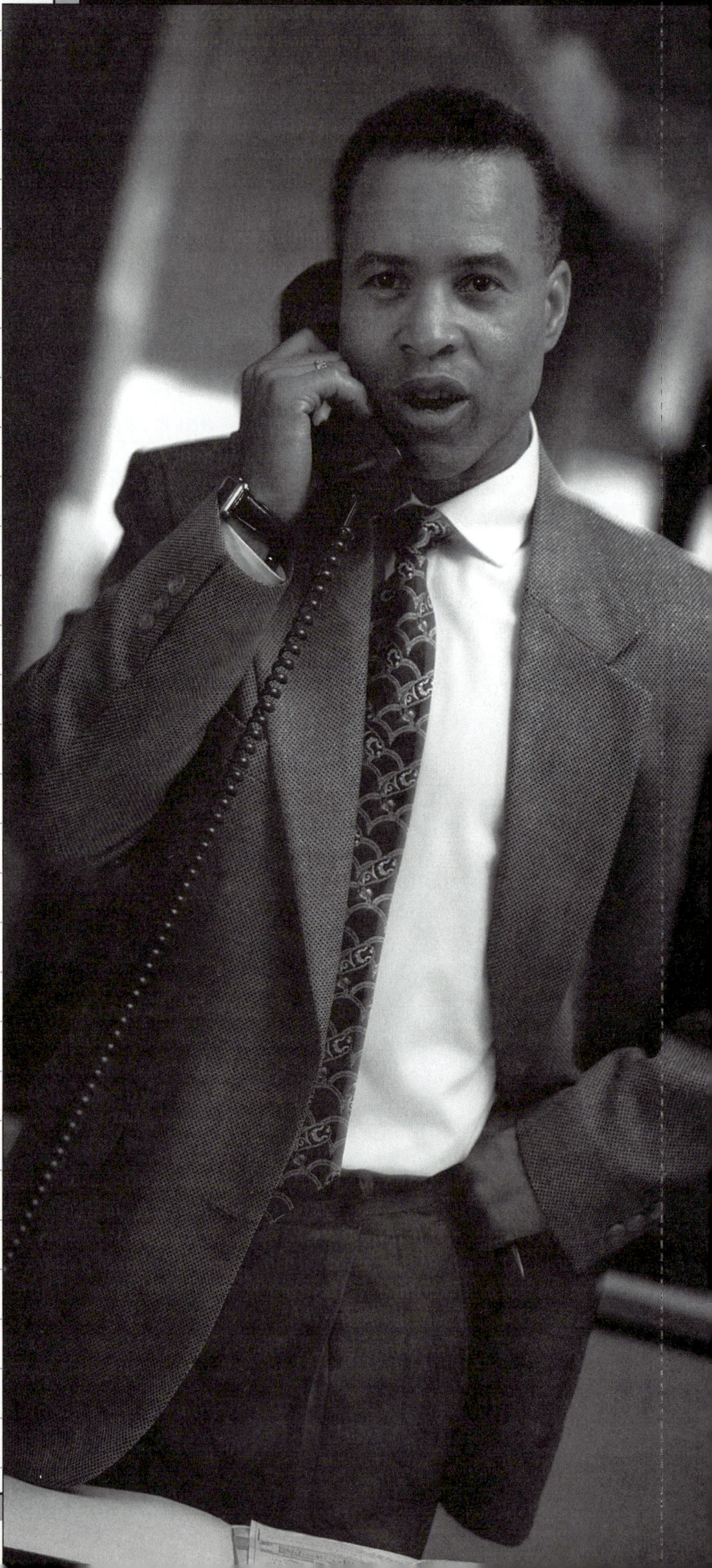

17

DRESS FOR SUCCESS
Making a Professional Impression

An old saying states that, "You can't judge a book by its cover." In a perfect world, that may be true, but in the working world, you are judged by the way you look. Your "cover" is the first impression you give to people. Compared to the other candidates for a job, you could have the highest level of education, be the most intelligent, have the best ideas, or have the best work ethic, but if you don't present yourself well—if you don't surround it all with a sharp looking "cover"—you may not get the opportunity to show off all your other wonderful qualities.

And once you've started a job, it's important to maintain a reputation of looking sharp on a daily basis. Your coworkers, and more importantly your boss, are paying attention to how you present yourself. If you take pride in your appearance, it reflects that you take pride in your work.

At first glance, it may sound superficial or unfair; however, we're talking not about how good-looking you are, but about how you present yourself. What matters is that you take the time to pay attention to details in your appearance. Your clothes and your grooming are aspects of your appearance that you have control over—where your efforts can affect the outcome—unlike the bone structure you were born with. Make the most with what you've got.

Of course, it's very difficult to give blanket dress code rules or grooming standards since what is appropriate for the workplace is as diverse as what your duties at your job are. Keep in mind that different companies, different parts of the country, and different job duties all factor in to deciding what is best to wear. And dress codes in the 1990s are constantly evolving—becoming more relaxed in many places. There are some basic rules to follow, however, and those generalizations are what will be discussed here.

So how do you package yourself in the most appealing way? How do you present yourself in a way that is both appropriate and desirable? How do you dress for success? Let's explore.

THE INTERVIEW

Obviously, the first chance you have to sell yourself in the business world is at a job interview. Before the interview, you must research the company, analyze your qualifications to figure out how you fit well in the company or the position, and think up some appropriate questions to ask the interviewer. But beyond that, you must make a good first impression. As superficial as it may sound, what you wear and how you present yourself at the interview are as important—or almost as important—as what you say. And if you think about it, the interviewer is going to see what you look like before she hears what you have to say. You get only one chance to make a first impression.

Grooming

First things first: Good grooming is vital. Be sure to show up to the interview feeling and looking as "fresh as a daisy." Get a good night's sleep and wake up in plenty of time for a morning interview. Your hair should be neat—it's probably best to get a trim a couple of days before the appointment. Long hair and facial hair for men are probably not the best—unless you are in a profession where more hair is acceptable. If women are going to try a new hairdo, like wearing it up, be sure to practice before the day of the interview. And do not overprocess your hair—bad perms or badly dyed hair can ruin an otherwise good appearance. Use mouthwash right before you leave your house to boost your confidence. Pay attention to your fingernails. Make sure they are trimmed and clean. Women should not wear a loud color of nail polish. Nor should women wear a lot of obvious makeup. Less is more—wear just enough to enhance your features. And everyone should take it easy on the cologne.

The Suit

As far as what to put on your clean body, wear a suit. Both men and women should wear suits. Sure, there are acceptable variations (which will be covered later), but nine times out of ten, you should wear a suit to a job interview. It should be a well-fitting suit. Use a tailor if it isn't. If it doesn't fit well, not only will it detract from your overall appearance but you will be physically uncomfortable as well. It's hard to wow them at an interview if your waistband is cutting into you. The suit should be a dark color; navy, dark gray, or dark olive green are suitable. And 100 percent wool is acceptable (and probably best) for all seasons. (Don't worry! Lightweight wool suits are available, so you won't be beading with sweat at a July interview!) Whether you wear a double- or single-breasted suit depends on your body type. Double-breasted ones tend to look a little better on tall people. Cuffs on the pants look very polished, and the bottom of your pants should "break" at the top of your shoe. Suit skirts for women should be a flattering length (not too short!) and, ideally, should be lined. If your skirt isn't lined, wear a slip that has a slit that matches the one in your skirt. And try to wear a slip that is the same color as your suit (or at least close).

The Shirt

The shirt under the suit is also very important. Men should wear a long-sleeved shirt; 100 percent cotton is recommended. They should also wear a short-sleeved white T-shirt under their dress shirt—it makes the shirt look "crisper." The shirt should be a not-too-wild color. White or light blue is the safest choice, but stripes and checks are becoming more popular, and acceptable. If in doubt, get someone else's opinion. And make sure the shirt has been laundered at a dry cleaners, if possible. It will look that much "sharper." Women should wear a polyester or silk blouse or shell in a flattering color. Off-white or pastels work well with a dark suit. Consider removing the blouse's shoulder pads, if they're thick, because with your suit jacket's shoulder pads, you could end up looking like a football player. Once again, fit is very important. Pay attention to the length of the sleeve. You look best if the sleeves of your shirt or blouse come just below your suit jacket.

Hosiery

Panty hose for women are a must. Skin-colored hose are probably best, but you may prefer navy, black, or off-white. Never wear panty hose that are darker in color than your shoes; your hose and shoes should match, or your hose should be a lighter color than your shoes. And always take an extra pair of panty hose with you to the interview! A run or snag in your hose can ruin a whole look. Men should always wear dark socks. A color close to the suit's color is best, and a subtle pattern is nice. *Never* wear white socks with a suit.

Shoes

Shoes should be a conservative color such as black or brown (or navy for women wearing navy suits). Loafer or lace-up shoes are good for men; pumps are preferable for women. The shoes should be in very good shape. The soles and heels should look new, and if they don't, take them to a cobbler for repair before the interview. Your shoes should also be polished the night before the interview. (Just be sure not to leave any excess polish on the shoes—a black streak on nude-colored pantyhose can be unnerving!) Women should pay attention to heel height—stay away from any over 2 inches—you don't want to teeter. Above all, wear shoes that are comfortable—it's hard to sell yourself while your toes are being pinched.

Accessories

Accessories are also important and are your best opportunity to express some individuality. Men can wear a tie that is both colorful and snazzy, but stay away from really bright colors and patterns that are obviously asymmetrical. Women can wear a colorful scarf and jewelry that show who they are. Pearls with a blouse look very elegant as do gold or pearl earrings. Earrings that are large or dangle a lot look out of place with a suit, so pay attention to scale. Both men and women should wear a professional-looking watch, and men should wear either a belt or suspenders. If you wear eyeglasses, make sure they are clean and not terribly outdated.

Extras

To an interview, you should also carry a smart-looking portfolio—one of those folders with a pocket and a pad of paper. It should be black or cordovan leather. If you don't have one, borrow one. You'll look and feel professional when you are asked for a resume and you present one out of a sharp-looking portfolio. Your resume, of course, should be equally impressive and printed on high-quality paper. Bring plenty of copies. Make sure you have a black pen with you, too, in case you want to take notes or are asked to sign something.

Women may want to carry a purse to the interview. If so, it should match your shoes and be very streamlined, not a slouchy, overstuffed bag. And be sure you can hold the portfolio and the purse and still have a hand free for shaking hands.

Dress Rehearsal

The day before the interview, have a dress rehearsal. Put on everything you plan to wear and have a friend look you over. Does your slip or skirt lining show? Are your pants too short? Are there any loose threads? Any stains or wrinkles? Are all the buttons sewn on? A rehearsal will inevitably save you time and trouble on the day of the interview. After the rehearsal, hang everything very neatly on thick hangers and use a lint brush on your suit. Press anything that needs it.

The Day of the Interview

Arrive at the interview early enough to give yourself extra time before the meeting. Make one last trip to the bathroom—blow your nose, spit out your gum, get a drink of water, comb your hair—and give yourself one last look in the mirror.

Besides grooming and clothing, there are a few more details related to your appearance that are very important to the impression that you give at an interview. When you meet someone, look her in the eye, introduce yourself, and give her a firm, confident handshake. Practice in the mirror if you want—and smile, smile, smile. A positive attitude and sunny disposition will always give the best first impression. Also, pay attention to your posture when you sit and stand. The most expensive suit you can buy won't look impressive if you're all hunched over. Sit up straight, but lean a little forward to convey that your full attention is on the interviewer.

What we've discussed so far may seem too detail-oriented or too fussy. But you need to stand out from the pack—you may be competing with dozens of other people for the job, so giving attention to details gives you a competitive edge. And, ultimately, you'll perform better at your interview because your appearance will be one less thing you have to worry about. You will be able to relax and let your inner qualities shine through.

What If a Suit Is Not Necessary?

Okay, so you're saying to yourself, "The job is construction work. Why the heck should I wear a suit?" And you're right. Certain situations arise when the job interview attire described above would look out of place. A rule of thumb is to wear clothing that is one step above what you would wear on the job. If you are applying for a manual labor job, a suit and tie is not necessary, and it would probably get you laughed off the site. But you should still dress up for the interview. Wear a nice long-sleeved shirt with a collar and khaki pants. If it is a job that you could start that day, take your work clothes with you and change into them once you've been offered the job. If the job you're applying for requires a uniform, you should still dress up for the interview. Wear something that you feel good in.

Technical workers, like computer programmers, are growing in number. They are professionals who do not fit into the "suit and tie" world either. More casual (and comfortable) clothing is certainly appropriate—especially when the job position doesn't require customer contact.

And finally, if you're applying for a creative job, the strict dress standards should be loosened up a bit. Actually, you may appear unimaginative if you don't loosen up. Creative positions don't need to stick to such rigid dress codes as those mentioned above. Show some flair and wear some color. Your clothing choices should reflect your creative talents. Women may want to wear a pantsuit with a colorful blouse. Men could try a mock turtleneck with a blazer and dress slacks instead of a suit and tie.

Whatever you decide to wear to an interview, remember that you got the interview because of your skills and talents. Just getting an interview scheduled is no small feat in this day and age. You should feel proud of yourself, and that pride should be reflected in what you wear.

THE JOB

Once you've landed the position, it's time to really think about your entire wardrobe. You had to come up with only one ensemble for the interview; now that you're an employee, you've got to get dressed at least five days a week. It'll save you time and money if you do some planning.

First of all, plan what you will wear the first week of work ahead of time. Starting a new job is stressful enough without having to worry about what to wear. Plus, if you plan strategically, you can look your best when you meet your coworkers for the first time. They'll remember you as a well-dressed, smiling, new arrival.

Also, during the first week, pay attention to what everyone else is wearing. Do all the men wear white or blue shirts? Are sport coats acceptable? Are Fridays casual? Do women wear pants? And, most importantly, pay attention to what your boss is wearing. You may want his job someday, so start looking the part early on. Dress at a level that is one job level above your own. (It'll save you a lot of shopping when you get that first promotion!)

Subscribe to a fashion magazine or two, or browse through them at the library, to get ideas for what to wear. Window-shop at fine boutiques and then look for similar items at more affordable stores.

Consistently tend to your appearance. Keep your hair and nails trimmed. Do wardrobe maintenance as often as necessary—get things dry-cleaned, sew on buttons, find a good tailor and a good cobbler, store out-of-season clothing properly, and so forth.

And one final (yet important) note, clothing should always be modest in the image that it portrays—revealing or scanty clothing is never appropriate in the workplace. Always keep in mind that what you wear conveys something about who you are; you wouldn't want it to be the wrong impression. When in doubt, don't wear it.

Affordable Good Clothes

Of course, all these suggestions must be tempered by your budget. You don't need to go into debt to look professional. There are certain strategies that can help you look like a million bucks without spending that much.

Shop for basic pieces at moderately priced stores. Look for classic lines in quality fabrics. Don't waste your money on trendy fashions. Buying the best quality you can afford is the smartest way to go about it. It's better to have a few traditional, high-quality outfits that you look and feel good in, than to have a closetful of cheap, out-of-style-in-a-month clothes. Watch for sales at department stores. Buy clothes this fall (at clearance prices) for next spring—since you're buying basic pieces, they won't go out of style. Try consignment shops—they are great places to pick up good-quality clothing at low prices, and there are many popping up that specialize in career clothing. If you have a well-dressed friend who is your size, ask for any hand-me-downs. And finally, don't worry about the price or brand name of what you have on—if you follow the guideline of sticking to simple, elegant pieces, the cost won't matter.

Business Casual

A new trend in the working world came about in the 1990s: business casual. Some companies allow business casual dress all week long, but most companies allow it on Fridays only. Hence, the new term *Casual Friday*. It has certainly been a welcome break from formal business attire, and many people argue that they are more productive at work when they are comfortably dressed. But what clothing is appropriate for business casual?

Let's start with what is not acceptable: sweats, T-shirts with printing, tennis shoes, and worn-out clothing (and usually jeans). In other words, it is not an excuse to look sloppy, but rather it is a comfortable break from a sometimes otherwise rigid dress code. A perfect outfit for a man on Casual Friday would be a plaid, cotton, long-sleeved shirt and well-fitting khaki pants with brown leather shoes. He should still shave that morning, and he should still tuck in his shirt and wear a belt. A woman's perfect outfit would be a tailored pair of slacks with a sweater and loafer-type shoes or a cotton dress that is a bit too casual for other days. Ask one of your coworkers before Friday to find out what to expect.

Again, pay attention to what others wear on those days. Perhaps overdress a little for the first casual day until you see what's appropriate. If your company allows for business casual attire either every day or just on Fridays, appreciate the rest from your ties and your panty hose, and enjoy!

Working from Home

Another convenient trend in the '90s is working from home. In this Information Age, it is possible for people to work from the comfort of their own homes and get their work done on-line. It's another welcome relaxation of strict dress codes.

Obviously, if you work at home, you don't have to adhere to any dress code. Some people have discovered, however, that if they are too lax in how they dress at home—for example, if they stay in their pajamas all day—their work productivity suffers. Do whatever works for you, but if you find yourself slacking off, try getting up early, showering, and putting on clothes that are comfortable, but presentable. Also, if there is the possibility of meeting with customers or clients on a particular day, you should obviously dress appropriately. You don't want your lax appearance to give them the notion that you aren't taking your job seriously because you are doing it from home.

Traveling for Work

Your job may take you out of town. Traveling can be a great break from the office routine, but it also means that you have to plan ahead for your wardrobe. Before you pack, make a list. Make sure you know the dress code of the office to which you're going. If you know what kinds of activities you will be doing outside of work, plan ahead for those, too. And find out what the weather will be like while you're there.

Invest in or borrow a good hanging bag—you can buy styles that fold over and have wheels. They are handy to carry onto airplanes, and they keep your suits and other good clothes relatively wrinkle-free. Leaving your suits in plastic bags from the dry cleaners is another way to avoid creases. Roll everything else that you can. Pack your toiletries in plastic bags—just in case one of them leaks. And take along some type of folder to keep all your receipts, maps, tickets, and travel information together.

SUMMARY

Remember, this chapter contains only suggestions on ways to dress for work or a job interview. They are not necessarily hard-and-fast rules. Dress styles are as varied as job positions. Ultimately, you have to dress in a manner that works for you and your place of work. You can't expect yourself to be someone you aren't, or dress in a way that doesn't feel right to you. For an interview, just remember the key is to pay attention to details to make yourself stand out from the rest of the applicants. And once you have the job, remember to reflect on the outside the kind of person that you are on the inside. Let the way you present yourself reflect your pride in your work and your accomplishments. And let your own "book cover" tell your story.

Applications & Exercises

Key Into Your Life: Opportunities to Apply What You Learn
Be Your Own Mirror

Think of passing by your cubicle or office each day at work and popping your head in to say hello to yourself. Try to see yourself as your coworkers do. What do you see?

_____

_____

_____

What's the first thing you notice about your appearance? Is it something positive that stands out? How's your posture? Do you smile at others?

_____

_____

Do you look like you took the time that morning to put yourself together? Did you pay attention to the details of your appearance?

_____

_____

Would your appearance impress your boss? Would it impress your customers?

_____

_____

Name three adjectives that describe your everyday appearance:

_____

_____

_____

What is your favorite thing about your wardrobe? Why?

_____

_____

_____

What needs improvement the most? What could you do to improve it?

_____

_____

_____

Would someone admire your wardrobe? Would they compliment you on your appearance?

_____

_____

_____

Key to Cooperative Learning: Building Teamwork Skills

A Picture Is Worth a Thousand Words

Meet with other students, where each student brings in some current magazines. Select six job positions (e.g., attorney, graphic designer, waitress). Separately, thumb through the magazines until everyone has cut out at least one picture of a person who is dressed appropriately for each of the job positions. Gather in your group again, and categorize each of your pictures with the job positions. Compare the pictures.

Do you all agree on what is appropriate? If not, how do you differ? What do you think causes your differences? Does it depend on the part of the country you're from? On your chosen profession?

_____

_____

_____

Do the women in your group agree with each other more than they agree with the men? Does your age affect what you think is appropriate?

_____

_____

_____

For what job positions do you agree on the appropriate dress? Do you all agree on appropriate dress for one of the positions? What type of position is it? Is it easier to standardize a dress code for a certain profession?

_____

_____

_____

Key to Self-Expression: Discovery Through Journal Writing

The Best That You Can Be

Just for the heck of it, put on your best work outfit—the one that you would wear if you had a job interview for your dream job or were meeting with the president of your company. Put on the clothes that make you look like a million bucks.

Now write in your journal about how you feel in those clothes. What about the clothes makes you feel good about yourself? Do they hide any flaws that you think you have? Are they flattering colors or a perfect fit? Are they comfortable? Try to determine what it is that makes you feel so special in that particular ensemble. Finish these sentences:

➤ These clothes seem to give me more confidence because . . .

➤ These clothes are different from my other clothes because . . .

➤ I could have more clothes like these if . . .

Key to Your Portfolio: Your Paper Trail to Success

Time to Take Inventory

It's closet-cleaning time. Time to evaluate just what you have in there. Put on some peppy music, get out your excavation tools, and get busy.

Remove everything from your closet and lay it on your bed. Now go through the big pile, separating each item into one of three categories: throwaways, giveaways, and keepers. Be ruthless. Have you worn it in the last two years? Is it out of style? Does it fit? Does it have holes or stains? Did you feel uncomfortable the last time you wore it?

Now, you know what to do with the throwaways. For the giveaways, get a big garbage bag and cart them off to your favorite charity or offer them to your friends. When you've got it narrowed down to just the keepers, carefully scrutinize your wardrobe. What items go together? What additional items do you need? Would a scarf help to "tie" two pieces together? Would one pair of dark gray trousers go with three different jackets? Does anything need alterations? Any loose buttons? Grab a pen and paper and make a list. Take careful inventory of what you have, what you need, and what you want. (And don't forget to vacuum the closet while it's empty!)

For Further Reading

Molloy, John T. *New Dress for Success.* (Warner Books, 1988).

Molloy, John T. *New Women's Dress for Success.* (Warner Books, 1996).

18 WORKING WITH YOUR MANAGERS AND YOUR PEERS
How to Be Effective with Others

In this chapter, you will explore answers to the following questions:

➤ Is IQ the most important element to succeeding on the job?

➤ Is there more than one way to deal with conflict on the job?

➤ How do I resolve conflict without making others feel like they've lost?

➤ Will it help my performance if I receive praise for the good things I've done?

➤ Will social skills be different as we move into the next century?

❓ Thinking It Through

Check those statements that currently apply to you:

☐ I'm not sure what "emotional intelligence" means.

☐ I have a hard time arguing with someone without becoming hurtful.

☐ I avoid conflict because I don't see the point in arguing about anything.

☐ I treat people in my profession the same way I'd treat my friends.

☐ I haven't really considered the importance of listening carefully.

COOPERATE

18

WORKING WITH YOUR MANAGERS AND YOUR PEERS
How to Be Effective With Others

Much of your contentment and success at work will hinge on your ability to get along with others. To effectively communicate your ideas and to marshal cooperation will require you to do more than focus on your individual task. You will need to sharpen your "people skills."

Therefore, it makes sense to maximize your interpersonal effectiveness, not only for climbing the corporate ladder but also for personal satisfaction. In his essay "Real Work," Abraham Zaleznik writes, "Money may be the lifeblood of a corporation but life itself consists of more than keeping the blood flowing; otherwise it would not be worth living." In fact, you may find that your work relationships are the most satisfying and meaningful part of your job. Jeff Williams of Creative Market Solutions testifies to this point: "Interpersonal skill is what gratifies me most on the job. When my team has won an award or when I have helped a secretary get promoted, these kinds of things are what make going to work worthwhile." Strengthening the quality of your work relationships will serve to increase your emotional well-being as well as your job performance.

EMOTIONAL INTELLIGENCE: THE NEW IQ OF BUSINESS

General Motors executive Russ Neighbors recently told Chicago-area college students that "Grades alone don't guarantee a good job. The key things are strong communication skills and a good attitude."

For the better part of this century, we heard the reverse of what Russ Neighbors purported. We falsely believed that mental aptitude, not qualities such as a good attitude, was the key to success. Promotions at work, therefore, relied on our mental prowess, and crowning achievements could only be expected of those whose minds were exceptionally fertile. Possessing an elevated IQ was the jewel of that crown. Many have taken IQ exams and were disappointed—even stigmatized—by the benign discovery that their brains were "average." For those of us who already suspected that we weren't in the class of astutely profound thinkers, IQ results were like the kiss of death to our futures. We weren't smart because we fell into the large gray area of the bell curve along with all the other "average" people.

Then came a breakthrough that turned our concept of brilliance upside down. Daniel Goleman, Ph.D., of Harvard University, delivered a refreshing message: Cognitive ability isn't the only kind of "smart." Drawing on groundbreaking brain and behavioral research, Goleman created the term *Emotional Intelligence Quotient* (EQ) to describe a different kind of human aptitude—an aptitude that can be more important than IQ. Goleman asserts that our view of human intelligence is too narrow; that is, it ignores a crucial range of abilities that affects how we do in life.

Emotional intelligence includes self-awareness, impulse control, persistence, zeal, self-motivation, empathy, and social deftness. These are the qualities of people who excel in real life: Those whose intimate relationships flourish, and who are "stars" in the workplace. These qualities are also the hallmarks of character and self-discipline, and of altruism and compassion—basic capacities needed if our society is to thrive. And in business, emotional savvy offers you the advantage of knowing what you and those around you are feeling and how to handle these feelings skillfully.

Emotion Unleashed

Why is EQ relevant to the workplace? After all, what counts is the bottom line. Interpersonal relationships are of only secondary importance, right? Not exactly. Of course, brain power is an asset in any job, especially in bookish endeavors such as medicine and law. But if you want to be a brilliant trial lawyer or dean of a law school, emotional intelligence will give you a crucial edge.

Career accomplishment can pivot on emotional competence. When it comes to being a successful salesperson or a popular, effective manager, people skills are critical. Take the case of Melburn McBroom (name changed), a commercial pilot known for his temper. One day in 1978 his plane was approaching Portland, Oregon, when he noticed a problem with the landing gear. So he went into a holding pattern, circling the field while he fiddled with the mechanism. While McBroom obsessed over the landing gear, the fuel gauges steadily approached empty. His copilots were so fearful of his wrath that they said nothing. The plane crashed, killing 10 people.

The cockpit is a microcosm of any working organization. When levels of emotional intelligence are low, companies, too, can "crash and burn."

While people with high IQs are ambitious and productive, they can also be cold, condescending, inhibited, unexpressive, fastidious, and uneasy with sensuality, says Goleman. "The brightest among us, can be emotional morons," he says. By contrast, those high in emotional abilities tend to be poised, outgoing, and cheerful. They have a strong commitment to people or causes, to taking responsibility for their actions, and to holding to an ethical outlook. They are cooperative and sympathetic with others; their emotional lives are rich. In short, they are comfortable with themselves and the people around them. Being at home with yourself and your place in the world greatly enhances your effectiveness at work. So profound is this revelation, that emotional intelligence is now the new IQ of business. A catalog of the qualities that constitute a high EQ follows.

FUNDAMENTALS OF EMOTIONAL INTELLIGENCE

Self-awareness: knowing what you feel and using your intuition to make decisions you can live with happily.

Management of feelings: controlling impulses, soothing your anxiety, and expressing anger appropriately.

Motivation: having zeal, persistence, and optimism in the face of setbacks.

Empathy: reading and responding to unspoken feelings.

Social skill: handling emotional reactions in others; interacting smoothly and managing relationships effectively.

IQ matters; but if you want to work effectively with your managers and your peers, you can't ignore emotional intelligence.

RESOLVING CONFLICT

Conflict is an inevitable part of life; unresolved conflict, however, doesn't have to be. Unresolved conflict fractures healthy work relationships, setting the stage for further interpersonal turmoil. The strain undermines organizational cohesiveness to the point of shrinking bottom-line profits. After all, how can a company thrive when conflict chokes the heart and soul of its employees? Conflict gets out of hand when workers don't know how to deal with it effectively. "People often make conflict worse by how they react," writes Amy Nathan in *Everything You Need to Know About Conflict Resolution*. Some of the common ways people react to conflict are listed next.

Blast it.   Some people see conflict as a win–lose situation. They feel that they are right—the other side is wrong—and they are out to prove it. They try to blast their way through a disagreement with threats, insults, and even bribes. Since they cannot admit any possible wrongdoing, the conflict never really gets resolved. More conflicts are likely to bubble up between the two parties again at some point.

Avoid it. Some people believe conflict is bad and try to avoid it as much as possible. When conflict comes up, they may ignore it, pretending it didn't happen. Or they may always give in and smooth things over. This may make things better for a while, but in the long run, it may actually make them worse.

Solve it. Instead of ducking conflicts or blasting their way out of them, some people try to face conflicts fairly. They don't try to "win." Instead, they look for the cause of the conflict. Then they try to find a solution that will work well for both parties. Sometimes compromise is necessary. Conflict resolution programs encourage people to react using this problem-solving guide.

Skills That Can Help

In the heat of battle, it's easy to say and do things you'll regret. Therefore, it is a good idea to have a conflict resolution strategy in mind *before* you're in a dispute. That way you are prepared to use your head, as well as your emotions, to solve the problem. Work, school, and virtually anywhere you find two or more people together will give rise to conflict situations, and conflicts can become intensely emotional. Conflict resolution programs teach people special skills to help them keep discussions from turning into put-down sessions.

"I" Messages

"You are so rude!" "You think only about yourself!" "You come up with the dumbest ideas!" Remarks like these won't be helpful in discussing a conflict. They heat things up rather than cool them down. A statement that starts with the word "you" can sound like an attack to the other person. For example, Rick is angry that his coworker handed out illegible copies of the companies' growth chart at a meeting Rick was officiating. The print was simply too small to read. Rick may feel like saying, "You are so stupid." And then his coworker would probably get ticked off and snap back with a negative remark of her own.

Instead, Rick needs to figure out exactly how he feels and why he feels this way. Then he should explain it using "I" as the first word in his statement. He might say, "I feel frustrated that the copies for the meeting are not legible. I wish you would make sure all handouts are easy to read."

Such a statement may help Rick's coworker think about what happened. She can focus on Rick's problem and how to solve it. That keeps the discussion on the problem. You can't change people's personalities, but you may be able to fix the problem.

A good "I" message has four parts. Below is Rick's "I" message broken into its parts.

1. Say how you feel: "I feel frustrated . . ."
2. State what event makes you feel that way: ". . . that the copies for the meeting are not legible."
3. Explain how that event affects you: ". . . because it makes the meeting more difficult for me to run."

4. Say what change would make things better: "In the future, please show me the handouts ahead of time so that I can be better prepared by making any necessary changes."[*]

The first and second parts of the "I" message give you a chance to state your feelings clearly and calmly and explain why there is a conflict.

The third part of the "I" message, the explanation, helps to keep the discussion on target. You're not just making a wild charge. You're backing it up with a clear explanation of how the other person's actions affect you. To do that, you have to think about the situation. That can calm you down and give you time to see what's really at stake. It can also help you keep from blowing things out of proportion.

The fourth part of the " I" message suggests a solution and gives you a chance to describe your own resolution ideas. This also allows the other person an opportunity to express his or her ideas for resolving the conflict.

Gaining a Perspective

One of the most vital conflict resolution skills is being able to see things from the other person's point of view. This sounds easy enough, but in reality, it is quite difficult to do. That's because no two people have identical perspectives, even when they are viewing the same event. Why is it, for example, that eyewitnesses to crimes give vastly different accounts? People give their versions of what they saw with conviction, and one person is often as certain that the culprit's hair was blonde as another is convinced it was black. Cultural backgrounds can also play a part in differences of opinion. For example, in some ethnic groups, it's okay to look someone straight in the eyes. In other groups, it's considered rude. The old adage, "put yourself in their shoes," is still the best advice for dealing with conflict.

When you find yourself in the middle of strife, your *interpretation* of the event often needs fine-tuning. Therefore, as much as possible, you must separate the facts from your feelings about them. John Crawley in *Constructive Conflict Management* suggests you ask yourself: What's happening? "Be clear in your own mind about what you see, how you judge and how you react to people and situations."

Identify Feelings

Our feelings serve a purpose; therefore, we need to listen to them. The first two steps in good conflict resolution models will help you to understand and take charge of your own feelings and behavior. Feelings alert you to what you want and also to what is blocking your desire. Thus, it's imperative that you learn to understand what you feel, and more importantly, why.

The unpleasant emotions that arise during conflict are like road signs; they can point you toward a remedy. For instance, when your desires are not fulfilled, you may become discontent and, consequently, less productive. So you need to determine exactly what it is that you want. In the example cited earlier,

---

[*]From Amy Nathan, *Everything You Need to Know About Conflict Resolution*

Rick depended on his coworker to provide legible charts. From Rick's perspective, his coworker let him down. "It is extremely important to identify something like this. In pinpointing what you need or want, you have positioned yourself for taking the final step in the process of conflict resolution," writes Ron Guzik, owner of Entrepreneurial Visions, in his article "Resolving Conflict at Work So Everybody Wins."

Make a Request

Guzik says that this final step, making a request, is rarely taken. This happens because you assume people will deduce your expectations from what you have said in the previous steps. This is the reason many conflicts are never resolved. It is easy to make too many assumptions. The golden rule of conflict resolution is: Never assume anything. Always spell out what you want to change in the future. "Somehow we expect people around us to read our minds and simply deliver what we need without our ever asking or explaining to them what it is," writes Guzik. "The more specific the request, the better. And try to frame the request in a positive form," he suggests. One possible request to a coworker in Rick's situation might be: "Don't ever hand out shoddy copies at my meetings." It would be more effective to say: "Please remember to show me the handouts before a meeting." The second request will increase your chances of having your coworker actually behave in the manner you desire, explains Guzik.

Making a specific request is also fair to others, and in any relationship, fairness is always welcome. Now they know what you want, and they don't have to figure it out for themselves, possibly coming up with the wrong assumption, which only adds to your consternation and theirs.

Conflict resolution, like any other skill, takes practice, so it makes sense to review conflict resolution strategies regularly. Guzik also offers a wonderful suggestion: After each conflict to which you are a party, sit down and think about what transpired. Visualize yourself having applied the conflict resolution model well in this situation and ask yourself: What should I have done differently? "Next time, try to do exactly that," writes Guzik.

DO YOU HEAR WHAT I HEAR?

Have you ever been talking with someone and had the distinct impression that he wasn't listening to you? How did that make you feel? Probably it made you feel unimportant and a little foolish for being so vulnerable. Conversely, when your words are taken seriously, you feel encouraged. You leave the conversation feeling energized and hopeful. That's because few things convey interest as much as active listening.

In the workplace, effective listening skills are extremely important. Surveys show that while you spend only 9 percent of your time writing, 16 percent reading, and 35 percent speaking, you spend a hefty 40 percent of your time listening. Some estimates of how managers spend their time put listening as high as 60 percent. Since we spend the majority of our time listening, it behooves us to make sure we are doing it well.

Body Language

An important feature of effective listening is *body language*. When you are talking with someone, turn your body toward that person, and focus your eyes on his or her face. You don't want this to be a "stare down"; just act naturally and don't forget to blink! Whether you sit or stand, let your hands rest comfortably at your sides or in your lap. Nod your head from time to time, and utter short phrases, such as "I see" or "Yes, that makes sense," so that the person knows you are following his or her train of thought. Furthermore, restrain yourself from performing any other task while you are talking with that person. Give him or her your full attention.

In addition to minding your own body language, you also need to tune into the nonverbal cues of others. Make a mental note of their tone of voice and facial expressions. Likewise, show by your facial expressions that you are following the tenor and mood of the message. This might mean smiling, for instance, or adopting a sympathetic expression and leaning slightly forward to express concern. Besides body language, there are other tips to help you become a skillful listener.

Reduce Distractions

Good listening is active and empathic. Your goal is to receive and understand the entire message of the person in front of you. In order to accomplish this, you will want to reduce distractions. If possible, move to a quiet place away from the noise of office machines and other conversations. If you are discussing a confidential matter, do so in private so you won't tempt others to eavesdrop. Another common distraction is interruptions, such as people stopping by who want to meet with you and telephone calls. When possible, have someone else assist people and take messages for you. If you must take the calls yourself, tell the callers that you will get back to them as soon as you can.

Another distraction to effective listening is our own impatience. Before people have finished speaking, we jump headlong into the conversation without fully understanding what the other party is saying. When you interrupt someone, you inadvertently place the focus on yourself. Resist the urge to interrupt, even if you think you know what your coworker or manager is leading up to. Let him finish what he wants to say.

Feedback

When your coworker has completed a thought verbally, summarize what she has just said. "Let's see, Cathy, if I've got this right. You are saying that you would like to divide the resource development department into two distinct areas: promotions and fund-raising. And that you would like to head up the promotion side of things." Then she will be able to let you know if you made an error in deciphering her message. Or she can refine what you've just said.

Remember the proverb, "silence is golden"? This sentiment rings true in everyday conversation. Don't be afraid of pauses and lulls when talking with your managers and your peers. Every second doesn't need to be filled with words. Often silence will permit the other person to talk, giving him the opportunity to express—on a deeper level—what he wants to say. Working toward your goal to be a better listener, you can also employ another technique that actually works in tandem with feedback: asking questions.

The Value of Asking Good Questions

The desire to hear the *whole message* is a key component to skillful listening. Too often, however, dialogue ends prematurely because you place the total burden of the interaction on the other person. You treat the dialogue like a spectator sport: You watch and listen to what's going on, but you don't participate. And since you are only passively listening, you neglect to draw out your managers' and peers' thoughts or intentions. Asking relevant questions conveys to the other person that you want to hear more and are investing yourself in the conversation.

Questions help draw out thoughts on the subject at hand so that you can listen more effectively. When you withhold questions, you unknowingly send vibes that say: "I don't have time for this," or "I don't care about this." Thoughtful questioning will demonstrate that you do care—about both the message and the messenger.

Through questioning you also glean relevant information, and gathering information is a major purpose of listening. Without getting answers to your questions, you may miss a vital piece of information. Good questions unearth potential problems as well as solutions. "Cathy, since you want to handle promotions, who would manage fund-raising?" This simple question allows your coworker to expound on her idea. Questions allow you to probe deeper so that you can accomplish genuine understanding.

Quite obviously, listening takes considerable effort and time. But the rewards are well worth it. Active listening helps you connect with other people. And it's these sorts of connections that forge effective work relationships.

THE POWER OF PRAISE

Steve Lauer, the manager of eight Subway Sandwich Shops in northern Colorado, was in a business quandary. His front-line workers, most of whom are under the age of 20 and earn slightly above the hourly minimum wage, frequently missed their shifts or quit after only a few weeks on the job. When the turnover rate at Lauer's fast-food operations hit 200 percent a few years ago, he made some changes. How did Lauer motivate these low-wage workers?

To stem turnover, Lauer established many pride-building practices for employees. One of these practices was to create a company culture that shows people they are appreciated. For example, Lauer placed special significance on an employee's one-year anniversary. Measures like this have helped reduce turnover rate at his stores to 125 percent in each of the past two years. His best stores have turnover under 100 percent. The average rate for fast-food businesses is 140 percent, according to a 1996 survey by the National Restaurant Association and the Deloitte & Touche accounting and consulting firm (*Nation's Business,* May 1997).

It's the Little Things That Count

The U. S. Department of Labor reported last year that 46 percent of those who quit their jobs did so because they felt unappreciated. Rosalind Jeffries, president of Performance Enhancement Group, a human resources consulting firm in Chevy Chase, Maryland, says, "Employees consistently cite a value-centered, collegial, creative, and responsive environment, *not money*, as factors that cause them to choose and remain with one organization rather than another." One reason a simple thank-you is so effective for building good work relationships is that appreciation does wonders for people's self-esteem. Praise also promotes unity and spirit in the workplace because you are acknowledging your managers' and coworkers' value.

Recognizing Accomplishments in Yourself and Others

It's difficult to give what you don't have. If you don't hold a very high opinion of yourself, you may not have the capacity to give a sincere compliment to your managers and peers either. A key to acknowledging others is derived from learning to praise yourself. Dogged determination on a job is fine, sometimes even essential, but to keep yourself energized, you must learn to mark the little milestones of your work's journey with rewards. Failing to "smell the roses" dulls the brilliance of life, especially in the workplace. Jack Canfield and Jacqueline Miller in their best-selling book, *Heart at Work,* assert that since we now spend so much of our lives at work, "we want that work to be connected with what we believe is important in the world. People want to feel that who they are and what they do matters." How can you believe that what you do matters if you never allow yourself to bask in your accomplishments? Perhaps your achievements aren't noteworthy in the eyes of the world. That doesn't matter. What matters is that you see your progress. And there's a predictable result of self-improvement: Eventually, others will notice it, too.

To gain a deeper sense of gratitude for others when they go the extra mile, first you must learn to take pride in your own accomplishments. When you've completed an assignment or done a job well, reward yourself for it. For example, when you've finished a tough project at work or school, treat yourself to a new CD or to a night out with friends. Giving yourself permission to acknowledge your successes with small rewards will boost your self-esteem. You'll be amazed by how invigorating it feels to do this! Once you've learned how to reward yourself for your own accomplishments, you'll find it easier to do the same for other people. Sincere praise will transform your relationships at work. Although you may have insecurities (we all do), your managers and peers will see that these insecurities aren't controlling you. Praise nourishes office camaraderie.

Challenge Negative Thinking

One of the obstacles to praise is our own negative thinking. Instead of nurturing your inner self, many of you kick yourselves with a lot of demeaning self-talk. When you experience a setback at work, you may automatically think: I'm a failure. Instead of generalizing like this, think of the isolated event. Tell yourself, for instance, "I didn't get the promotion this time, but that doesn't mean I won't ever get one." This will help you develop a more optimistic outlook on life. Also, ask yourself, "What can I do in the future to make myself more qualified?" This puts the ball in your court, which may help you feel more in control.

We also chide ourselves for not having done as thorough or perfect of a job as we should have. Much of this mental abuse revolves around the guilt-laden word *should*. "I *should* have told the customer about the possibility of a delay in the shipment." "I *should* have double-checked those figures before sending them to human resources." This browbeating erodes your self-esteem. Instead, use should messages constructively. Let the word serve as a form of self-advice. Perhaps you *can* do something differently next time that will increase your effectiveness with others. A healthy self-concept is critical to motivating ourselves and others. Yes, we need to reflect and learn from our mistakes, but to continue rolling in the muck and mire of regret is self-defeating. And if you can't truly appreciate yourself, how will you be able to appreciate anyone else?

Show Enthusiasm

Though researchers have long focused on negative emotions like depression and anxiety, there hasn't been as much attention given to the study of pleasant emotions. Only recently have psychologists begun serious study of emotions such as enthusiasm. Already, though, scientists know enough to confirm what Norman Vincent Peale intuitively sensed back in 1952 when he first published his now-classic book, *The Power of Positive Thinking.* That is, that the character traits of enthusiastic people are typically associated with greater peace of mind, higher self-esteem, a stronger sense of well-being, and even better physical health and increased success in the workplace. An upbeat spirit is contagious. When you feel great yourself, you can't help but pass praise on.

Be Sincere but Creative

It's very important that your praise be sincere, not feigned or exaggerated. Manipulative flattery actually undermines work relationships because people won't see you as authentic. They will read through your empty words of praise for what they are: self-serving devices. To help ensure sincerity, state exactly what the other person did that you liked: "Yolanda, that was a fantastic presentation of our materials. I'm sure you'll be a great hit on the road." Or, "David, thanks so much for providing the sales figures. Without your attention to detail, I couldn't have adequately explained how our company will benefit next year."

At first, praising others may feel stiff and contrived. Don't give up! With a little practice, you'll enjoy brightening someone's day.

PROFESSIONAL INTIMACY

Many things keep people apart. Differences in race, beliefs, and opinions (to name only a few) can build walls between you and those with whom you work. Charlotte Roberts, coauthor of *The Fifth Discipline Fieldbook,* says, "No matter how fervent our desires for team learning and collective intelligence, they are often undermined by the boundaries between people." Today's companies, asserts Roberts, must permit the display of human feeling in the workplace with full acknowledgement of the whole person at work, not just his role. Roberts emphasizes the necessity for making a commitment to getting to know people "behind the mask of their job title, role or function," a commitment that she refers to as *intimacy.*

Intimacy stems from the Latin *intimatus,* which means to make something known to someone else. In other words, the original meaning of intimacy did not mean emotional closeness but the willingness to pass on honest information. Therefore, your ability to share what you know, as well as what you can do, are at the heart of intimate work relationships. Following are several tips that will help you develop professional intimacy with your managers and peers.

Share Relevant Information

When something comes across your desk, such as a memo, always ask yourself these two questions: "What is obviously important about this particular piece of information?" and "Who else would want to know about it?" Then, according to your answers, follow through. If people believe you are hiding information in order to put them at a disadvantage, you'll create a whirlwind of ill will. If, however, you're generous with what you know, your respect level will soar.

Also, keep in mind that your managers and peers are busy people, just as you are. Therefore, if you plan to share information with them in person, tell them what they need to know and skip the peripheral, unimportant stuff. For example, which of the following messages would you rather listen to? "When I finished gathering the figures for my report, I decided to walk over to human resources to turn them in. On my way there I ran into Carol, and she told me that one of our big accounts may be moving to Texas." Or, "Carol just told me that one of our big accounts might move to Texas." The second message is easier to receive because it is not bogged down with irrelevant details. When you make it a habit of getting to the point, your managers and peers are more likely to listen to you.

Share Credit

A second way to foster professional intimacy among your coworkers and employers is to *share the credit.* Intimacy can't exist when one person—especially the boss—takes credit for the work. In groups (or work teams), one person may have been the originator of an idea, but it takes everyone's input to develop a thought into a concrete plan. Attempting to hog the credit breeds resentment and mistrust among your managers and peers.

Be Transparent

You will be more effective at work if you project openness and honesty—including the confidence to say what you believe in and to admit when you are uncertain. Being a transparent person doesn't mean you must divulge family secrets or unveil the details of your personal life. What is significant are your true opinions about an idea. Therefore, if someone asks you your opinion, answer honestly.

While transparency offers a rich sense of involvement, it also implies vulnerability. As a team player, you will be mentally, emotionally, and socially "exposed." You will not be free to sneak things by, to withhold information, to pretend you know something that you don't, or to propose self-serving policies that undermine team goals. In intimate situations, you must be trustworthy because you know that you are bound to your team in the long run by your shared purpose. "The lack of trust pervasive in most organizations is not a *cause* of lack of intimacy, but a symptom of it," writes Roberts.

Share Laughter

Some days our problems at work become larger and larger until we all feel "pinched," like our feet do when wearing shoes that fit too tightly. Humor can loosen things up. Intimate relationships are formed when we can laugh together. For years *Reader's Digest* has run a column titled, "Laughter, the Best Medicine." This little phrase offers a great prescription for office stress. Learn to laugh at yourself and at trying situations. Laughing with coworkers will help you to develop a bond, which will help you weather stressful times together.

Lend a Hand

How can your managers and peers feel close to you when you are absorbed with your own interests and never theirs? One of the most effective ways to demonstrate that you care is by offering to help your coworkers when they are overwhelmed. First, ask them how you can help. If they are stumped, suggest something. Perhaps you can send a fax for them, look up a piece of information that they need, or run an errand. Even offering to get them a cup of coffee shows you care about their plight.

If you're in a managerial position, maybe one of your staff could be put on temporary loan to your colleague for a day or so without undue disruption to your operations. (If your group interlocks in any way in an overall departmental job with another group, be sure that your part of the job is never so late as to cause another group's delay.) Looking out for the welfare of others melts barriers between you and your peers.

Embrace Diversity

"Few things trouble our world so persistently as the conflict between different races and backgrounds," wrote evangelist Billy Graham in his foreword to the book *Breaking Down Walls* by Raleigh Washington and Glen Kehrein. Some people in our society, and even in our business, say: "Stay with your own kind; you'll be happier." We doubt it. Those who have taken the risk of building cross-cultural and other diverse relationships testify to the ways their lives are enriched.

We no longer live in racial, religious, or any other kind of total isolation. Thankfully, we are learning together that different doesn't mean inferior. What will it take to build these diverse relationships? Washington and Kehrein believe it will take a combination of attitude and action. Next we'll discuss ways to increase your level of commitment to diverse relationships in the workplace.

Develop Sensitivity

1. Read literature about and by members of racial groups different from your own. Reading is one of the best ways to build sensitivity.

2. Do not dismiss unintentional insensitivity that stereotypes groups of people. Racial or sexual jokes and slurs may seem unimportant to you, but they have an impact on the workplace. To say it was "nothing" and unintended will be taken as rationalization and justification. If you have offended someone, apologize for the action. Your humility can pull the two of you closer together.

3. Affirm your coworkers' and managers' own cultural identities. For example, if you have a Jewish colleague, give him a greeting card on the first day of Hanukkah. He'll remember this small act of kindness.

Show Respect

Respect allows for differences. Everybody brings something of value to the work environment, creating a relationship of equals. If you have a cross-cultural relationship at work, specifically identify strengths that the other person brings to your relationship. Then thank that person for that gift to your relationship. Acknowledging your need for their expertise and competence translates into respect for that person. When your managers and coworkers know you respect them, a dividing wall is broken down.

Take the First Step

Be willing to reach out to someone who is racially or culturally different, even if you risk misunderstanding by that person. One way to reach out is to move beyond saying hello; for example, initiating a conversation that goes beyond superficial chitchat. You could begin by asking about the artwork or photographs she has displayed in her office. If appropriate in your work setting, invite your coworker to lunch so you can get to know him better.

SOCIAL SKILLS FOR THE TWENTY-FIRST CENTURY

By the end of the century, one-third of the U. S. workforce will be "knowledge workers," people whose productivity is marked by adding value to information—whether as market analysts, writers, or computer programmers (*Harvard*

Business Review, Oct. 1977). Peter Drucker, the eminent business maverick who coined the term "knowledge worker," points out that knowledge workers' expertise is highly specialized, and that their productivity depends on their efforts being coordinated as part of an organizational team. While people have always worked in tandem, notes Drucker, with knowledge work, "teams become the work unit rather than the individual himself." This suggests why the skills that help people harmonize should become increasingly valued as a workplace asset in the years to come.

Interpersonal Stars

Just how well people can develop a network—in effect, call on workers in various areas of expertise to solve a problem—is a crucial factor in on-the-job success. Consider, for example, a study of star performers at Bell Lab, the world-famous scientific think tank near Princeton University. The stars studied were from a unit that creates and designs the electronic switches that control telephone systems—a highly sophisticated and technical piece of electronic engineering. Because the work is so difficult, it is done in teams that can range from 5 to 150 members. No single engineer knows enough to do the job alone; getting the job done means tapping other people's expertise. To find out what makes the difference between members who are highly productive and those who are only average, the authors of the study, Robert Kelley and Janet Caplan, had managers and peers nominate the 10 to 15 percent of engineers who stood out as "stars."

Kelly and Caplan reported the following in the *Harvard Business Review:* "Based on a wide range of cognitive and social measures, from standard tests for IQ to personality inventories, there's little meaningful difference in innate abilities. . . . [A]cademic talent was not a good predictor of on-the-job productivity." After detailed interviews, critical differences emerged in the interpersonal strategies the "star" performers used to get their work done. One of the most important differences turned out to be a rapport with a network of key people. Things go more smoothly for the stars because they put time into cultivating good relationships with people whose services might be needed in a crunch to solve a problem or handle a crisis. "A middle performer at Bell Labs talked about being stumped by a technical problem," Kelley and Caplan observed. "He painstakingly called technical gurus and then waited, wasting valuable time while calls and e-mail messages went unreturned. Star performers, however, rarely face such situations because they do the work of building reliable networks before they actually need them. When they call someone for advice, stars almost always get a faster answer."

Many things people do at work depend on their ability to call on an informal network of fellow workers; different tasks can mean retrieving information from a variety of people, depending on their line of expertise. And as knowledge-based services and intellectual capital become more central to corporations, improving the way people work together will be a major leverage point.

Our job in this module has been to help you keep in proper perspective the degree to which good relationships can help you in getting the total job done. Put purely and simply, one of the best tools for maintaining balance in your career is building good work relationships. If you actively keep this thought in your mind, your chances for total success will be multiplied.

Applications & Exercises

Key Into Your Life: Opportunities to Apply What You Learn

1. Conflict Resolution

Visualize your most recent or most striking conflict situation, then respond to the following:

1. Briefly describe the problem you faced.

_____

_____

2. How did you *feel* about the problem?

_____

_____

3. How did you *respond* to that feeling?

_____

_____

4. Did you make a *request,* and if so, what was it?

_____

_____

5. What was the *outcome* of the conflict?

_____

_____

6. What could you have done *differently?*

_____

_____

2. Listening

Be on the lookout for someone who needs a listening ear. Pay attention to their nonverbal cues and then record what happened.

Name of the person you spoke with:

_____

What they talked about:

_____

Something you learned about this person:

_____

List any nonverbal cues you noticed:

_____

_____

Other insights:

_____

_____

3. Praise

Think of someone you know who needs encouragement. Write down what you want to say to them.

_____

_____

After you've said it to them, record their responses.

_____

_____

Is there a way you could have worded the praise in order to enhance its effectiveness? If so, rewrite it.

_____

_____

Key to Cooperative Learning: Building Teamwork Skills

1. Asking Questions

With a group of other students, brainstorm to find at least five thought-provoking questions that you can ask someone at your school. After you have tried to answer these questions within your group, set up meetings with a counselor, administrator, job placement advisor, and so forth for their insight. (Ask no more than two questions of the same person.)

Question #1:

_____

Question #2:

_____

Question #3:

_____

Question #4:

_____

Question #5:

_____

MEETING 1

Name of the person you met:

_____

Position at your school:

_____

Something you learned about this person:

_____

_____

_____

Something new you found out that can help you with your studies or your working life:

_____

_____

_____

Other insights:

_____

_____

_____

MEETING 2

Name of the person you met:

_____

Position at your school:

_____

Something you learned about this person:

_____

_____

_____

Something new you found out that can help you with your studies or your working life:

_____

_____

_____

Other insights:

_____

_____

_____

MEETING 3

Name of the person you met:

_____

Position at your school:

_____

Something you learned about this person:

_____

_____

_____

Something new you found out that can help you with your studies or your working life:

_____

_____

_____

Other insights:

_____

_____

_____

Key to Self-Expression: Discovery Through Journal Writing

1. Healthy Dialogue

Remember the conflict you recorded in Exercise 1 in "Key Into Your Life"? Review your answer to question 6—what you could have done differently. Write down a dialogue on the same subject, touching on the same problems and frustrations, but handle the conflict in a way that everyone can walk away from feeling some measure of success. Write the dialogue for all parties, and be fair. This exercise will help you to control your anger when you are in a similar situation, and will remind you what you need to do to solve conflict in a win-win fashion.

19 COMMUNICATING EFFECTIVELY
Groups, Meetings, and Presentations

In this chapter, you will explore answers to the following questions:

➤ What is a group?

➤ How do groups make decisions and solve problems?

➤ What is the key to leading a successful meeting?

➤ How do I encourage participation in meetings?

➤ Why is the audience the number one consideration when giving a presentation?

➤ How should a presentation be organized?

❓ Thinking It Through

Check those statements that currently apply to you:

☐ I don't know what to expect when working in a group.

☐ I'm not sure how to be an effective group participant.

☐ Meetings often seem to be a waste of time and I don't know how to help change that.

☐ I avoid giving presentations because I don't think I can do a good job.

☐ I need help organizing and presenting information to a group.

321

E X P R E S

EXPRES

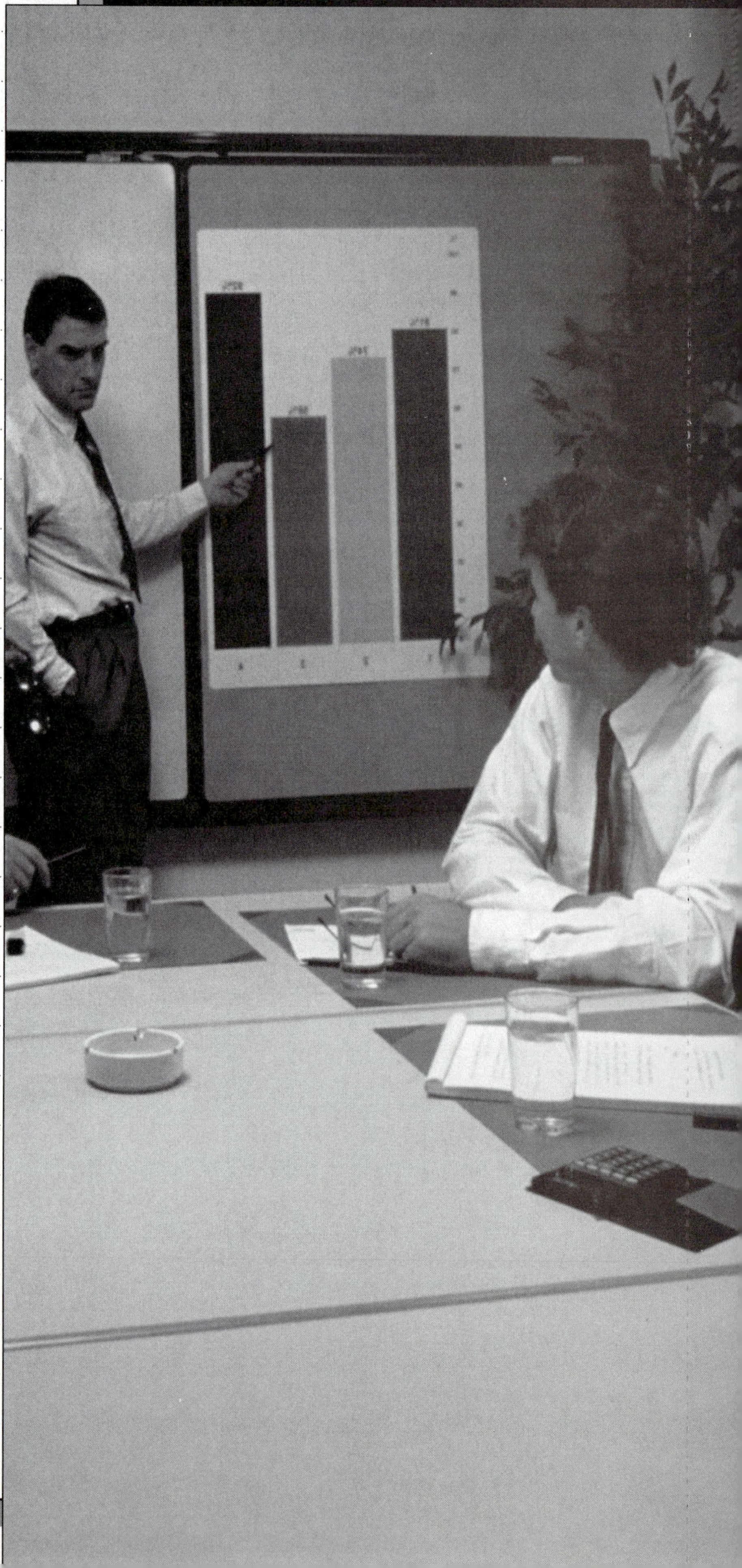

19

COMMUNICATING EFFECTIVELY
Groups, Meetings, and Presentations

We hear a lot about communicating effectively these days. Talk shows, radio programs, and popular books all discuss the merits of communicating well. Why is it such a big deal? Well, as Lee Iaccoca, the former CEO of the Chrysler Corporation once said, "You can have brilliant ideas, but if you can't get them across, your brains won't get you anywhere." In this chapter, we will discuss how to get your ideas across in three specific contexts: groups, meetings, and presentations. Let's get started.

GROUP COMMUNICATION

Ricardo Ramirez has just landed his dream job in the marketing department of a major magazine publisher. He knows it is a big organization, and wonders how he'll ever feel at home. But it's a fabulous opportunity, and he can't wait to start. On his first day, he is escorted directly to the conference room where he is introduced to his new "group." He smiles and makes polite conversation, but wonders, "My *group*? What does that mean? What do these people expect of me? What should I expect of them?"

New hires encounter this situation on a daily basis. Businesses increasingly rely on small groups within their organizations to perform specific functions and meet important goals. Take a quick look at today's want ads, and you'll frequently find companies looking for "team players," or "someone who works well in a group." As you move up the ladder of success in the workplace, research shows that you will find yourself participating in various group meetings the majority of the time. One study showed that the average CEO in the United States spends about 6 hours of every day participating in group meetings—that's around 1,560 hours per year! Since you'll be doing a lot of group work in whatever profession you choose, it makes sense to understand how groups work, and how you can be a successful group member.

What Is a Group?

According to communications professor Gerald Wilson, a group is "a collection of three or more individuals who interact about some common problem or interdependent goal and can exert mutual influence over one another." In other words, groups involve people working together and depending on one another to accomplish an agreed-upon goal. Members of groups share ideas, make decisions, solve problems, and foster relationships. Everyone has been a part of a group at some point. You may have been a Boy Scout, a cheerleader, or a member of a sports team. You have undoubtedly been assigned to a work group as part of a class project in school. As an adult, you may be a part of a political action group or some kind of support group. These are all legitimate group experiences.

In the workplace, you will most likely be assigned to a particular *work group*. You may have also heard the term *teams* used frequently. These terms are interchangeable for our purposes. The potential benefits of groups are immense. According to one study, a team environment can "break down departmental barriers, provide developmental challenges, free up management, and improve customer service."

What to Expect in Your Group

When you first join a group, you will probably be concerned with two things: (1) Will we like each other? (2) Will we accomplish the work we are here to do? In the first controlled study of group development, researcher Robert Bales discovered that these two concerns predominate all groups. He called the first concern the *socioemotional dimension* and the second the *task dimension*. Most

group members want to do some socializing, but they also want to get some work done. When there is only one dimension, the group cannot be productive.

Bales also noted that when groups initially form, they tend to emphasize the socioemotional dimension. They ask questions about each other and discuss interpersonal issues. Then, as socioemotional needs are met, the group can move on to the task dimension. This relationship-task cycle tends to continue throughout the life of the group. When groups have been particularly successful in the socioemotional realm, they are said to have high levels of cohesion. Let's examine cohesion in depth.

Group Cohesion

Clearly, it's not enough to just know how to do your job. If you're working in a group setting, the people in your group help determine whether your work is successful. In other words, relational dynamics are very important in the group context. It's common sense that people who like each other tend to work well together. As a general rule, research confirms that highly cohesive groups are more successful at reaching their goals than groups with low cohesion.

However, it is possible to have too much of a good thing in terms of cohesion. Gerald Wilson, author of *Groups in Context,* explains it this way: "At some point it is possible for a task group to be too cohesive. If cohesiveness is more intense [than task orientation], productivity suffers."

You have probably experienced this firsthand. Often, a group assembles to plan a project or presentation. Everyone is involved in the conversation, and everyone seems to genuinely like each other. Eventually, the social aspect takes over, and the task can go by the wayside. These are the meetings that essentially turn into "parties."

In any group, it is important to strike a balance between accomplishing tasks and fostering healthy relationships. Promoting an optimal level of cohesiveness is essential to the success of any group. According to communications professor Ron Adler in *Communicating at Work,* there are eight conditions in groups that lead to healthy cohesiveness. As a rule, groups tend to be more cohesive when they

1. *Emphasize shared or compatible goals.* Group members tend to increase cohesion when they are all on the same page. When groups know where they're going and have similar goals, they draw closer together.

2. *Strive for progress toward these goals.* It's fine to share the same goals. But it's another thing to reach them consistently. Group members tend to feel closer when they feel they are progressing toward a target. If they consistently fail, they will feel discouraged and feel less attracted to the group. No one likes to be on a losing team.

3. *Promote shared norms or values.* Groups function best when the members have similar beliefs and values. Think about your current group of friends. If you think about it, you are probably similar in terms of values and beliefs. Let's say you are all moderate drinkers, tend to be junk food junkies, and have no real religious affiliations. But one of your friends decides he needs a change, and he becomes a health food nut, gives up drinking altogether, and joins a religious club on campus. This will undoubtedly have an effect on the dynamics in your group of friends. However, it is important to note that research shows that some variation is healthy and challenging. Otherwise, a group can get pretty boring.

4. *Minimize feelings of threat among members.* Change is inevitable even in groups. Classmates transfer to other colleges. Coworkers get promoted, demoted, and transferred. Company policies change. Technology advances. All of these may make group members feel threatened. It is important that groups recognize threatening dynamics and work toward helping each other adjust to changes in the group culture.

5. *Create interdependence among members.* Groups whose members need each other to reach a group goal will be more cohesive than those in which members work independently toward group goals. An in-depth study of the Xerox Corporation revealed that some teams were designed so that members were required to work together to accomplish certain tasks. Other teams completed tasks as individuals, but called themselves teams. The study concluded that teams whose members worked together rather than individually learned more about effective group operations and were happier team members.

6. *Encourage competition from outside the group.* If you have ever played sports, you probably know that competition with an opposing team boosts relationships within your own team. Setting up group contests within organizations tends to make groups bond together and accomplish tasks faster.

7. *Enhance mutual perceived attractiveness and friendship.* Again, cohesion happens when group members like each other. Focusing on developing friendships within the group enhances feelings of closeness.

8. *Create shared group experiences.* As a general rule: Groups who play together, stay together. It is important to create fun experiences that help the group develop shared memories. Many companies provide special events to help this process. One popular trend in corporations is a "retreat" in which groups get away for a weekend to attend workshops, plan for the future, and most importantly, play together.

Leadership of Groups

"A group may not need a specific leader, but it always needs leadership," states Stephen Lucas in *The Art of Public Speaking.* Leadership in a team environment is very different from leadership in the traditional workplace. You may work in a group with a designated leader, or you may find that no one is officially in charge. This is very different from the traditional hierarchical workplace. In the traditional model, managers assign tasks, direct work throughout the process, and make sure employees are working on the tasks at all times. They also provide rewards and/or punishment to individuals, depending on their performance.

In a team environment, leadership is generally less structured and more participative. Rather than simply taking orders from a boss, group members discuss ideas, attempt to persuade one another, and make team decisions. Many work groups today are called *self-managed teams.* In a self-managed team, the group members are all responsible for managing one another. This requires accountability and initiative on the part of each individual. Companies such as General Mills, 3M, and Federal Express have successfully implemented self-managed teams, and productivity levels have soared at all three organizations.

However, many organizations continue to operate with designated group leaders. The leader helps her group establish a purpose and mission, and coaches the team toward the accomplishment of that mission. However, the most effective teams are allowed to make their own decisions about how to carry out the mission. The leader specifies the ends, not the means. In other words, the team gets to choose its own path toward the team's goals. Obviously, this requires more active participation from all group members and creates shared responsibilities.

Columbia University professor Ruth Wageman suggests the following three primary roles that designated leaders play:

1. *Designer.* When the group is initially formed, a leader should help set a direction for the group, design task and reward systems, make sure everyone has adequate resources, and establish responsibility requirements. In essence, the design process involves putting together a general "blueprint." Then, the team members decide how to fill in the blueprint with their own creativity and personal styles.

2. *Midwife.* After the team is launched, the leader helps the team establish performance goals. The leader also encourages group members to make decisions about how they will use their resources and authority to achieve objectives. Helping the team set goals and make decisions leads them in the direction of self-management.

3. *Coach.* This third role will be the primary role that takes over for the remaining life of the team. Good coaches spend time interacting with the team, rewarding the team when they perform well and helping the team broaden its decision-making skills. In the problem-solving process, coaches facilitate discussions without imposing their own views of a solution. In other words, coaches make sure the team is running smoothly and give direction as needed. But again, the major bulk of responsibility lies within the team itself.

So if the leaders aren't telling everyone what to do, just how do decisions get made in groups? Let's take a look.

Decision Making and Problem Solving in Groups

As group members perform their everyday tasks, they face decision after decision. Some can be made individually, but many require group participation and consensus. There are a number of decision-making models that groups can adopt when they need to make highly structured decisions. One of the most popular approaches is the Reflective Thinking Method. This method was developed by philosopher John Dewey, and offers a step-by-step approach to solving problems and making decisions. The five steps in the process are (1) defining the problem, (2) analyzing the problem, (3) establishing criteria for solving the problem, (4) generating potential solutions, and (5) selecting the best solution. Next we'll discuss each step in more detail.

Define the problem.   Obviously, it is important to know what the problem is before you try to solve it. Usually, a problem is phrased in the form of a question. Basically, the group is asking itself, "What should we do?" It is important to phrase the question correctly, however. Communications professors Stephen Lucas offers the following guidelines (see box) for asking the right kinds of questions.

Guideline	Ineffective Question	Effective Question
Make sure the question is as clear and specific as possible.	What should we do to improve morale around here?	What should we do to increase employee satisfaction by 50 percent in the next six months?
Phrase the question to allow for a wide variety of answers.	Should we sue Company XYZ?	What steps should we take in order to solve our problem with Company XYZ?
Avoid biased or slanted questions.	What should we do about the idiotic new vacation policy?	What revisions should be made in the new vacation policy?
Tackle just one question at a time.	What should we do to increase our market share and brand recognition?	What should we do to increase our brand recognition?

Analyze the problem.   After the problem has been identified, analysis should begin. Do a little research. Find out how big the problem is, who it affects, what other solutions have been tried, and so forth. Don't put the cart before the horse. Investigate your problem thoroughly before you go any further.

For example, let's say your work group has been faced with the task of developing an orientation class for new employees. The existing class has been largely ineffective. So the problem statement is: "What revisions need to be made in the current training design?" To investigate the problem, you could

➤ talk to other companies who have successful training programs in place

➤ do some library research about training trends

➤ interview employees about what they liked or disliked about the former orientation style and solicit their suggestions for improvement

Establish criteria for solutions.   Let's say you are currently in the process of looking for a job. If you're like most people, you spend some time thinking about what type of job you want. You think about the title you would like to have, what industry you want to work in, how much money you need to make, and where you want the job to be located. In short, you establish criteria before you really begin the hunt.

This process should also take place in the group decision-making process. Set up some standards for acceptable solutions. For example, your team may have a budget of $20,000 to work with. So one criterion for solving the problem would be that it must cost less than twenty grand. Decide as a group what your solutions must achieve and what factors limit the solutions you choose.

In our new employee orientation scenario, possible criteria may be that the solution (1) must cost less than $20,000; (2) must be available in two months; (3) must decrease the new employee error rate by 25 percent; and (4) must result in a three-day class rather than a week-long class.

Generate potential solutions.   Now the fun begins. In this step, group members brainstorm possible solutions. Ideas should flow freely without evaluation or elimination. The point here is to generate as many ideas as possible. Evaluation and elimination come later.

Following are some of the potential solutions for our training group: (1) Hire a consultant who specializes in new employee orientation; (2) develop a computer-based training class; (3) require written exams in order to pass the training class; (4) prescreen applicants better to make sure they have the aptitude for the job; (5) set up a certification program; and (6) develop video-based training.

Select the best solution.   In this step, solutions are examined one by one and weighed against the criteria established earlier. The group will eliminate some options, and the list will narrow as the process goes along. When the list is sufficiently narrowed down, members decide on the very best solution(s). Ideally, the members should reach a consensus, meaning everyone agrees with the decision. However, it is not always possible to reach a consensus. Many groups reach a stalemate and opt for a vote. Voting should take place only after it has been determined that consensus cannot be reached.

The Reflective Thinking Method works well in groups that like structure and agree to follow the steps correctly. However, not all groups like this much structure. Some groups don't adopt a formal model for decision making. Rather, they just start discussing the task at hand and see what happens from there. Surprisingly, even unstructured problem-solving discussions tend to have a general pattern. Communications scholar Aubrey Fisher studied audiotapes of 10 different groups and found that they all progressed through four distinct stages: orientation, conflict, emergence, and reinforcement.

1. *Orientation.* During the orientation stage, group members are polite and tentative. Everyone is attempting to understand the task in front of them. No one wants to be viewed as aggressive or boorish, so statements may seem a bit vague and noncommittal. Group members are usually pleased with the harmony that predominates this phase, and they feel confident that things are going to run very smoothly.

2. *Conflict.* In the conflict stage, group members have more well-developed opinions than during the first stage, and they begin to argue their own points of view. Gone are the tentative statements and ambiguous remarks. In this stage, opinions fly, egos may be bruised, and coalitions may form. Some groups actually get stuck in the conflict stage and find it necessary to disband the group altogether.

3. *Emergence.* However, most groups make it through this stage and come to a decision-making point. The willingness to make a decision leads them into the emergence phase. In this phase, conflict subsides, and members return to a more tentative communication style. They use phrases like "Perhaps this would work" or "Let's try it." The coalitions weaken, and those members who still have objections tend to not express them.

4. *Reinforcement.* The final stage of the process is reinforcement. In this stage, members endorse the decision that has been made, and the group bands together to defend the decision against any outsiders who attack it. The tension of the previous stages is gone and social harmony returns. Group members feel like things are "back to normal"; an atmosphere of lighthearted laughter and joking may return.

Even though a large number of groups tend to follow this progression, it is important to remember that not all groups neatly move through these stages. Some groups may get "stuck" in a phase and never move ahead. But many groups predictably move through these stages whenever a new decision arises. Even groups that have worked together for years may fall back into polite, orientation-stage behavior when a new decision needs to be made. Now that you know about these stages, you can rest easy when your group is in heavy conflict or when everyone acts overly polite. You'll know that this stage will pass, and you can be planning ahead for the next stage.

HOW TO MAKE THE MOST OF YOUR GROUP EXPERIENCE

➤ *Back up your group*—Once you are familiar with the team's mission and goals, it is important to get behind them. Let your group know that you are excited to carry out the team's mission. Let everyone know how you would like to participate in the accomplishment of the group goals.

➤ *Check your ego at the door*—By now you know that conflict will definitely happen on any team. Don't be offended when your ideas are refuted or your suggestions aren't accepted. Everyone has some ideas that are great, even brilliant—and everyone occasionally offers a rotten idea. Remember, Babe Ruth had more strike-outs than home runs. Capitalize on your strengths, not your weaknesses.

➤ *Do your part*—When you are assigned a task, surprise your group with how well you did your job. Get it done on time. Exceed their expectations. Let them know how hard you are working to make everyone a success.

➤ *Observe, observe, observe*—Take in everything you can about productive behaviors in your group. Emulate the good behaviors. Learn from the bad ones.

➤ *Disagree (sometimes)*—Groups whose members always agree tend to make poorly thought-out decisions. If no one offers an alternative perspective, the results are often disastrous. Sometimes, you can be helpful to your group by playing the devil's advocate. Just make sure you do it appropriately. When you disagree with something, be sure you always attack the idea, not the person who presented it.

➤ *Work on your people skills*—Do everything you can to be a good communicator in your group. Verbally encourage individual team members and let them know how important they are to the group. Make eye contact. Listen attentively. Make it your mission to be an exceptionally positive force on the team.

MEETINGS

Groups frequently assemble to discuss specific topics or concerns. In this segment, we will discuss group communication in a particular setting: the meeting. Meetings frequently take place within the team setting, but can also occur at a companywide level. In large companies, several different teams might meet regularly to make sure the work functions of each team are complementary and to achieve organizational goals. Meetings are a reality of corporate life; they can present an opportunity to learn a great deal about what's going on in the company. It's also a time to connect socially.

However, meetings tend to get a bad rap because so many of them are poorly done. We have all been in boring, unproductive meetings. Many of us have counted the tiles on the floor, daydreamed, or fallen asleep in a seemingly endless meeting. But meetings don't need to be boring. A good deal of literature has emerged in recent years about making meetings more exciting and productive. If you're lucky, your future managers will have read some of these books and will strive to make your meetings more interesting. Or maybe you can share some of your knowledge and become a hero to your boss.

Leading Meetings Successfully

If you find yourself in a position of leadership at a meeting, there are several important things you need to know. First of all, it is important to decide what situations call for a meeting. The major reason people have meetings is to interact. If there are no plans for interaction, then you could probably just draft a memo. Usually, people meet to share information, solve problems, make decisions, or celebrate company victories. Always ask yourself if the task at hand requires human interaction or if the information can be dispersed in writing. Nothing makes people crankier than feeling like a meeting is unnecessary, so avoid this mistake at all costs.

Setting an Agenda

Once you have decided that a meeting really is necessary, distribute an agenda to the participants a few days before the meeting. The following items should appear on the agenda:

1. beginning and ending time for the meeting
2. who will attend
3. where the meeting will be held
4. the purpose of the meeting
5. any tasks that need to be completed before the meeting
6. phone number where participants can call to let you know if they'll attend
7. a list of items that will be discussed (*Hint:* Put the "mentally taxing" items first, when everyone is alert and energetic.)

When participants receive an agenda, they can be fully prepared for the meeting. They will also have better attitudes about the meeting because they know that it is a well-planned event. They know the goal of the meeting and have an idea of what will be accomplished by the time the meeting adjourns. Take a few minutes to write an agenda for every meeting. You'll be happy with the results.

Encouraging Participation in Meetings

Facilitation skills. When you lead a meeting, it is important to help everyone get involved in the discussion process. You can help this process along through taking on the role of a facilitator. In this role, you gently guide the conversation and encourage balanced participation. There are four important functions that superior facilitators carry out.

WHAT SUPERIOR FACILITATORS DO

1. *They clarify.* They make sure they are understanding statements by rephrasing what has been said, and perhaps by asking the participant to explain the perspective using an example. This allows any misunderstanding to be "nipped in the bud."

2. *They remind.* Facilitators gently remind participants to stay on track, and they let everyone share their perspective. When someone is monopolizing a conversation, or not participating at all, facilitators try to remedy the situation. For example, if Pedro is monopolizing, and Sydney isn't saying anything, the facilitator may say, "I feel like I have a clear understanding of your take on the issue, Pedro. Sydney, what are your thoughts?"

3. *They make connections.* Facilitators look for common threads among group members. They look for points of agreement or similar approaches to a particular problem. This helps to unify the group, and it leads to a course of action. For example, a connecting comment might be, "Sydney feels like the press releases are not effective. Colson, you've expressed this same thought in the past. What do you have to add?"

4. *They summarize.* Facilitators summarize what has been communicated, what has been decided, or what action is planned. At the end of a meeting, facilitators also reiterate what positive accomplishments have been made in the meeting. This gives everyone a sense of satisfaction, knowing the time has been well spent.

Creating a Fun Meeting Environment

In addition to creating a safe place for interaction to occur, some facilitators go a step further. They look for creative ways to help participants have fun with the material being discussed. According to one author, "the use of games and exercises to teach hard business lessons is becoming widely accepted among proponents of adult learning theories." Try a simple icebreaker like a brain teaser to get everyone's mind in high gear. Or divide the participants into small groups for a few minutes and ask them to come up with a metaphor that describes the company climate.

There are a lot of resources in bookstores about adding creativity to your meetings. Explore the literature on structured experiences and workplace games. Then, add a little creativity of your own—and dare to have fun in your meetings.

Being a Meeting Participant

When you are a participant in meetings, you may think that you can just "show up." Not true. You are part of the success of the meeting, no matter how small you think your role is. Review the points we discussed earlier in the "How to

Make the Most of Your Group Experience" section. These ideas apply to meetings as well.

PRESENTATIONS

One of the functions you may be asked to perform in your professional life as well as in college is giving a presentation. From groups of just a few people to convention meetings of several thousand, knowing how to give an effective presentation is critical to your success. Research from both the academic and popular press confirm that good communicators move up the corporate ladder more quickly than their less skilled counterparts. Want proof? Consider the following:

➤ Alumni surveyed by the College Placement Council one, seven, and ten years after they had graduated testified that communication was critical for job success, regardless of the field. Most respondents said that communication was more important than the major subject they had studied!

➤ A University of Michigan study asked 1,156 graduates "Which courses best prepare one for business leadership?" Business communication ranked the highest overall, and 71 percent ranked it as the most important course. All of these graduates were recently promoted chairs, presidents, and vice presidents in their respective companies.

➤ When 170 business and industrial firms were asked to list the most common reasons for not offering jobs to applicants, the most frequent replies were "inability to communicate" and "poor communication skills."

Hopefully, you are now convinced that this segment is an important one. You absolutely must have good presentation skills in order to be successful in any field. Many students don't take full advantage of their public speaking classes while in college. When they get into the job market, they find that their ability to advance is impeded by their inability to communicate. So they attend seminars, read books, and hire coaches in hopes of gaining this much-needed skill. Don't make this same mistake. You have the opportunity NOW to develop your presentation skills. So let's get started.

Your Audience: Your Number One Consideration

Believe it or not, the purpose of giving a presentation is not to make yourself look good. The purpose of public speaking is to gain a desired response from listeners. Successful public speakers focus on the *audience,* not on themselves. Your first task as a public speaker is to find out as much as you can about your audience, so you can gain your desired response. What happens if you don't put your audience first? Well, your speech might be a complete flop! For example, consider the following story:

> *Bill Reynolds is a social worker who was asked to give a presentation to some recent immigrants from South America. He was scheduled to deliver an 8-week orientation to help the immigrants adjust to American culture. On their*

first Friday evening meeting, he tried to create a casual atmosphere, and he talked a little bit about American cultural norms. He even served hamburgers and fries to show a typical American meal choice. He tried to lighten things up by telling some jokes, but they seemed to fall flat. He then moved on to a discussion of politics and the American economy. However, the audience seemed increasingly uncomfortable, so he cut things short. As a parting comment, he suggested that future meetings be held on Sunday afternoons, and finished his comments by gesturing with the "A-OK sign." At this point, the audience looked shocked, began whispering to each other, then filed out of the room quickly.

What went wrong for Bill? Well, just about everything. If he had researched just a few simple questions, he could have avoided most of the problems. First of all, Bill's audience was made up of very orthodox Catholics. They were uncomfortable with the meal because it was a Friday. Many Catholics abstain from eating meat on Fridays. His suggestion that future meetings be held on Sundays was also a problem because the group believed strongly in keeping the Sabbath. His jokes fell flat because he used some slang terms that were not understandable to this group. His discussion of politics was entirely over their heads, as they were mainly high school–educated laborers. Finally, when he made the A-OK sign, he might as well have given them the middle finger. This gesture is very offensive in many South American countries.

Bill had good intentions, but his presentation was a complete failure due to poor audience analysis. This is an extreme example, but it illustrates the types of things that can go wrong if you don't investigate your audience. Most professional speakers have a list of detailed questions they ask each client before they begin planning the presentation. One successful speaker reported that he routinely asks 60 questions of each client before he begins writing his presentation!

So what type of questions should you ask? Start with some simple demographic questions. Ask about the gender, age, ethnicity, educational level, cultural background, and religious affiliations of the audience. Then, ask what groups they belong to and what political affiliations they might have. Find out if the audience is required to attend your presentation, or if they plan to come voluntarily. In short, find out as much as you can, so that your presentation is uniquely tailored to them. They will feel honored that you cared enough to find out about them, and you will feel more confident about your presentation.

Setting a Speaking Goal

A presentation goal is very simple. It is a statement of what you want the audience to understand, believe, or do by the time you have finished speaking. It is a way for you to focus your presentation, and have a firm sense of why you are presenting in the first place. Rather than aimlessly sharing some ideas, a presentation goal gives you an overarching purpose that guides all of your comments. It is always helpful to place your goal at the very top of your outline or speaking notes. The statement begins pretty much the same way each time you speak: By the end of my presentation, I want my audience to _____. Simply identify what you want from your audience before you begin assembling your speech, and you'll feel much more focused throughout the entire process. Here are some examples of well-worded presentation goals:

"By the end of my presentation, I want my audience to

➤ understand the new company procedure for reporting sexual harassment."
➤ believe that our school district needs more qualified science teachers."
➤ donate money to the March of Dimes."
➤ sign up to volunteer for Habitat for Humanity."

How will you know if you have achieved your goal? If you are asking for an action, it will be fairly clear. The response will be tangible. Audience members will be signing up to volunteer, taking out their wallets, or signing on the dotted line. But if your goal was to help the audience understand or believe something, how will you know? Simple—ask. Excellent speakers always solicit feedback from the audience after they have concluded their presentations. They make certain that their goal has been met. Your college speech class will undoubtedly provide opportunities for you to receive oral and written feedback from your instructor and your peers. Take advantage of this time, and always ask if the audience understood your goal. If they didn't understand the goal, you probably didn't achieve it.

Organizing Your Presentation

If you failed to communicate a presentation goal, chances are you simply had a problem organizing your message. Planning a clearly organized presentation is essential to its success. You must chart a path through your speech that is clear and easy to follow. So where do you begin charting this path? With a map, of course.

Semantic mapping.   Developing main ideas from just one topic idea can be very overwhelming. Most of us simply don't think in terms of nice, neat outlines with a main point, a sub-point, and a sub-sub-point. Instead, most of us tend to just start writing, hoping some good ideas spill onto the paper. Further, we hope that the ideas will be well organized and brilliant. Sadly, this approach just doesn't work, especially in the context of speech writing. You aren't just writing an essay. Rather, you are preparing a *talk,* which means clarity of ideas is most important.

One approach that helps get the ball rolling is semantic mapping, or mind mapping. This technique involves placing your main topic at the top of a page, and then breaking the topic down by branching out. This is a brainstorming process, so don't edit your ideas. Just start filling in the branches until you think you have sufficiently narrowed your ideas down. Then, pick three to four branches that represent your best ideas on the topic. These become the main ideas for the body of your speech.

For example, if your topic is date rape, break down the different areas that should be discussed until you feel they are narrow enough to be covered within the time allotted for your speech. If your speech is 5 to 7 minutes long, determine the most important nuggets of information that you want the audience to understand. Remember, your job is to be clear, keep them interested, and accomplish your goal. They can always ask you for more information after the presentation is over.

Once you have mapped out some ideas, determine the very best order in which to place your main ideas. Many speech texts list endless options for orga-

PRESENTATION GOAL: By the end of my presentation, I want my audience to understand date rape.

DATE RAPE

What it is   The profile of a date rapist   Consequences of date rape   What to do if it happens to you

nizing your ideas. There are no formulas for which type of organizational pattern to pick for which type of speech. The key is this: Any organizational pattern is better than no pattern. Play around with different ways to organize your message. Practice the different patterns out loud. Ask a friend or roommate which pattern sounds the best. Then, trust your instincts. If you have really put some effort into making your message clear and you have tried it out on one or two other people, chances are you're on the right track.

Supporting Material

So you have your goal, you know what your main ideas will be, and you have an organizational pattern mapped out. What's next? Well, if you want to keep the audience curious, you must find a way to make your ideas interesting and believable. This is accomplished through supporting material in the form of examples, analogies, illustrations, facts, statistics, or expert testimony. These are all elements that are used to help the audience relate to your ideas.

For example, let's continue with our date rape speech. One of the main ideas is a description of the consequence of date rape. You may be tempted to just list the different consequences, then move on to your next idea. But this doesn't meet our criteria for supporting material. Remember, each idea you present should be interesting and believable. One way to make this section interesting would be to discuss a case study that describes some of the consequences experienced by a date rape victim. This makes the issue more real, and helps the audience empathize with the people behind the issue.

Then to make your point believable, bolster your example with data. In this case, you might cite some expert testimony from a psychologist who works with date rape victims. You could also cite a study of date rape victims that discusses the percentages of people who experience aftermath consequences. So remember, for each main idea, (1) make it interesting (anecdote, example, illustration) and (2) make it believable (fact, statistic, expert testimony).

Introduction

When you finish the body of your speech, you are well on your way. You have the main substance ready to go, but you are missing two extremely vital elements: the beginning and the end. Research shows that audiences make decisions about speakers very quickly, so we'll discuss introductions first. Your audience will begin forming opinions about you as a speaker one to two minutes after you begin. They will decide whether to keep listening, start daydreaming, or fall asleep. So it's incredibly important that your introduction is effective.

Also, if you're like most people, it is very easy to remember the beginning of a speech and fairly easy to remember the end. This phenomenon is called the primacy-recency effect. Our brains seem to be wired in such a way that we remember firsts and lasts. What does this mean to you as a speaker? Simply put, it means that the first and last thing you say better be good because your audience will most likely remember these elements of the presentation.

Spend time thinking about a creative way to gain the attention of your audience. Use attention grabbers such as rhetorical questions, startling statistics, interesting stories, humorous anecdotes, or inspiring quotes. Just remember to connect your attention grabber to the main topic of your speech.

The Big Finish: Concluding Your Presentation

Just as the introduction of a presentation must be polished and well thought out, the conclusion is your final chance to shine. It will probably be remembered by your audience (thanks to the primacy-recency effect), so make sure it is done with style. You have probably heard speeches in which the speaker forgets to develop a strong conclusion. She or he may have finished by saying, "The end" or "That's it." Nothing ruins a good speech faster than a poor conclusion.

When you finish discussing the final point in the body of your speech, briefly summarize what you have talked about. After you have summarized, deliver a closing image. The final line of your speech should leave the audience with a sense of finality as well as something to "chew on." It is very much like the attention grabber in the introduction of a speech. You can end your speech with a quotation, a story, a humorous anecdote, or even a rhetorical question. Just make sure it is memorable.

You have undoubtedly heard Martin Luther King, Jr.'s famous speech entitled "I Have a Dream." If you think for just a moment, you can probably remember the final line. He concluded his speech by quoting an old spiritual: "Free at last, free at last, thank God almighty, we are free at last." This memorable finish encapsulated the spirit of the entire speech, and it sent the audience soaring. Study the concluding lines of your favorite speakers. You'll find a wealth of great ideas.

Delivery

Composing a presentation is much like writing a musical composition. Musicians would never write an entire musical score, and then play it at the end, when everything is on paper. Rather, they write a few bars, play it, edit, and start again. They know how it sounds at every stage in the process. Composing a presentation is a similar process. It is advisable to "talk" out your ideas as you are writing them so that you know your material sounds good out loud. After you have decided on your main ideas, talk aloud about one idea. Then, jot down the good stuff, and move on to the next idea. Then, when you have put all the pieces together, practice five to seven times from start to finish. By this time, you will know whether your speech is a beautiful symphony or a discordant mess. You will also reduce your anxiety about speaking because you will be intimately acquainted with your material. Remember, your job as a speaker is to have a conversation with the audience, not to read them an essay. Serious practice is the key to achieving this objective.

Following is a "Top 10 List" for delivery do's and don'ts:

1. Make sure that you look your audience members straight in the eye when speaking. Lock on to one person for a few seconds and then move on to another section of the room. If you just can't make direct eye contact, look at foreheads. No one will know the difference.

2. Place your hands at your sides or on the podium. Gesture naturally, don't plan your gestures or they will seem stilted. But *do* remember to gesture; otherwise you will seem overly stern.

3. Integrate some movement if it feels natural. A good time to take a few steps is when you are moving from one idea to the next. This visually emphasizes that you are shifting gears. Do not move aimlessly or you will appear to be pacing.

4. "Plant" your feet shoulder-width apart. This will help you avoid rocking or swaying.

5. Hold your shoulders back and stand up straight. This helps you look confident (even if you don't feel confident).

6. Speak in a natural, but energetic, fashion. Practice varying the inflection of your voice so that you don't sound monotone.

7. Avoid the tendency to make your inflection go up at the end of sentences. Make sure statements sound like statements and questions sound like questions.

8. Speak at a natural pace. The tendency is to rush when you get nervous. If you feel yourself speeding up, force yourself to pause for a couple of seconds and begin again at a slower pace.

9. Breathe!

10. Smile!

Visual Aids

Let's face it: We live in a visually oriented society. We watch endless hours of television and movies, and we have access to innumerable images on our computer screens. We are accustomed to watching as well as hearing. The implications for you as a speaker are obvious. It's a good idea to enhance what you are saying with visual aids. However, it is important to note that *aid* is the key word in the phrase. Visuals should *aid* the speaker; they should never become the main event. Too many speakers develop slick graphics and hope that it will make up for the fact that they are boring to listen to. This is poor logic, and it has been proved false time and time again. Make sure that *you* are the main event and that your visual aids act as a helpful "sideshow."

In order to use visual aids effectively, there are several points you should consider:

1. *Don't overload the audience.* The visuals should emphasize important points and add pizzazz to the presentation. It is a good idea to keep your visuals down to one per minute so the audience doesn't feel overloaded.

2. *Talk to the audience, not the visual.* Stand to the side of the visual you are presenting and gesture sideways toward it. Never, never turn your back on the audience.

3. *If in doubt, enlarge it.* When using text or slides on overheads, make sure your type size is at least 18 points. If you think a photo might be too small to see, have a color transparency made.

4. *Always prepare visuals ahead of time.* In other words, don't use chalkboards. They are difficult to see and don't produce a sharp image. Instead, use slides, overhead transparencies, or computer-generated displays. Make sure you arrive early to practice using your visuals.

5. *Hide your visuals.* Until you're ready to discuss them, that is. Don't leave a visual sitting in front of the podium, and don't distribute a handout before your presentation begins. People are easily distracted. Show your visual only when you are discussing it, and then get rid of it as soon as you are finished.

6. *Use color—wisely.* Color adds energy to your visuals, but don't get too excited and try to use every color in the rainbow just to keep things interesting. Inconsistent color schemes distract the audience.

7. *Explore the wonderful world of computer graphics.* Creating effective visuals is easier than ever with presentation software programs. One of the more popular programs is PowerPoint, which is probably available at your school. It is very easy to learn and use.

Applications & Exercises

Key Into Your Life: Opportunities to Apply What You Learn

For each of the following topics, draw a semantic map to narrow the topic down and identify the main points. Then, write a preview statement based on the semantic map.

EXAMPLE:

Topic: Stress
Semantic Map:
Preview Statement:

STRESS

Causes   Symptoms   Treatments

Today, in our examination of stress, we'll look at causes, how to recognize its symptoms, and finally, what you can do to treat it.

_____

Topic: Skiing
Semantic Map:
Preview Statement:

_____

_____

_____

Topic: Movies
Semantic Map:
Preview Statement:

_____

_____

_____

Topic: Travel
Semantic Map:
Preview Statement:

_____

_____

_____

Key to Cooperative Learning: Building Teamwork Skills

In groups of four or five, think about a current problem on your campus or in your community. Pretending that your group has the power to solve the problem, use the Reflective Thinking Method to (1) define the problem, (2) analyze the problem, (3) establish criteria for solutions, (4) generate possible solutions, and (5) select the best solution.

Key to Self-Expression: Discovery Through Journal Writing

You are probably a member of at least one group right now. Based on our discussion of positive group behavior, evaluate your contributions to your group. What are you doing to help promote group cohesion? What is your role in the problem-solving process? In what ways would you like to develop in your role as a group member? What positive behaviors have you observed among group members? Negative behaviors?

Key to Your Personal Portfolio: Your Paper Trail to Success

Based on the concepts you have learned about making presentations, develop a speech for your class. It can be based on any topic of interest to you. Be sure to carefully review the final section of this chapter, "Presentations," before you begin. After you have delivered your presentation, distribute a feedback form to your audience members, so you have written evaluations from several people. Then, based on the critiques, complete the following form:

What are your strengths as a speaker?

_____

_____

_____

Copy some positive comments from your feedback forms here:

_____

_____

_____

_____

In what areas do you need improvement?

_____

_____

_____

Copy some suggestions for improvement from your feedback forms:

_____

_____

_____

_____

What specific plans do you have for improvement? (List at least three)

_____

_____

_____

References

Adler, Ronald B. *Communicating at Work: Principles and Practice for Business and the Professions.* (New York: McGraw-Hill).

Benini, Carla. "In room interaction." *Meetings and Conventions* (May 1995): 125.

Foss, Sonja. Lecture notes. University of Colorado at Denver, Department of Communication. Denver, CO.

Kinlaw, Dennis. *The ASTD Trainer's Sourcebook: Facilitation Skills.* (New York: McGraw-Hill, 1996).

Lucas, Stephen. *The Art of Public Speaking,* 5th ed. (New York: McGraw-Hill, 1995).

Mendzela, Elisa. "Effective teams." *CPA Journal* (September 1997): 68.

Wageman, Ruth. "Critical success factors for creating superb self-managing teams." *Organizational Dynamics* (Summer 1997): 49.

Wilson, Gerald L. *Groups in Context: Leadership and Participation in Small Groups,* 4th ed. (New York: McGraw-Hill).

20 WHAT YOU SHOULD KNOW ABOUT SEXUAL HARASSMENT

Assessment and Protection

In this chapter, you will explore answers to the following questions:

➤ How is sexual harassment defined currently, and what are the different types of sexual harassment?

➤ What events helped to bring the subject of sexual harassment into the national spotlight?

➤ What is the "reasonable woman standard"?

➤ What is the scope of sexual harassment in the workplace?

➤ What is the cost of sexual harassment in the workplace?

➤ How should you deal with harassers?

? Thinking It Through

Check those statements that apply to you right now:

☐ I'm not sure I understand why things have changed so much in recent years regarding this issue.

☐ My workplace subjects me to mild harassment that is nonetheless annoying.

☐ I'm concerned that if I speak up about harassment problems with coworkers I'll be retaliated against.

P R O T E C T

T

WHAT YOU SHOULD KNOW ABOUT SEXUAL HARASSMENT

Assessment and Protection

In many workplaces, it used to be commonplace to make sexual jokes and propositions. Today, however, men and women are beginning to understand that such conduct at work may be unacceptable and could be against the law. Four key events in 1991 threw the national spotlight on sexual harassment, which has led not only to an increase in legal action but also to major shifts in the way we think about gender discrimination.

In the fall of 1991, the issue steamrolled into public consciousness when a University of Oklahoma law professor, Anita Hill, accused Clarence Thomas of sexual harassment, an allegation that delayed but did not stop Thomas' appointment and confirmation to the U.S. Supreme Court. Another focus that year was the U.S. Navy's Tailhook scandal involving sexual harassment of women attending a convention for naval aviators.

It wasn't business as usual in the courtrooms that year either. The passage of the Civil Rights Act of 1991 allowed jury trials for sexual harassment cases and "increased the nature and amount of compensatory and punitive damages that employers may be held liable for," according to Joyce Kaser, author of *Honoring Boundaries: Preventing Sexual Harassment in the Workplace* (Human Resource Development Press, 1995). Additionally, a 1991 U.S. Ninth Circuit Court of Appeals case, *Ellison vs. Brady,* recognized a "reasonable woman" standard rather than a "reasonable person standard," promoting the understanding that women may view mild sexual harassment as a prelude to violent sexual assault and feel it creates a hostile work environment.

A WORKING DEFINITION OF SEXUAL HARASSMENT

Sexual harassment is a form of sex discrimination and is against the law. Title VII of the Civil Rights Act of 1964 prohibits discrimination in the workplace based on race, color, religion, national origin, or sex. Title VII is enforced by the Equal Employment Opportunity Commission (EEOC). The EEOC defines sexual harassment as:

➤ unwelcome sexual advances;
➤ unwelcome requests for sexual favors; or
➤ unwelcome verbal or physical conduct of a sexual nature.

On the broad spectrum of sexual discrimination, sexual harassment is one of the more extreme and flagrant manifestations. Unlike some forms of sexual discrimination that result unintentionally from neutral policies or practices, sexual harassment arises out of deeply ingrained attitudes about sexual identities and sexual attitudes. Yet, as many recent court decisions illustrate, there may often be a fine line between what is acceptable workplace behavior and actions that cross the line to create an offensive environment, particularly to women.

Authors Anne C. Levy and Michele A. Paludi explain in their book *Workplace Sexual Harassment* the reason for this difficulty in semantics: "The term *sexual harassment* can be confusing because it has both a legal and a logical definition. To be termed sexual harassment by the law, harassing conduct or behavior must reach a level that the courts have defined as *beyond trivial or merely offensive.* Situations in a workplace may well be termed sexual harassment yet not reach the level of legally defined sexual harassment. What must be made clear to all workers, however, is that harassment because of another's gender does not belong in the workplace, whether such behavior does or does not meet the legal standard."

The "Reasonable Woman" Standard

The *Meritor Savings Bank v. Vinson* case is an extreme example of a hostile work environment. Not every case, however, is so easy to distinguish. Recently, the U.S. Ninth Circuit Court of Appeals reinstated a suit filed by a California woman, saying that in gauging whether the hostile work environment affected the employee's psychological well being, Title VII requires a "reasonable woman" standard. "The experience of men and women is so radically different," said Alison Wetherfield, of the National Organization for Women's Legal Defense and Education Fund, "that a gender-neutral, reasonable person standard does not work." The case, *Ellison v. Brady,* involved a coworker's continuing romantic overtures to Kerry Ellison, an employee of the Internal Revenue Service. There were neither threats nor physical contact between the two, but the man expressed in writing on two or three occasions his interest in a relationship, and in conversations he "pestered her with unnecessary questions." Although the lower courts deemed the behavior as trivial and merely part of the dating ritual, the appeals court viewed the situation from a woman's perspective and decided a hostile work environment had been created for Ms. Ellison.

The effect of actions on a "reasonable woman" also was weighed in a Florida case where a judge ruled that calendars and posters featuring nude or scantily dressed women created an atmosphere of sexual harassment that unlawfully stereotyped women as sex objects *(Robinson v. Jacksonville Shipyards).* Such recent court decisions are not radically changing how courts view sexual harassment, but they are refining the standards used to decide what precisely constitutes a "hostile" working environment.

Intent versus Impact

The way the "reasonable woman" standard gets played out in real life may be captured in the phrase *intent versus impact.* This means that some things men do, perhaps even unintentionally, are experienced by women as sexual harassment. "A discriminatory environment is created not by what is in the mind of the person carrying out the behavior, but rather by what effect it has on the person viewing the behavior," write Levy and Paludi.

Today, courts often look to sociologists and psychologists for help in understanding the effects of certain behavior on a plaintiff. Office behavior perceived as mere fun and games by the perpetrator may feel threatening and condescending to the receiver. Testimonies from social scientists are key in helping judges and jurors view the conduct from the alleged victim's perspective.

IDENTIFYING HARASSERS

The stereotypical case of a male supervisor harassing a female employee is only one example of sexual harassment. While it is primarily a problem for women, men are affected as well. In May 1992, for instance, a Los Angeles court ordered a manufacturer to pay a man $1 million in damages for sexual harassment by his female supervisor, an officer of the company. A recent report published by BNA Communications, Incorporated, a Maryland consulting firm, maintains that 15 percent of men believe they have been sexually harassed in the workplace. While their numbers are still relatively small, cases involving female supervisors harassing male subordinates are on the rise, according to *Nation's Business* (March 1995).

Furthermore, the victim and harasser may not even be of opposite genders. Thus, for example, a male supervisor's sexual advances toward a male employee may also constitute sexual harassment. As of this writing, the Supreme Court was studying a Louisiana case to decide whether on-the-job sexual harassment is illegal when the harasser and victim are the same sex. Bubbling to the surface of this scrutiny is whether the harassment was homosexually motivated, since both the harasser and victim are homosexual men. This case reveals the complexity of defining sexual harassment. Courts today grapple with a wide range of variables in determining exactly what sexual harassment entails.

In the midst of the confusion, however, one thing remains clear: Men and women have a right to a workplace free from all sexually offensive behavior—whether or not a court would consider it sexual harassment. And each worker is the judge of what behavior is sexually offensive to him or her.

TYPES OF SEXUAL HARASSMENT

The six types of sexual harassment include the following:

1.   Quid Pro Quo

Quid pro quo harassment, a legal term that literally means "this for that," occurs when a supervisor or manager seeks to exchange employment benefits for sexual favors, for instance, threatening to withhold perks if a request for sexual favors is rejected. Quid pro quo examples are the most clear cut; for example, "Sleep with me or you're fired." In the case of quid pro quo harassment, the company is liable for damages whether or not it knew about the supervisor's improper conduct.

The rationale for holding employers strictly liable in quid pro quo cases is that the supervisor is considered to be the employer because the harassment is accomplished by the authority that the employer specifically delegated to him or her. Until 1986, quid pro quo was the only legally recognized form of sexual harassment.

2.   Hostile Work Environment

The second—and less clear—form of sexual harassment is **hostile work environment.** A hostile work environment exists where supervisors and/or co-employees create an atmosphere so infused with unwelcome sexually-oriented conduct, such as sexual jokes, suggestive comments, unwanted physical contact, and pornographic displays, that an individual's reasonable comfort or ability to perform is affected. With hostile environment cases, the firm is liable if it knew or *should have known* of the circumstances and their effect on the employee. Claims based on a hostile environment make up the majority of cases.

Today's legal standard was set in the 1986 case, *Meritor Savings Bank v. Vinson,* in which a bank supervisor forced intercourse on the plaintiff, as well as exposed himself to her and other employees. The supervisor, however, had not made an offer of workplace benefits. The U.S. Supreme Court held unanimously that Title VII of the Civil Rights Act of 1964 authorized sexual harassment suits based on a claim of "hostile or offensive working environment," even if the plaintiff in such a suit did not suffer loss in employment benefits. The crucial factor in any sexual harassment dispute is whether the harasser treats members of one gender differently from members of the other gender.

Hostile work environment sexual harassment cases are more complex because the definition of what constitutes an offensive atmosphere is often based on subjective measures, namely the perspective of the plaintiff. Trade journals and business publications often report on new cases that expand the currently accepted parameters of sex discrimination liability. *Business Week* noted that the rules were changing faster than most people could comprehend:

> A revolution in the law on sexual harassment underlies all the hub-bub over Thomas and Hill. It was as recently as 1980 that the Equal Employment opportunity Commission first identified two types of sexual harassment. Companies easily understand the obvious kind: "Sleep with me, honey, or you're fired." But they often don't quite get the murkier, second form: *hostile environment harassment.* Here, as in the Thomas affair, questionable behavior may be subtle and cumulative, ranging from lewd jokes to nude calendars or even obsessive staring. Now, courts are ruling that the conduct has to be judged, not by the old "reasonable man" rule, but from the eyes of a "reasonable woman." And they're stretching the definition so fast that many employers can't keep up.

3.   Sexual Favoritism

Sexual favoritism involves a supervisor playing favorites and rewarding only those who respond to sexual advances. Employees who do not go along with the supervisor's game, and are therefore denied the best job assignments, pay raises, promotions, etc., may claim harassment. A federal court ruled that a female employee was a victim of sexual harassment because she wasn't asked for sexual favors, assuming that those who were, were receiving job perks.

4.   Indirect Harassment

An employee who witnesses sexual harassment on the job, but isn't a victim, can claim sexual harassment. For example, a California state court ruled that an "environment of sexual harassment" was created by a doctor who grabbed other nurses in full view of the claimant who was not harassed.

5.   Harassment by Nonemployees

In both quid pro quo and hostile environment cases, the employer may be held responsible for the harassment of nonemployees, for instance, contractors, vendors, or even customers, if the employer:

➤ knew or should have known of the conduct
➤ failed to take immediate and appropriate corrective action
➤ has control or responsibility over the nonemployee.

6.   Harassment Based on Gender

Behavior can be considered sexual harassment even if it doesn't involve overtly sexual behavior. This type of harassment is directed at a woman explicitly because of her gender. For example, a court ruled that a female dispatcher experienced sexual harassment because she suffered persistent and hostile treatment by male police officers. One officer admitted that he felt she should not have been given the dispatcher position because it was a man's job. He made derogatory comments about her work performance over the police radio, which was listened to by other dispatchers around the county. He also subjected her to pranks. Other officers purposefully used lewd language around her, even though she let them know it offended her. Her complaints to superior officers did not result in any corrective action. Eventually, she resigned from her job.

THE SCOPE AND UNDERREPORTING OF SEXUAL HARASSMENT

In the wake of the Hill–Thomas hearings, several polls and surveys have been released, with results generally showing that sexual harassment is not uncommon in the workplace and that it often goes unreported. It is estimated that 50 to 85 percent of American females will experience some form of sexual harassment during their academic or working lives (*Business & Finance,* March 1995). The National Association of Female Executives, a 250,000-member organization of businesswomen, conducted a telephone poll of 1,300 of its members and found that 53 percent said they had been sexually harassed or knew of someone who had been sexually harassed. Sixty-four percent of those who had been sexually harassed said they did not report the incident. Of the 36 percent who reported the incident, 52 percent said it was not resolved to their satisfaction.

A *New York Times*/CBS News telephone poll of 512 men and women found that 38 percent of female respondents said *yes* when asked if they had been "the object of sexual advances, propositions, or unwanted sexual discussion from men who supervise you or can affect your position at work." Of those who had been victims of harassment, only one-tenth of those women said they had reported it. The same poll found that 53 percent of men said they had "done or said something that a woman might interpret as sexual harassment, even if it was unintentional."

Linda Singer, an attorney with Lichtman, Trister, Singer, & Ross, foresees a possible continuation in underreporting, although she believes awareness of the problem of sexual harassment is increasing. "People do not report sexual harassment out of embarrassment, guilt, and fear—fear of retaliation, fear that people will think less of the person, fear that it will affect the job, fear of being thought to provoke the conduct, and fear that they are not a 'team player,'" she said.

Clearly, there is misunderstanding about what constitutes sexual harassment. Sexual harassment can occur even if there is no touching, and it can be committed by coworkers, Singer claimed.

According to a fact sheet provided by the National Women's Law Center, Washington, D.C., despite growing awareness of the problem of sexual harassment, most women do not report it. Reasons for not reporting sexual harassment include the following:

➤ fear of job loss;
➤ need for future job references;
➤ concern about being labeled a troublemaker;

➤ fear of blame for inviting the behavior; and

➤ reluctance to invite public scrutiny of one's private life.

Rather than report the harassment, many women either endure it or leave their jobs, the fact sheet states.

ADVICE ON DEALING WITH HARASSERS

With record-breaking settlements trumpeted in the news, it might appear that women have gained the upper hand in the struggle against sexual harassment. Certainly, a handful of working women have treated some corporate Goliaths to a costly lesson in office-appropriate behavior. Take the 1996 sexual harassment case against Wal-Mart: A judge ordered the retail giant to pay former employee Peggy Kimzey $5 million in punitive damages (a relative bargain compared to the $50 million originally awarded by the jury).

While this case illustrates an encouraging trend—America's growing intolerance of sexual harassment—countless women and men are still subjected to unwanted advances in the workplace, and in many cases, lawsuits are not the answer. In reality, taking a sexual harassment complaint to court is "almost useless, unless you have a clear-cut, well-documented case and lots of time on your hands," said Cydney Pullman, coauthor of *Sexual Harassment at Work: A Training Workbook for Working People* (the Labor Institute).

Here's another important truth: You may not even have grounds for a complaint or lawsuit. Traumatic as it may be for the victim, offensive conduct in the workplace frequently falls short of the legal definition of "sexual harassment." Men may grouse that a few innocent comments can now land them in court, but in truth, the law protects only women who can prove extreme or ongoing abuse. That leaves a wide range of behavior that doesn't legally qualify as sexual harassment but can make a working person's life miserable.

How should you handle conduct that either constitutes harassment or falls into that vast gray area? Experts now discourage limiting yourself to the three classic responses: Bear it in silence, quit the job, or sue. These days you can choose from many more options without sacrificing your job, your sanity, or your future.

The adage "An ounce of prevention is worth a pound of cure" is good advice for individuals and organizations alike, particularly as it relates to sexual harassment in the workplace. Each year, companies spend thousands of dollars defending themselves in sexual harassment cases. Others, lucky enough to have escaped such claims (so far), are taking preventive measures by creating a sexual harassment policy that not only allows sexual harassment complaints but encourages them.

Legal experts say the best way for a company to deal with sexual harassment is to come up with a tough, clearly understood policy that is disseminated throughout the workplace. In addition, it behooves a company to identify both women and men of different races to which employees can report harassment. This is important because women are often apprehensive about reporting sexual harassment to a man. Furthermore, it isn't always helpful to assign the handling of sexual harassment complaints to one person. What if that person is the harasser? Finally, prevention is bolstered when a business commits to training everyone in the company on what is acceptable and what is not.

Before you take a job, any job, do a little investigative work. Find out if the company you want to work for is "women-friendly." The Labor Institute's Cyndey Pullman says you can often get a reading on the "corporate culture" during your interview process. For example, does the company have a sexual harassment policy, one with a good reporting mechanism? If possible, talk with other employees, especially women, and ask them about the nature of the office environment. Perhaps egregious sexual harassment doesn't go on, but are women called *Darling, Honey,* or *Sugar?* It's true sticks and stones will break your bones, but name calling also hurts because of the condescending attitude often accompanying such words.

Are only women expected to make coffee, run errands, and tidy up the office? It isn't that women should never carry out these activities, but if the men are never called upon to do them, the company's attitude toward women employees may be suspect.

Anita Hill said there are no blanket rules for dealing with a harasser. She recommends you first assess the situation. Sometimes it works to say, "Please, stop." Sometimes that escalates the behavior. "People think if I had told Clarence Thomas to bug off, that would have ended it. But I said 'no' in a variety of ways. It didn't work. I thought: 'Maybe it's my perfume.' 'Maybe I shouldn't laugh at his jokes.' . . . You blame yourself," Hill said in a recent interview with *Chicago Sun-Times* reporter, Jeffrey Zaslow.

The organization 9 to 5, National Association of Working Women says that sexual harassment is not about sex. It's about power. Typically, such behavior is designed to humiliate and control. They suggest taking the following steps if you are being sexually harassed on the job:

1. *Say* no *clearly.*   Inform the harasser his attentions are unwanted. Make clear you find the behavior offensive. If it persists, write a memo asking him to stop; keep a copy for yourself.
2. *Document the harassment.*   Write down each incident including the date, time, and place. Detail what happened and include your response. Keep a copy at home. This information will be useful if you need to take legal action.
3. *Get emotional support from friends and family.*
4. *Document your work.*   Keep copies of performance evaluations and memos attesting to the quality of your work. The harasser may question your job performance in order to justify his or her behavior.
5. *Look for witnesses and other victims.*   You are probably not the first person mistreated by this individual. Ask around; you may find others who will support your charge. Two accusations are much more difficult to ignore than one.
6. *Explore company channels.*   Use the grievance procedures or channels detailed in your employee handbook. If you're in a union, get the union steward involved right away.
7. *File a complaint.*   To pursue a legal remedy, contact your state discrimination agency or the federal Equal Employment Opportunity Commission. (Look in your phone book for the field office nearest you. The federal agency covers workplaces of 15 employees or more. State law may protect you if you're in a smaller workplace.)
8. *Consult an attorney.*   You do not need an attorney to file a claim, but you may want to speak with a legal service or private attorney specializing in employment discrimination.

Under the Civil Rights Act of 1991, victims of sexual harassment are entitled to damages for pain and suffering as well as to any lost pay. If you win, you may also recover legal fees.

THE COST OF SEXUAL HARASSMENT

As the U. S. evolves from an industrial/manufacturing economy toward an information/services one, human resources—people—are becoming the true engine of added value. Skilled, experienced, and committed employees frequently provide a company its competitive leading edge. Most firms today subscribe to the idea that it makes eminent sense to invest in human capital resources to enhance productivity.

Yet, many companies do not understand the productivity aspect of sexual harassment. While it is well known that harassment essentially is an abuse of power, few people appreciate the adverse effect it has on employee productivity. Corporations are beginning to realize that investment to minimize sexual harassment in the workplace can yield startling economic returns.

Women constitute 46 percent of the workforce, and their productivity is critical to the nation's economic health. It is imperative U. S. companies grasp an important fact: Great economic benefits can be derived from establishing and maintaining a harassment-free workplace.

To date, there has been only limited research on the dollar costs of sexual harassment. The data that do exist are compelling, however. In the typical Fortune 500 company with 23,750 employees, sexual harassment costs $6,700,000 per year in absenteeism, low productivity, and employee turnover. This represents $282.53 per employee, according to a 1988 survey conducted by *Working Woman*. (The first scientific sampling of its kind in the private sector, this 49-question survey was answered by directors of personnel, human resources, and equal-opportunity offices representing 3,300,000 employees at 160 corporations.)

The economic impact falls into three main categories. First, sexual harassment can degrade employee performance. At the very least, victims are forced to waste time blocking and parrying unwanted attention. It is distracting (and disturbing) for the victim and certainly erodes the working relationship, both manager-to-subordinate and peer-to-peer. At the same time, the harassing employee is wasting valuable company time on personal pursuits. Generally, sexual harassment diverts human energy from achieving business objectives.

Second, harassment can breed resentment and mistrust in the workplace. Camaraderie and cooperation are replaced by negative tension that can impair the concentration of *all* employees. A widespread cynicism can suffuse the workplace; productivity suffers; and absenteeism increases. How can an employee work enthusiastically for a company that tolerates hurtful, demeaning behavior? Twelve percent of females who face sexual harassment report stress-related health problems, 27 percent claim undermined self-confidence, and 13 percent see long-term career damage, according to the EEOC.

Third, harassment contributes to costly turnover. Women are nine times as likely as men to quit because of it, five times as likely to transfer, and three times as likely to lose their jobs. Fully 25 percent of females who believe they have been harassed have been dismissed or quit. (When someone is attacked personally, her livelihood and future are threatened.) Every woman who leaves because of harassment represents a large loss of the investment in training her, compounded by the costs of employee replacement. Consider the following true story, which illustrates these realities.

> The first time Cathy's boss, Joe, asked her to lunch she felt a little uncomfortable about it. She accepted, however, because she didn't think it was in the best interest of her job to say "no" to a supervisor.
>
> At the start of their meal, Joe instructed Cathy to check on the warranty of the office printer. Apparently, it wasn't working properly. Cathy instantly breathed a sigh of relief, and she privately chided herself for having had such unfounded apprehensions. She reasoned Joe was simply taking her to lunch to discuss business in a more pleasant atmosphere. From that point on, however, Joe shifted conversational gears. For the remaining 55 minutes of their lunch break, he talked about subjects unrelated to their work. He spoke passionately about his kids and his love for art, and he confided in Cathy that he and his wife were having marital problems.
>
> A month passed before Joe asked Cathy to lunch again. This time she tried to refuse, but he insisted. He said he needed her input about "important matters." Yet, during the second outing, Joe didn't bring up office work at all. Instead, he talked about his impending divorce and how lonely he felt. After these two initial meetings, Joe began "asking" Cathy to lunch regularly, sometimes up to three times a week. Over lunch he would divulge personal disappointments, and he told Cathy he had always found her attractive.
>
> She tried to put a stop to their luncheon engagements, explaining she preferred using her lunch breaks to refresh herself by spending time alone, including reading or writing to friends. Joe wouldn't take no for an answer, and he said, "Consider this part of your job description."
>
> Increasingly, Cathy dreaded coming to work and began to feel a knot in her stomach. After six months, this knot developed into a full-blown ulcer. A short time later Cathy quit her job without telling her employers the real reason why. She told a trusted coworker in confidence, "I felt controlled and unable to do my job effectively. It was as if he were suffocating me."

The company lost a valuable employee in Cathy. She had been with her company for five years and, according to one supervisor, was "the best employee we ever had." Businesses are rapidly becoming aware of the heavy economic costs of sexual harassment and are searching for solutions. The clearest laws and company resolutions can go only so far in preventing sexual harassment. The real solution lies in changing individuals' perceptions and attitudes, and here the company can play an influential and decisive role. Many forward-thinking businesses are going beyond the minimum legal requirements. These employers are initiating thoughtful, company-wide awareness training programs to help men and women understand the pain and indignity of sexual harassment. They also realize that respect for and sensitivity to people's differences are the keys to avoiding sexual harassment.

Such initiatives are being implemented not only because they are "the right thing to do" but also because they make sense economically. These can be extremely cost effective. For a small company, the price can be as little as $5,000; for a large one, it can range up to $200,000.

The lesson for the U.S. is an obvious one: Working women could be the nation's trump card in the intensely competitive world market of the 21st century. Certainly, American corporations should do everything in their power to exploit more fully the skills of half the workforce. Aggressive elimination of sexual harassment, along with all forms of discrimination in the workplace, will enable more women to be more productive for longer periods of time.

More insidious and pervasive than blatant harassment are the underlying sexist attitudes that often lead to offensive and discriminatory behavior. Therefore it is unlikely that sexual harassment can be eradicated in a single generation. Until that day comes, employees need to use good judgment and forethought. Smart people don't wait until the building is on fire to find an exit. Sexual harassment at work is something women, as well as men, need to think about—in advance.

WHERE TO GO FOR HELP

Books

The following books are available in bookstores:

Workplace Sexual Harassment by Anne C. Levy and Michele A. Paludi. Help with understanding sexual harassment from both the legal and psychological perspectives.

Speaking Truth to Power by Anita Hill. Hill explains her experiences working for Thomas in two government jobs.

Sexual Harassment at Work: A Training Workbook for Working People by Cydney Pullman. A comprehensive guide for managers and employees about smart ways to deal with sexual harassment.

Publications

The Webb Report is a monthly newsletter on sexual harassment. It is aimed at small-business owners, human resource managers, and government officials. At $120/year, it is available from the Pacific Resource Development Group, Inc., 800-767-3062.

What Every Employee Ought to Know About Contributing to a Harassment-Free Environment, a 64-page booklet about what harassment entails and how to prevent it. Available at $5 per copy (plus shipping and handling) by calling CCH, Inc., 800-835-5224, ext. 2091. Quantity discounts available.

Organizations

9 to 5, The National Association of Working Women: Call for information, 800-522-0925

The Equal Employment Opportunity Commission: Consult the U. S. government (blue) pages of your telephone book for the number of the regional office nearest you.

Publications and conferences of the *Society for Human Resource Management* (SHRM) frequently feature sexual harassment topics. For information on membership, contact SHRM at 606 N. Washington St., Alexandria, Va. 22314-1997, 703-548-3440.

Applications & Exercises

1. Preventing Sexual Harassment

Sexist attitudes often lead to sexist behavior. The first step in dealing with sexual diversity is to develop a general awareness of the problem by exploring people's assumptions about men and women that often result in destructive practices. Read the following statements and write down an obvious assumption for each one.

➤ "She doesn't need to work; she has a husband to support her."

_____

_____

➤ "He doesn't need family leave time. The mother is home with the new baby."

_____

_____

➤ "Men are much more logical and rational than women."

_____

_____

➤ "Women are much more creative and reliable than men."

_____

_____

➤ "Let's try to hire a man for this position. Men are much more stable."

_____

_____

➤ "I'm so glad you're getting married. Now you have a woman [or "a man"] to take care of you."

_____

_____

2. Television as a Reflection of Society

Watch a clip from an early television show, such as *The Honeymooners, Father Knows Best,* or *Leave It To Beaver.* Think about the messages being communicated concerning male/female roles and in what ways we see similar messages communicated today. How are messages different today?

_____

_____

_____

_____

_____

3. Is This Sexual Harassment?

For each of the following examples, circle the response (Yes, No, or Maybe) that you feel is appropriate.

➤ A coworker of Emma's asked her for dates repeatedly and often made suggestive comments about her appearance. This attention made her feel very uncomfortable, but because he made the requests and comments in an off-hand way, she brushed them off and lived with them. But after his promotion, he became her supervisor. He made it clear that if she would go out with him and "get to know him better," her chances for success in the office would improve dramatically. If she didn't, he could make her job unbearable.

Yes   No   Maybe

Explain: _____

_____

_____

_____

➤ Everyone in your office knows about a group of people who are willing to go along with the manager's sexual behavior—squeezes, brushups, kisses, creeping hands—because they get the best assignments and promotions. The employees who won't submit to his sexual advances get the least desirable work and are passed over when better jobs open up. They are disgusted with these types of working conditions.

Yes   No   Maybe

Explain: _____

_____

_____

_____

➤ A woman brought in a fortune cookie left over from her Chinese take-out lunch. She wrote a new fortune which said, "I like it hot and spicy," and put the cookie on a male coworker's forklift. The story traveled around the plant. Someone then put a *Playgirl* magazine in front of her locker. She thought this was going too far and complained to her supervisor, who shrugged and said, "You can't have it both ways."

Yes   No   Maybe

Explain: _____

_____

_____

_____

➤ An owner of a foreign car dealership hires three women to hand out flyers advertising car sales. The women are required to sit on the hood of a fancy sports car wearing sexy outfits—very short, low-cut, Lycra dresses and spike heels. The women complain because passersby are making obscene remarks and propositioning them. The owner says he's not responsible for what people say and threatens to fire the women for refusing to fulfill their job requirements, including wearing the "uniforms" he's selected.

Yes   No   Maybe

Explain: _____

_____

_____

_____

_____

➤ Faye and Betty like to consider themselves "one of the guys." They enjoy hearing and telling raunchy jokes, as do a group of their male coworkers at the plant. Coworker Harold, though, doesn't think women should be subjected to such off-color jokes and tells the boss he thinks the men are acting inappropriately around the women. The boss tells the men to keep it clean around the women.

Yes   No   Maybe

Explain: _____

_____

_____

_____

_____

➤ Raul is on an overnight business trip wit his boss, Sarah. As they are finishing up a late dinner, Sarah makes it clear that she is attracted to Raul and invites him back to her room. Raul, who is married, declines the invitation. Sarah expresses regret but does not bring up the topic again in the office or on subsequent business trips.

Yes   No   Maybe

Explain: _____

_____

_____

_____

_____

21 EXECUTIVE COMMUNICATION
Improving Speaking and Writing Skills

In this chapter, you will explore answers to the following questions:

➤ How do I learn how to communicate more effectively?

➤ Why is communication so important in the business world?

➤ How will I know where to start when I have to write a speech?

➤ How should I edit my work after I've finished writing it?

❓ Thinking It Through

Check those statements that currently apply to you:

☐ I never thought that communication was important in business.

☐ When I sit down to write a speech, I don't know where to start.

☐ I have a difficult time speaking in front of people.

☐ When I am finished writing, whether speech or memo, I don't want to have to go back to it for editing.

PRESENT

21

EXECUTIVE COMMUNICATION
Improving Speaking and Writing Skills

Communication is an important part of professional life. Effective communication means effective management: Effective managers know their business and can communicate it. They create dynamic business associations with colleagues and employees, and build rapport, or harmony, with the people they relate to. Clearly, there is a relationship between being able to communicate and getting ahead. Used skillfully, communication can influence the behavior of others and produce enhanced results in all aspects of corporate life—from internal employee relations to a positive perspective of the company globally.

Yet communication skills are not always deemed important when designing degree plans for formal education. Communication courses fall into the category of "soft" skills, which often take a backseat to the "hard" information that leads to technical and scientific competence. However, with the emerging global economy and the technical ability to exchange information instantaneously, communication competence is becoming as essential as technical expertise. Author and communication expert Brent Filson interviewed dozens of CEOs about the importance of good communication skills in the workplace. Gerard R. Roche, chairman of Heidrick & Struggles, Inc. (an executive search firm) offers the following perspective:

> I address a number of business graduate schools a year, and I tell them that their courses are so overloaded with analytical studies and accounting and financial analysis and statistics and all these quantitative, measurable subjects that the students and the schools neglect one of the most important management skills of all: the ability to communicate.

Another CEO, John H. McConnell of Worthington Industries, adds, "Take all the speech courses and communication courses you can. Because the world turns on communication." There is a tremendous market today for communication improvement seminars, and most of the business is for companies training their employees to communicate better on the job. With this in mind, let's look at writing and speaking specifically as it applies to the workplace.

In order to communicate clearly, skilled executives must be able to transfer their thoughts into writing and speaking. Oral and written communication are accomplished through two different mediums—the spoken and the written word. The main difference is personal contact. Speaking involves face-to-face contact; when people hear and see you at the same time, everything about you is part of the communication experience.

While speaking gives you the advantage of using your entire being—vocal nuances, body language, and other nonverbal behaviors—to emphasize your message, you have only one opportunity to reach the audience. On the other hand, when you make a point in writing and the readers don't immediately understand, they can reread and investigate the material. Let's look at the ways in which executives communicate, beginning with speaking.

EXECUTIVE SPEAKING

Importance of Speaking in a Leadership Role

Public speaking uses spoken language to influence human behavior. Beyond the words the speaker chooses, speaking involves seeing the similarities and differences in people, including yourself. Think about presentations that you have attended. What are the characteristics that made the experience a positive or negative one? How did you feel about the speaker, the message, the effectiveness of the talk? Did the speaker move you to take action or persuade you to take his position?

Many executives are not effective speakers, and that undermines their leadership positions because the audience perception is not favorable. Common critiques of poor presentations indicate that many speakers have low energy, read their speeches, fumble questions, have no sense of purpose or audience, and seem uncomfortable. You can avoid all of these by learning the basics of public speaking and adopting the attitude that a speaking engagement is an opportunity to assert a positive leadership presence. Let's look at the techniques for purposeful, powerful speech making.

Components of a Good Speech

A good speech builds on the flow of ideas that moves the listeners to action. Though it is important to write out your presentation as you develop it, it is not a written document and does not follow the rules of formal grammar. Delivery relies on informal, or conversational, style.

Purpose of the Speech

For executive communicators, all speaking is purposeful. Whether giving an impromptu talk or a formal presentation, your message—your commitment—should always be clear. This is what makes you the leader.

Speeches inform or persuade. What is your intention? If your intent is to inform, you must be clear, precise, and organized. If your intent is to persuade, you must go a step further and motivate your listeners to agree with you, change their behaviors or attitudes, or take action from your message. Use your speech to communicate change or a vision for the future, influence industry and investors, enhance sales and marketing, promote business growth, and build teamwork. The key to success in public speaking is knowing your intention and organizing your ideas around it—the audience expects you to know what you are talking about and to show it.

Organization of the Speech

Preparation and organization are the keys to successfully presenting your message. Impromptu talks may appear to be off-the-cuff, but a successful manager has prepared in advance for any speaking opportunity. Many executives use everyday conversations to practice material and "test the waters." Impromptu talks are planned but flexible and immediate.

How do you prepare, regardless of the circumstances? The old sales adage applies here: Tell them what you are going to tell them, tell them, then tell them what you told them. A good speech has an engaging opening, a concise, informative body, and a powerful closing.

Beginning.   A good beginning is essential. It captures the attention of the audience, states your purpose, and sets the tone. Openings can be dramatic or subtle. Use questions, statistics, quotations, and anecdotes to grab the attention of the audience. You want to engage your listeners and get them to think about your message—this is the time to challenge their assumptions. Always remember to focus on your message—you want to clash with issues, not your audience.

Body.   The body of the speech is the place to make your points and carry your theme. Be dramatic and passionate. The more open you are about your position, the more your audience will trust you and be drawn into your position. Involve the audience in your enthusiasm. Use humor and visual aids to engage listeners and aid their retention. Build your background: Find stories and examples to support your position. Find something in common with the audience: People who have shared experience relate to each other, so relating to the audience brings them closer to you. Challenge them with questions. Show them what's in it for them. Organization is important—if you are focused and summarize as you go, the audience will stay with you.

Ending.   The ending is your close. "Tell them what you told them" . . . and why. Express your appreciation for their support, and call for action. What do you want them to do? The ending should be brief and optimistic. Highlight a positive aspect about your position and leave them inspired to follow your lead.

Writing the Speech

The task of organizing your ideas in written form can seem overwhelming. Where do you start? The important thing is to start. Get your ideas down on paper. The way in which you want to organize will become apparent as the process of writing down your ideas unfolds.

One technique is to write the body of the speech first. Write down the points, the theme, and the support details you want the audience to know. Next, write the conclusion. Restate your mission, call for action and ask for commitment. Then, write your introduction. Once you know where you will end, you can concentrate on the most effective way to begin. Finally, create a dynamic title. As you organize, remember the reason for your presentation.

The last, and most important step, is editing. Learning experts find that people will listen to you for 90 minutes, but they will retain only what is said in the first 20 minutes. Confine your message to this amount of time.

Who Is the Audience?

Leading communication theorist Kenneth Burke wrote, "You persuade a man only insofar as you talk his language by speech, gesture, tonality, order, image, attitude, ideas, identifying your ways with his." The arguments you use, the rapport you establish, and your approach to the issues are already impacted by what the audience believes before you begin. The more you understand your audience before you communicate with them, the more you can handle circumstances intelligently. Not all audiences are open-minded, especially in the business world. You must select what you say and how you say it based on your analysis of the audience. Audience analysis is an important part of your preparation.

Find out all you can about the people you are communicating with so that you consider their interests, needs, attitudes, knowledge, beliefs, values, and backgrounds in your speech. If your ideas are seeds you want to plant, it's a good idea to know the soil conditions in order to plan your approach!

With regard to your topic, where is your audience on this spectrum?

Knowledgeable · · · · · · · · · Not Knowledgeable

Favorable · · · · · · · · · Unfavorable

Willing · · · · · · · · · Unwilling

Using this gauge to rate the receptivity of your audience will help you assess your approach and modify your message to win them over.

What are some of the other characteristics of the people who make up your audience? Consider cultural values, age, gender, occupation, education, group affiliation (for example, union or professional society), geography, and special areas such as disabilities. Again, the more you know about your audience, the more successful your presentation will be.

Delivery

The most organized and powerful collection of words in the world will fail to achieve results without a powerful delivery. Words make up less than 10 percent of the oral communication process. Vocal quality and body posture comprise the rest; body posture contributes over 50 percent. It's not only what you say, but how you say it!

Purpose.   A good delivery is vital because it builds rapport and connects you and your message with the audience. You connect with the audience physically by how you look, sound, and make eye contact. You connect with them mentally by presenting ideas and challenging them to think about your presentation. You connect with them emotionally by identifying with them and their experiences.

Vocal quality.   Vocal quality sets the tone of your presentation. A good speaking voice is pleasant and natural and conveys friendliness and sincerity. It balances volume, pitch, and rate. Varying these elements offers several options for creating the dynamics you want. For example, volume adds emphasis—the louder, the more assertive. Differences in pitch convey emotion and conviction—the higher, the more excitable. Changing your rate, or speed, of speech helps you change the mood, add emphasis, and avoid sounding boring.

Body posture.   Body language brings the most important dimension to your speech. You show as well as tell, and the audience will believe your face and body as much or more than your words. Look people in the eye, keep your body open to the audience, and get out from behind the podium. Create a presence that your audience can trust. Use hand gestures to indicate size, shape, direction, and location. Use your hands and arms to show comparisons. Punctuate importance and urgency with a fist. Remember, body movement is not an outlet for nervous energy. It is a way to emphasize what you are saying.

Practice your speech.   The best way to be prepared is to practice, practice, practice. There may be several unknowns about the actual presentation event, but if uncertainty of your material is one of them, you are at a disadvantage. Practice your material until you know it well and can concentrate on your delivery style and connecting with the audience. Videotape your practice; then watch yourself. Are you projecting the image, the intensity, and the message that you want? Would *you* believe, trust, and support this speaker if you were in the audience?

Remember that the audience is a mirror of the presenter. If you want to know how you are doing, observe the audience. How are they responding? If you are comfortable and at ease, they will be. If you wish you were somewhere else, so will they. Inspire them to share your passion by projecting that you know their business as well as you know your own. Be confident about the future. If you have done your homework and know your audience, the rapport you establish will help them see things your way.

Questions and answers. Questions and answers allow you to get feedback from your audience and provide additional information about your message. Listen attentively, be neutral, and answer with respect. Questions and answers at the end of your presentation provide the opportunity to interact personally with the audience, focus on the issues, and demonstrate further your sincerity and commitment to obtaining their support.

Remember, the only speech worth giving is one you believe in. Put your whole mind and body into it. Ask yourself, "What are you fighting for?" Believe in the cause because, if you don't, how will you convince your listeners?

CROSS-CULTURAL COMMUNICATION

At one time, international cross-cultural contact affected only a small portion of the world. New technology in transportation and information systems places us in instant and sometimes constant contact with people globally. Not long ago, only 5 percent of all American businesses faced international competition. Now, 75 percent of U. S. business is involved in international commerce. American executives communicate daily with people from other cultures. If cross-cultural communication is to enhance business relationships and increase productivity, it is imperative that the executive who anticipates speaking to another culture makes careful preparations.

Techniques for Presenting to Cross-Cultural Audiences

Research the culture—know your audience. You don't need to know the culture as well as a native executive, but make a sincere effort to understand the people.

Common ground. Most North American and Northern European cultures focus on the bottom line—on doing business first and then becoming friends. However, many cultures value friendship first and then business. What is necessary to establish a relationship with each audience so that both sides are comfortable before proceeding to the issues?

Make the effort to establish common ground based on cultural values. If you are addressing an East Asian or American Indian culture, both of which believe in living harmoniously with nature, you want to be cautious about making recommendations that exploit the environment. Points of controversy and challenges are better met if you establish common ground.

Humor.   Author Virginia Woolf wrote, "Humor is the first of the gifts to perish in a foreign tongue." Humor is certainly a powerful communication tool, but it does not translate well. Plays on words are rarely understood because they are taken literally. If you use humor, direct it toward yourself, never at the audience or their culture. For one culture, jokes about the elderly or religion may be fine, but for another, these subjects are sacred. Try out your humor in advance on people who understand the culture that you are trying to reach.

Body language.   Body language is vital to communicating with cross-cultural audiences. The listeners may not understand the spoken language, so they will assess your message as much by what they see as what they hear. Every culture has taboos regarding gestures, and you can discover these by researching. The most important thing is to be natural and sincere. Your open, friendly manner will assure the audience that your verbal and nonverbal messages come from the heart and are meant with respect.

Speak slowly and in plain English.   Some executives are fortunate to know the language of the people they are addressing. Others have the text of their speech translated phonetically and memorize it. Most use simultaneous translators. Whatever the circumstances, speak plainly. Idioms and sarcasm, like humor, may fall flat because the audience does not share your cultural context. Avoid jargon and puns unless you are sure the audience is familiar with them. Make your points with simple illustrations and anecdotes.

Audience reaction.   Often, audiences from other cultures show little or no reaction to a presentation, and speakers wonder if their message is sinking in. If you do not get the reaction you expect, carry on. Continue to project respect and sincerity and don't be frustrated. Likewise, there may be no questions from the audience, even if you invite them. Many cultures are taught to respect authority, and it is unthinkable to question the authority of the speaker. To encourage discussion and questions, ask the audience to discuss your points in small groups and interact personally with the groups to address concerns directly.

Summary for Executive Speaking

Public-speaking skills are a valuable and indispensable tool for every successful executive. Seize every opportunity to speak; speak to inspire your employees and coworkers and to solidify your leadership. Uwe S. Wascher, head of General Electric Company's $5-billion-a-year plastics business, recommends: "If you want to be a business leader, you have to learn to speak in front of people. Speaking is one of the ways you carry out your management responsibilities. If you want to be the person who determines strategies, then you have no other choice but to be a good speaker. If you aren't, you lack something as a manager."

Learning to speak well is not a secret. With knowledge and practice, the most reluctant executive can become an effective speaker. Whether a student with little business experience or a seasoned veteran of the corporate world, you can use each opportunity to speak to enhance your personal and corporate success.

EXECUTIVE WRITING

Power of the Written Word

Consider the following classic example of business writing:

A plumber found hydrochloric acid excellent for cleaning drains. He wrote to a Washington bureau to find out if it was harmless. The bureau replied as follows:

The efficacy of hydrochloric acid is indisputable, but the chlorine residue is incompatible with metallic permanence.

The plumber wrote back, thanked the bureau, and said he was very glad that they agreed that it was effective. Another reply came:

We cannot assume responsibility for the production of toxic and noxious residues from hydrochloric acid, and we suggest, therefore, that some alternative procedure be instituted.

The plumber answered that he was getting fine results thus far. Would the bureau like to suggest the use of hydrochloric acid to other people? Finally, someone in Washington wrote:

Don't use hydrochloric acid. It eats the hell out of the pipes.

In a business day, the volume of information being exchanged is staggering. Memos, bulletins, letters, documents, reports, reviews, proposals, and articles all represent opportunities to communicate on paper. How do you capture the same passion and intent in writing that you strive for in speaking? As in the example, there is a tendency for writers to use "business-speak," language cluttered with stuffy expressions that, rather than move the message along, cater to the ego and self-importance of the writer.

Like speaking, writing in the corporate world is more than putting ideas down on paper. It involves moving ideas through your organization so that people will act on them. Let's look at some of the points to keep in mind when writing for business.

Basics of Good Business Writing

Many work environments today make it easy to avoid writing. E-mail and conference calling facilitate instant communication. Thoughtful, analytical writing is slow by comparison.

As in speaking, business writing focuses on information and persuasion. Remember, you are writing to convey a meaning—to inform or persuade—not to impress the reader. The best, and most challenging, approach is to keep your writing simple and conversational.

Business writing should be clear so your reader doesn't need additional interpretation. Grammar and structure are important, but managing the words reflects how you manage the situation and the people. What kind of management will the readers respond best to? What are the risks? How strongly do you want to express yourself? How directly do you want or need the document to influence action?

Be "present" in your writing. State your message with conviction. Use first-person voice rather than third-person to convey presence. For example,

... it appears that it would be prudent to determine a solution to the catalog distribution situation as soon as possible.

This is more effectively stated:

We need to find a solution to the catalog distribution problem immediately.

Organization is important. Communications consultant Edith Poor suggests that executives use a "management of thinking" approach to producing effective documents. Use the following six steps to focus and manage your thinking when you are organizing your thoughts.

Message	What is the major point? What must be included in the content? What *must* the audience remember?
Audience	Who is the audience? How many are there? What is their relationship to you and yours to them? What do you know about them? What don't you know? What motivates them?
Purpose	What must you accomplish? What is the desired outcome? What will happen if you don't succeed? What action do you desire from the audience?
Situation	Why are you the author? What political, professional, and personal concerns make this easy, or difficult, for you?
Introduction	What is the core issue you are addressing? What background is needed to support the issue? How much does the reader need to know? You may be an expert, but does the reader need to be?
Question	What is the central question? Does your document address it?

Using these questions, remember the format: "Tell them what you are going to tell them, tell them, then tell them what you told them."

Tone—The Voice on Paper

Written documents lack vocal variety and body language that set the tone of an oral presentation. You have to compensate for these by a careful choice of words. A positive tone in writing is achieved by using lively, pleasant, conversational language. Tone is important because it influences how readers will receive and respond to your communication. You can smooth out a situation or create adversaries. Keep the following in mind:

➤ Avoid jargon and "business-speak." Use language that is clear and uncomplicated. For example,

> A comprehensive review of your school-based substance abuse program will be conducted by a team of field auditors from our department next week.

Can be made clearer by writing,

> We'll be reviewing your substance abuse program next week.

➤ Use positive words that do not imply criticism or accusation. Instead of the following:

> You failed to return my phone call.

You can write:

> Did you receive a message that I called?

➤ Focus on changing behavior rather than expressing anger. Remember that the other party does not have to be wrong for you to be right, so use a positive approach to criticism. Suggest a course of action. For example,

> The quality of the monthly report you submitted is totally unacceptable.

Can be stated as:

> The quality of your recently submitted monthly report is not up to your usual standards. Let me know if there is anything I can do to help you fix it.

➤ Use the first-person voice and be pleasant and courteous. Change the following:

> There will be a meeting in the conference room about the parking situation at noon today.

To:

> Let's meet in the conference room at noon today to discuss the parking situation. Please let me know if that is inconvenient; otherwise, I will assume you will be there.

Examining Audience

Consider the points we listed earlier about analyzing an audience for oral presentations. Now, remember that the audience is reading your message, but they cannot read your mind or ask you questions. They are not at hand to give you feedback. Therefore, you need to know their background knowledge and receptivity. They rely on your words to understand your message and what is required of them. Think about the political climate of the company—the context within which your message will be received. What are people's beliefs about the company and about you? Think about the document from the reader's perspective.

Editing—An Important Tool

Pascal once wrote, "I have made the letter longer than usual because I lack the time to make it shorter." Editing is a challenge because we think every thought that our minds create is priceless. Remember the hydrochloric acid memo—edit to get the job done, not to impress yourself or your readers!

When you edit, look for ways to format the information so it will visually assist the reader to get the necessary information.

> At the meeting on Friday, we will discuss customer requests to return merchandise, the return of unused merchandise, and factory merchandise receipts.

This same information can be formatted as shown next.

> At the meeting on Friday, we will discuss:
>
> —customer requests to return merchandise
>
> —return of unused merchandise
>
> —factory merchandise receipts.

Good editing results in a document that states its message in the simplest, clearest way. Put yourself in the reader's place. Do you understand what is being asked of you? Have someone who understands your intent give you feedback. Read the document aloud to assess the clarity of its message.

Get Those Creative Juices Flowing

Sooner or later everyone experiences writer's block. Perhaps you must prepare a speech or write a document that includes sensitive, controversial content sure to impact your colleagues. You must rally the troops around a reorganization of the company or pump up a discouraged sales force. You sit, pen poised over paper, and you're stuck. Writer's block is no fun, and the harder you try, the less you accomplish. Whether organizing ideas for a speech or writing a document, it is helpful to understand the ways in which our mental processes can be assisted when inspiration is scarce.

We process our thoughts in two ways. One is our creative unconscious that flows with original ideas, insights, and discoveries. The other is our critical conscious, which reviews and often censors what the creative mind produces. We need both of these processes; however, we need them to work together.

One effective way to direct the creative processes of the mind is a technique called *mind-mapping*. It is an activity for the creative unconscious that generates a wealth of ideas to which the conscious mind can add structure.

Mind-mapping is a brainstorming process similar to free association, and it helps writers become "unstuck." Trying to write in a linear fashion—from the beginning through to the end—can be a frustration for the most knowledgeable of people. Inspiration rarely leaps out and grabs us, and we lose valuable time waiting for it. You cannot force ideas, so try this.

Select a topic word or phrase, the central idea, write it in the middle of a sheet of paper, and circle it. Let this word trigger other words or images. Write and circle them surrounding the center (see Figure 21.1). Follow each train of thought out from the center, connecting each new circled thought to the preceding circle. Let the thoughts radiate until all of the associations you can make are exhausted. Don't censor yourself; just spill your ideas onto the paper. Keep going until you experience a definite sense of what you want to write about. Then stop generating ideas and begin writing. If your writing stalls, go back to the mind-map and get another idea.

Try it now. Write the word "fear" on a piece of paper and circle it. This word is sure to bring up many associations. Make as many associations as you can—let them flow. Avoid judging or choosing—let go and write. When you feel that you know the direction you want to go, start writing. Use the associated ideas to feed your writing flow.

As an executive or manager creating written documents for corporate and business settings, you might feel that mind-mapping is more suited for abstract concepts than the concrete topics an executive has to deal with. Don't judge. Write down your nucleus and go for it.

Figure 21.1.   *Sample of mind-mapping.*

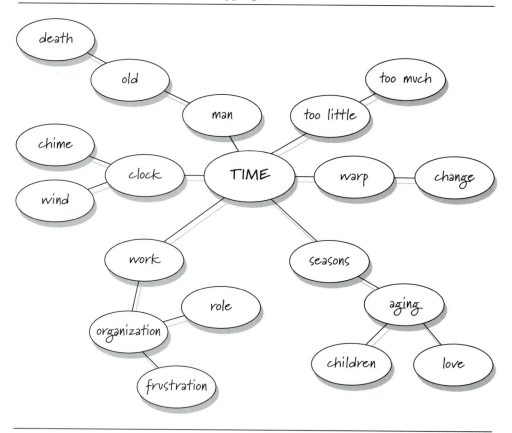

SUMMARY

Successful business leaders use communication skills to be effective managers. Good public-speaking and writing skills are essential for successful communication in all aspects of education and business, especially in the corporate world. Whether you are in school or working, there are plenty of opportunities to practice and perfect these skills so that you can use them to enhance both personal and professional communication.

Brent Filson, author and president of Filson Communications, sums it up best when he says, "To be a successful executive, it's not enough to know your business. You must communicate your business. It's not enough to be a leader. You must communicate leadership. Communication isn't simply moving information. It's moving people by using information; it's transmitting a conviction from one person to another."

374 Chapter 21 Executive Communication

Applications & Exercises

Key Into Your Life: Opportunities to Apply What You Learn

1. Imagine that you will give a 5-minute persuasive presentation on a topic of your choice. Write down four or five topics that bring out real passion in you—topics that you believe in and could speak persuasively about.

   _____

   _____

   _____

   _____

2. Choose one and, on a separate piece of paper, brainstorm ideas around this topic using the mind-mapping technique described in this chapter.

3. Now, organize your ideas by writing them down so that they flow. Remember to:

   ➤ State your purpose. What do you want to accomplish with your message? You may not necessarily include this in your speech, but you want to be sure you are clear about it yourself.

   ➤ Write the body of the message first. Write all the points, the theme, and supporting details. Include an anecdote or story to help the audience relate to you and to help them remember what you are saying.

   ➤ Write the conclusion. Restate your theme; ask for action from the listeners.

   ➤ Write the opening. Use a question or idea that will engage the listeners immediately.

   ➤ Create a title.

4. What characteristics would your ideal audience have? What if you had an unreceptive audience? How could you improve the way you state your message to appeal to people who might not agree with you? Think about how to establish common ground or use humor to your advantage.

   _____

   _____

   _____

   _____

5. What is the best way to sell your speech? How will you dress, what tone of voice will you use, how will you stand and move? Ask yourself, "What am I fighting for?" Be aware that words are not the only way in which to convey your message.

   _____

   _____

   _____

   _____

6. Practice your speech. Use a mirror, a video camera, or a tape recorder. Find an audience of friends or family who will listen and offer constructive feedback. Based on what you think of yourself and what others have to say, make adjustments and practice the presentation again.

Key to Self-Expression: Discovery Through Journal Writing

A journal can serve as a log for you to keep track of your personal growth as you record how you feel about each successive time you make a presentation, and it can become a resource as you begin to keep stories and experiences that can be used in future presentations. Becoming a competent speaker is a process. Every time you speak, whether it is a formal occasion or an impromptu one, you become more relaxed and confident and discover things that you want to remember for the next time. Recording your progress is a good way to discover what you have learned.

Always be on the lookout for pertinent experiences or stories that reinforce or illustrate the issues and concerns you find important. You may not know what topics you'll speak on down the road, but experiences that impact your life will fit into a variety of presentations. Record personal experiences and stories that you hear, and keep clippings or photocopies of written items that cross your path. Jot down notes about presentations and speakers that you have particularly enjoyed. What did the speaker do to engage you? Why was the presentation influential? Keep notes and learn from them. This becomes a rich and personal resource for your own future presentations. Remember, stories that have meaning for you personally are important assets for helping you to establish rapport with your listeners.

Key to Your Personal Portfolio: Your Paper Trail to Success

One way to develop and hone speaking and writing skills is to take advantage of all opportunities to do them. Speak and write as often as possible. There are lots of places to look for opportunities.

➤ *Academic, service, and social organizations.* These groups are often looking for program speakers. They also often have newsletters or flyers that need to be written. Don't be shy about getting involved. It helps you personally and adds to your resume of experience.

➤ *Classes.* Remember, you can practice speaking skills in impromptu situations as well as formal ones. Participate in class, or offer to moderate a class for the instructor.

➤ *Social situations.* Tell stories or present your opinions to friends at social gatherings. Watch their reactions and adjust your behavior. They don't need to know that you are seeing them as an audience, but you will learn about speaking skills and probably increase your social standing by being more outgoing as well!

References

Blake, Gary, and Robert W Bly. *The Elements of Business Writing.* (New York: Macmillan, 1991).

Filson, Brent. *Executive Speeches.* (New York: John Wiley & Sons, 1994).

Poor, Edith. *The Executive Writer.* (New York: Grove Weidenfeld, 1992).

Walters, Lilly. *Secrets of Successful Speakers.* (New York: McGraw-Hill, 1993).

index